D0930389

MICROECONOMIC THEORY
OF THE MARKET MECHANISM:
A General Equilibrium Approach

Macmillan Series in Economics

Lawrence R. Klein
Consulting Editor

MICROECONOMIC THEORY OF THE MARKET MECHANISM:

A General Equilibrium Approach

Robert E. Kuenne

GENERAL ECONOMIC SYSTEMS PROJECT

The Macmillan Company / NEW YORK

Collier-Macmillan Limited / LONDON

reproduced or
or mechanical,
on storage and
he Publisher.

-10012

NTARIO

(58462)

FOR MY MOTHER
MARGARET EDITH KUENNE

Preface

This book is the fourth volume to emerge from the General Economic Systems Project, the purposes of which are to further the study of large-scale decision models and to increase their applicability to the analysis of real-world problems.

To fulfill these objectives it is the overriding purpose of this work to introduce a general equilibrium outlook into the structure and teaching of the intermediate microeconomic theory course. The book's appeal to the instructor, therefore, will reside in the importance he attaches to this revision of method and outlook. The ultimate justification of the book must be sought in its success in effecting this methodological and substantive revision necessary to highlight and feature the wholeness of the market economy. Both student and instructor require an explanation of the importance the author attaches to these purposes.

First, in teaching the microeconomic theory course to undergraduates using existing textbooks—many of them very fine technically—I have been struck by the great amount of time spent in teaching fine points of technique of little real significance to the student's needs. Over the years we have accumulated a huge clutter of partial analytical tools and specific analyses to which we have become habituated, and which serve to scatter the focus of the course. I have attempted as an integrated decisionmaker relying upon intricate interrelatedness of variation to eliminate most of the furbelows of partial analysis by following as closely as possible a clear line of development of the market economy. That (alas!) I have not had the complete courage of my convictions will be found in my brief presentation of the nearly worthless concepts of elasticity, but these have sunk so deeply into the teaching of economics that I felt I could not eliminate them completely. However, because I have spent much time in evaluating the displacement of equilibrium, in which the slopes of functions at points rather than their elasticities are all-important, I trust that a substantial, implicit correction of emphasis has occurred.

Second, in accordance with my desire to stress the holistic presentation of the economy, I have included the complications of time and of money from the beginning of the analysis, albeit in simple manners. This makes some demands on the student, but my experience has been that he is quite capable of accepting them in the stage of laying the foundations of the models, and the payoffs accruing to having these realistic elements inbuilt *ab initio* are very great indeed. The general equilibrium approach used in the book, therefore, includes the integration of capital goods and money from the beginning.

Lastly, I have stressed the methods and purposes of modelbuilding a great deal more than is customary in intermediate texts. The purpose of this emphasis is to give the student a feel for the uses and limitations of rigorous modelbuilding, and more especially for the problems of manipulating models to derive useful insights. In doing this, however, I have attempted to eliminate most difficult mathematical presentations—except for a few pages in Chapter 9 where I found that a section on welfare maximization conditions was indispensable—in favor of literary, geometric, or elementary analytical presentation. This has resulted in a certain haziness and softness of definition in portions, but my objective in the book to stress the philosophical aspects of economic theory and the economic outlook, rather than mere technique, reinforced my pedagogical desire for simplicity.

My hope, in pursuing these three departures from current practice, is to have written a book that will aid the student in obtaining an understanding of the market mechanism as a social decisionmaker. In de-emphasizing the partial approach, I have sought to give him some insights into the market economy's philosophical implications, some understanding of its total operating characteristics, and some judgments concerning its welfare aspects.

I am indebted to Professor Robert Pollak for his careful reading of the manuscript, but he must be excused my academic sins of omission and commission.

R. E. K.

Genequil
Thompson's Point
Charlotte, Vermont

Contents

PART III / *The Complete Model*

Image the whole, then execute the parts—
  Fancy the fabric
Quite, ere you build, ere steel strike fire from quartz,
  Ere mortar dab brick!

—ROBERT BROWNING

PART I

The Methods of Economic Analysis

CHAPTER 1

Economic Modelbuilding:
Methods, Concepts, and Limitations

IT IS THE PURPOSE of this book to display the economy of a modern market society as a huge, integrated, decisionmaking machine, functioning within the society to make economic choices and to effect them. Like any other machine, it absorbs *inputs*, processes them in accordance with its own internal structure, and yields *outputs*. If we are to understand the workings of the machine, therefore, it is our task to study the characteristics of the inputs, the structure of the mechanism as it relates to the transformation of these inputs into outputs, and the nature of the outputs. In such a study of these three aspects, a host of questions will arise, which may be grouped under two headings: (1) a *positive* set, concerned with the *how* of the machine's operation, and (2) a *normative* group, which bears upon the *how well* of the machine's performance.

For example, we might ask what kinds of inputs are fed into the machine; where they are obtained or how they are produced; how they are used by the machine or through which parts of the machine they pass for processing; what kinds of outputs are produced; and what kinds of intermediate products appear between the absorption of raw inputs and the production of final output, as well as how all of these flow through the machine's transformation process. These questions are concerned with positive aspects of performance, and are therefore included in the first group.

On the other hand, we may inquire about the efficiency of the machine's performance; the social welfare or equity implications of its outputs; the possible malstructuring of some of its parts and how they might be improved; or the malfunctioning of some of its components and suggested redesigns. These questions imply the presence of value judgments to be used as criteria for the assessment of performance and structure, frequently with an eye toward changes in the machine, and are found therefore under the second heading.

Another approach to the study of the mechanism may be clarified by an appeal to medical terms. If we use a machine or an organism as a subject of analysis, we may distinguish a study of (1) the *anatomy* of the subject and (2) its *physiology*. The first type of examination is made when the subject is at rest, and concentrates upon the production of a figure or other description, that reveals the form and structure of each component and the linkages it possesses to every other component that integrate the parts into a whole. This type of knowledge is that gained by dissection, by the study of the machine's or organism's structure, and is summarized by the blueprint or the anatomical chart.

The physiology of the organism or machine, on the other hand, pertains to the subject in motion, performing its assigned tasks. Its concern is with the nature of the flows between organs or components, their functioning, and, by a study of the functioning of the organs or components in their interrelatedness, the performance of the system as a whole. We may seek to obtain information about such functioning by approaching the subject while it is performing in a steady, repetitive way and disturbing this steady-state performance by changing the value or nature of an input. We may then observe what effects the "disturbance" or "displacement of equilibrium" has upon the flows of inputs through the mechanism, the functioning of the organs or components, and the flows of output from the mechanism. By carefully controlling the disturbances so that the mechanism does not have to cope with too many at one time, we may be able to gain valuable analytical information about its modes of performance or its physiology.

Alternatively, we may change the structure of the machine or organism, thereby changing the lines of input flow through it and constraining the performance of one or more organs or components, in order to see what effects these changes have upon the flow of outputs, intermediate products, or both. By striving to attain information about "the laws of motion" governing the subject, or, broadly, its physiology, we may gain the insights needed to answer both positive and normative groups of questions categorized above.

If we approach the modern, complex economy of an industrial nation with such purposes and with such an outlook upon the nature of our tasks, we are immediately struck by the immensity of the job. The first of these counsels of despair will undoubtedly concern the bewildering amount of detail in the realistic economic mechanism—in inputs, in components, in paths of linkage among components, and in outputs. The inputs will include the preferences of perhaps millions of individual consuming units, the amounts of hundreds of thousands of primary factor services available to the economy, the technology governing the production possibilities of millions of products, the expectations of future events held by millions of consumers and firms. The component parts of the machine may be viewed as literally millions of markets, or places where goods, securities, and factor service inputs are bought and sold. These components are linked by paths along which information and goods flow from every other component, compounding the complexity that inheres in the mere number of parts in the mechanism. And, finally, the outputs emerging from the machine are the prices and amounts exchanged of hundreds of millions of goods, securities, and factor services.

If we are to implement our *vision* of the economy as a mechanism for generating economic decisions, we must obviously resolve at the start to abstract from much of the detail of the mechanism. We cannot hope to produce an anatomical chart or blueprint of the economy in all of its detail: our chart will be more in the nature of a sketch than a blueprint, displaying major features of interest for those who wish to use it. Similarly, our physiological description must be much simplified in the sense of eliminating most of the detail inherent in reality. We cannot *reproduce* the machine and its functioning as an end-result of our analysis and synthesis, but can hope only to produce a *model* that vastly simplifies the mechanism it represents and that yields at best the major anatomical and physiological features of it. Hopefully, the model will give *insights* of use to policymakers into these features of the realistic economy, not exact and detailed reproductions to scale.

Having reconciled ourselves, however reluctantly, to these necessary simplifications, let us now turn to some of the fundamental decisions we must make in designing the model.

Some Fundamental Decisions in Economic Modelbuilding

THE ECONOMY: MECHANISM OR ORGANISM?

The first decision that we must make after deciding to map the economy is the type of model we will produce, and in the initial stage of our analysis this depends upon our view of the economy. Does it resemble a *mechanical* entity, placed within the whole social complex but removable from it for purposes of analysis; with a stable structure that can be changed within broad limits by its designers; which functions under the regime of inner laws built once-for-all into that structure; and which is essentially insulated from external impacts except those it is designed to accept as inputs? Or can it be viewed only as one *organ* of the larger social organism, related holistically to that organism and incapable of worthwhile physiological analysis removed from it; subject to disturbance from many forms of external influences and possessing some potential to adapt its structure to them inasmuch as its inner processes are life processes that do not freeze its structure for all time, but give it the capability of adaptation to external impacts? Further, does it possess within itself an inner law of change through time, such as growth and decay, or some more complicated *process* involved with the mere passage of time?

Let us seek to clarify these distinctions by broadening our outlook a bit. We may define a *society* as a family of *systems*. These systems may be divided for convenience into three types:

1. the *culture system*, or the whole complex of values, beliefs, symbols, goals, traditions, and ways of looking at the world that the society embraces;

2. *social systems*, or those systems in which two or more persons interact meaningfully for the accomplishment of individual and social ends, and in which the individual acquires *role-expectations* for his own and others' conduct; and

3. *personality systems*, most particularly those characteristics of the individuals in the society that interact with the culture and social systems to determine the *actions* of the individual. Included in this category are all kinds of activities (thought, for example), which have some social (as opposed to purely individual) meaning.

These three sets of systems are intimately interconnected, mutually affecting and being affected by all other systems. The economy, for example, is a member of the set of social systems, and contains within itself other social systems such as corporations, labor unions, markets, and the like. These component systems interact with other social systems such as governments, contain individuals who have been mightily affected by the culture system within which they move, and enforce upon these individuals certain prescribed manners of behavior toward others. But, if we found in our initial view of the economy that its detail was overwhelming and that any meaningful analysis required greater simplification, our difficulties would be compounded a millionfold were we to attempt to analyze as one entity in full detail the largest system—society.

Our decision, therefore, to remove one social mechanism—the *economy*—from the matrix of other systems in order to study it, was a step toward simplification even prior to our decision to lessen economic detail. The word *remove* implies that many of the lines of mutual influence must be made paths of one-way causation, along which feedbacks from the affected social system to the economy are not permitted. Now, if the economy, and more broadly, the society, can be treated in the light of a *mechanism*, this removal of the economy and the necessary distortions it requires are less punitive analytically, for the frozen structure of the market mechanism does not change as we lift it out and cut its affiliations with many other systems. We have merely blocked off from it a variety of inputs, which it formerly received and which may have been processed by it, but to which its inner structure did not respond nor its in-built rules of operation alter in response. That is, if our "vision" of the economy is Newtonian in inspiration, reflecting a view of the economy as in the nature of a solar system, following stable laws of motion essentially unaffected by the laws of other solar systems, and with a structure which, if changing through time, is so stable that the changes can be ignored for long time periods, we may regard our operation as non-distorting.

A great temptation exists to adopt this view of the market economy for a simple but compelling reason: there exists a body of logical and mathematical techniques, developed by physicists, engineers, astronomers, and mathematicians in their analyses of physical systems, which is ready to hand for the physiological analysis of an economic mechanism. We can bring economic analysis under the regime of forces striving for an equilibrium, study changes in the equilibrium when inputs are changed to get insights into the assumed mechanism, and observe the performance of the mechanism as it functions through time, by applying mechanical statics and dynamics to its analysis. This approach pushes our analysis into a search for the principles of converting inputs to outputs that inhere in the structure of the mechanism, and therefore into an analysis of the rigid construction of the machine. The physiology of the system is, for purposes of such analysis, wholly self-contained (given inputs from the outside), and very closely related to the anatomy of the system. The outlook diverts our analytical attention from features of performance of the economic system that are *structural* responses to outside stimuli or changes inspired by inner laws of development within the system itself. That is, it ignores most *organic* aspects of the system.

If we consider the economy to be analogous to an organ in the organism that is society, the removal of the organ by definition is a dissection of the social body and automatically the organ ceases to function, or, at least, to function in its normal manner when all its linkages to other systems are intact. If we cut the ties of the economic system to the legal system, and in so doing, fail to take account of such entities as the body of antitrust law, the functioning of firms and markets may be quite different from what actually occurs in the American economy. Removing linkages with other social systems has the same effect as this abstraction from the legal system. If we cut the ties of the economy to the culture, which contains, for example, a set of attitudes toward work which we label the *Puritan work ethic*, any study of labor supply in the economy may be misleading. Further, any vision of the economic system that does not allow structural change in a living process—for example, the changes in attitudes to work, that arise as a labor force gains experience and more income, or the responses of price to changes in demand as oligopolists in a market become more accustomed to the reactions of their rivals in a learning process that can only be characterized as organic changes in the structure of the market—may yield results that are fundamentally deficient.

Thus, we may discern two basic and antagonistic *visions* of the nature of the economic system. The first, which we may call the *mechanistic* view, has been in the ascendant among professional economists at least since the time of David Ricardo, although there were some strong strains of the second, or *organic*, view in the work of such leading theorists as Alfred Marshall. The organic view has been best expressed by *historicist-institutionalist* analysts like Thorstein Veblen, John R. Commons, Wesley Clair Mitchell, Cliffe Leslie, and the German historical school of economists. But its failure to become dominant among economists may be ascribed to a number of factors.

First, and perhaps most importantly, the adherents of the organic view have not succeeded in devising a body of analytical methods with the degree of rigor and with the success in the derivation of fruitful theorems about reality that the mechanistic school has done. Indeed, many of the organic view's adherents have attempted to show that it is impossible to develop such a body of formal methods, so that practically speaking only intensive *ad hoc* studies of historical process can derive insights into the functioning of the economy, the results of which possess only a limited capability for generalization given the organic changes in the system constantly occurring. The approach to a study of history without a body of formal techniques admittedly requires a more subtle mind, a much broader spectrum of detailed knowledge of the history of society, and promises fewer concrete and purportedly generalizable results, than the adaptation of mechanical statics and dynamics to social phenomena. In an age of "science" and logical positivism the appeal of the mechanical view to the body of professional economic analysts has been much more powerful.

Second, to an important degree the clash between the mechanistic and organic views occurs because of a difference in viewpoint about the *problems* that should be attacked by the economics profession. The adherent of the mechanistic viewpoint tends to focus upon shorter-run questions, such as how prices are formed by the mechanism under various constraints concerning adjustments, how quantities are arrived at in periods that are quite short historically, decisionmaking for the consumer and firm over short periods, and so forth. For such periods even the adherent of the organic approach might agree that the economic system does not change fundamentally under its own organic laws of change, nor does it have time to react greatly to external impacts from the culture or other systems. For short periods, therefore, speaking historically, the social organ may be viewed adequately as a mechanism. The historicist-institutional school argued that these are not the problems in which the field of economics should be interested, and therefore stressed the need to treat the economy organically. There was, then, a good deal of *problem relativity* in the conflict, to the extent that many economists would no doubt agree that short-run problems are best attacked by the mechanistic model, whereas historically long-run problems are best attacked by organic models.

Thirdly, there is an important difference in implications for policy in the two viewpoints, which has biassed professional economists toward the mechanistic methods. Analytical treatment of the economy as a mechanism develops in the analyst an attitude of *social engineering* concerning normative approaches to his subject. If his approach to analysis is that of dealing with a mechanism, his attitudes toward social problems arising from its functioning may well be that they seem capable of being handled by proper alterations in the structure of the mechanism. The abstractions of the mechanism from its ties with other social systems tend to be ignored or at least subordinated, so that the analyst with understandable desires to effect policy changes is consciously or unconsciously drawn to the mechanistic framework of analysis.

On the other hand, those who embrace the organic viewpoint tend to be more cautious in their approach to policy recommendations. At one extreme they view man as caught up in a web of cultural and other institutions that impede the rational adjustment of society to its externally imposed needs and make futile any social engineering attempts to improve his lot in the short run. It is ironic that although institutionalism was in revolt against the social Darwinism rampant at the end of the century, and although it was mightily affected by reform movements like Progressivism and Populism and by such policy-oriented intellectual movements as philosophical pragmatism, John Dewey's instrumentalism, and Roscoe Pound's sociological jurisprudence, the fundamental organic outlook which underlay it prevented it from becoming a strong proponent of legislated or educated reform.

In this book we shall adopt the mechanistic outlook upon the nature of a market economy, but with the explicit recognition that when longer-run problems of the system are involved, or when one asks broader questions concerning the impact of the economic system on other systems in society, the organic approach should be explored as an intuitively more plausible outlook. Our set of problems, however, will be of the shorter-run types, concerning the operation of the market mechanism in its allocation of resources and its production and distribution of products. It is our belief that for such problems the mechanistic viewpoint is at once more appropriate and more fruitful.

THE COMPONENTS OF AN ABSTRACT MODEL

Having made this decision to build a simplified model of a system, which we conceive for present purposes at least to be mechanical in its operating principles and structure, how shall we proceed to accomplish the task? If we were to perform this work for a concrete mechanism—an airplane, a ship, a piece of machinery—our manner of procedure would be quite clear. But the mechanism we seek to represent is an abstract one, and as such is largely a creature of the human mind's ability to discern and synthesize abstract relations and patterns. Of what stuff are models of such abstractions made?

We shall define four sets of components in an abstract model whose interaction and consistency yield the outputs of the model in the form of *solutions.* Let us take these component sets in turn.

THE DATA SET. Whenever we start to create a model of social systems, we face an immediate and inescapable decision: how ambitious is our model to be? By this we mean explicitly, how much of the variation that is manifest in the society do we wish to attempt to explain by the model's performance, and how much do we intend to fall outside the domain of the model's competence? All of those phenomena that are external to the operation of the model we shall term the *data* of our model. Because they are external to the model—in the sense of having values or attributes determined in some manner not specified by the structure of our model—we shall assume that these values or attributes are given at the start of the analysis and are subject to change at the arbitrary whim of the analyst.

We may distinguish between two bodies of data: (1) *irrelevant* data, or that body of givens which, in the specifications of the model, are not required as inputs, so that they play no direct role in the operation of the model, and (2) *relevant* data, which are inputs into the model. For example, the positions of the planets in the solar system are data for economic models, being physical phenomena which no social model would attempt to explain, and it is difficult to imagine a model of economic phenomena which would require such data to enter as inputs. On the other hand, in most economic models the level of population in the society is a datum, explained on the basis of other-than-economic principles, but it is easy to see that it would be a relevant datum for many types of economic models. It should be noted that the notion of which data are relevant and which are irrelevant is not defined directly in terms of reality but rather of some specific model of that reality; that is, it is decided by the theorist as an implicit or explicit element of his constructions.

The relevant data, as inputs to the model, are ultimately the raw materials from which are fashioned, by the structure of the economic model, the outputs of the model. These data, being excluded from the body of the phenomena that are to be *explained* and being denoted occurrences that have a significant impact upon these phenomena, are given the status of determinants of the solution. Even when some of the relevant data are frozen throughout all analyses, or manipulations, of the model, so that their changes can have no impact upon the solutions and changes in the solutions of the model, they nonetheless exercise an influence upon these solutions.

The analytical ambition of a model is indexed by the size of the relevant data set relative to the size of the *variable* set, or that set of phenomena whose values or attributes are the outputs of the model mechanism. That is, the relevant data set plus the variable set in economic analysis should include all phenomena that are believed to be in the economist's province to explain, in addition to phenomena outside this domain that have a peculiarly strong impact upon economic phenomena. The most ambitious model an economist could construct would be a model whose variable set included all of the former and whose relevant data set contained all of the latter. As he becomes less ambitious in his analytical purposes, the modelbuilder removes phenomena from the variable set and places them in the relevant data set. For example, in one model, the price of beef and the price of pork might be included as variables of the model, whereas in another the price of beef might be placed in the relevant data set as a *given* and the price of pork be determined for that given value of beef. We should term the former a more ambitious model than the latter.

THE SET OF POSTULATES. A second set of components in a model is the set of assumptions that govern the external environment's specific contributions to the model's functioning and the model's behavior. On the basis of the distinction used in the previous sentence let us subdivide the postulates into two sets: (1) *data-constraining* postulates, or those which require that the relevant data set possesses certain values and attributes for a given analysis, and which therefore qualify the solutions to the model to be applicable to reality only when the values of the data approach those asserted by these postulates; and (2) *variable-constraining* postulates, or those which directly or indirectly constrain values of or establish relationships among the variables. The distinction between these two types of postulate is not always a clear one, but the division is sufficiently distinct to be valuable.

In the first category of assumption, for example, the analyst might set the relevant data at prescribed levels: in an economic model population, capital resources, and raw materials available to the economy could be set at specific numerical levels; the preference functions for consumers over the field of choice they face might be specified in function form; or the technological relationships confronting firms might be specified in function form. Or the analyst may state explicitly or implicitly that for the period of his analysis he assumes that no social upheaval such as war will occur to disturb his model.

Suppose, now, that with a specific economic model the analyst obtains a solution for his variables and tests these values or attributes against reality. Suppose, further, their conformance to reality is quite poor. One possible difficulty is that this first set of postulates—the data-constraining postulates —has been violated because the values and attributes of the data in reality depart from the values specified by the postulates in substantial degree. In any realistic analysis the description of the data set out by the postulates and values of the data in the real world will differ from one another, and as a consequence, a very real danger is run that every failure of the model's solution to predict reality may be ascribed by the analyst—affected with the vested interest of creation in his own model—to this lack of conformity. However, scientific devotion must force the analyst to face the possibility that real values and qualities for these phenomena are within acceptable distances from the values and attributes assumed by the postulates, and that the model itself is a poor depiction of the forces at work in the real economy. This danger in modelbuilding must be pointed out to the student and the following conservative corrective suggested: it is probably a good working hypothesis that whenever a model fails to predict accurately, the variable-constraining postulates should be suspect unless a strong and specific case can be stated to indict the data-constraining postulates.

The model *is*, in at least one important sense, the second set of postulates, or that set whose definition is required to obtain the relationships among the variables and the data or otherwise directly constrain the values the variables may assume. These relationships are the abstract counterparts of the components of the physical machine, for they define the manner in which the model absorbs data inputs, relates them to the outputs of the model, and determines their final form as outputs. It is perhaps the most difficult task of formal theorizing to specify a complete and consistent set of postulates that will suffice and just suffice (1) to yield information concerning the desired variable set that is (2) capable of being validated or invalidated by empirical test and (3) that will survive this ultimate test of usefulness. These final results of the model are, indeed, the variable-constraining postulates in another form: that is, these postulates give rise to relationships among variables and data that are merely convenient statements of the mutual implications of the postulates themselves. The whole purpose of the model is to restate the mutual implications of the variable-constraining postulates in a more convenient manner, where convenience means more conducive to deriving the limitations on the variables contained in the whole system of variable-constraining assumptions.

The formal techniques of modelbuilding are most vitally concerned with this one task: deriving methods for discovering the constraints placed upon the ability of the variables and attributes to vary by the mutual interaction of this set of assumptions. The basic reason for the need of such techniques is the difficulty which the human mind experiences when it seeks to juggle a whole set of postulates without formal aid in order to discern what implications they have for the values of the variables.

Let us pause for a moment to use a simple example for illustration of our meaning. Suppose we make the following data-constraining assumptions for a consumer:

Assumption 1. The consumer faces a set of fixed, positive, finite prices for goods which he cannot affect by his actions.

Assumption 2. The consumer has a fixed positive amount of income to spend in the period under analysis, and he may not spend more than this amount.

Assumption 3. The consumer's preferences for goods are unaffected by prices and can be represented by a function whose value rises when a new collection of goods is preferred to an old, remains the same when the old and new collections are equally desirable, and falls when the old is preferred to the new. This function is smooth (has no sharp points) and continuous (has no breaks or gaps). Moreover, at every point on the function an increase in one or more goods—all other goods in the old collection being held constant—causes a rise in the value of the function. That is, at no time can the consumer become satiated in any good, any group of goods, or all goods.

Assumption 4. Find two baskets of goods, X_1 and X_2, such that the consumer is indifferent between them. Now, draw a straight line connecting these two baskets in the space in which they are points, and that straight line will contain baskets of goods that are weighted combinations of the two given baskets. We require that when X_1 is equally preferred to X_2, every basket X^* on the line (except X_1 and X_2) be preferred to X_1 and X_2, and we require these conditions to hold for any choice of baskets X_1 and X_2 that are equally attractive to the individual.

It is easily seen that these assumptions place restrictions on the data set, which consists of given prices, income, and a preference function. The latter is constrained to be smooth, continuous, always rising as we move outward from the origin, and to be *strictly quasi-concave*, as specified by Assumption 4 and to be discussed further in Chapter 2.

We may now add the set of variable-constraining assumptions:

Assumption 5. The amounts of goods taken by the consumer in the solution must be zero or positive.

Assumption 6. The consumer makes his goods choices by seeking to obtain as high a value on the preference function as he can, given Assumptions 1 through 5.

Assumptions 1 through 6 imply the following proposition: if the price of one good is raised slightly, all other goods' prices remaining fixed, and if money income is also raised by exactly enough to allow the consumer to buy the same basket of goods he bought before the price rise, he will not in fact buy this same basket, but will buy a new basket of goods in which the amount of the good whose price has risen will always be less than in the old basket.

Our desire at this point is not to deal with the meaning of the proposition for consumer behavior, but merely to show the reader that although this proposition inheres in the statement of Assumptions 1 through 6, it is not immediately apparent in reading them. The student will then appreciate the need for a formal body of techniques that will allow such propositions to be drawn with efficiency from such sets of postulates. And this body of techniques is perhaps the most important content of the art of theorizing. In this book our major concern in the chapters to follow will be to present to the student the methods which economists have developed to derive such propositions or theorems as well as to present the theorems themselves, for the methods seem to us to be as important as the *theorem-outputs* of the model.

If the data-constraining and variable-constraining assumptions in fact imply the solutions we seek to obtain, furnishing the inputs to the mechanism and specifying the mechanism's structure, what qualities must they possess for the purpose of gaining insights into the real world economy? It will be useful to discuss some of these.

First, they must be consistent with one another, so that the implications of the sets of assumptions do not contain both *A* and non-*A*. As a useful analogy, we may cite the following simple illustration: it is impossible to require a relationship to be a straight line and to pass through any three points specified in the data-constraining assumptions. In general, both requirements cannot be met, and therefore the assumption sets imply an inconsistency, so that no solution exists.

Second, the set of assumptions must be sufficiently binding upon the variables to make the solution or solutions small enough in number to be interesting. This does not mean that the set of assumptions must be such as to admit one and only one (that is, a unique) solution: no a priori reason exists for believing that the real economic mechanism which we are seeking to understand always gives a unique solution. But if, in analogy, our assumptions merely require that a straight line pass through a given point, obviously an infinity of relationships among variables can meet this requirement, and so the solutions are infinite in number. Because the purpose of our assumptions is to restrict variation within reasonable bounds in order that it can be tested against reality, this type of model is not very interesting. We may call such a model an *underdetermined* system, meaning by this that the restrictions implied by the assumption set are not narrow enough to render interesting results.

Third, we may tolerate a set of postulates that is repetitive or redundant, in the sense of implying the same restriction upon the variables more than once. Such a system does not suffer from the same difficulty as the model suffering from inconsistencies among its postulates, but the interrelationships among the variables and data that are the reflections of the assumptions (and which will be discussed subsequently) should be culled to eliminate such redundancies.

Fourth, we may also tolerate some degree of *unrealism* in the set of data-constraining and variable-constraining postulates. In the case of the first set of postulates, we have already discussed the inability to expect that in the real world conditions will always hold at the given levels specified for the data, or that the characteristics specified for functional data forms will be exactly fulfilled. In our consumer example, more than one price may vary during any usable real world period; consumers' incomes may not remain constant; some consumers' preferences may not be specifiable by a representation of the type we have assumed, and where specifiable, may not be independent of prices, smooth, continuous or quasi-concave. As far as the second group of postulates is concerned, it is equally possible that we may be making assumptions that are patently untrue on their face: for example, our assumption that the consumer sets about to find a maximum on his preference function constrained only by the unalterable data he faces would strike most of us as a false interpretation at least of conscious behavior, and perhaps even of unconscious consumer behavior.

But these points should come as no shock to us, after our discussion of the basic need to abstract from detail and to simplify if we are to have any realistic hope of obtaining a useful model. For the example at hand, it is quite clear that the motivations of typical consumers in their decisionmaking are much too complex and subject to whim and caprice to be depicted photographically by a maximizing procedure. Suppose that we took seriously the criticism that Assumption 6 above was so unrealistic as to be unacceptable, and that we spent a long period in obtaining information on actual consumer behavior in order to frame more realistic postulates about consumer motivation. It would probably be true that we could not obtain an alternative postulate of such behavior that could be readily generalized, or, that could be generalized in a graceful way permitting analysis to continue. Therefore, we would face a situation that arises in modelbuilding quite frequently: *either we simplify and abstract from realistic complications to get a manipulatable model, or we give up the hope of such analysis.*

The justification for making such intellectual compromises or capitulations is that the items of ultimate interest are the solution outputs of the model, not the postulates that make them possible. It is quite possible to obtain predictions from a model concerning realistic economic variation that are very useful when some of the postulates are unrealistic. In the natural sciences, for example, the assumptions that bodies fall in a complete vacuum, or that elastic strings do not change their lengths, or that pendulums are suspended by weightless strings, yield quite good realistic predictions.[1] Although the projection must be proved by experience, the same type of result may be obtained in the social sciences.

Indeed, some economists have taken the extreme position that the value of a model must be judged wholly or at least primarily from the validity of the propositions it yields. If they are reasonably close to reality in a large number of trials, then the model is said to be useful and should be used regardless of

---

[1] There are important exceptions to this assertion which serve to check our eagerness to eliminate frictions from physical systems, and thereby imply bounds to such eliminations from economic models. The classical hydrodynamics of Euler, as refined by Helmholtz, Kelvin, and Rayleigh, postulated the movement of bodies through a fluid of zero viscosity, so that resistance to such movement was nil. Because this assumption was approximated in reality only when the boundary layer of the fluid formed under the influence of viscosity stayed in contact with the moving object, and because the airplane in flight detached this boundary layer, the classical theory could not be used to explain the flow of air around the aircraft. Alongside the classical hydrodynamics and its frictionless abstractions, therefore, arose a science of *hydraulics* to cope with such practical problems as were encountered in aerodynamics, with techniques characterized much more by the *ad hoc*, practical, and ungeneralized.

In economics, too, where abstracted frictions in fact cannot be ignored and tend to make *classical* theory inapplicable, the analogue to hydraulics tends to arise as a related but separable body of techniques, as we shall see in our discussion of rivalrous competition.

For a discussion of the problem in hydrodynamics, see O. G. Tietjens, based on lectures by L. Prandtl, *Fundamentals of Hydro- and Aeromechanics*, Dover edition, New York, 1957, pp. 2–4, 107–110, and *Applied Hydro- and Aerodynamics*, Dover edition, New York, 1957, pp. xv–xvi. For calling my attention to this illustration, I am indebted to Jacob Viner, who cited it in his "International Trade Theory and Its Present Day Relevance," *Economics and Public Policy. Brookings Lectures*, 1954, Washington, D.C., 1955, pp. 127–128.

the unreality of the postulates.[2] This position is extreme from several points of view. If the propositions or outputs of the model are merely the inter-dependent and indirect implications of the postulates, then the postulates standing singly must be viewed also as the most directly derived propositions of the model. There seems little a priori reason, therefore, for excusing them from the empirical tests which the less immediately derivable propositions must be put through. For, if one asserts that one class of propositions is excused from the need for verification but another class is not, one has placed himself under the obligation of drawing up general criteria for dis-tinguishing between the two classes.[3]

If this is indeed a just outlook, then if one of the postulates does not yield results taken alone which are validated by reality, the likelihood that the more complicated deductions of the model will so conform must decline below what it would be if such validation did hold. And even if the outputs of the model time after time yield useful results, the likelihood of failure the next time must be higher if this lack of empirical validation of the postulate occurs.[4] If the postulates of a model are not directly testable, this same line of reasoning must also make final solutions more suspect than if they were so tested and were validated.

The extreme position concerning the irrelevance of realistic postulates in economic models, therefore, is one to which we could not subscribe; but neither is an opposite extreme that would put near-exclusive reliance upon the testability and realistic content of these postulates. Our position is between these extremes: realistic and testable postulates add to the credita-bility of positive results of an economic model, and are desirable, but failure to obtain them does not of itself deny the usefulness of the propositions obtained from a model.

THE SET OF FUNCTIONAL RELATIONSHIPS. A third set of components of an abstract model contains the counterparts of the structural assemblies of a concrete mechanism. They are derived wholly from the set of postulates and are therefore not independent components, but it is they that are the immediate generators of the outputs. This set contains the functions relating the variables of the model to themselves and to the data of the model, as these relations are implied by the body of postulates. These functional relationships, when they reflect a set of postulates that is sufficient and

---

[2] See, for example, Milton Friedman, "The Methodology of Positive Economics," in *Essays in Positive Economics* (Chicago: University of Chicago Press, 1948), pp. 3–43.

[3] See Tjalling C. Koopmans, *Three Essays on the State of Economic Science* (New York: McGraw-Hill, 1957).

[4] The point has been made most forcefully by Jack Melitz, "Friedman and Machlup on the Significance of Testing Economic Assumptions," *Journal of Political Economy*, LXXIII (1965), pp. 37–60.

self-consistent, yield the solutions to the model, or the values of the variable set that, ideally, can be tested against reality. Because these functions summarize the constraints which the postulates put upon the data and the variables in a more convenient form than the postulates themselves, most of our attention in modelbuilding ordinarily is focussed upon discerning the properties of these functions in order to gain insights into the general properties of solutions to the model.

In economic modelbuilding, there are several postulates that have a direct bearing upon the derivation of these functional relationships, whose discussion we have delayed until this point in order to emphasize their roles in generating the interrelationship functions. These are employed so frequently that we will do well to take a brief look at them before we use them in later chapters.

1. *Maximization or minimization*. The assumption is frequently made that consumers and firms maximize their satisfactions and profits respectively subject to various constraints among the data, or that firms minimize costs. We have encountered this in our simple example of the consumer above, and have employed it to illustrate the use of nonrealistic postulates. The reason why these assumptions concerning motivation and behavior are so frequently used is simply that the logic of maximizing a criterion variable over the field of choice provides us a simple way of deriving the interrelationships among variables and data, whose existence is so important to our models. Beyond this, by assuming that the decisionmaking unit *has in fact achieved a maximum or minimum*, we can obtain important information about the shape of the functions in a small neighborhood about that position, and this information may be put to valuable usage in deriving insights about the physiology of the model.

This line of reasoning adds more support to our argument in the preceding section, that, although simple and perhaps for the largest part unrealistic, the assumption of maximization for economic units is most attractive because of its double function of giving us the interrelationships we need and some general information about the shapes of the functions at strategic points. No other alternative assumption has been found to be so fruitful in generating these interrelationships and supplementary information.

2. *Diminishing marginal rates of substitution*. The assumption of diminishing marginal rates of substitution among goods for consumers, and among inputs and ouputs in production, is a direct assumption about the shape of functions useful in assuring that maxima or minima are attainable by the methods we use to find them and to obtain information about such shapes for manipulating the model. This assumption merely means that if we hold

all but two goods or factor services constant, as we increase the presence of one such object it becomes a poorer and poorer substitute for the other variable object as a producer of consumer satisfaction or of output.

3. *Equilibrium*. A most frequent and direct restraint upon the values of variables in the solution is that contained in the concept of equilibrium. That is, it is enforced upon the values determined in markets that the solution yield values such that every person desirous of selling in the ruling market environment be able to find a person desirous of buying in such a market, and vice versa.[5] In such a situation, no effective participant in the market has any reason to upset the status quo. Obviously, such a postulate has much intuitive appeal, and is a powerful limitation upon the ability of the solution values to vary. Consequently, such market equilibrium assumptions are frequently used.

4. *Stability of equilibrium*. An assumption also employed on occasion is that an equilibrium, once achieved, is *stable*. That is, if the equilibrium is disturbed, so that the model departs from it, the inner workings of the model will return the market to the same equilibrium. If we assume this will happen, then the shapes of the interrelationships of the model are constrained to assume certain forms, and such information may be used to good advantage in working with the model to gain insights. Stability analysis is a particularly valuable tool in models in which individual decisionmaking units employing a maximization technique are not present, for then the assumption that the market equilibrium is stable provides a basis for gaining information about the functions which a maximization assumption cannot.

THE SET OF VARIABLES. The interrelationships, derived from such postulates as these, may ideally be solved out so that the values of the variables are functions only of the data of the model. In our example of the preceding section concerning the consumer, the set of interrelationships obtainable from the postulates given (which we shall not deal with here but will derive explicitly in Chapter 2) may be solved out (at least ideally) to obtain such relations as

$$X_j = F_j(P_1, P_2, \ldots, P_n, Y) \qquad [1\text{--}1]$$

where $X_j, j = 1, 2, \ldots, n$, is the amount taken in the solution of the j-th good, P_j are prices of these goods, and Y is the income of the individual, and where, in the background and present only implicitly, is the preference function of the individual. These solution functions of [1–1] are called *demand functions*, and depict the solution values of the variables of the model as functions

---

[5] We shall complicate this overly simple definition of market equilibrium in later chapters.

wholly of the data of the model. Therefore, given any set of data-constraining postulates specifying allowable values for prices and income, the amounts the consumer will take of any good by the logic of the model are determined. At this point, therefore, we have arrived at the fourth and last set of components of the model.

The outputs of our model, given any allowable set of data inputs, are the values of the variables which we have decided to determine in the model. The solution functions illustrated by [1–1] are a direct bridge from data to the outputs of the model, overarching the intermediate steps of defining variable-constraining postulates and deriving from them the interrelationships among variables which we require. As such they do teach the lesson that in the final analysis it is the data and assumptions of the model that do the determining of the solution values of the variables. As we said earlier, the fewer the variables in the set relative to the whole set of economic variables the less ambitious the model.

With this consideration of the components in a model behind us, let us now ask a quite important question with direct bearing upon what we wish to accomplish in this book. The question is this: Suppose we wish to build a model that is the most ambitious construct economists could concern themselves with. Of what would the relevant data set and variable set consist? We shall answer this question in the next section.

THE CLOSED MARKET EQUILIBRIUM MODEL

Although the consensus is only a conventional one, most economists would probably agree broadly on the limits of the economist's tasks. By this we mean that from the whole set of phenomena that arise in the functioning of society—with its interrelated groups of social systems, the culture, and personality mechanisms—the economist is given a rather well-marked territory of variation with which to cope by developing models that allow some insight into its causes. Working back from the variable set of this most ambitious model which economists would build if they could, we would therefore find a set of interrelationships among variables and data for this model, a set of postulates for it, and a set of relevant data. If we could build it, this model would be *closed* to outside *economic* factors: that is, all recognized economic variation would be in the variable set, by construction, and the only factors determining the solutions would lie in the social and physical areas of noneconomic phenomena. In this sense we may refer to it as a *closed* model.

We may view the task of the investigators in any subfield of social or physical phenomena as that of ultimately developing a closed model of their domain of variation—that is, a model whose determinants are forces outside that subfield, so that all variation recognized as relevant to the subfield is explained by this closed model. Only if this model were attained, and it were incapable of improvement in its structure and predictions, would the work in that subfield be done. In this sense, therefore, our discussion of the *ideal* closed economic model is a view of the ultimate ambitions of the economist, and from that view many of the smaller analytical problems and models of economic phenomena can be given scale and perspective.

The variable set of this ultimate model would be the prices and amounts exchanged of every good and factor service, of every type of security, and of money, at every point in time after an initial period through some horizon period, and with values for variables relevant to every consumer and firm in the economy. Most of those variables that have an economic content can be expressed as prices or as quantities at points in time or over some period of time; as a consequence of this great convenience, we shall treat the variable set of this most ambitious model as consisting of prices and quantities exclusively.

We should like a model that would explain *all* such variables in its solution (1) over time such that every variable has a value in the solution for each period or point distinguished in the flow of time, or (2) that at least we obtain the solution values for those periods after which the time path of variables remains unchanged if no alterations in data or postulates are imposed. We shall distinguish between these two types of model more fully later, but let us not pause in our discussion of the closed economic model to distinguish them at this point.

The interrelationships in such a model would feature the following types.

1. *Demand relationships* for each consumer and each good, which would imply the amounts he desires of each good in equilibrium.

2. *Demand adjustment relationships* for each consumer and each good, which would show how the consumer adjusted his purchases over time to attain the equilibrium amounts given by the demand relationships when he was not in equilibrium. These relationships would show the rates of speed and directions of adjustment of quantities purchased as a function of the consumer's current quantities taken and their departure from the equilibrium quantities he desires to purchase. Thus, these relations would reveal how the consumer's purchases of goods in period t are related to his purchases in $t - 1$, giving us potential linkages over time of his decisions.

3. *Supply relationships* for each consumer, which would imply the equilibrium supply of factor services under his control, given income and prices.

4. *Supply adjustment relationships* for each consumer, which are analogous

to those on the demand side except that they refer to the adjustment of his supplies of factor services.

5. *Demand relationships* for each firm and each good or service used as an input by the firm, which would imply for the firm the equilibrium amounts of inputs it would purchase for any specified set of prices.

6. *Demand adjustment relationships* for each firm and each input, which specify the firm's rates of reaction in its demands for inputs over time when its purchases are not in equilibrium.

7. *Supply relationships* for each firm and each output, which determine the firm's desired outputs for the period whose length has been adopted in the analysis.

8. *Supply adjustment relationships* for each firm and each output, which state the rates at which the firm adjusts the output to reach its equilibrium amounts over time.

9. *Market demand relationships* implying the amounts demanded of each good and factor service in equilibrium by all actors in the economy, obtained from relations 1. and 5.

10. *Market demand adjustment relationships*, which show the rates of adjustment of amounts demanded in the whole market by consumers and firms of every good and factor service, obtained from relations 2. and 6.

11. *Market supply relationships* for all consumers and firms and for each good and factor service obtained from relations 3. and 7.

12. *Market supply adjustment relationships*, which show the adjustment of supplies in nonequilibrium states over time, obtained from relations 4. and 8.

13. *Market equilibrium relationships*, stating that in all markets the amounts supplied must equal or exceed the amounts demanded.

14. *Market equilibrium adjustment relationships*, requiring that the rates of change of all economic variables in the solution must have reached zero, so that constancy prevails in all economic phenomena.

15. *Equilibrium price relationships*, which state that for some goods like capital goods, money, and securities, prices in equilibrium must bear certain relationships among themselves that are based on the equilibrium interest rate.

These fifteen sets of interrelationships would provide the immediate basis for the derivation of our solutions and would be the structural components of our closed economic model.

The data-constraining postulates would include the following among their number.

1. Restrictions on the shape of the consumer preference functions and a statement of the laws of change over time of these functions, if any.

2. Restrictions on the shape of the firms' technological functions, and a statement of the laws of change over time of these functions, if any.

3. The initial amounts of primary resources available to the economy and laws of change in the quantities over time of those which are not producible under the spur of economic forces.

4. The expectations of prices held by consumers and firms and their laws of change from period to period.

5. The *market power* of each consumer and firm in the economy, stating their abilities to affect the prices of the goods and services they buy and sell in markets.

The variable-constraining postulates of greatest importance would be the following.

1. All variables would have to meet certain restrictions in the solution—in most cases, they must be constrained to be positive or nonnegative.

2. All markets would have to be in equilibrium and reveal no nonzero rates of change over time in the variables.

3. Consumers must maximize satisfaction, subject to constraints, and firms must maximize profits, subject to constraints, in the solution.

4. Net rates of return on all assets must be equal in the solution.

Lastly, the most important of the relevant data set's elements would be the following.

1. The existence of consumer preference representations for each consumer.

2. The existence of consumer price expectations for the future.

3. The existence of a technological relationship among inputs and outputs of producible goods for each firm and all such goods.

4. The existence of firms' price expectations in the future.

5. The existence of maximum amounts of primary inputs, that is, non-producible inputs or inputs that are not produced under the economic regime of profits (such as labor).

6. The existence and rules of operation of all social mechanisms with a direct impact upon the economic mechanism, with the relevant laws of change of these external social mechanisms. Among these, the most important would be the demands for goods and services, the taxation policies, the borrowing and lending policies, the rules for creation of money, and so forth, of all levels of government. Further, the operations of all economic mechanisms external to the economic mechanism must be taken as given, such as those setting the levels of import demand by foreign countries for the products of the economy under analysis, and including the possibility that the laws of change for their activities would be specified.

For our present purposes of studying the operation of the market mechanism, *every* theoretical analysis of economic problems may be viewed as starting from this closed market equilibrium model, and, through a suitable choice of a subset of the variables in the variable set, being narrowed down in its ambition to the size indicated. This means that variables are converted to data, that data-constraining postulates are increased at the expense of variable-constraining postulates, and that the body of relevant data is increased in size by the addition of the converted variables. Having obtained a large and detailed map (not a photograph) of the entire terrain of economics, we can now place every economic analysis within that domain, and study its relation to the surrounding terrain.

Moreover, at this point we may see clearly that any economic analysis with hopes of empirical relevance must be a simplification of this closed model, for the latter is much too cumbersome for successful manipulation. As we indicate the types of simplification we shall employ in this book, we shall take the opportunity to explore the meaning of these measures and to look over the alternatives available.

Some Problems and Limitations of Modelbuilding

How shall we reduce the scale of the closed economic model so that we may present a reasonably brief textbook of economic analysis, yet retain the large overview of the economy that the closed model depicts? What alternative simplifications might have been made to those we have adopted? What are the meanings of these neglected alternatives, and how does their neglect qualify the results of the methods we have used in this book? These are the problems that will now be discussed. In their discussion, some of the unavoidable limitations of modelbuilding as a technique of gaining insights into the operation of a modern industrial economy will become apparent.

STATIC ANALYSIS VERSUS DYNAMIC ANALYSIS

A most fundamental problem in designing a theoretical model must concern the choice between a static and a dynamic model. A dynamic model is one whose interrelationships (and therefore whose solutions) involve *time* in an essential way, that is, in such a way that it is impossible to state those interrelationships or the solutions without its presence. The solution to a dynamic model, therefore, is a path through time: it is a function that yields different values for the variables for every integer-valued time period over some horizon. For example, the solution to a model that predicts the value in period t of a principal V_0 invested in period $t = 0$ at a compound interest rate of $i \times 100$ per cent effective for $t \geq 1$ is given by

$$V_t = V_0(1 + i)^t, \qquad [1-2]$$

where the model is expressed as the simple relationship

$$V_{t+1} = V_t(1 + i) \qquad [1-3]$$

and the initial value V_0 is given among the data.

The equation [1–2] is a *particular* solution to the model of [1–3] because the accumulated value in any period is given in terms of the data V_0, i, and t only, because when the values of V_t and V_{t+1} are substituted from [1–2] into [1–3] the latter is satisfied for all values $t = 1, 2, \ldots$, and because when $t = 0$ in [1–2] the given value V_0 is obtained. The model [1–3] is dynamic because time is intimately involved in its definition, inasmuch as the problem of compound interest could not be posed in the absence of time.

The solution to the model presented in [1–2] obviously is a path through time. When working with such dynamic models, or continuous time variations of them obtained by allowing the length of the time period to shrink without limit, we are most interested in the solution path's configuration when plotted against time, for it can exhibit quite different modes of behavior. We have illustrated them in Figure 1–1 and will discuss briefly idealizations of the types of paths that are possible in simple dynamic models. In the presentation of the chart we have assumed that the time periods t are very small in duration in order to make the curves smooth and more easily understood.

1. *Monotonically increasing and unbounded values.* This type of path is illustrated by the concept of compound interest and by curve A of Figure 1–1. If we assume that $V_0 > 0$ and that $i > 0$, V_t climbs without limit as time goes on, and never attains a maximum.

2. *Monotonically decreasing and unbounded values.* This type of solution, charted by curve B, occurs when values fall through zero and approach $-\infty$ as time rises indefinitely.

3. *Constant values.* This type of solution is illustrated by curve C, and would occur in the compound interest example if $i = 0$. It is the simplest of the monotonic curves.

4. *Monotonically increasing values converging to a limit.* Curve D illustrates this kind of behavior. It might be typified in the real economy if the state were to pass a law declaring that a sum V_t might accumulate to no more than a fixed value K. Then the value V_t would increase until it hit the ceiling and become constant thereafter at K.

5. *Monotonically decreasing values converging to a limit.* Curve E depicts this type of path or sequence of values. If $V_0 > 0$ and $i < 0$, so that the saver

was forced to pay negative interest for the safekeeping of his money, the value of his holding would fall toward zero as time went on. The limit approached by *E* on Figure 1–1 would then be zero rather than a negative value as we graphed it.

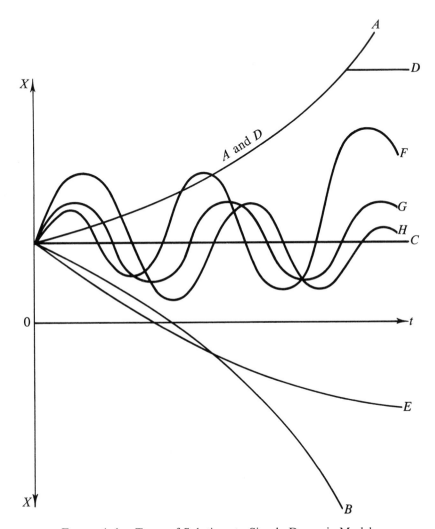

FIGURE 1–1.   Types of Solutions to Simple Dynamic Models.

6. *Explosive cycles.* This diverging sequence of values is graphed in curve *F*, and illustrates cyclical behavior that increases in amplitude through time.

7. *Undamped cycles.* This type of cycle, which neither grows nor shrinks in amplitude, is illustrated in curve *G*.

8. *Damped cycles.* This last type of behavior, in which the amplitudes of the cycles decrease over time, is illustrated in curve *H*.

If we were to solve an economic model of the simple dynamic sort, we should obtain a solution that had the major features of one of these types of solutions, if a solution existed. But if the solution is of that configuration shown in curves *C*, *D*, *E*, or *H*, it is clear that for some value of *t* sufficiently large the solution gets arbitrarily close to limiting or *stationary* values, or, indeed, attains them, and the rates of change in the values are zero (or very close to it).

Where such dynamic solutions may be assumed to exist, we may term them *stationary* solutions, and where dynamic solutions of the other forms in Figure 1–1 result we may term them *nonstationary*. Let it be noted that the terms *stationary* and *nonstationary* refer to the characteristics revealed by the time paths yielded by the solution of the dynamic equation system.

But another form of interrelationship set can be used in the analysis of processes through time by assuming that all of the interrelationships contain only variables relevant to the same point in time; thus, different time periods are not explicitly interconnected through associations among the variables. For example, suppose we broke up the time periods involved in the compound interest example and, rather than treating them in a unified way as a sequence whose solution values were obtained simultaneously in [1–2], assumed instead that the data for each period included the principal and interest accumulated up to that point in time. That is, for $t = 5$, the datum $V^* = V_5 = V_0(1 + i)^5$ is given, and the value V° is the solution to

$$V^\circ = V^*(1 + i). \qquad [1\text{--}4]$$

In period $t = 6$ a new datum $V^* = V_6$ is used, and so forth, so that we may treat what is essentially a time process as a series of related *slice-of-time* analyses in which temporal relationships are omitted from the interrelationships among the variables and limited to those among the data. Each solution value of [1–4] is stationary, in the sense that it remains constant through time unless the datum V^* is changed, in which case the new solution value is attained instantaneously and is stationary in the same sense. Such analysis is termed *static*.

Static analysis is, therefore, a type of analysis of temporal processes in which time is eliminated explicitly from the interrelationships among the variables and relegated to effecting changes in the data, but which may be used to analyze time processes by a series of snapshots rather than a motion picture of the process. It is incorrect to say, therefore, that static analysis is a type of analysis that eliminates time and that dynamic analysis is a method that includes time. Rather, the two basic methods of analyzing economic variation are distinguished by the structure of the interrelationship functions used in the models with which the analysis proceeds. Static analysis excludes all explicit intertemporal relations among the variables in the variable set, whereas the interrelations in the dynamic model include meaningful relations among values of variables at different points of time. Thus, the accumulated value of a principal at compound interest in a static analysis is *made to appear* independent of yesterday's accumulated value by making the latter a datum relevant to today, whereas in a dynamic analysis these relationships are included as linkages among the variables.

Needless to say, a dynamic analysis is much more difficult to undertake than a static analysis, for in the former the laws of change of the variables must be assumed known, but in the latter the analyst's freedom to change the values of the data from period to period without explicit knowledge of the laws of change makes the process through time more easily manipulated. Moreover, the mathematical methods available to deal with static models are much more developed and simpler than those available to treat dynamic models. For these reasons, we shall neglect dynamic problems in greatest part, and not strive to obtain postulates that explicitly relate values of variables at different points of time. For example, the capital stock of an economy is an economic variable, because it is determined by motivation concerning the profit urge and consumer preferences relative to saving. But its values at each point of time t are interrelated, inasmuch as it is a stock that is added to or subtracted from each period. Its laws of change, therefore, should be part of the solution to a dynamic system. But we shall treat capital accumulation in a static model, by dealing only with the addition to or subtraction from the stock—that is, the investment of the period—and assume that the capital stock with which we begin every period is given as a datum.

From the interrelationships of the closed market equilibrium model, therefore, we shall eliminate relations 2., 4., 6., 8., 10., 12., and 14., or those which include these intertemporal relations among the variables. All rates of adjustment are postulated to be infinitely rapid, because in this event only the values of variables of the current period enter into the interrelationships among the variables.

STABILITY ANALYSIS

We may pause a moment to clarify a frequently abused term in model-building, inasmuch as we have spent some time in spelling out the difference between dynamic and static analysis. We may distinguish between two types of *stability* in dynamic analysis: (1) the stability of a *model* or a *process*, and (2) the stability of an *equilibrium*, or stationary solution to a dynamic model. Let us treat each in turn.

A dynamic model is globally stable if, from every set of acceptable initial values for the variables—that is, for every acceptable set of data including the values of the variables in $t = 0$—the model attains or approaches some stationary solution (not necessarily the same for all initial points) or set of solutions. This term, therefore, is used to characterize the nature of the solutions to dynamic models, and indicate whether and under what conditions an acceptable (i.e. stationary) solution occurs.

On the other hand, if we begin with the assumption that we are already at a stationary solution, and if we move the model away from it by choosing a new initial position which departs from that solution, then study the path to see if the same equilibrium is reestablished, we are concerned with the stability of an equilibrium. If an equilibrium reestablishes itself for any permissible displacement to an initial position, the equilibrium is termed *stable in the large*. If this stability holds only for relatively small displacements in the neighborhood of the equilibrium, it is termed *stable in the small*.

If a model has a unique equilibrium and that equilibrium is stable in the large, then obviously the model will be globally stable. But if a model has more than one equilibrium, no equilibrium can be stable in the large but may be stable in the small; however, the model may be globally stable, because it is possible that one of the multiple equilibria will be attained for any allowable initial position or that the set of equilibria will be approached by particular solutions. Thus, an equilibrium may be unstable, so that once departed from it can never be reattained, but some other equilibrium or set of equilibria can be attained, preserving the stability of the system.

Lastly, let us note that whether we use the term *stability* to describe a quality of an equilibrium or a system, it can only be relevant to dynamic systems—that is, to systems that have explicit time assumptions in their interrelationships. Stability characterizes a path or set of paths in the time dimension, and if these paths do not exist in the solution, or exist only in the implicit sense that we move the solution through time in a constant manner, stability analysis does not apply. Thus, to analyze the stability of a static model or of that model's equilibrium is impossible, and when we seem to do this we are in fact implicitly building a dynamic model and analyzing its properties. We shall in this book, therefore, spend little time in analyzing stability properties, inasmuch as we have explicitly ignored most dynamic properties of the economy for the sake of simplicity. However, in Chapter 7, in order to illustrate the nature of such analysis, we shall deal with the stability of a single market.

THE PROBLEMS OF MODEL SIZE

We have indicated our intention to build a static closed market model of the type described in the section, "The Closed Market Equilibrium Model," earlier in this chapter. The level of ambition of that model—in the sense of the definition of ambition as the relation of the variable set's size to that of the relevant data set's content of economic phenomena—is clearly quite great.

Our purpose in building such a model is to present the market mechanism as a whole: as a functioning mechanism, accepting inputs of data, transforming them by feeding them into its working parts which consist of complicated interrelationships among the variables and data, and generating a whole-solution output. In our view only in this way can the student obtain the feel of the highly interdependent nature of the causation in a modern economy. Indeed, were we able to do so, we should like to extend this vision of holism to that of society, showing the interactions among the economy and all other social mechanisms, as well as the cultural system and personality mechanisms. Only by visualizing the whole initially can we execute the partial analyses with full understanding of what has been abstracted from and what limitations flow from that abstraction.

But we must at the same time point up a fundamental limitation of such large-scale (or general equilibrium) models: for the purposes of explicit analysis, or the deriving of specific propositions about the nature of solutions in order to gain insights into the real economy, they are largely valueless, unless we are able to fill them with explicit numerical data. This fact may best be illustrated by discussing at some length the way in which we shall *use* models to derive general insights into the physiology of the real economy.

COMPARATIVE DYNAMICS. Let us deal briefly with the manner of using dynamic models for such analysis, because we shall do little further in this book with such systems. Suppose, however, that we began with such a dynamic model and with a specific set of data, including the values of the variables at some initial point of time. By assumption, let us say that the model yields a stationary solution for this data set. Now, if a datum is changed—a methodological right of the modelbuilder—how will the model react to it? Will it yield a new stationary equilibrium, and if so, how will the solution values differ from the original stationary equilibrium? Will the model merely return to the old equilibrium? Will the model yield a solution that is not stationary?

This method of analysis of a dynamic model by displacements of its equilibrium due to shocks administered to its data set is called *comparative dynamics*, because it derives properties of the model by comparing the model's solutions for controlled differences in data. It may be seen, for example, that if the only datum we change in such displacements is the set of original values of the variables (or the original position of the model), we are treating the stability of an equilibrium or of the system. Thus, stability analysis is a specific form of comparative dynamic analysis.

But, of course, it is not the only type. We might ask, for example, what would happen to the solution of a model if we increased the time necessary for the supply of a good to respond to an increase in demand: would it change the solution from one yielding stationary equilibria to one that oscillates in explosive fashion? Or, we might ask what would happen to the equilibrium prices of goods if transactions were permitted to occur before the equilibrium was reached?

Economic analysis generally has not made much use of comparative dynamics until recent years. Stability analysis may be considered an exception, although except for quite simple models it has not been much used until recently. For other types of shocks administered to a dynamic model of some complexity, it may be justly stated that the economist is only now beginning to investigate the possibilities of comparative dynamics. Its mathematics are quite complicated and, although it is early in the game, to date it has not given us very interesting propositions about economic variation in the real economy. Of course, by virtue of our remaining for the most part with static models, we shall not deal to any great extent with comparative dynamic methodology. It is important to see, however, that the counterpart of the analytical methods we shall develop for static models does exist for these more complicated theoretical structures.

COMPARATIVE STATICS. The same method of shocking the model by changing a datum and observing the qualitative or quantitative changes that occur in the new equilibrium may be applied to static models, and, indeed, we shall rely most heavily upon this method to gain insights into the analytical structures that we build. We shall assume that a model is in equilibrium; then, we may ask, "If the price of a good rises, and consumer A readjusts his choices to achieve a new equilibrium, will he take more of that good in the new solution, less of the good, or the same quantity? Will Firm 1 produce more of the good, less of it, or the same quantity in the new equilibrium?"

Asking questions of this sort and seeking techniques to answer them are essential parts of modelbuilding, for only if we can cope with variations of this nature can the models be of much use, assuming as is ordinarily the case that we cannot actually fit the interrelationships to actual data. These laws of change of the model give us the insights into the real economy which it is the purpose of the model to furnish. The sterility of merely obtaining general statements of the interrelationships among data and variables and of asserting or even proving that there exists a unique and stable solution may be illustrated very simply.

Assume that for a market we have a demand curve (which in this simple model is an interrelationship between the amount demanded and the price of the product, all other prices and incomes of consumers being data and given at fixed values) and a supply curve (or an interrelation between the amount supplied of the good and its price, all other prices being given and held constant). If we go further and constrain the data in such a way as to guarantee the existence and uniqueness of the intersection of the two functions, we may then assert with confidence that the solution will yield a price and quantity exchanged. But is this not a rather uninteresting piece of information, unless we can gain further information about the market? If we could actually fit the curves to data in the market, of course, the quantitative answers concerning price and quantity would be of interest. But we must remain at the abstract (that is, nonstatistical) level of analysis in most of our probing into the workings of the economy.

For example, if a policy maker came to us and said that he expected the demand curve to rise next period, and asked us to help him in his planning by predicting whether the price of the good would rise, fall, or remain constant in response, we could not tell him the answer with the knowledge at hand. All we could assert was that after the demand curve shifted a new equilibrium would be attained, but we could not characterize for him the differences between the two equilibrium solutions. Would he not think that all of our modelbuilding yielded few insights indeed if we could not answer such questions?

Obviously, we need more information before we can give answers to such questions, and the nature of the information we need is quite clear from this simple example. The demand curve will shift upward (or to the right) to intersect the supply curve at some new static equilibrium point. Now, whether price is higher, lower, or the same in the new equilibrium, and whether the amount exchanged is higher, lower, or the same, depends upon the slopes of the demand and supply curves, and not the slopes at every point of the curves but merely in the region which the shift of the demand curve makes relevant. For example, if we knew that in the neighborhood of the old equilibrium the slope of the demand curve was negative and the slope of the supply curve was positive, then for very small shifts in the demand curve we could predict that price would rise in the new equilibrium and the amount exchanged would also rise. And this methodological insight from the simple model we have been discussing can be generalized: in order to work out the laws of change from a static model, we must gain knowledge concerning the slopes of functions in the regions where the data changes shift the functions. Comparative statics is dependent upon our ability to obtain such restrictions upon the slopes of the functions.

What sources are available to us for limiting in the general case the slopes of the functions in the neighborhoods of equilibria, in order to cope with small shifts in data? We depend largely upon three sources, which we shall discuss briefly and illustrate in later chapters.

1. *Direct assumption.* In this case we simply assume the qualitative or quantitative nature of the slopes in which we are interested. For example, in the case of the market which we have been discussing, we might merely assume that the demand curve is sloped negatively in the relevant region and the supply curve is sloped positively; or, less restrictively, we might assume that the difference between the demand curve's slope and the supply curve's slope is negative. The source of these assumptions is wholly intuitive or based upon some prior knowledge.

2. *Maximum or minimum assumptions.* Frequently in modelbuilding, as we have already noted, it is possible to derive the interrelationships from an explicit maximum or minimum analysis, as for the consumer obtaining a maximization of satisfaction or the firm minimizing costs or maximizing profits. When we may make this analysis, by assuming that a true maximum or minimum has been reached, we gain certain information about the slopes of the function being maximized, and this information can be used to evaluate comparative statics shocks.

3. *Stability assumptions.* We may simply assume that an equilibrium or a process is stable in the large or in the small. If true, stability analysis allows us to conclude that the slopes of the functions at the equilibrium or everywhere will meet certain restrictions, and these restrictions may permit us to evaluate certain qualitative changes in the equilibrium. For example, if we assume that the market equilibrium we have been discussing is stable in the small, then a stability analysis will reveal that the necessary and sufficient conditions for this stability to occur are that in the neighborhood of the equilibrium the slope of the demand curve minus the slope of the supply curve must be negative. Using this information we can determine that an upward shift in the demand curve must raise price in the new equilibrium, but may increase, decrease, or keep constant the amount exchanged.

The reader will have gained some knowledge of the importance of being able to manipulate the static models we build by the methods of comparative statics if we are to be able to derive theorems from the models that can be checked against the real world. It should be kept in mind that the theorems we obtain may be incorrect: we may find, for example, that an upward shift of the demand curve in the real world *decreases* price, and our model may therefore not be very useful. Yet the important function of a model is to yield theorems that can be so tested, and for this purpose the methods of comparative statics are indispensable.

But a fundamental difficulty arises in the use of comparative static methodology with ambitious models: the difficulty of evaluating the directions of movement of variables between equilibria rises much more rapidly than the number of variables in the variable set, when we can use only the information concerning slopes available from the three sources discussed earlier. Knowledge of the signs of the slopes of the functions in the neighborhood of equilibrium, or even of the sign of the difference between slopes, may be sufficient to evaluate the qualitative characteristics of changes in the solution when only one or two variables are involved. But if the number rises to four or five or more, it is almost certain to require some knowledge concerning quantitative characteristics of the slopes to arrive at conclusions. As a consequence, if we are to employ our model for analytical uses, we are led to less ambitious systems.

We shall accomplish this simplification in a manner that does not sacrifice the opportunity of building the larger model for purposes of perspective and for obtaining insights into the physiology of the economy by less rigorous methods. We shall simply build that closed general market system by constructing submodels with fewer variables, using them to analyze economic phenomena in less ambitious ways, and then, after these uses, fitting them into previously developed submodels and ultimately ending with the completed general system. Let us employ this framework in the explanation of the plan of this book.

The Organization of the Book

In Part II we shall build three types of submodels: in Chapters 2 and 3 we shall construct submodels of consumer behavior; in Chapters 4, 5, and 6 we shall build systems of entrepreneurial behavior, and in Chapter 7 we shall treat the theory of market behavior. For the reasons just developed, most of the fruitful theorems derived in a *rigorous* fashion from the analysis will be obtained from these submodels treated independently of their counterparts. But their limitations in the analysis of realistic phenomena and the usefulness of general equilibrium models will also be shown there.

However, in Part III we shall choose submodels from each of the three varieties, put them together into a final assembly, and arrive at a closed general system. This will be accomplished in Chapter 8. We shall employ this large model in less rigorous fashion to gain insights into the monetary and capital phenomena of the real economy. And, in Chapter 9, we shall use this large model to make welfare judgments of the market mechanism, concluding our work by asking to what extent these welfare conclusions can be applied to the real economy.

Selected Readings

1. C. E. AYRES, J. DORFMAN, *et al.*, *Institutional Economics* (Berkeley: University of California Press, 1963). Lectures on the major American institutionalists, and a commentary on their analyses by a noninstitutionalist. Excellent as an introduction to the nonmechanistic school.

2. ROBERT E. KUENNE, *The Theory of General Economic Equilibrium* (Princeton: Princeton University Press, 1963), Ch. 1. An expanded treatment of the methodology and the problems of model size presented in this chapter.

3. JACK MELITZ, "Friedman and Machlup on the Significance of Testing Economic Assumptions," *Journal of Political Economy*, LXXIII (1965), pp. 37–60. A presentation and critique of the methodological position that judges theories primarily by the correspondence of their theorems to reality.

4. TALCOTT PARSONS and E. A. SHILS, editors, *Toward a General Theory of Action* (New York: Harper & Row, 1962), Ch. 1. An outline of a general model of society drawn upon extensively in our discussion of the section, "The Economy: Mechanism or Organism."

5. HERBERT A. SIMON, "Theories of Decisionmaking in Economics and Behavioral Science," *American Economic Review*, XLIX (1959), pp. 253–280. The concept of "satisficing" as an alternative motivation in modelbuilding to that of maximizing is presented in imaginative fashion. The student should read this with our discussion of the fruitfulness of assumptions in models as a background.

PART II

The Component Submodels

CHAPTER 2*

The Theory of Consumer Behavior: I

THE HUMAN PSYCHE—that complex of ambitions, fears, hopes, and will so resistant to analysis—is the ultimate generator of human behavior and the fundamental interest of the social scientist. The economist shares this final interest, but formal economic analysis has centered its immediate ambitions upon the prediction of *actions* rather than upon the motives or functioning of the minds that generate them. These latter the economist believes to be largely data in his systems, perhaps to be furnished him by the psychologist and social psychologist. However, a goodly portion of this abstraction from the individual's or the group's attitude formation, as it is relevant to economic choice and more especially as it is formed or conditioned by the actions of such social mechanisms as government or corporations or by those of other individuals, must be explained by the economist's failure to find simple explanations of this process. For example, the explanation of a consumer's choice of goods would undoubtedly be improved if the economist could build into his models a simple but useful set of mechanisms that predicted the consumer's responses to advertising or the fads of his social group.

As a consequence of this primary interest in observable behavior and its prediction, of the need for simple motivational assumptions to yield behavioral theorems, and of the complexity of the underlying psychic processes, such motivational psychology, learning models, and response patterns as economics has included among its postulates have been implicit more often than not, and where explicit rather simple-minded. Assumptions concerning the consumer's motivation, for example, have ranged from a whole-hearted adherence to a naive Utilitarianism, asserting that the consumer makes his choices in a conscious pursuit of a pleasure maximum, to a noncommital

* A convenient summary of the definition of all symbols used in this book will be found on pp. 331–332.

behaviorist basis, which urges that the consumer does what he does, and that what he does for whatever reasons happens to conform to certain logically arbitrary definitions of rationality. The processes by which the consumer absorbs information concerning goods, or alters his preferences with experience, or adjusts his consumption in response to the expectations or example of his associates, have received only implicit treatment.

But, whatever these explicit or implicit assumptions, the primary interest has been in the predictive richness of the models that incorporate them. As we have explained in Chapter 1, economic theory predisposes one to accept simplicity in its postulates, because that is ordinarily the only way to obtain predictive results. In this chapter and the next, therefore, we shall present in some detail the submodels that have been developed by economists to predict in general terms what choices the consumer will make among available alternatives before he in fact makes them. The student should scrutinize the postulates of these submodels, and consult his experience and his introspective faculty to judge their plausibility; but he should also recall the discussion in Chapter 1 concerning the possible partial dependence of useful theorems upon unrealistic or implausible postulates.

The Sets of Postulates and Data

In order to make our analysis as clear as possible and as simple as its inherent complexity will permit, we shall spend some time defining the environment of the models we shall build. After this preliminary task has been accomplished, we shall proceed to list and discuss the sets of postulates and data that bear specifically upon the consumer's behavior.

THE INSTITUTIONAL ENVIRONMENT

STATIC METHODOLOGY. The consumer and the entrepreneur in our models make decisions on one *market day* for the following one week period. That is, in order to give definiteness to our theory, we shall assume that all consumers come to the various markets on Monday, sell what they desire to sell and buy what they wish to buy by signing contracts at the end of that day to deliver what they have sold and receive their purchases at specified times during the period Tuesday through Sunday. By the end of this last day, (1) all contracts have been fulfilled, (2) all goods that have been merely borrowed or leased are returned to their owners, and (3) all financial transactions associated with fulfillment of contracts have been effected. On the following day, the market is reopened, contracts once more let, and the economic week inaugurated. In this manner we may treat the continuous realistic time process as a succession of self-contained weeks in which decisions are assumed to be made at discrete intervals of one week, and in which time is recognized by making the values of the variables determined in Week 1 the data of Week 2, and so forth. The student should review our discussion of the simple problem concerned with compound interest, in which we indicated the manner in which a continuous dynamic process could be converted into a comparative statics process.

We have chosen, therefore, to depict the realistic economy by means of static models. The data sets of the models are defined for the given market day, the values we seek are for variables associated with that market day, and the interrelationships among data and variables do not contain time. The solution of each week affects the data of the following week, shocking the system and enforcing upon the following week's solution a different set of values. This interweek change continues until the values of the variables in Week n do not change the data of Week $n + 1$ from what the data were in Week n. When this occurs the model has achieved a long-run stationary solution through a succession of short-run or weekly equilibria. This static method, it will be recalled, contrasts with dynamics in that were we to employ the latter the whole set of weekly solutions would be determined simultaneously from knowledge of the values of the variables in Week 0.

FACTORS AND FACTOR SERVICES. We shall simplify our analysis at the expense of reality by assuming that all factors of production—including capital goods—are owned by consumers, and that the flows of services from the factors are sold each week in free markets to obtain consumer income. If the reader prefers he may assume that instead of actually owning capital goods in the physical sense, consumers hold titles to these goods. The important content of the assumption is the implication that these capital goods (as well as land and labor) are perfectly mobile among firms on each market day. There exists in our economy a separate market for each kind of capital good service, land service, and labor service, in which the factors are leased for one week against a payment that includes depreciation allowances and a net return.

Despite the fact that equipment leasing is practiced by some firms for such capital goods as automobiles and trucks, by far most firms own their own capital goods, and the services of these capital goods do not flow through a market. Why then do we adopt such an unrealistic assumption? The reason is a good illustration of the point made in Chapter 1 to the effect that the best postulate is not always the most realistic one. We are interested in discerning the deeper, longer-run forces active in the market economy, and in tracing out the impacts they have on the values of economic variables. In the long run, capital is mobile among uses because capital goods wear out and return their value as liquid capital, to be embodied physically once more in the best use the market affords. Our assumption allows these long-run solution characteristics to enter our analysis, showing us how capital goods are allocated among uses in the idealized longer period, when mistakes made in the short run can be rectified. However, we shall abandon the assumption momentarily when we come to a consideration of the demand for capital goods in Chapter 7.

We shall include among capital goods a fixed stock of paper money. Money is a type of capital good performing services for its holders each week, for which services they are willing to pay a price. Consequently, we shall assume that among the factors held by each consumer is a stock of cash, whose services he sells by lending balances on the money market for one week at a price that is the rate of interest. In this way money becomes a consumer-held asset yielding saleable services just as land, or labor, or capital goods proper. We may, therefore, introduce money into our analysis of consumer behavior in a symmetrical manner with other sources of income.

Let us symbolize the factors of production other than money as Z_i, and the stock of them available to the economy on a given Monday market day as Q_{z_i}, where $i = 1, 2, \ldots, m$. We shall designate the collection of all factor stocks by $\mathbf{Q}_{z_i} = [Q_{z_1}, Q_{z_2}, \ldots, Q_{z_m}]$.

The Q_{z_i} are *stocks* of assets on the market day: that is, they exist among the data of the model as stockpiles at a *point* in time, having accumulated over all previous periods. Each week a unit of Z_i yields a flow of service z_i, which has a time duration; that is, the unit in which z_i is measured is a *week's worth* of labor service, or capital good service, or land service. The distinction between stocks and flows is a quite important one, and it should be understood at this point. Let the student visualize a tank that serves as a reservoir, with an inlet pipe and an outlet pipe; then if we pour water through the inlet and let it emerge from the outlet pipe, the quantity of water emerging from the system is a *flow* through time, which can be measured only in such dimensions as *gallons per hour*. On the other hand, the water in the reservoir is a *stock*, which must be measured at some *point* in time—say at 3:00 p.m.—in *gallons*. Having different time dimensions, the two concepts are not comparable, and must be treated differently.

Finally, let us symbolize money by U, the stock of it in the economy by Q_U, and its service by u. We shall assume, for the sake of completeness, that the consumer may derive satisfaction from the consumption of the services of factors and money. In this way, for example, we may introduce most easily leisure and cash balances into the analysis of his behavior.

CONSUMER GOODS. Much more important as objects of consumer purchase, however, are the produced goods Y_j, $j = 1, 2, \ldots, n$, which are the goods we ordinarily designate as *consumers' goods*. The demand of all consumers as a whole for any of these n goods we shall symbolize by X_j', which is a week's flow of Y_j contracted for on Monday and delivered from Tuesday through Sunday. The prediction of the values that such variables as these attain is, of course, a major aim of our analysis of consumer behavior.

SECURITIES. We have already noted in passing that one type of security the consumer may buy to hold during the week is what we will call *the promissory note*. That is, the institutionally determined manner in which a consumer lends or leases cash balances for one week is to go to the money market and to buy the promissory notes issued by those who want to provision themselves with cash balances for the week. These promissory notes are redeemed on Sunday by the return of the money to the consumer, while the contractual obligation to pay interest on the note is fulfilled sometime during the week. These are short-term obligations in the sense that the consumer receives back at the end of the week a wholly liquid asset—money—so that the economy has not employed the loan to commit resources to any illiquid form. Realistically, our short-term money market is represented by the various money markets of the economy where firms and consumers borrow to build up balances of cash. They may be viewed as buying their own promissory notes when they retain cash balances for their own use.

Let us now create a second type of security, designated by the symbol E. We will refer to this instrument as a *long-term security*, even though it is redeemed in capital goods (excluding money) at the end of every week, because it is used to obtain resources for conversion into forms that are fixed over long periods of time. We define a unit of this security—let us call it a *bond*—as a promise to deliver each week for an infinite number of weeks a net payment of one unit of money—let us say one *dollar*—to the consumer who purchases it. The market for bonds will price them, and consumers who wish to save or dissave during the week will demand positive or negative amounts of them, where negative amounts imply consumer issuance of bonds. The bonds are issued by firms that produce and sell reproducible forms of capital goods or by consumers who wish to substitute larger present consumption for smaller future consumption. At the end of the week, the bonds are redeemed in equivalent values of capital goods (or titles to them), and the consumer adds or subtracts these goods to or from the stocks of them he already possesses. In our economy this will be the basic manner of saving.

Saving, therefore, is an explicit purchase of perpetual future income by the consumer. By treating it as a good we are implicitly assuming that the consumer has attitudes toward the purchase or sale of present income and consumption for the sacrifice or receipt of future income and consumption that are coordinate in his preferences with attitudes toward all types of goods received for consumption today.

A SUMMARIZATION. Let us summarize the institutionally given environment in which the consumer (and firm) makes decisions. Each Monday, every consumer comes to a group of markets, in some of which he is a buyer and in some of which he is a seller. A separate market exists (1) for every factor service z_i, (2) for every saleable capital good, Z_i, (3) for every consumer good, Y_j, (4) for promissory notes through whose instrumentality money balances, u, are lent, and (5) for bonds, E. At the end of the market day, the consumer has signed contracts to deliver factor services, factors (if he has sold any of his stock of assets by issuing bonds), and cash balances to buyers at specified times during the forthcoming week. By the end of the market day he has also signed contracts to purchase consumer goods and bonds (his purchase of factor services is ordinarily merely a deduction from his own sales of them, although he may be a net buyer of some) to be delivered by the sellers at specified times during the week. By the end of the week, on Sunday, all contracts have been fulfilled, and the money balances and factors that were leased by the consumer have been restored, while his security purchases or sales have been cancelled by equivalent values of capital goods received or delivered. On Monday a new market day is entered and the weekly cycle begins its contracting phase again.

THE CONSUMING UNIT'S PREFERENCES

We shall assume that decisions concerning consumption purchases and supplies of factor services are made by certain *consuming units*, in most instances, families, whose preferences we must now consider as part of the data of the model. When these units are multi-person aggregations we shall neglect the decisionmaking that occurs within the group, and treat each unit as a single person—*the consumer*. We shall designate a set of consumers, C, with elements $c = 1, 2, \ldots, s$, and treat each member as an individual.

THE FIELD OF CHOICE. The first decision we must make to begin our analysis of the preferences of Consumer c is how to handle his decision dealing with the amount of cash balances he desires to hold during the week. Although we may treat such decisions as wholly analogous to those concerning consumer goods and bonds, to do so requires us to introduce prices explicitly into the analysis of preferences, and complicates it unduly. Moreover, our models will abstract from the uncertainties of price movements and other speculative elements, so that decisionmakers will desire cash balances wholly for transactions purposes. Let us therefore, at least as a first approximation, exclude cash balance decisions from the present analysis, and treat them separately; at the present time we shall view the consumer's demand for cash balances, X_{cu}, as already determined.

There are, then, m factor services, n consumer goods proper, and bonds that are potentially purchasable this week by Consumer c for use. A basket, $\mathbf{X}_c$, in the consumer submodel will feature values $[X_{c1}, X_{c2}, \ldots, X_{cn}, X_{cz_1}, X_{cz_2}, \ldots, X_{cz_m}, Q_{ce}^*, Q_{cU}^*]$, where Q_{ce}^* is the amount of capital goods in value terms with which the consumer *ends* the current week, and where Q_{cU}^* is the stock of money with which he *ends* the week. The equilibrium basket, $\mathbf{X}_c^\circ$, which Consumer c chooses for the current week, is merely one such basket that he might have chosen.

The student is familiar with geometrical diagrams with one, two, or three axes along which units of some variable are measured. For example, let the x-axis measure units of X_{c1}, or Consumer c's demand for Y_1; let the y-axis measure units of X_{c2}; and let the z-axis measure X_{cz_1}, or Consumer c's demand for factor service z_1. Then we may define a three-dimensional *consumer goods space* as we have done in Figure 2–1. If consumers had only three options for purchase, any basket of goods $\mathbf{X}_c$ that has zero or positive values for the components of the basket may be represented as a *point* or *vector* in the nonnegative octant of this space. We have illustrated one such basket on Figure 2–1. We limit ourselves to this nonnegative portion of the space, of course, because under the conditions of our model negative absorptions do not exist.

Now let the student construct—in his mind's eye, of course—such a space with $n + m + 2$-axes along which X_{cj}, X_{cz_i}, Q_{ce}^*, and Q_{cU}^* can be measured. Every feasible basket $\mathbf{X}_c$ will be represented as a point or vector in this $n + m + 2$-dimensional space, and the nonnegative *orthant* will contain all such feasible points. We shall call this nonnegative portion of the consumer goods space the *field of choice* for the consumer.

Each axis of the field of choice consists of the whole interval from 0 to ∞. This distorts reality somewhat by making all goods indefinitely divisible, because it assumes that for *every* real value along the axis there exists a feasible component for a basket. For example, the value $X_{c,23} = 5.764$, where Y_{23} is automobiles, asserts that it is possible to be given five and a fraction of them. This distortion of reality is not really an important one for our analysis, but the assumption does simplify it and makes such continuity a worthwhile idealization of reality.

CONSUMER POSTULATE 1: THE COMPLETE WEAK ORDERING. We shall now take the first step along the road that will permit us to construct a preference function for Consumer c on this space to represent his attitudes toward

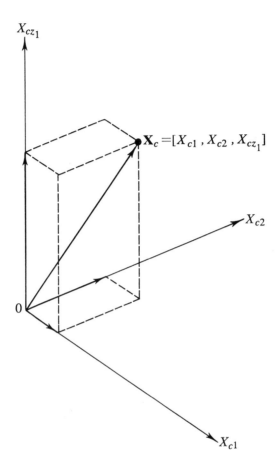

$$\mathbf{X}_c = [X_{c1}, X_{c2}, X_{cz_1}]$$

FIGURE 2–1. A Three-Dimensional Field of Choice.

these potential choices of basket. To begin this construction we must assure ourselves that the consumer can in fact give us certain information concerning baskets of goods in the field of choice. Let us symbolize the field of choice—that is, the set of all conceivable baskets Consumer c might take under all possible values for the data—simply as X, inasmuch as it is the same for all consumers. For convenience let us also omit the subscript c from the baskets that are elements of this set in the analysis below, it being understood that we are studying the behavior of Consumer c.

We shall now state a proposition:

PROPOSITION. Given *any* two baskets $\mathbf{X}^1$ and $\mathbf{X}^2$ in X, Consumer c will find $\mathbf{X}^1$ at least as attractive as $\mathbf{X}^2$.

Let us imagine that we are given X and its exact duplicate X, and let us draw a basket $\mathbf{X}^1$ from the first X and a basket $\mathbf{X}^2$ from the second X. If we confront Consumer c with them or any other pair so chosen, and if the proposition can be stated to be true or false in every instance (and so for every pair of baskets), the proposition is called a *binary relation in X*. The expression, "at least as attractive," to the consumer means, in simple language, that if he were offered either $\mathbf{X}^1$ or $\mathbf{X}^2$, and if the proposition were true (which we symbolize by $\mathbf{X}^1 \mathscr{R} \mathbf{X}^2$), he could not be made happier in this situation than he would be if he received $\mathbf{X}^1$.

We postulate that the consumer's potential behavior is such that the proposition is a binary relation in X. It is implied, therefore, that the consumer is able to make a comparison between any pair of baskets, not necessarily different, in his field of choice, and state whether the proposition is true or false. Then we have a relation among all the pairs of X for the consumer, defined by the proposition. We assume that this relation satisfies three properties:

1. *Reflexivity.* Let $\mathbf{X}^1 = \mathbf{X}^2$, which means that every component of $\mathbf{X}^1$ equals the same component of $\mathbf{X}^2$. Then, if the proposition holds the binary relation is said to be reflexive; that is, every basket is at least as attractive as itself. If this property were violated most of us would think the consumer quite peculiar, and this requirement of the consumer's preferences does not lead to much dispute.

2. *Transitivity.* Suppose that for the three baskets of goods $\mathbf{X}^1$, $\mathbf{X}^2$, and $\mathbf{X}^3$ in X the following is true: $\mathbf{X}^1 \mathscr{R} \mathbf{X}^2$ and $\mathbf{X}^2 \mathscr{R} \mathbf{X}^3$. We require that $\mathbf{X}^1 \mathscr{R} \mathbf{X}^3$. If a basket is at least as attractive as a second, and that second is at least as attractive as a third, then we require that the consumer be at least as attracted to the first as the third. This axiom is a bit more controversial than the first—one can imagine situations in which the consumer could be led to contradict himself simply through his inability to make comparisons rapidly—but it would probably again strike most of us as an elementary and intuitively plausible expectation of consumer behavior. If in fact the consumer did assert that he found six apples at least as attractive as six peaches, and six peaches at least as attractive as six pears, but later asserted that he found six pears at least as attractive as six apples, most of us would think that the consumer had violated a rather elementary rule of procedure, if we were assured his preferences had not changed in the midst of the experiment. We would expect that if the contradiction were pointed out to the subject, and if he were *rational* in the sense of being uncomfortable in accepting a contradiction, certain anxieties which arose in him from having seemingly accepted a contradiction would lead him to alter his behavior and eliminate it.

3. *Indifference.* Suppose for Consumer c that $\mathbf{X}^1 \mathscr{R} \mathbf{X}^2$, but at the same time $\mathbf{X}^2 \mathscr{R} \mathbf{X}^1$, so that each basket is at least as attractive as the other. Then we assume that the two baskets are equivalent in the sense of the relation, which relationship we symbolize by the expression $\mathbf{X}^1 \mathscr{I} \mathbf{X}^2$. By this we imply that the consumer is indifferent to the free receipt of either basket, feeling equally well off in either event. With this assumption we have introduced the possibility of the consumer finding baskets of equivalent satisfaction to himself. With the assumption of reflexivity it assures us that the consumer is indifferent between two baskets of exactly the same structure, and with the transitivity assumption it assures that if $\mathbf{X}^1 \mathscr{I} \mathbf{X}^2$ and $\mathbf{X}^2 \mathscr{I} \mathbf{X}^3$, then $\mathbf{X}^1 \mathscr{I} \mathbf{X}^3$, so that the indifference relationship is transitive.

If these three postulates are true the consumer will be able to order or to rank in ascending or descending array all of the baskets in X, with the possibility of ties being allowed. That is, the consumer has a complete (all pairs of baskets in X are covered) weak (the relationship of indifference may lead to ties) ordering (ranking). Indeed, these three assumptions concerning the proposition imply and are implied by the existence of a consumer's complete weak ordering over a field of choice. Therefore, we assert our first postulate concerning the consumer's preferences:

CONSUMER POSTULATE 1. The consumer is capable of constructing a complete weak ordering over the field of choice.

CONSUMER POSTULATE 2: THE MAXIMIZING MOTIVATION. The consumer will not in fact be choosing from the entire field of choice, because the data which we shall impose upon him—positive prices for at least some goods and finite amounts of resource services and assets under his control—will restrict him to some *attainable* subset, including the possibility that no non-null basket of goods can be obtained by him in the current week. For a specified data set let X_a be the attainable subset of baskets available to the consumer this week. We are then assured that on this subset the consumer can give us a complete weak ordering in terms of his preferences.

Let us now define another relation between two baskets of goods based upon those which we have already derived. Suppose $\mathbf{X}^1 \mathscr{R} \mathbf{X}^2$ and it is *not* true that $\mathbf{X}^2 \mathscr{R} \mathbf{X}^1$. Then Consumer c cannot be indifferent between the baskets and must *prefer* $\mathbf{X}^1$ to $\mathbf{X}^2$. We may symbolize this by writing $\mathbf{X}^1 \mathscr{P} \mathbf{X}^2$. We now have the relation of strict preference between goods baskets.

In the attainable subset X_a let us define a maximal subset $X_{a/m}$ such that the consumer is indifferent to every basket within it and, at the same time, every basket within it is strictly preferred to every basket that is in X_a but not in $X_{a/m}$. That is, the consumer will always get more satisfaction by moving from a basket within the attainable set and outside the maximal set to a basket within the maximal set, but he gains nothing (and loses nothing) by moving from one basket in the maximal set to another in that set.

Our assumption concerning the consumer's maximizing behavior can then be stated by asserting that when a maximal set $X_{a/m}$ exists, the consumer will always choose a basket of goods from it in the solution to the consumer submodel. We state it formally:

CONSUMER POSTULATE 2. Given an attainable subset X_a in X, and given a maximal set $X_{a/m}$ in X_a, the consumer will always choose a basket $\mathbf{X}°$ from the maximal set.

RATIONAL CONSUMER BEHAVIOR. We may now define quite neatly our concept of a rational consumer as one who can give us a complete weak ordering over X and who, for any given attainable set X_a, chooses a basket of goods from the maximal subset when (as in all but the most abnormal cases) it exists. More formally, we may state:

DEFINITION. A consumer is rational if he conforms to Consumer Postulates 1 and 2.

Does this definition imply that our consumer is a hedonist or a computer whose choices are made by summing an index of utility? Obviously, we have not yet even mentioned any measurement of satisfaction, so that we have not yet even thought about the second implication. True to the initial assertions of this chapter, we have not delved into the consumer's psyche to ask why he prefers this to that, nor has our general specification of his preferences thus far allowed us to determine much about his personality. We surely cannot say, for example, whether he has a taste for alcohol or music that dominates his choices in some sense, or whether his choices are activated by what we would call hedonist impulses.

Indeed, to illustrate how neutral are our postulates in terms of motivation, let us put the analysis wholly in behaviorist terms. We define the following set of operations by which the economist gathers information about consumer preferences. We offer Consumer c two baskets as hypothetical alternatives and ask whether he is indifferent between them or prefers one to the other. We record his answers (having assumed that he can always give an answer), and save time by implying certain of his preferences from our assumption of transitivity. Thus, if he has told us that he prefers $\mathbf{X}^1$ to $\mathbf{X}^2$ and $\mathbf{X}^2$ to $\mathbf{X}^3$, we do not bother to ask him about his preferences between $\mathbf{X}^1$ and $\mathbf{X}^3$, but record them as implied by transitivity relationships. In this way the economist gathers or infers the information about Consumer c's preferences over (some practicable portion of) the field of choice. No questions have been asked and no theories are implied about the underlying psychological motivation of the consumer, nor even whether he consciously or unconsciously goes about defining his preferences in the absence of the economist's procedures.

Now, let the *economist* assume a set of data that yields an attainable subset X_a for the consumer. From it let the *economist* determine the consumer's maximal subset $X_{a/m}$, and let the *economist* predict that under the regime of the hypothetical data the consumer will choose any basket in the maximal set. Let him then ask the consumer what basket he would choose in the specified circumstances: if the consumer does in fact choose a basket from the maximal set, the consumer has done what our postulates assert he would do; if not, he has violated our assumptions of rationality. But be it noted that in this analysis it is the *economist* who is doing the maximizing, not the consumer. The economist has constructed a useful device to predict what the consumer will do—the maximal set—while the consumer is merely doing "what he wants to do."

The student may feel that this is not a satisfying interpretation of these procedures, and that is his privilege. However, it is important to see that it is possible to analyze the consumer's preferences without any assumption concerning the nature of his satisfactions, and without any implication that he is maximizing purposively—either consciously or unconsciously—or even acting "as if" he is maximizing, whatever that means. Economic theory may therefore escape the criticism that has plagued it since its unhappy alliance with Utilitarianism and the hill-climbing consumer.

MEASURING THE CONSUMER'S PREFERENCES. The postulates we have thus far assumed assure us a *rational* consumer by definition, which implies that he has a complete weak ordering over the field of choice. This ordering, at the present time, consists of a huge file of information concerning his expressions of preferences between pairs of baskets, or deductions from such expressions by virtue of the transitivity assumption. Our modelbuilding tasks ahead require the employment of these preferences to obtain maximal sets by mathematical techniques, and it will be a pronounced convenience if we can measure preferences by associating with each basket a real number that can be compared with the real numbers associated with other baskets. We are, for example, somewhat in the position of a heating engineer who can make pairwise comparisons between rooms in a building and completely order them from warmest to coldest. If he could associate with each room some real number—measured let us say in *degrees*—whose magnitude were meaningful in indexing heat sufficiently accurately so that a comparison of the numbers for two rooms would immediately tell him which was warmer and, perhaps, by how much, he could replace all of the pairwise comparisons by a function that associated the numbers with the rooms. If the task ahead of him were to balance the heating system and equalize the degree of heat in all rooms, the reader will sense the great convenience a *temperature scale* would possess for him.

Measurement of Consumer c's preferences, therefore, is a set of operations that associates with every basket in the *domain* or field of choice a number with sufficient *uniqueness* to allow the economist to make comparisons among them and thereby predict the consumer's maximal set. Let us discuss the nature of the measurement process in more detail.

Cardinal Measurement. The measurement operation with which we are most familiar is one we shall term *cardinal measurement*, and, indeed, the chances are that our familiarity with it is so great that we think of nothing else when *measurement* is mentioned. Yet, frequently it yields a precision that we do not need.

Suppose a carpenter is building a house, the length and width of which have been marked by pairs of stakes in the ground. The carpenter must saw boards and perform other tasks that would be immensely simplified if he could obtain numbers for length and width that were useful for his purposes. Assuming that he is innocent of knowledge of existing measurement devices, we can see immediately that one commonsense method of obtaining such numbers is to cut an arbitrary and convenient length of board and designate this a *unit*, lay it off against length and width, and count the number of times it can be placed between both pairs of stakes. If it were laid down 20 times in the lengthwise direction and 10 times in the width direction, the carpenter could use these numbers and the arbitrary unit stick to perform his tasks.

In fact, the carpenter has made two arbitrary decisions in this measurement process—arbitrary in the sense that he could have selected other values equally well. The first of these decisions was that of an *origin* for his dimension index; implicitly he chose a value of 0 as origin, so that if the stakes had been so placed as to allow no portion of the unit stick to fall between them, the dimension would have been recorded with that null value. The second decision, of course, was the length of the stick used as a unit; presumably it might equally well have been one half or three quarters of its chosen length, or two or three times that length. Except for these two arbitrary decisions, however, the measurements obtained by the carpenter are *unique*.

That is, the numbers derived from our carpenter's procedure may be depicted as adding an initial value of 0 to a number, say b, of unit lengths:

$$N = 0 + b(1). \tag{2-1}$$

The operations performed by the carpenter could have yielded other numbers which differed from those of [2–1] only by a different origin (say a in general) and a different unit. For example, if the carpenter had chosen 10 as an origin, and if his unit stick had been only half as long as that of [2–1], the number he would have obtained would have been

$$N' = 10 + 2b(1) = 10 + 2N. \tag{2-2}$$

That is, all of the possible measurement indexes the carpenter could conceivably have obtained would have differed from one another only by a factor of proportionality and/or a constant.

Because these characteristics define linear transformations of one index into another, we say that the carpenter's indexing operations result in measurements that are *unique up to a linear transformation*. Indeed, for the purposes of the carpenter's work, the measurement procedure would probably be even more constrained, for it is hard to imagine the carpenter choosing any other origin than that of zero. That is, there is a *natural* zero origin—there is something impressively absolute about the distance of a point from itself—so that the carpenter may be expected to choose $a = 0$ in all circumstances. This will make his measurements most convenient, for then index values of 20 and 10 will indicate to him correctly that one dimension is twice that of the other, whereas if he had used 10 as an origin, his values of 20 and 30 would not have directly yielded this useful information. Therefore, we would expect the carpenter's measurement procedures to have given indices unique up to a multiplicative constant, so that only his arbitrary unit —a foot, or a yard, for example—would have been different.

In the field of thermometry, however, the absolute zero was not so immediately apparent, if in fact it exists. Therefore, we find two common measurements of temperature that are unique up to a linear transformation: that is, yielding the same measurements except for a difference in choice of origin and units. These are, of course, the centigrade and Fahrenheit scales, where we may transform centigrade degrees into Fahrenheit degrees by the transformation

$$F° = 32° + 1.8\ C°. \qquad\qquad [2\text{--}3]$$

Since the time of their establishment, an absolute zero was thought to have been found for the phenomenon of temperature—at $-273.1°\ C$ and $-459.6°\ F$—but colder temperatures have been encountered, so that the absolute zero origin has not yet been established.

This kind of measurement procedure—unique up to a multiplicative constant or up to a linear transformation—is characterized by the fact that the increments between measurements are meaningful as to magnitude as well as to sign. For example, if the carpenter had chosen the foot as his unit length, and had derived a measurement of 50 feet for the length of the house and 25 feet for the width, the difference between these measurements, $50 - 25 = 25$ feet, can be compared numerically with its generating measurements. In this case, we can say that the width is one half the length of the house, and the statement is meaningful. If the carpenter had chosen the inch as his unit of measurement we should have had a length measurement of

600 inches and a width measurement of 300 inches, but these are the same measurements except for choice of unit, and the same comparative results would occur. Had the carpenter not chosen 0 as an origin, the magnitudes of length and width and the differences between them could not be compared so conveniently, but the absolute value of the difference would remain meaningful.

Ordinal Measurement. The type of measurement just discussed is very desirable in its *uniqueness*, for it allows us to perform operations upon the measurement index of great usefulness. It permits the carpenter, for example, to multiply the length and width measurements by height measurements for volume calculations, if his measurements are unique up to a multiplicative constant, and permits him to add up his total lumber requirements. However, outside of the realm of the physical sciences it is frequently difficult to devise operations that will yield such a measurement index, or even one that is unique up to a linear transformation. How, for example, do we go about obtaining such uniqueness in measuring salesmen's abilities, students' performance in courses, or the quality of published books? Thus far, at least, man's ingenuity in devising measurement procedures has not yielded cardinal indexes of these qualities. Indeed, the nature of the attributes or qualities themselves may make such uniqueness unattainable.

How great a penalty this imposes depends upon the degree of uniqueness we need for the tasks ahead. For example, if the carpenter merely had to know which dimension or distance between the stakes was larger, obviously he would not have to measure in a cardinal fashion. This involves merely a ranking of the distances, or, to say the same thing, the ability to derive merely the *sign* of the difference between them. If the length is greater than the width, this is to say that if we had a measurement index, its value for the length distance would have to be greater than its value for the width distance. Of course, the cardinal index yields this properly signed difference too, but the important point is that it may be the only piece of knowledge that we require for the operations we have in mind.

Suppose the carpenter had derived a cardinal index in feet, and the dimensions were 50 and 25 feet. If we were merely interested in recording that length is greater than width, *any* two numbers chosen such that the value associated with length was larger than that associated with width would yield the ranking information. For example, the values 80 and 79, or 3,000,000 and 23, or 2 and 1 would do the job demanded. Note that the signs of the differences between these index values are in every case the same— $80 - 79$, or $3,000,000 - 23$, or $2 - 1$ are all positive—and so they preserve the ranking of length and width equally well. But, of course, the absolute magnitudes of the differences are different in a nonlinear sense, and so cannot be meaningful. Therefore, we can perform no operation upon any such index that depends upon the absolute magnitudes of the differences being meaningful.

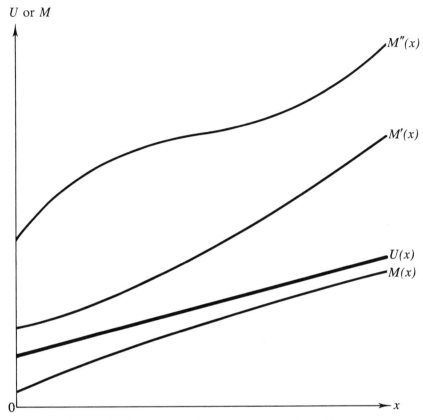

FIGURE 2–2.   Linear and Monotone Transformations.

The numerical values we have chosen to demonstrate indexes that would preserve the ranking of the carpenter's measurements are examples of a class of measurement indexes that are *unique up to a monotone transformation.* By this is meant that the values rise, fall, and remain stationary together, and, if they can be related to a cardinal index, rise when it rises, fall when it falls, and remain stationary when it moves sideways. Such indexes are *ordinal* indexes, as opposed to cardinal, and measure in the sense of preserving the order or ranking of the objects with which they are associated with respect to the attribute or quality they are used to index. For example, on Figure 2–2, if the cardinal index values are assumed to lie along the curve graphed there as $U(x)$, where x are the objects in question, then any of the indexes graphed as $M(x)$, $M'(x)$, and $M''(x)$ will preserve the ranking given by $U(x)$, because they all rise when it rises (and would fall when it falls or remain the same when it does if we chose to graph such behavior of $U(x)$). In these characteristics, $M(x)$, $M'(x)$, and $M''(x)$ are positive monotone transforms.

From our discussion of Consumer Postulates 1 and 2 the student will remember that all of our references to the operations involved in obtaining Consumer c's preferences among baskets in a field of choice concerned ranking and ordering according to the binary relation implied by the proposition. Our purpose in recording these preferences is to isolate maximal sets for any feasible data set, and these maximal sets are collections of baskets that are equally attractive among themselves and more attractive than those baskets in the attainable set but outside the maximal set. These purposes can be accomplished wholly by ranking all baskets in the field of choice, and, *if we can* obtain an index of measurement for convenience, it need only be unique up to a monotone transformation—an ordinal index.

Assuring the Existence of a Measurement Function. The assumptions that the consumer has a complete weak ordering over the field of choice and that he chooses from a maximal set are not sufficient to guarantee that his preferences can be represented by a continuous, real-valued function which is order-preserving. If the function $y = f(x, z)$ is continuous we mean that if we choose any point $[x', z']$ in the domain of the function, where the value of the function is y', we may set up sequences $[x_s, z_s]$, that converge on $[x', z']$ from any direction permitted by the definition of the domain, and the sequences y_s will converge to y' as a limit. On Figure 2–3 Curves A, B, and C are continuous at every point, whereas Curves D and E are discontinuous at the point P, because sequences approaching P from the left and right would yield sequences of values for the functions that converge to different limits, or might yield no values at all for the functions if they are not defined at that point. Were we to have a preference function that yielded different rank values for the same basket, or that yielded no ranking at all, obviously we might encounter difficulties in our analysis.

For example, Consumer c might be a person for whom one quart of milk a week—no more and no less—had a positive psychological value. Now, imagine a sequence of goods baskets which has fixed amounts of other goods, and increasing amounts of milk, the latter varying by small amounts in approaching the critical value of one quart. Then, if we assume a preference function exists, the values of that function for the sequence would remain constant as the amount of milk increases to .75 quart, .80 quart, ..., .99 quart, and so forth. We may get arbitrarily close to 1 quart, and the index value will remain constant, but as soon as we reach one quart it will jump discontinuously to some higher value and remain there as the amount of milk increases (if the consumer can dispose of the unwanted quarts without cost or inconvenience). If we were to approach the critical value from *above*, on the other hand, we can approach the value as a limit—the function is *right-continuous* but not *left-continuous*, both of which are necessary and sufficient for continuity. Therefore, the function is discontinuous at all points for which the quantity of milk in the basket is unity. We may illustrate this behavior by Curve *E* of Figure 2–3, where *P* is one quart of milk, beyond which the function "plateaus out."

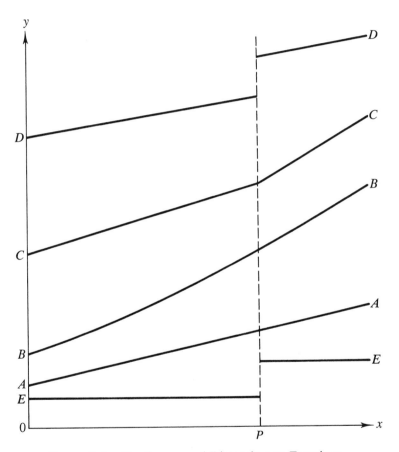

FIGURE 2–3. Continuous and Discontinuous Functions.

To help us in eliminating such *jumps* and *plateaus* in the preferences of Consumer *c* (and note that they can occur even though no gaps exist in the field of choice, for we have considered all goods to be indefinitely divisible) we adopt an assumption which assures us that he will always prefer more of any good to less:

CONSUMER POSTULATE 3. Given any basket **X** in *X*, the consumer will prefer it to any other basket in the field of choice that contains no more of any good but less of one or more, and he will prefer it to any other basket containing at least as much of all goods but more of one or more.

As we shall see, this postulate does not entirely eliminate the possibility of discontinuity which we have illustrated, but does reduce its probability of occurrence. On the other hand it does eliminate the possibility of plateaus by assuring that the consumer never becomes satiated in any good and will always welcome more of any good. The function must rise, therefore, as more milk is given the consumer in our example; it cannot "plateau out" any-where. However, as we shall see, it is possible to invent pathological consumer preferences that may exhibit sudden jumps at critical baskets.

The postulate serves to give us other information about the preferences of the individual. Consider any basket **X**^{1} in Figure 2–4: the assumption that a complete weak ordering exists assures us that the field of choice may be divided into three disjoint (that is, nonoverlapping) subsets, such that every basket in *X* falls in one such set. First, the set *B* (better) which is preferred to **X**^{1}; second, the set *W* (worse) to which **X**^{1} is preferred; and third, the set *I* (indifferent) to which **X**^{1} is indifferent.

Now, on the basis of Consumer Postulates 1 through 3 alone it is impos-sible to divide *X* into these subsets, or indeed even to know if the set *I* con-tains more baskets than **X**^{1} itself. But we can say certain things about *B* and *W*:

1. The set *B*, which is preferred to **X**^{1}, must contain the baskets along the lines **X**^{1}*F* and **X**^{1}*G*, considered as being extended indefinitely, and all such baskets in the wedge they bound. This must be true because all such baskets (except **X**^{1}) have more of at least one good and at least as much of every other as **X**^{1}.

2. By a similar chain of argument, the set *W* must contain the baskets along the lines **X**^{1}*H* and **X**^{1}*J* and in the wedge between them, except of course for **X**^{1}.

3. **X**^{1} cannot be in *B* or *W*, but must lie in *I*, by reflexivity and the defini-tion of indifference.

4. *B* and *W* cannot intersect: that is, a basket cannot be both preferred to and less attractive than **X**^{1}.

5. *I* can have no *width*. If a basket is in *I*, adding any amount to it of any good, or subtracting any amount of any good from it, must take us into *B* or *W* respectively. This, of course, reflects the denial of plateaus in the function.

6. *I*, if it contains more baskets than **X**^{1}, must slope from left to right

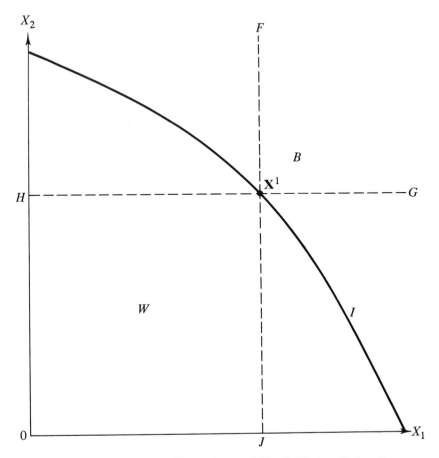

FIGURE 2-4. A Possible Partition of the Field of Choice Under Consumer Postulate 3.

negatively. If it did not, as the student may check for himself, the postulate of nonsatiation would be violated.

7. Because I, if it contains more than a single element and behaves well, is the boundary between B and W, it is implied that neither B nor W can be separated by a wedge of the other. For this to happen, the boundary of the sets must reverse direction and this violates the nonsatiation assumption. Note this does not imply that the set I might not change from concave downward to convex downward, or vice versa. It merely means that if perpendicular lines parallel to the axes are drawn through any basket in I, no other basket in I can touch or cross those lines.

8. The sets B and W must be *connected*: that is, roughly speaking, there cannot be an enclave within either set that belongs to the other set. For any

point in either set, we must be able to build a chain of line segments (a *polygonal line*) to any other point in the set without ever leaving the set. If an enclave of W existed in the set B, a straight line segment connecting a point in the enclave to a point in the main portion of W would pass through B and contain points in B. Obviously, we may construct the straight line in such a way that a basket in the enclave has at least as much of all goods and more of some as some point in B, which violates the nonsatiation postulate.

With our Consumer Postulates 1 and 3 we have assured ourselves that we will be able to partition the field of choice into the sets B, W, and I; that the three sets will not intersect; that I, when it is the boundary between B and W, will slope negatively and be continuous and *nonthick* between them; and that B and W will be connected sets. But what we are not able to prove is that the boundary between B and W will not be owned by one or the other of these sets, rather than by the set that contains $\mathbf{X}^1$. In economic terms, we are not assured that indifference curves exist.

We may illustrate the case where indifference curves do not exist in Figure 2–5. Suppose Consumer c were a confirmed drunkard, to the outlandish extent that he preferred any basket of goods with more whiskey to any basket with less, although for two baskets with equal amounts of whiskey he would prefer that one which had more of other goods to that which contained less. On the x-axis of Figure 2–5 we have graphed quantities of whiskey, and on the y-axis we have graphed amounts of *all other goods*. Then we have drawn in any basket $\mathbf{X}^1$. All baskets on the line segment $\mathbf{X}^1F$, except the end point, must be in B because they contain more of all other goods than the given basket. All points on the line segment $\mathbf{X}^1G$ must be in W, because they contain less of all other goods except at the upper end point. All baskets to the right of $F\mathbf{X}^1G$ contain more whiskey than the given basket and thus must lie in B, and all baskets to the left of this line have smaller amounts of whiskey and lie in W.

In this case, therefore, we can obtain all of B and W. B is the upper segment of the line and all points to the right of the line, whereas W is the lower segment of the line and all points to the left of the whole line. I, therefore, contains only the point $\mathbf{X}^1$, and no indifference curve exists for this or any other basket. The boundary between B and W at every point which is drawn except $\mathbf{X}_1$ is owned by one or the other of these two sets. This means that the consumer's preferences jump discontinuously from baskets that are less attractive than a given basket to baskets that are more attractive, and cannot be represented by a continuous ordinal preference function. Except for paths that lead through the point $\mathbf{X}^1$ on Figure 2–5, one does not *pass through* the value of the preference function for $\mathbf{X}^1$ in going from points in W to points in B.

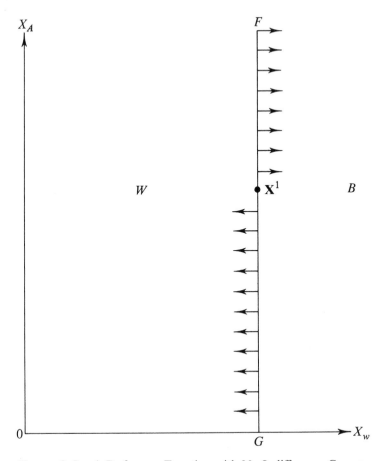

FIGURE 2–5. A Preference Function with No Indifference Curves.

Because it will be simpler to work with a consumer model in which we have continuous indifference curves, we shall merely postulate that the consumer's preferences do yield them. That is, we assert that for any basket X the boundary between B and W will be I, which is connected, so that it consists of one piece. Because I must be a single basket in width, it will be a continuous function of its components. We therefore assert:

CONSUMER POSTULATE 4.   For any basket X the sets B and W are bounded by the set I, which is connected and does not intersect B or W.

The student may see that it is now possible to define a continuous ordinal function—one that is unique up to a monotone transformation—to describe the consumer's preferences by the following line of reasoning. Take any basket X, which we are assured by Consumer Postulate 1 has been ordered. Now associate with X and its indifference set I a number such that the number is higher than any number assigned to sets *I* that are not as attractive as it and is lower than any number assigned to sets *I* that are more attractive. Consumer Postulates 1 and 4 will assure us that the sets *I* exist for every basket in the field of choice. Consumer Postulate 3 assures us that for every *I*, if we specify all quantities of goods but one in some basket contained in *I*, the quantity of the remaining good will be uniquely determined (because the sets *I* cannot be thick). Therefore, each *I* is a function whose arguments are quantities of each good and whose value is an index number associated with it. One and only one value of the function is determined for each basket.

Further, Consumer Postulates 3 and 4 assure us that the function is continuous—that it does not make sudden discontinuous leaps and that there are no gaps in it. Therefore, we may associate with every basket a number that is unique and depict the consumer's preferences by a continuous, real-valued ordinal function

$$M_c = M_c(\mathbf{X}), \qquad \mathbf{X} \in X. \qquad [2\text{--}4]$$

Restricting the Shape of the Preference Function. The preference function may now be imagined as a smooth hill in $n + m + 3$-dimensions, rising indefinitely as we go out from the origin in any direction, with no plateaus and no *holes* in it. We have restricted the shape of the function importantly in the sense that we know that we will rise indefinitely if we start at the foot of the hill and walk up its face in any direction. But suppose we stop at a certain height on the hill and begin to walk on its face, being careful to stay at the same height. We should then be walking along a given *I* set. In three dimensions we know from Consumer Postulate 3 that we would be moving at all times from northwest to southeast, or vice versa, but such a restriction is consistent with the contours drawn in Figure 2–6. If our purpose in deriving the preference function is to facilitate the determination of the maximal set $X_{a/m}$, does it make any difference which type of contour is characteristic of the preference hill?

It does, both from the viewpoint of plausible expectations concerning the preferences of typical human beings and from the standpoint of the techniques available to isolate the maximal set. For example, Indifference Curve *A* of Figure 2–6 is linear, which implies that for baskets of the two goods along the contour the consumer finds a given quantity of one of them (no matter how much of it he has consistent with being on the contour) a perfect substitute for a unit of the other. Rare indeed would be such goods, and certainly we would not expect such linear segments to characterize the entire surface, for the linearity implies that if the prices of these equivalent quantities are different, the consumer will find his maximal set at a corner point, buying all of one good and none of the other. Inasmuch as the intuitive

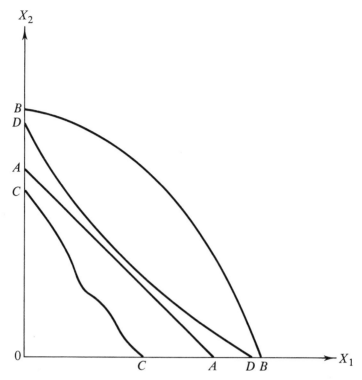

FIGURE 2–6. Possible Shapes of Indifference Curves Under Consumer Postulate 3.

plausibility of this behavior does not seem great, and because observation does not yield examples of one-good consumption, we must doubt the existence of large linear segments in indifference curves or such entirely linear curves as Indifference Curve *A*.

Curve *B* exhibits similar troublesome philosophical and behavioral properties. As we shall see, the consumer's maximal set will always lie at a corner basket with such indifference curves, implying that he buys only one good. Moreover, the techniques which we have for feeling out the maximal set make the operation a tricky one for such curves. Our techniques tell us to move up the hill subject to the constraints of our data, yet we may be fooled into moving down the hill and away from the maximal set without realizing it if the contours are shaped like Indifference Curve *B*.

Indifference Curve *C* with its meanderings is simply inconvenient to work with, affording us the prospect of suffering the same fate as Curve *B* leads to or of becoming hung up on one of its little cusps in a mistaken belief that we have reached a global constrained maximum rather than a local one.

Indifference Curve *D* is a most convenient shape for the indifference curve, both technically and from the viewpoint of plausibility. It asserts that as we obtain more of one good, we must sacrifice less and less of other goods to obtain the same level of satisfaction. This seems plausible introspectively and from our observation of consumer behavior, inasmuch as neither consideration leads us to expect that a consumer will frequently spend all of his resources on only one good. On the other hand, such shapes do not rule out the possibility that some goods will not be bought in the maximal set. Technically, if the indifference curves are so shaped, if all goods are taken in the equilibrium, and if we do move upon the portion of the hill permitted until we move parallel to the base plane, our decision that we have reached a constrained maximum will always be true.

Because our present desire is to build a consumer model that is simple and will yield insights into the nature of consumer decisionmaking, let us simply postulate that the indifference curves are shaped universally like Indifference Curve *D*. What does this imply about the shape of the consumer preference function [2–4]?

For simplicity imagine such a consumer preference function in three dimensions, with good Y_1 along the *x*-axis, quantities of Y_2 along the *y*-axis, and the index values M_c along the *z*-axis. Assume that the function has the general configuration of a derby hat, which does not reach its maximum over the field of choice but rises indefinitely with the same configuration. We have drawn a portion of such a preference function in Figure 2–7. It is the peculiar feature of this shape that if one took a plate of flat sheet metal or of cardboard, and placed it on the function, the sheet would touch the surface of the function at only one point and, except for that one point, the entire surface of the function would lie *beneath* the sheet metal or cardboard. When a function meets this test at every point in its domain—that is, when at every such point (1) the surface of the function either touches the plane or lies beneath it, and (2) it touches the plane at only one point—we say that the function is globally (everywhere) strictly (only one point of the plane touches) concave.

The peculiarly appealing characteristics of such a function are immediately apparent from the following operations. Suppose we took a plane of sheet metal, placed it above the function perpendicular to the base plane and oblique to the *x*- and *y*-axes, in the manner depicted in Figure 2–7. Imagine cutting the derby hat obliquely with the edge of the metal plane by pushing the sheet through the function until the sheet touched the base plane. If one viewed the profile of the cut from the side he would see that the profile had the shape of a rounded-out, inverted letter *U*, as will be seen from *ST* on the diagram. In fact, the data which we impose upon the analysis will constrain the consumer's choice by presenting him the opportunity of purchasing any basket of goods on *ST*, the profile of this cut. Obviously, if the consumer climbs the profile to the top of it at *H* and stops moving when he starts to go downhill, he will have attained the maximum preference index value available to him.

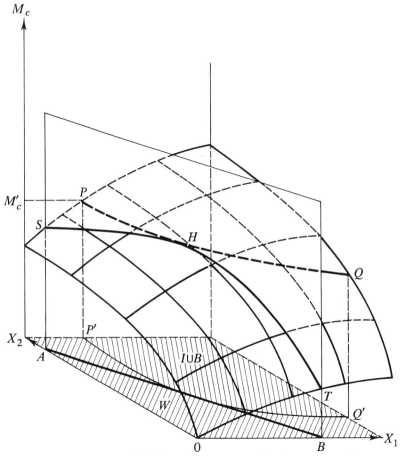

FIGURE 2–7. A Globally Strictly Concave Preference Function.

Imagine, now, that we are suspended in air directly over the plane of sheet metal that is cutting the hill, so that it appears merely as a straight line. Then the reader's imagination will see that attainment of the maximum height on the hill consistent with remaining on the plane of sheet metal will appear to be at the only point where a contour of the hill, *PQ*, just touches the sheet— being neither cut by the metal nor separated from it. These contours may be obtained by slicing the function with a knife parallel to the base plane: that these will bow out in the manner of Indifference Curve *D* of Figure 2–6 is clear from the shape of the derby hat. Because the hill is continuous and has no plateaus, the piece of sheet metal at whatever point is used to slice the function in the manner described must be touched by one and only one such contour. If we project this contour onto the base plane we obtain the indifference curve $P'Q'$ which is tangent to the budget line AB under H.

We might, therefore, assume that the consumer's preference function must be globally strictly concave to obtain contours of the desired form, or indifference curves that bow out toward the origin. But we really do not need this strict a condition. Imagine, for example, the bell of a trumpet halved

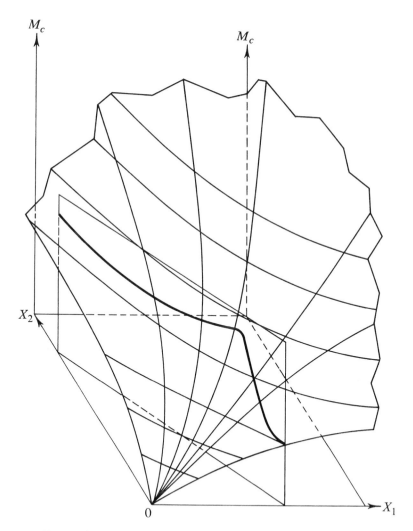

FIGURE 2–8.   A Strictly Quasi-Concave Preference Function.

longitudinally, and assume that the preference function of an individual takes on this shape rather than that of the derby hat. We have illustrated this configuration in the preference function of Figure 2–8. This function is not globally concave: in general, the piece of sheet metal could not be placed at a point on the surface such that the remainder of the surface lay underneath the sheet. Yet, if we sliced this function parallel to the base plane to get indifference contours, they would have the same shape as the globally strictly concave function, as the solid-line contours on Figure 2–8 reveal. Further, if we cut the function with the sheet placed obliquely with reference to the *x*- and *y*-axes, we should find the same type of solution looking at the tableau from above as we did in the previous case. That is, the new function acts *like* a concave function *in these respects*, and, indeed, we will call it a globally strictly *quasi-concave* function.

Instead of defining the function by virtue of its position relative to a plane touching its surface, we must define it in either of two simple ways that are equivalent.

1. If the function is sliced parallel to the base plane at value M'_c the set of baskets in the field of choice, as depicted on the base plane, will be divided into two subsets. The first of these will be W—all baskets that yield a preference index less than M'_c and that are therefore less attractive than any basket in the second set, which is $I \cup B$, the union of I and B, or all baskets whose preference values are at least as great as M'_c. The function [2–4] is globally strictly quasi-concave if and only if the set $I \cup B$ is strictly convex, by which we mean that a straight line connecting any two points of the set must lie wholly within the set with all points in the interior of the set or with only one or both of the end points of the line on the boundary.

These conditions—which are quite simple—are illustrated in Figure 2–7. The set I, or the indifference contour $P'Q'$ for the value M'_c of the preference function, divides the field of choice into the sets W and $I \cup B$. All interior points of this latter set, or those points in B, connected pairwise will give rise to lines that lie wholly within B and therefore within $I \cup B$. And, if two points are selected on the indifference curve and a line is drawn connecting them, the line segment will touch the indifference curve only at the end points and lie wholly within $I \cup B$. If only one of the two points lies on I, the line connecting them will have only that point in I and all other points in the interior of $I \cup B$.

It is immediately apparent, therefore, that these conditions are merely formal statements of the requirements that the indifference contour bow out toward the origin of the base plane and that it not have any linear segments: that is, that it be *strictly convex*. And, because we impose this requirement globally, such shapes must hold for all indifference contours of the preference function.

2. More simply, perhaps, if not so revealing of its properties, a globally strictly quasi-concave function is defined when the following conditions are met. Select *any* two baskets in the field of choice X such that one is strictly preferred to the other, and connect the baskets with a straight line in X (the base plane). Then, the M_c values of every basket along the line except for the end point corresponding to the less-preferred basket of the original pair, must be greater than the value of this less-preferred basket. If the two selected baskets have the same M_c values, every basket along the line except those at the end points must have higher M_c values than the original points.

It should be noted that a globally strictly concave preference function is globally strictly quasi-concave, as Figure 2–7 illustrates, so that the former

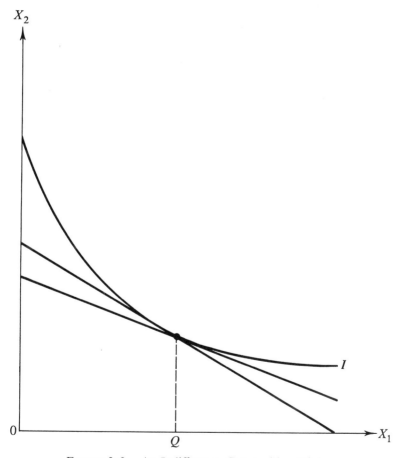

FIGURE 2–9.   An Indifference Curve with a Kink.

condition implies the latter; but, of course, the converse is not true, because the condition of quasi-concavity is less restrictive. We shall, then, impose only those restrictions which we need to obtain curves of the form of Indifference Curve *D* in Figure 2–6 and *P'Q'* in Figure 2–7:

CONSUMER POSTULATE 5.   The consumer's preference function is assumed to be globally strictly quasi-concave.

There remains only one more restriction to impose upon the function for the purposes of convenient analysis. Consumer Postulate 5 gives us strictly convex indifference curves by which we mean that a line drawn tangent to a curve at any point will be elsewhere below the indifference curve. We have not guaranteed the smoothness of those indifference curves, however. By this we mean that our postulates would allow kinks to occur in the curves, at which points the slopes of the indifference curve are not well defined. This is illustrated in Figure 2–9, where we have touched the indifference curve at such a point *Q* with straight lines of different slopes—any one of which could be associated with the shape of the curve at the kink, so that the slope is ambiguous. The existence of this kind of problem is not overly troublesome, but it can complicate a simple model. For example, in our analysis we shall want to change prices by small amounts, and if we do so it might so happen that we merely revolve the price line around the kink, the consumer's maximal set remaining constant. It would be much more convenient to assume that the consumer's marginal rate of substitution between goods changes continuously and smoothly, so that small changes in the data can be expected in general to inspire solution changes whose direction it is the goal of the analysis to gauge. Therefore, we complete our postulates constraining consumer preferences with the following:

CONSUMER POSTULATE 6.   The indifference contours are assumed to be smooth; that is, at every point, nonzero first and second derivatives exist.

With this set of six postulates we have assured (1) the existence of a complete weak ordering, which can be represented by (2) a smooth, continuous ordinal function which is strictly quasi-concave globally and rises monotonically in all directions, (3) whose contours are therefore smooth, strictly convex, and continuous, and (4) the value of which is maximized to obtain the maximal set for the consumer.

SPECIFICATION OF PRICES

A further postulate which we must specify as a constraint upon the data is the statement of a set of prices $\mathbf{P} = [\mathbf{P}_j, \mathbf{P}_{z_i}, P_e, \mathbf{P}_{Z_i}, r]$, where these are in order the prices of the *n* consumer goods proper, of the *m* factor services, of bonds, of capital goods, and of the week's service of a dollar of cash balances (the interest rate). All prices are measured in dollars, so that implicitly we have set the price of a dollar bill, P_U, equal to one (dollar). All of these prices arise, of course, in the markets we have described, but for our submodel, which does not include prices in the variable set, we must assume them as given by the data. We specify formally:

CONSUMER POSTULATE 7. The price vector $\mathbf{P} \geq 0$, by which we mean that every price in the vector is either positive or zero in value with the possibility that all prices might be zero, is specified at given values. It is unaffected by any consumer's actions. Further, and for purposes to be made clear later, we assume that the profits of every firm, π_v, $v = 1, 2, \ldots, o$, are specified in the vector $\boldsymbol{\pi}_v \geq 0$, where V is the set of all firms in the economy.

The Set of Variables

The set of variables for which we seek values from the model includes the following elements.

1. X_{cj}. Consumer c's demands for consumer goods this week.
2. X_{cz_i}. Consumer c's demands for factor services this week.
3. X_{cu}. Consumer c's demand for cash balances this week.
4. Q_{ce}^*. Consumer c's demand for bonds to be held at the end of the week, which is equivalently Q_{ce}, the number of bonds with which he begins the week, plus X_{ce}, the addition to or subtraction from his bond holdings during the week.
5. Q_{cU}^*. Consumer c's demand for money to be held as an asset at the end of the week, equivalent to Q_{cU}, his stock at the start of the week, plus X_{cU}, his additions or subtractions during the week. We shall continue to designate any basket containing all such goods except X_{cu} by $\mathbf{X}$, omitting the subscript c for convenience, but we shall distinguish the basket the consumer takes in the solution as well as all other baskets in the maximal set by $\mathbf{X}_c^\circ$.

The Set of Interrelationships

It remains for us now to derive a set of interrelationships among the data of the model on the one hand, and the variables on the other, whose mutual constraining properties will yield us one or more solutions $\mathbf{X}_c^\circ$ forming the maximal set $X_{a/m}$. Because we have chosen to treat the consumer's demand for cash balances outside of the treatment given other variables in the set, let us turn to the derivation of this relationship first.

A CASH-BALANCE TRANSACTIONS DEMAND FOR MONEY SERVICES

Let us reconsider the environment in which the consumer is functioning. At specified times during the period Tuesday through Sunday he will be called upon to make payments for goods he receives from sellers and he will receive money payments for the goods and services he sells. The economy could construct a complicated set of credit and debit balances to keep track of these "I owe you" and "You owe me" types of relations, to be cleared at the end of the week in order to be sure that no one tries to take more from society than the value of the things he sells. But this might be a costly method of accounting, because resources have to be used to check receipts and disbursements against names. On the other hand, a relatively cheap way of performing this same task of assuring a deliverer of goods that the receiver has a social claim to them without clearing at the end of the week is to receive the value of all deliveries in tokens whose very possession is a guarantee of the valid right to the goods.

Money performs this function, therefore, of facilitating transactions. If every person upon receipt of each of his purchases gives to the deliverer an equivalent value in money, exchange will go smoothly. Now, if at every moment that Consumer c had to make such a payment for a delivery he also received an equal amount of money for some delivery of his own, he would have no need of cash balances. That is to say, under these conditions he would not have to contract on the Monday market day to buy the services of a cash balance of money to hold. The flows of money as receipts would just match the flows of money as payments. If the individual owned a cash stock, therefore, he could rent out its services to the full extent of his holdings to others not so fortunate.

But suppose the forthcoming transactions did not mesh so well. Suppose that at 4:00 p.m. next Friday he will have accumulated over the week from his excesses of flow receipts over flow disbursements $50 but he will be obligated to make a payment of $125. He must then hire cash balances on the Monday market day of $75 in anticipation of this net disbursement, and, of course, he must pay the interest rate on this amount for the service it provides. Therefore, the demand for cash balances by the consumer is determined by the pattern of receipts and deliveries of goods and services over the coming week. However, to specify this pattern would involve us in a long analysis of doubtful generality, and so we shall adopt a Gordian-knot solution, which is much simpler. We shall simply assume that the individual's demand for cash balances is some easily determined function of the value of his expenditures on consumer goods and money balances themselves. That is,

$$X_{cu} = F_{cu}(\sum_j X_{cj}P_j, r), \qquad [2\text{–}5]$$

where we assume that the consumer does not buy most factor services (except those of money) but merely withholds them from sale, and so does not have to hold cash balances against their delivery, and where the consumer holds no balances against his transactions in bonds because deliveries of assets to redeem them occur at the end of the week. Let us write [2–5] in a more general form, following the convention we shall use throughout this book of putting all data behind semicolons to distinguish them from variables:

$$X_{cu} = F_{cu}(\mathbf{X}_{cj}; \mathbf{P}_j, r). \qquad [2\text{–}6]$$

Let us simplify further by assuming that [2–6] is a simple *linear* and homogeneous function of the value of expenditures, with the factor of proportionality given among the data. By this we merely mean that if the consumer were to make no expenditures he would need no cash balance (this is the quality of homogeneity) and that for positive expenditures consumers require a given proportion of their value in cash balances. That is,

$$X_{cu} = \frac{K_{cu} \sum_j X_{cj}P_j}{1 - K_{cu}r}, \qquad [C\text{–}1]$$

where K_{cu} is given among the data of the consumer submodel, and where the denominator term arises from the fact that the consumer must hold cash balances against his hiring of cash balances.

Thus, Consumer c may hold 20 per cent of the value of his purchases in cash balances hired at the beginning of the period, for this may give him enough cash to cover his deficiencies at all points in the week. Obviously [2–6] is a more general relationship, but it would have to be derived from a knowledge of the institutional environment and the specific timing of receipts and expenditures we have discussed above. We shall, in the interest of simplicity, adopt [C–1] as the form we shall use for the interrelationship linking the demand for cash balances to the relevant data and other variables, where the expression [C–1] symbolizes *consumer interrelationship 1*. Formally:

CONSUMER POSTULATE 8. The consumer holds the proportion K_{cu} of his expenditures on consumer goods and interest in the form of cash balances, and K_{cu} is defined among the data of the model.

Now we must make an important distinction that will help to clear up confusions frequently present in monetary analysis. In our model, the demand for cash *balances* is a demand for a *flow* of cash services, and it is related only to the *flow* of cash receipts and expenditures. But a second type of demand for money is present in our model and must be distinguished from the present demand. The consumer owns a *stock* of money, Q_{cU}, at the start of the week which he lends out, and he may very well wish during the week to increase his holdings of such stocks on the following Monday, just as he might wish to increase his holdings of stocks of factors Z_i the following Monday. The reason for both accretions is the same: if the consumer enters the next market day with larger stocks of money, factors, or both, he can increase his leasings of their services and obtain more income.

Just as we have not yet discussed the consumer's savings actions where those savings are in the form of bonds, so we have not yet discussed his saving in the form of money stock accretions. But in our model this type of money acquisition is a completely different phenomenon from that we have just treated. It is the acquisition of money as an asset, to be held like any other asset. As such, the decisions to save or consume in the first instance, and to buy bonds or buy money assets in the second, have not yet been treated.

DERIVING THE OTHER INTERRELATIONSHIPS IN THE SET

With this vital cash balance interrelationship among the variables and the data determined, let us turn to the more general problem. We have seen that Consumer Postulate 2 requires that the choice of a basket of goods be from the maximal set $X_{a/m}$. Therefore, in accordance with our discussion of ways of deriving the interrelationships in economic modelbuilding, we will obtain them, and through them the set $X_{a/m}$, by maximizing the ordinal preference function subject to (1) the cash balance constraint [C-1] and (2) an expenditure constraint. Let us proceed to a definition of this second constraint.

STOCK-FLOW EQUILIBRIUM vs. FLOW EQUILIBRIUM. The consumer in our model is faced with two types of decisions—those concerning *stocks* and those concerning *flows*. The former must affect the decisionmaking of future periods; the latter, under the conditions of our model, are relevant only to the present week. During our weekly market days it is quite possible for the consumer to achieve a *flow* equilibrium but not be in *stock* equilibrium. The simplest way to give a quick idea of what is involved in this statement is to imagine the following example. Suppose that in Week 1 the consumer is in a complete equilibrium, in the sense that his holdings of stocks of assets of all kinds are yielding a flow of income and consumed services which he desires to receive each week indefinitely at the current **P**. That is, he is not tempted to sell off some bonds this week or to reduce his stocks of money in order to purchase flows of goods this week, at the expense of reducing his flow of income for all future weeks, nor, on the other hand, does he wish to sacrifice any of his flow of consumer goods this week to accumulate more assets to yield him more income for all future weeks. He has, in short, made mutual adjustments in income flows and asset stocks such that he does not wish with the data set ruling to substitute either flows or stocks for the other. Moreover, in Week 1 he is spending this desired flow of income in the optimal way by purchasing $\mathbf{X}_c^\circ$ (which we may now take as including X_{cu}°, or optimal cash balances).

Imagine, however, that in Week 2 the consumer is presented by his Aunt Harriet with \$1,000 in government bonds as a gift. This pleasant disturbance of his previous stock-flow equilibrium probably means that he is now holding more asset stocks than he desires, and will therefore lead him to begin to substitute flows of consumption for the asset increment fully or to some partial extent. Let us assume, for example, that he desires to liquidate the entire \$1,000 of new bonds by increasing his consumption. He will probably not spend all of the windfall in Week 2 and return to his previous income level in Weeks 3, 4, ..., for this might mean that the total satisfaction he gets for the prospective income is not at a maximum. Over time, it might yield him more satisfaction to increase his consumption by \$100 for each of the ensuing ten weeks, on the principle of diminishing marginal satisfaction from income. For each of the ten weeks, then, he adds \$100 to his income and spends the sum optimally, so that his choices among goods for that given sum are maximal. He is in short-run equilibrium as far as flows of consumer goods are concerned during each of the weeks, yet he is not in long-term or stock equilibrium, because his holdings of stocks exceed his long-term desires. Only when the consumer is back to his Week 1 situation, with the same holdings of assets and the same income, will he have reattained a stock-flow—that is, a long-run and a short-run—equilibrium, if in fact he does elect to eliminate all of the asset increment. Alternatively, he might have desired to increase his asset stocks permanently by \$200 of the windfall; when under this new assumption about his preferences he had liquidated all but this amount he would have attained a new stock-flow equilibrium.

In our model if $X_{ce}^\circ = Q_{ce}^* - Q_{ce}$ or $X_{cU}^\circ = Q_{cU}^* - Q_{cU}$ is positive or negative, so that the consumer is adding to or subtracting from his stocks of capital goods or money, the consumer has not yet reached a stock equilibrium. If these values are both zero, he has reached such a stock equilibrium. We shall discuss the general case in which the individual may or may not be in such an equilibrium. We shall assume that the consumer delivers any assets he sells and receives any assets he buys at the end of the week, so that he does not lose income during the current week from the assets he sells nor gain income during the current week from the assets he buys. Therefore, the wherewithal which a consumer has to spend this week is composed of (1) the value of all of his assets, which we denote his *wealth*, W_c, and (2) his *income* from those asset stocks which we symbolize by Y_c.

We add the following data-constraining postulate to the system:

CONSUMER POSTULATE 9. Each consumer c enters the market day of the week under analysis with a stock of assets $\mathbf{Q}_c = [Q_{cz_i}, Q_{cU}]$, each component of which is positive or zero. Further, he has the nonnegotiable right to receive the proportion α_{cv} of Firm v's profits π_v, $v = 1, 2, \ldots, o$.

Given $\mathbf{P}$, therefore, we may define the value of his physical assets as the equivalent bond value of his capital goods:

$$Q_{ce}P_e = \Sigma_i Q_{cz_i}P_{z_i}. \qquad [2\text{--}7]$$

The consumer's wealth, therefore, is

$$W_c = Q_{ce}P_e + Q_{cU}, \qquad [2\text{--}8]$$

or the bond-value equivalent of his physical holdings plus his initial stocks of money.[1] His income is defined as

$$Y_c = \Sigma_i Q_{cz_i}P_{z_i} + Q_{cU}r + \Sigma_v \alpha_{cv}\pi_v, \qquad [2\text{--}9]$$

or the stocks of assets he holds multiplied by the value of their services plus a profit-receipt term. Note that the consumer's income is defined in terms of the maximum money receipts he *might* receive if he sold all of the factor services at his disposal. Further, we may view the consumer as hypothetically selling all of his assets each market day, then buying back the value of assets he wishes to retain at the end of the week.

We shall at this stage consider the constraint that will restrict the consumer to an attainable subset of baskets within his field of choice to be limited wealth (as defined in [2–8]) plus income (as defined in [2–9]). Economically, this permits the consumer to substitute income in the current period for income in future periods. We shall seek, therefore, to find a weekly flow equilibrium when the consumer may not be in stock equilibrium.

WEALTH AS A CONSTRAINT. We have imposed upon the consumer, by Consumer Postulate 9, fixed quantities of assets as well as the need to face a nonnegative set of prices fixed under the regime of Consumer Postulate 7. By another postulate—a variable-constraining postulate in the terminology of Chapter 1—we must insist that the consumer spend no more than the wealth and income he possesses at the end of the market day.

CONSUMER POSTULATE 10. The consumer's selections of flows during the week, valued at current prices, plus the value of the asset stock with which he ends the market day, must be less than or equal to his wealth and income on

---

[1] Strictly speaking, we should include the capitalized value of the shares of firms' profits held by the consumer. But because these are nonnegotiable and therefore must be held at the start and finish of each period, we will net them out for simplicity.

the market day. That is, our second interrelationship among data and variables is

$$\sum_j X_{cj}P_j + \sum_i X_{cz_i}P_{z_i} + X_{cu}r + Q_{ce}^*P_e + Q_{cU}^* \leq W_c + Y_c. \quad [C'\text{-}2]$$

The net change in units of assets, X_{ce} and X_{cU}, may vary in the negative direction to the value $-Q_{ce}$ and $-Q_{cU}$, if the consumer were to liquidate his entire holdings of wealth during the period, and may rise in the positive direction to equal the value of the flows of services he sells, if he were to invest all of his income.

Note that we do not require the consumer to spend all of his wealth and income this week, but merely require that he not overspend. Actually, as we shall see, our postulates will assure us that the equality sign in $[C'\text{-}2]$ will hold in equilibrium, but we shall derive this as a theorem of the model, not assume it explicitly.

With the exception of X_{ce} and X_{cU} all of the quantity variables for Consumer c must be nonnegative. We may eliminate the inconvenience of potentially negative-valued variables by using, in our definition of **X**, the values Q_{ce}^* and Q_{cU}^* instead of X_{ce} and X_{cU} respectively, as we have done in the section, "The Field of Choice," earlier in this chapter.

CONSUMER POSTULATE 11. All elements of $\mathbf{X}_c^\circ$ are nonnegative. This follows from the definition of the field of choice, X.

THE CONSTRAINED MAXIMUM. We may now obtain the remaining interrelationships among the variables and the data by employing the assumption that Consumer c must choose from the attainable subset X_a defined by his cash balance constraint $[C\text{-}1]$ and his wealth-income constraint $[C'\text{-}2]$, and that the basket he does in fact select will be from the maximal subset $X_{a/m}$. Therefore, by maximizing the function M_c in $[2\text{-}4]$ subject to $[C\text{-}1]$ and $[C'\text{-}2]$ we obtain this maximal set and $\mathbf{X}_c^\circ$ a solution.

Let us use three dimensions to demonstrate how we do this. In Figure 2–8 we have drawn an ordinal preference function which is globally strictly quasi-concave over a field of choice containing baskets with various quantities of two goods, say Y_1 and Y_2. For a given P_1 the given wealth-income $W_c + Y_c$ could buy $(W_c + Y_c)/P_1$ units of Y_1 if it were wholly spent on Y_1, and, similarly, for a given P_2, $W_c + Y_c$ could buy $(W_c + Y_c)/P_2$ units of Y_2 if it were exhausted on that good. On Figure 2–10, where we have reduced the function of Figure 2–8 to two dimensions through the use of contour lines or indifference curves, we have marked these maximum amounts of the two goods on their respective axes as B and A respectively.

Now connect these two extreme points with a straight line, AB. This line shows us all baskets that could be purchased if wealth-income were totally exhausted on the goods, for the slope of the line reveals for a unit loss of

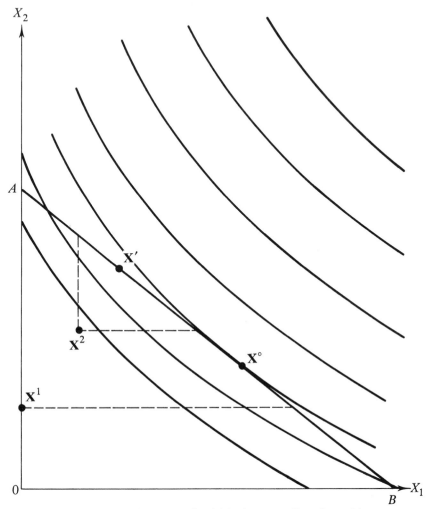

FIGURE 2–10. The Constrained Maximum as Seen from Above.

Y_1 how much of Y_2 the consumer would have to buy to exhaust his wealth-income once more. For example, if P_1 and P_2 were \$2 and \$4 respectively, then a unit loss of Y_1 would require that .5 unit of Y_2 be purchased if wealth and income are to remain exhausted. Thus, the slope of the *budget* or wealth-income line—the intersection of the plane with the base of Figure 2–7—is defined by $-P_1/P_2$. It shows the rate at which the market will transform by exchange units of Y_1 into units of Y_2 for Consumer c, and, because the slope is constant over the whole function, the rate of transformation via exchange is depicted as constant and unaffected by the amounts of goods so transformed by the consumer, following Consumer Postulate 7. We have already seen that the *position* of the budget line—where its axis-intercepts occur—is determined by the amount of wealth-income the consumer has to spend.

But the budget line merely shows the baskets available to the consumer if he were to spend all of his wherewithal. He may also purchase any basket that lies along the line segments OA and OB, or in the interior of the triangle AOB. If he sold all of his physical assets and gave away this money along with that held as money stocks and that obtained as money income, he would take the basket that lies at the origin, containing no goods. Less spectacularly, he may choose other baskets in the three sets just described that do not exhaust his wherewithal by simply destroying or otherwise disposing of his means.

Therefore, the consumer's attainable set X_a consists of all baskets of the triangle AOB, including those that lie on its three boundaries. By Consumer Postulate 2, the consumer will choose a basket from that subset of AOB which yields the highest values of M_c for the baskets it contains of any in the triangle. Now, no basket in the interior of AOB or on its boundaries OA and OB (except possibly where they intersect the AB frontier) can be in the maximal set, by virtue of Consumer Postulate 3, for any such basket will always have at least one other basket in the attainable set that is preferred to it. For example, consider $\mathbf{X}^1$ on OA and $\mathbf{X}^2$ in the interior of AOB in Figure 2–10. If we make each of these points an apex for a 90° angle, and extend the sides of the angles until they reach the budget line, any point within or on the right triangles so formed (except the original basket at the apex, of course) will be preferred to the original basket. This reflects the requirement stated in Consumer Postulate 3 that no good can become a nondesired good within the field of choice, so that the consumer always will prefer more of it to less, other goods remaining constant in quantity.

This being true, no basket that lies in the maximal set can be found in the interior of the attainable set or on OA or OB except as end points. Thus all of the baskets in the maximal set must be found along the budget line. Therefore, because the consumer will choose some basket in that set, he will exchange *all* of his wealth-income (do not forget this usually means buying back most or all of the assets with which he begins the week). It is thus deduced from the postulates that the equality sign of $[C'-2]$ will in fact rule in the solution—Consumer c will not waste his wealth or income.

But let us get another perspective on this budget line. In three dimensions the wealth-income constraint is a plane—let us think of it as the piece of sheet metal illustrated in Figure 2–7—whose edge follows the budget line of Figure 2–10. Indeed, as we have seen, Figure 2–10 is the image of Figure 2–7 we obtain if we view the latter from directly overhead, where the edge of the sheet metal plane alone is capable of being seen. This means that the piece of metal has sliced away that portion of the hill that lies between the sheet and the origin of the space, for it indexes baskets that do not exhaust the wealth-income of the consumer. If we remove the metal, we will have before us the profile of the hill where it has been sliced. The student may imagine its outline by thinking of the profile he would obtain if he sliced a derby hat or round loaf of bread in the same manner with such a metal sheet (see Figure 2–7), or if he were to stand a trumpet on its bell end and saw through it obliquely. The side profiles of such cuts are given in Figure 2–11 in *a.* and *b.* respectively.

The baskets of the maximal set must lie along this profile edge, for we have seen that they must lie on the piece of sheet metal, and only these edge baskets meet that requirement. Indeed, our problem as we have phrased it is to get as high upon the hill, M_c, as we can, never getting off the metal plane. Therefore, we are bound to the baskets along the profile. If, therefore, we start from an end point of the profile and climb to the top of the profile hill —that is, if we climb until we can go no higher—we will have the basket or baskets that are the most preferred of those available to Consumer c. If the profile rises smoothly from either of its end points, approaches a rounded peak, and then falls smoothly toward the other axis, we will have the ideal conception of the profile. For then, at the apex of the profile, there will be a very tiny segment of it, before the climber starts to go downhill but after he has stopped going up hill, at which he moves parallel to the base plane.

At that point—and for the basket over which he stands—he has reached the highest point on the hill accessible to him. If, facing the origin of the space, he leaped forward, he would be jumping into the void of baskets that have more preferred counterparts on the profile. He is forbidden to climb onto higher portions of the hill because he does not have the wealth or income to attain them. Constrained to move sideways in either direction along the metal plane, therefore, he finds that when he is at the top if he moves in either direction he goes downhill. In short, he has attained a constrained maximum.

There is another possibility, however, even for M_c functions that are globally strictly concave (illustrated in Figure 2–11c) or quasi-concave. The climber may, starting at one of the intercepts of the plane of sheet metal with an axis on the base plane, continue to climb along the sheet of metal until he comes to its edge over the basket at OA or OB in Figure 2–10. Then, instead of having achieved an *interior* maximum point he has achieved a *corner* maximum. The distinguishing characteristic of such a maximum is that when he is standing at it there is no place to go forward on the edge of the sheet metal and it is downhill all the way along the metal plane's face behind him. At the point of the maximum on the function there really is no

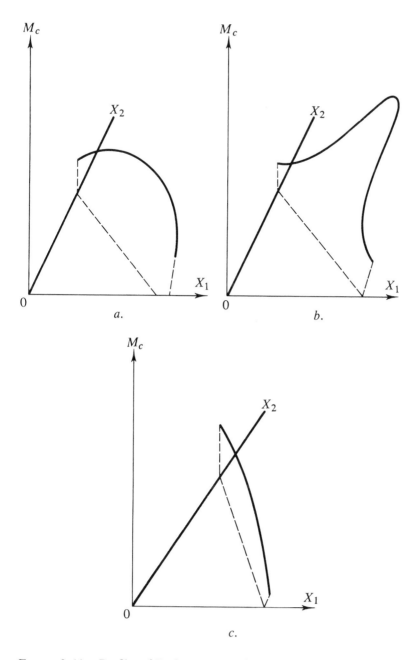

FIGURE 2–11. Profiles of Preference Functions Cut by the Budget Plane.

well-defined slope that is parallel to the base plane: rather, it is a point of constrained maximum because the climber has reached the end of his ability to move upward along the metal plane.

The economic distinction between the two types of maxima that are possible with such a smooth, continuous, strictly quasi-concave function as we have postulated is that the corner maximum means that at least one of the goods is not purchased in the consumer's equilibrium selection. It is an immediate implication of this fact, therefore, that because the consumer will also be on the budget constraint, if all prices and wealth-income are positive he can never in the equilibrium be at a corner point in which he consumes nothing. At most, if $n + m + 2$ goods are available to him, he can consume zero quantities of no more than $n + m + 1$ goods. On the other hand, an interior maximum means that some of *all* goods are taken in the equilibrium.

The fact that the slopes of a function at corner points are not in general well defined causes technical troubles for us. Instead of telling our climber to ascend the hill along the plane of metal until he stops going up hill, then to test the point by stepping off in *both* directions along the plane of metal to make sure he would begin to go downhill—it is easy to give him mathematical instructions to do this—we must tell him to continue climbing in search of this point and to stop short of it only if he bumps into a wall before he has attained a point of zero slope. Surprisingly, the mathematical ways of telling the climber to do this—to take into account the fact that he may bump into a wall—are complicated, and make our task of isolating the maximal set for Consumer c more difficult.

It is difficult to work in three dimensions as we have been doing, although it is a good preliminary step to view these relations in three-dimensional space for an initial understanding. Suppose that we again view the hill and the metal sheet from directly overhead. Then we may convert the metal sheet into what appears to be a line on the base plane (see Figure 2–7 again). Also, by making slices of the hill parallel to the base plane at given values of M_c and projecting the profiles so obtained onto the base plane, we may obtain a map of the hill in two dimensions. This we have done in Figure 2–12. How would our two types of maxima appear to us from this direct overhead view?

If the student will once more employ Figures 2–7 and 2–8 and his imagination to answer this question for an interior maximum, he will see that if the M_c function is shaped like a rising portion of a derby hat or a halved trumpet, the metal sheet will divide the hill into three sections. The first section will contain all portions of the hill whose contour lines have penetrated the metal sheet or have not reached it from the side of the origin. The second section of the hill is that part whose contour lines have not been touched by the metal

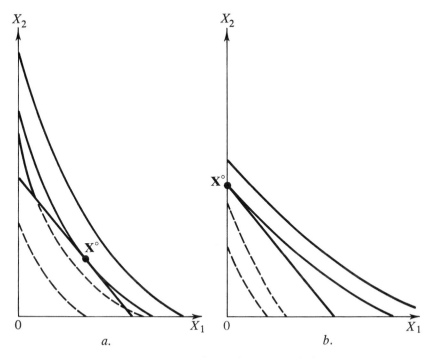

FIGURE 2–12.   Interior and Corner Solutions.

sheet and which lies behind it. But a third section of the hill neither penetrates the metal sheet nor lies at a distance from it. In short, this third section just touches the metal sheet.

For the corner maximum the shape of the hill and the location of the metal plane must be such that the only contour line that merely touches the sheet must do so on an edge of the function along a goods axis. That is, from this point of support the hill would tend to veer sharply away from the sheet. Except for this, however, nothing else about the shape of the hill need differ. Indeed, for any such function as those with which we are dealing, there are some budgets and prices that will result in corner maxima, which is merely to say that if one's wealth-income is low enough and the price of a good is sufficiently high, at some point one will have none of it in his equilibrium basket of goods. Realistically one expects every consumer to be in equilibrium at a corner point, for no one buys some of all goods available to him for purchase.

Let us now translate this into the perspective of two dimensions and Figure 2–12. For the interior maximum we are merely saying that at the point of maximum satisfaction the critical contour line will just touch the budget line—be tangent to it—whereas lower contour lines will go through it or fall short of it from the front, and higher ones will not touch it from the back. This is illustrated at basket $\mathbf{X}^\circ$ in Figure 2–12a. The same behavior for the corner maximum is illustrated in Figure 2–12b, although strictly speaking no tangency of budget line and contour occurs.

We may say some important things about this (interior or corner) maximum position. First, it will exist, because there are no holes in the field of choice and therefore the attainable set, our function has no holes either, and with positive wealth-income and prices the metal sheet must penetrate the hill whereas with zero income-wealth we must lie at the origin of the hill. Second, the indifference contours cannot be *thick*, or be greater in thickness than one basket, for reasons we discussed in our presentation of Consumer Postulate 3. Therefore, the indifference contour that touches the metal sheet cannot be behind it as well as touching it. It must *merely* touch it without penetrating. Third, the maximal set will contain only one point—the critical indifference contour will touch the budget line at one point only—because we have assumed the M_c function to be *strictly* quasi-concave everywhere. This

FIGURE 2–13. Indifference Curve with a Linear Segment and Nonunique Equilibrium.

means that not only will the contours of the hill bend away from the budget line on both sides of the point of contact with the budget line, where an interior maximum occurs, and on one side where a corner maximum occurs, but that there will be no linear segments in the contour line, as illustrated in Figure 2–13, every basket in which segment is in the maximal set.

These results of our consumer postulates mean that we can obtain the maximal set from a two-dimensional contour map of the consumer's preferences for this two-good problem, rather than deal with three-dimensional space. It will lie at the point of tangency or support of a contour line with the budget line. We have found our constrained maximum in geometric manner.

THE ALGEBRAIC INTERRELATIONSHIPS. It will be well to do in nongeometric mathematics what we have already done in geometric form in order to illustrate what we said in Chapter 1 about the derivation of the set of interrelationships in a model. We are given the preference function we have constructed to depict the consumer's preferences over goods, as written in [2–4], we are given the demand for cash balances in [C–1], and we are given the wealth-income constraint of [C′–2]. Mathematically, our problem is to obtain a constrained maximum.

We now ask what conditions must hold true if we have found our desired point; for example, if it is an interior maximum, and if we move on the surface of the budget plane and of the preference function, it must be true that the slope of the function along the direction of the metal plane must be zero at that maximum. But we have seen how to translate this into two dimensions: the slope of the critical indifference curve and the budget line must be equal. If it is a corner maximum, this equality need not characterize the meeting of the budget line and the critical indifference curve; rather, the slope of the critical indifference curve at this point, measured in the direction of the axis for a good that is taken in positive amounts in equilibrium, must be equal to or less than the slope of the budget line in an algebraic sense.

Let us examine this more closely. Choose any basket in the field of choice, $\mathbf{X} = [X_1, X_2]$, and locate the value of M_c for it on the surface of the hill. Now, at that point, there are three slopes of relevance for us. If we hold X_1 constant and increase X_2 slightly, we obtain the increase of the function in the M_c direction for a change in Y_2. We shall symbolize this slope by the expression $S_{m/2}$. We may also hold good Y_2 constant in quantity, increase X_1 slightly, and obtain the slope $S_{m/1}$. Or, lastly, we may hold M_c constant, change X_1 slightly, and observe the change in X_2 which, by construction, is necessary to keep us on the same height of the hill.

When we are concerned with the slope of an indifference curve, it is, of course, with the last slope that we are working. The indifference curve slope at any point, therefore, we designate $S_{2/1}$ or $S_{1/2}$, depending upon which direction we wish to measure in. Let us distinguish the slope at a point where the curve touches a budget line at a maximum value by the degree mark (°), so that we have $S_{2/1}^{\circ}$ or $S_{1/2}^{\circ}$ there.

The budget line has only one slope of interest to us in this two-good example, and it remains constant throughout the length of the line. Let us designate it $B_{2/1}$ or $B_{1/2}$. Then our third set of conditions for a constrained maximum may be stated for both an interior or a corner solution in the following form:

$$S_{2/1}^{\circ} \lesseqgtr B_{2/1} \quad \text{if } X_1 > 0,$$
$$S_{1/2}^{\circ} \lesseqgtr B_{1/2} \quad \text{if } X_2 > 0. \qquad [C^*\text{–}3]$$

We have employed the asterisk on $[C^*\text{–}3]$ merely because we are dealing at this stage with only two goods and will generalize the conditions in short order.

We must also make explicit the fact that our consumer is constrained to remain within his attainable set X_a, as defined by the need to purchase cash balances and to spend no more than his wealth-income. As we have indicated, although we have structured our postulate set in such a way that he will in fact spend all of his wherewithal, we must give him the option of not doing so. Therefore, we put in the inequality sign as well as the equality sign. If we substitute the expression for cash balance demand of $[C\text{–}1]$ into $[C'\text{–}2]$, we would obtain

$$X_1^{\circ}P_1 + X_2^{\circ}P_2 \leq W_c + Y_c - \frac{K_{cu}(X_1^{\circ}P_1 + X_2^{\circ}P_2)}{1 - K_{cu}r}r. \qquad [2\text{–}10]$$

That is, the value of the goods purchased plus the interest paid on the implied cash balances that must be held against them must be no greater than the consumer's wealth plus income during the week. We may rewrite $[2\text{–}10]$ as

$$X_1^{\circ}P_1 + X_2^{\circ}P_2 \leq (W_c + Y_c)(1 - K_{cu}r), \qquad [C^{*'}\text{–}2]$$

which is the budget relationship among the data and the variables which must hold at equilibrium.

We must be more explicit, however, by defining the conditions under which the inequalities of $[C^*\text{–}3]$ and $[C^{*'}\text{–}2]$ will hold. In $[C^*\text{–}3]$, for example, when will the corner solution occur? Economically, it defines the state when the consumer takes none of one of the two goods in equilibrium. Therefore, we state the condition that if the inequality sign holds in equilibrium, the consumer must consume none of the good; but, if it issues that the equality sign rules, and with it a tangency solution, then the quantity of the good taken may be positive or zero (to cover the possibility that the equality of slopes happens to occur at the corner). These conditions may be neatly summarized in the following relation:

1. $X_2^{\circ}(S_{2/1}^{\circ} - B_{2/1}) = 0,$ if $S_{2/1}^{\circ} \leq B_{2/1}$

2. $X_1^{\circ}(S_{1/2}^{\circ} - B_{1/2}) = 0,$ if $S_{1/2}^{\circ} \leq B_{1/2}.$ [C*'-4]

If the student will study these equations he will see that they require exactly what we have stated in words.

There is also, however, an inequality in [C*'-2]. We must state the conditions under which we will allow the consumer to waste his wealth-income by not spending it, for in this two-good case we shall assume that if he does not exhaust his wherewithal the unspent portion is lost forever. For our two-good example, the only rational way in which this unusual occurrence could take place would be if the consumer were satiated in *both* goods. In terms of our preference function, this means that at X_c° the function turns down in the direction of *every* good. For our case, both $S_{m/1}^{\circ}$ and $S_{m/2}^{\circ}$ must be negative or zero (in which latter case further purchases of both goods would yield zero satisfaction to the consumer) in order for the consumer to be satiated completely before his wealth-income is spent. We may state these conditions explicitly:

1. $X_1^{\circ}P_1 + X_2^{\circ}P_2 - (W_c + Y_c)(1 - K_{cu}r) = 0,$
$$\text{if } S_{m/1}^{\circ} \geq 0 \quad \text{and/or} \quad S_{m/2}^{\circ} \geq 0,$$

2. $X_1^{\circ}P_1 + X_2^{\circ}P_2 - (W_c + Y_c)(1 - K_{cu}r) \leq 0,$
$$\text{if } S_{m/1}^{\circ} \quad \text{and} \quad S_{m/2}^{\circ} \leq 0. \quad [C*-2]$$

The critical indifference curve must bend away from the budget line in the upward direction, not into it, and we have required it to begin to do so on both sides of a single point of contact. This is actually to specify that the indifference curve at equilibrium (and to be safe we have specified that all indifference curves at all points on them) be *strictly convex*. That is, if we draw a tangent or supporting line to such curves at any point the entire curve will lie above the tangent except at the single point at which it lies on the line. As we have seen, if this is true we are assured that the indifference curve will not turn down somewhere and recross the budget line, which might imply that better baskets are in the attainable set. We state therefore:

All indifference curves at all points are strictly convex.   [C*-5]

If we rewrite [C-1] for the example at hand, we obtain

$$X_{cu}^{\circ} = \frac{K_{cu}(X_1^{\circ}P_1 + X_2^{\circ}P_2)}{1 - K_{cu}r}, \quad [C*-1]$$

which we have incorporated in [C*-2].

Lastly, we must restrict the solutions so that they are not negative, reflecting Consumer Postulate 11, for negative values would not make economic sense. We write:

$$X_1^\circ \geq 0, \qquad X_2^\circ \geq 0. \qquad\qquad [C\text{*--}6]$$

Having stated conditions [C*--1] through [C*--6] for our simple illustration with two goods, let us now generalize them for all the goods and services of our Consumer c's field of choice. First, if we make sure that [C*--3] is met for every equilibrium slope in the Y_1 direction, where it is known before the analysis that the consumer will take positive amounts of Y_1 in his equilibrium basket, it will also hold for slopes in the direction of other goods also taken in positive amounts. For example, suppose $S_{2/1} = 6$ and $S_{3/1} = .5$. Then by the definition of a slope, $S_{1/3} = 2$ and $S_{2/3} = S_{2/1} \times S_{1/3} = 12$. Now suppose $B_{2/1} = 6$ and $B_{3/1} = .5$; then $B_{2/3} = 12$, and thus the equalities are preserved in slope directions other than those using Y_1 as denominator. We may, therefore, use only these latter.

Our relations then become:

1. $S_{j/1}^\circ \leqq B_{j/1},$ $\qquad j = 1, \ldots, n$

2. $S_{z_i/1}^\circ \leqq B_{z_i/1},$ $\qquad i = 1, 2, \ldots, m$

3. $S_{e/1}^\circ \leqq \begin{cases} B_{e/1} & \text{if } r \leqq 1/P_e. \\ B_{U/1} & \text{if } r \geqq 1/P_e, B_{U/1} = P_1 r. \end{cases}$ $\qquad [C\text{--}3]$

This third condition merely states that the consumer will desire to acquire wealth in capital goods form if the rate of return on capital goods (bonds) is higher than the interest rate, in money form if the interest rate is higher, and in either form if the returns on both types of asset are equal. In the second case the slope of the budget line will be $P_1 r$. We shall explain this in greater detail in the next section.

The budget constraint enters into the analysis at this point:

$$\sum_j X_j^\circ P_j + \sum_i X_{z_i}^\circ P_{z_i} + X_u^\circ r + Q_{ce}^* P_e + Q_{cU}^* \leqq W_c + Y_c. \qquad [C'\text{--}2]$$

The constraints to define the conditions under which zero values occur for amounts demanded are given as:

1. $X_j^\circ(S_{j/1}^\circ - B_{j/1}) = 0,$ $\qquad j = 1, \ldots, n$

2. $X_{z_i}^\circ(S_{z_i/1}^\circ - B_{z_i/1}) = 0,$ $\qquad i = 1, \ldots, m$

3. $Q_{ce}^*(S_{e/1}^\circ - B_{e/1}) = 0$ $\qquad \text{if } r \leqq 1/P_e$

4. $Q_{cU}^*(S_{e/1}^\circ - B_{U/1}) = 0$ $\qquad \text{if } r \geqq 1/P_e.$ $\qquad [C\text{--}4]$

Note that the first set of conditions requires that good Y_1 be a good that will be purchased in positive amounts in equilibrium.

The consumer is restricted to not spending his entire wherewithal this week only if he is satiated in all goods:

1. $\sum_j X^\circ_j P_j + \sum_i X^\circ_{z_i} P_{z_i} + X^\circ_u r + Q^*_{ce} P_e + Q^*_{cU} - W_c - Y_c = 0$
   if *any* $S^\circ_{m/j}$, S°_{m/z_i}, $S^\circ_{m/e}$ is positive;

2. $\sum_j X^\circ_j P_j + \sum_i X^\circ_{z_i} P_{z_i} + X^\circ_u r + Q^*_{ce} P_e + Q^*_{cU} - W_c - Y_c \leqq 0$
   if *all* $S^\circ_{m/j}$, S°_{m/z_i}, and $S^\circ_{m/e}$ are zero.   [C–2]

We impose the condition of strict quasi-concavity upon the $n + m + 3$-dimensional preference function, which is sufficient to yield the convex indifference surfaces that we imposed in three-dimensional space:

The preference function is globally strictly quasi-concave.   [C–5]

We have already defined the cash balance demand as

$$X^\circ_u = \frac{K_{cu} \sum_j X^\circ_j P_j}{1 - K_{cu}r},   \qquad [C–1]$$

And, finally, we impose the nonnegative-value requirements:

$$X^\circ_j \geqq 0, \quad X^\circ_{z_i} \geqq 0, \quad X^\circ_u \geqq 0, \quad Q^*_{ce} \geqq 0, \quad Q^*_{cU} \geqq 0.   \qquad [C–6]$$

We have in the restrictions [C–1] through [C–6] the necessary and sufficient conditions for the derivation of a maximal set of baskets—in our case a unique basket, because our indifference surfaces contain no linear segments—as well as the institutionally determined cash balances desired by Consumer c during the coming week. These are stated in the manner of equations or inequalities that restrict the values which the variables may take, given the values of the data. They are, therefore, the interrelationships among the variables and the data that form the third component set of our model. To illustrate the discussion in Chapter 1, we call to the student's attention the peculiar importance of the maximization postulate in deriving them. The economic meanings and implications of the maximization procedures will be expanded upon in Chapter 3.

STOCK DISEQUILIBRIUM AND THE NATURE OF THE SAVINGS DECISION. The reader will have noted that we included the demand for securities and money stocks in the interrelationships, although we recognized that if the consumer were in stock equilibrium, X°_{ce} and X°_{cU} would be zero, indicating that he was neither increasing nor decreasing his stock of future income claims, nor seeking to hold his wealth in a different form. Let us now consider, however, the nature of the individual's demand for savings or supply of dissaving—that is, changes in the value of the asset stocks he holds—when he is not enjoying this stock equilibrium.

We postulate, therefore, that the consumer will enter the week with a vector $\mathbf{Q}_c = [Q_{cz_i}, Q_{cU}]$ and end the week with a vector $\mathbf{Q}^*_c = [Q^*_{cz_i}, Q^*_{cU}]$, and we have also defined Q_{ce} and Q_{ce}^* (implicitly) in [2–7]. Thus, $\mathbf{Q}_c$ and $\mathbf{Q}_c^*$ are vectors of the real stocks of assets held by the consumer at the beginning and the end of the week respectively, whereas $Q_{ce}P_e$ and $Q_{ce}^*P_e$ are the values of stocks of real capital goods proper at the beginning and end of the current week respectively, acquired through the purchase of securities during the previous and current weeks.

The consumer may add to his stock of wealth in two ways: by purchasing securities at P_e per unit or by purchasing money (that is, *hoarding*) at the end of the week at the price of 1 per unit, or he may reduce his stock of wealth by selling securities at P_e or by selling money at 1. Both of these paper assets are claims on future income to begin in Week 2 and to be earned in perpetuity, and we shall for convenience endow our consumer with an infinite time horizon. That is, we shall assume that our consumers do not look forward to some time in the future when they will liquidate their holdings of wealth, perhaps because they do take strongly into account the future welfare of their heirs.

Then, a unit of security, E, is a riskless guarantee of the receipt of 1 dollar every week until Doomsday, and a unit of money, U, is the guarantee of the earnings on a dollar lent at short term, or r, in perpetuity, beginning the week following the acquisition of the asset. The price of a unit of money asset is set at 1, because all other prices are measured in units of it, but P_e is set on the bond market, and we must now consider what its price will be. On a free market, P_e should approach the value of an infinite stream of dollars valued in current dollars. If we define the current value of such a stream to be V, we desire to understand how it is determined in order to see into the determination of P_e.

What, then, will V be in a market society? If there is a net rate of return on capital goods in the economy, i_k, then a dollar receivable at the end of Week 1 will be worth on the market day of Week 1 only $1/(1 + i_k)$ dollars, where i_k is the rate of return ruling in Week 1 on capital goods. Similarly, on the market day of Week 1 the current worth of a dollar received at the end of Week 2 will be $1/(1 + i_k)^2$ dollars, and so forth, where for simplicity we assume that everyone expects i_k to remain constant over all future time at the level determined on Week 1's market day. Therefore, the value of a stream of such receipts will be the sum of the individual current values of the elements in the stream:

$$V = \frac{1}{(1 + i_k)} + \frac{1}{(1 + i_k)^2} + \cdots. \qquad [2\text{–}11]$$

For convenience let us define

$$A^t = \frac{1}{(1 + i_k)^t}. \qquad [2\text{–}12]$$

Then we may write that the value of a stream of one-dollar payments receivable for n time periods will be

$$V = \sum_{t=1}^{n} A^t.$$ [2–13]

We may reduce this to a simplified form by recognizing that [2–13] is a geometric progression. Then, if we multiply V by A and subtract this product from V, we get

$$V - AV = A - A^{n+1},$$ [2–14]

and factoring out and transposing,

$$V = \frac{A(1 - A^n)}{(1 - A)}.$$ [2–15]

Substituting for the A-terms from [2–12], we may get finally,

$$V = \frac{(1 + i_k)^n - 1}{i_k(1 + i_k)^n}.$$ [2–16]

Suppose, now, that we allow n to grow indefinitely and approach infinity, as we convert [2–16] from an annuity to a perpetuity. Then, if we divide numerator and denominator by $(1 + i_k)^n$ and take the limit of the expression we obtain

$$V = \frac{1 - (1 + i_k)^{-n}}{\dfrac{i_k(1 + i_k)^n}{(1 + i_k)^n}} \to \frac{1}{i_k}.$$ [2–17]

That is, the value of a perpetual flow of one dollar per week (to begin the following week) approximates the reciprocal of the net rate of return on capital goods. In the long-term security, or bond, market, therefore, the price of the bond, P_e, which is the *actual* price of the perpetual flow of a dollar of net income set by competition, may be set equal to V, the theoretical valuation of this flow, and from this price the implied net rate of return on capital goods, i_k, can be deduced.

As we have explained, bonds are supplied by (1) firms who wish to sell new capital goods which they are going to produce, and (2) consumers who wish to reduce the stock of capital goods they possess, and they are demanded by (1) consumers who wish to increase the stock of capital goods they hold, or, more realistically, who wish to increase the titles to such goods that they hold. At the end of the week, we have assumed that the suppliers of the bonds redeem them in equivalent value amounts of capital goods. As long as the consumer gets equivalent money values of such capital goods for the savings he put into bonds, he is indifferent, providing the net earnings on this value are independent of its structure. Of course, in the complete model, towards which we are building, all assets will earn the same rate of return and this independence of structure will characterize assets.

Now, because in the model in which we allow the consumer to be in stock disequilibrium we impose the constraint that he stay within his total where-withal—wealth plus income—rather than income alone, we may view the consumer on each Monday market day as hypothetically selling all of his wealth on the market and selling all of the factor services at his command, then buying back the quantity of bonds, money, factor services, cash balances, and consumer goods he wishes for the week.

The consumer under these conditions will hypothetically purchase bonds until the marginal rate of substitution of bonds for the good with which we are measuring (Y_1 in our submodel) meets the condition of [C–3–3] subject to [C–4–3, 4]. In short, we may treat his demand for savings as a symmetrical good with factor services and consumer goods.

For what is a bond in this analysis? It is a unit of perpetual net revenue—a dollar of weekly income received indefinitely—with a price P_e. The consumer is asked to balance the satisfaction of receiving one more unit of such income against the satisfaction of consuming another dollar's worth of any other alternative purchase. This is another reflection of the consumer's preferences, but because of its importance and of the fact that it requires the balancing of satisfactions received steadily in the future against goods that are receivable once-for-all in the present, economists have spent some time in the discussion of the peculiarities of the preferences that lie behind such choices.

To explain the discount on future goods which i_k constitutes they have provided the hypothesis that the vast majority of men are psychologically prone to live in the future only when it arrives. That is to say, the theory is that most men have a *positive time preference*: they tend to prefer to consume in the present rather than the future, and to discount the satisfactions or dissatisfactions which they will experience in the future. Even, therefore, offering them more goods tomorrow for a given number of goods today leads to a diminishing satisfaction and to a limit to savings.

In this way therefore we can determine in the solution set a demand function for the number of units of bonds the consumer desires to hold at the end of the week:

$$Q^*_{ce} = D_{ce}(\mathbf{P}, \mathbf{Q}_c, K_{cu}, \boldsymbol{\alpha}_c, \pi_v) \quad \text{if } i_k \geq r,$$
$$= 0 \quad \text{if } i_k \leq r. \tag{2–18}$$

The complication is caused by the existence of money. As we have indicated already, the consumer will desire to hold all of his wealth in money form if the rate of interest, r, is higher than the rate of return on capital goods, i_k. This means that the effective price of a perpetual weekly flow of \$1 is not

$1/i_k$ but rather $1/r$. Because the slope of the budget line in the E direction, $B_{e/1} = P_1/P_e = P_1 i_k$, when money is the effective asset, it follows that $B_{U/1} = P_1 r$. Thus we may write

$$Q_{cU}^* = \frac{D_{ce}(\mathbf{P}, \mathbf{Q}_c, K_{cu}, \boldsymbol{\alpha}_c, \boldsymbol{\pi}_v)}{r} \qquad \text{if } i_k \leqq r,$$

$$= 0 \qquad \text{if } i_k \geqq r. \qquad [2\text{--}19]$$

The relative rates of return on the two types of asset dictate the form the desired wealth holdings will take, in the present model being exclusively one or the other. Of course, both rates will be equal in equilibrium in our complete model, and consequently the consumer will be indifferent in equilibrium as to which form of asset he holds. Moreover, the exact amount of money versus capital goods going to the consumer will be indeterminate in this final equilibrium as far as individual consumers are concerned.

The consumer in general, however, will begin with stocks of both equivalent units of perpetual net revenue and money, and we are interested only in incremental adjustments which he makes to these stocks, namely X_{ce} and X_{cU}. With this analysis we have worked into the consumer's submodel the provision for changes in stocks, and we have done so in a manner that preserves the symmetry of capital goods and money with other goods and services in the model.

THE SOLUTIONS FOR THE VARIABLE SET

From these interrelationships we may obtain the values of the variables for any allowable data set. If we solve out these interrelationships to obtain each variable as a function of the values of the data only, we would obtain the following relations. Let us now place the individual consumer's subscript on the variables to distinguish these functions from the market functions to be defined in Chapter 7.

1. $X_{cj}^\circ = D_{cj}(\mathbf{P}, \mathbf{Q}_c, K_{cu}, \boldsymbol{\alpha}_c, \boldsymbol{\pi}_v), \qquad j = 1, \ldots, n$

2. $X_{cz_i}^\circ = D_{ci}(\mathbf{P}, \mathbf{Q}_c, K_{cu}, \boldsymbol{\alpha}_c, \boldsymbol{\pi}_v), \qquad i = 1, \ldots, m$

3. $X_{ce}^\circ = D_{ce}(\mathbf{P}, \mathbf{Q}_c, K_{cu}, \boldsymbol{\alpha}_c, \boldsymbol{\pi}_v) - Q_{ce} = Q_{ce}^* - Q_{ce}$

4. $X_{cu}^\circ = \dfrac{K_{cu} \sum_j X_{cj}^\circ P_j}{1 - K_{cu} r}$

5. $X_{cU}^\circ = W_c + Y_c - \sum_j X_{cj}^\circ P_j - \sum_i X_{cz_i}^\circ P_{z_i} - X_{cu}^\circ r - Q_{ce}^* P_e - Q_{cU}$

6. $W_c \equiv Q_{ce} P_e + Q_{cU}$

7. $Q_{ce} \equiv (Q_{cz_i} P_{z_i})/P_e$

8. $Y_c \equiv Q_{cz_i} P_{z_i} + Q_{cU} r + \sum_v \alpha_{cv} \pi_v. \qquad [1]$

In [I–6] we have defined the consumer's wealth again so that we have it in the system of equations, in [I–7] we have defined the bond-equivalent of the stock of physical assets, and in [I–8] we have repeated the definition of income.

Note that in [I–5] we have defined one of the values of the variables (and we chose X_{cU}°, the equilibrium increment in money stocks, wholly arbitrarily) as a residual. This merely means that because the individual will in fact spend all of his wealth-income in the solution, because of Consumer Postulate 3, once we have determined $n + m + 2$ values of goods in the equilibrium basket, the remaining value will follow from the fact that he spends all of his wherewithal.

The functions of [I–1] through [I–5], which are not merely definitions as are the identities of [I–6, 7, and 8], yield our prediction of the consumer's demands over his field of choice, summarized in the basket $\mathbf{X}_c^{\circ}$. We may, for convenience, determine his *supplies* of factor services and money balances by simply subtracting his demands for these goods from his holdings of them:

9. $\bar{X}_{cz_i}^{\circ} = Q_{cZ_i} - X_{cz_i}^{\circ}, \quad i = 1, \ldots, m$

10. $\bar{X}_{cu}^{\circ} = Q_{cU} - X_{cu}^{\circ},$ \hfill [I]

where we shall, throughout this book, symbolize *supplies* or *outputs* by $\bar{X}$, or "X-bar."

Our task is, therefore, completed in the sense that we have demonstrated (1) the structure and construction of a model and (2) the end-result or the purpose of it to predict the values of phenomena under given states of the relevant environment. We have taken a good deal of care in this chapter to work slowly through the exercise in order to provide an illustration of the mechanistic method discussed in Chapter 1. We have (1) isolated the phenomena that are treated as relevant data and defined the institutional environment within which the consumer makes his decisions, (2) defined a set of consumer preference and behavior postulates, as well as a set of data-constraining postulates, (3) restated the elements in (1) and (2) in the form of a set of relationships among the data and variables of the model, and, finally, (4) solved out the system in (3) to obtain, in System [I], for given states of the environment, the model's prediction of the consumer's preferred basket.

But our task has only begun in another sense. We stressed in Chapter 1 that one of the most important tasks of the modelbuilder is to *manipulate* his model after having constructed it, in order to gain some insights into the phenomena it purports to explain. In the case at hand, for example, as economists we cannot really hope to fill the above model with statistical data and thereby to obtain *quantitative* answers from System [I]. Rather, as economic theorists, we must seek to find out as much about the nature of the system—the nature of the demand and supply functions for goods and services—as we can *without* having specific functions before us. Does the postulate set contain within itself further information that is not apparent in System [I] as it stands?

System [I] is the *anatomical chart* of the consumer model, in the sense we spoke of in Chapter 1: can we get some view as well of the *physiology* of the model? System [I] gives us no real insights into reality as yet: it merely asserts the rather sterile proposition that our set of assumptions will yield *some* acceptable values for all variables in the consumer's choice—a proposition interesting as a beginning, but certainly not as an end of modelbuilding. Therefore, in Chapter 3 we shall turn to methods of employing economic models in an attempt to derive more specific propositions from them concerning consumer behavior.

Selected Readings

1. ARMEN ALCHIAN, "The Meaning of Utility Measurement," *American Economic Review*, XLIII (1953), pp. 26–50. An elementary and still valuable presentation of the problems of measuring preferences.

2. KENNETH ARROW, *Social Choice and Individual Values* (New York: John Wiley, Second Edition, 1963), Chs. III, V. The classic but difficult statement of the problem of obtaining a group preference representation from individual preferences.

3. HARVEY LEIBENSTEIN, "Bandwagon, Snob, and Veblen Effects in the Theory of Consumer's Demand," *Quarterly Journal of Economics*, LXIV (1950), pp. 183–207. An elementary attempt to integrate into demand theory some aspects of consumer behavior we have ignored.

4. RUTH P. MACK, "Economics of Consumption," Ch. 2 in Bernard F. Haley, editor, *A Survey of Contemporary Economics* (Homewood, Ill.: Irwin, 1952). A balanced overview of the problems in consumer theory, most valuable for its statistical portrait of American consumers.

5. PETER NEWMAN, *The Theory of Exchange* (Englewood Cliffs, N.J.: Prentice-Hall, 1965), Ch. 2. An excellent presentation of the theory of consumer choice to which our analysis is greatly indebted.

CHAPTER 3

The Theory of Consumer Behavior: II

We have discussed in an introductory manner in Chapter 1 the problems and some of the techniques involved in obtaining propositions about the behavior of consumers in the real world from our models. We are seeking to obtain from what we have called the *anatomy* of the model insights into its *physiology*, or its functioning. We have reached the stage where we can attempt to manipulate the consumer model for these purposes. Because our model is static in the sense of Chapter 1, we will be involved with the method of *comparative statics*, which keeps the structure of the model (the interrelationships) unaltered, changes inputs of data in a controlled fashion, and derives propositions concerning changes in the solution values. In this way it is possible to attain insights into consumer behavior which the mere anatomical chart of System [I] does not yield.

We may illustrate the nature of the propositions we seek by means of a few examples. It has already been pointed out that we will not attempt to fill the data set with quantitative observations collected from an empirical study of the consumer because of the huge task this would entail, although more limited empirical studies of the consumer's behavior have been attempted. Therefore, the propositions which we hope to derive must be qualitative, predicting only directions of movements in the solutions for changes in the *parameters* or data in known directions. Obviously, this blunts the precision of our results, and, indeed, ensures that in most cases we will not be able to obtain results at all. As a case in point, if the question of whether the amount of beef taken by Consumer c rises or falls when the price of pork is lowered depends upon whether the numerical value of his purchase of beans is greater or less than the numerical value of his purchase of mutton, obviously we will not be able to evaluate the sign for the change in beef purchases, for by assumption we do not have the numerical values of the variables discussed.

We must be prepared, therefore, for many cases where our tools will not be sharp enough to yield unambiguous results. Even in such cases, however, it may be instructive to see upon what variables the answers depend.

Suppose the consumer is at an equilibrium, all quantities of Q_c, his asset endowment, remain the same, and all prices and profit receipts are constant except the price of labor service—the wage rate. Assume that the wage rate for the kind of labor service Consumer c controls rises: will he offer more of his labor services for income, will he take more leisure and work fewer hours, or will he hold constant the amount of leisure he now demands? The ability to obtain an answer to this kind of question concerning the nature of Consumer c's demand for leisure and attitudes toward work is most important for social purposes, if we may assume Consumer c is reasonably representative of the typical worker, If, for example, we increase the income tax, will it induce the laborer to work harder, will it interfere with his incentives to work, or will it leave these incentives undisturbed? Such questions must be posed to models such as ours and answers sought by comparative static techniques.

Or suppose we increase the stock of money assets with which the consumer begins the period. Will he increase his purchases of clothes as a result? Will he increase his demand for cash balances as a consequence? Will he add the new money to his permanent stocks of assets and employ only the income from lending it for purchases? These questions also may be answered by a study of his solutions under the conditions postulated, although *we shall assume in the formal analytical portions of this chapter that the consumer is in stock equilibrium.*

Before we turn to the formal methods of attacking such questions however, let us discuss some qualities of the demand (and supply) functions of System [I] which are evident without much analysis.

Some Obvious Propositions About Consumer Behavior

Several general propositions about consumer choice may be derived from an unaided study of the set of interrelationships [C–1] through [C–6], as well as their solutions in System [I]. First, it is clear from the set of interrelationships that the demand for any one good or service is related to the demand for any other good or service, at least to some extent. In [C–3] this interdependence enters the analysis because the slope of the consumer's preference function for every good enters into the determination of the solution, and these slopes change with the baskets at which they are observed. A second type of interdependence among the goods arises in the [C–2] interrelationship, because the purchase of any one good diminishes the amount of wealth-income remaining to purchase other goods. Although this second type of interdependence is most dramatically displayed in the derivation of the Q_{cU}^* as a residual, it pervades the system.

These types of mutual interdependence among the variables are indirectly reflected in the demand and supply functions of System [I]. Each demand and supply is assumed to be functionally related to every price in the data set. It is implied, therefore, that a change in any one price would be likely to exert some net change upon any demand and supply quantity in the new consumer solution. We cannot in general make a change in the relevant data of the model without affecting every variable in the model.

Though a simple result of our analysis, it is an important one. It is not to assert that because there is likely to be *some* impact of a change in the price of mandolin picks upon the basket of goods taken by the consumer it cannot be neglected without substantial danger to the analysis. It is merely to emphasize the fact that in more important cases unless we take into account that more than one quantity will change we may get into trouble. We cannot change the price of beef and study its impacts upon the demand for beef without realizing that the amount of pork demanded must also change. Demand functions, and supply functions, realistically, may be expected to have many prices as arguments.

A second characteristic of the demand and supply functions for goods other than cash balances and money in System [I] is gleaned from the interrelationships that yielded them. The economist refers to it as the fact that they are "homogeneous of degree zero in all prices, profits, and the stock of money." Suppose all money prices (except r) were doubled to the consumer and, at the same time, his receipts of firms' profits and his money assets Q_{cU} were also doubled. Now, from [C–1] it will be noted that the consumer's demand for cash balances also doubles, which indicates that the demand for *nominal* balances is linear and homogeneous, or homogeneous of degree 1, in all prices.

We say that a function is homogeneous of degree n in its arguments, if, for any positive factor λ we obtain

$$F(\lambda x, \lambda y, \ldots) = \lambda^n F(x, y, \ldots). \qquad [3\text{–}1]$$

That is, if we multiply each argument of the function by some positive value λ, the function rises by the factor λ^n. If a function is homogeneous of degree zero in its arguments, then $\lambda^0 = 1$ and the value of the function does not change. If a function is homogeneous of degree one—or linear and homogeneous—then $\lambda^1 = \lambda$ and the value of the function rises by the same factor as the arguments.

If the demand for cash balances rises by the same factor as that by which all prices rise, the demand for *real* balances—that is, the demand to hold command over real commodities and services in money form—does not change, for although the demand for money balances has doubled, so have all prices. Therefore, the consumer can hold command over the same quantity of goods as previously. We may say then that the demand for *real* cash balances is homogeneous of degree zero in all prices. From System [I–10] it may be seen that the supply of nominal balances is homogeneous of degree one in all prices *and the stock of money*, whereas, on the basis of the same reasoning as that employed for the demand for cash balances, the supply of *real* balances is homogeneous of degree zero in these variables.

From [C–3] it is clear that if all prices double, the $B_{j/1}$, which are the slopes of the budget constraint in the relevant goods directions, and therefore are determined by price ratios, are unchanged. Similarly, of course, $B_{z_i/1}$ and $B_{e/1}$ will be unaffected. $B_{U/1}$ will double, and, where it is relevant, the consumer must acquire twice the former stock of money assets. The real value of wealth remains the same, therefore. Inasmuch as the slopes of the indifference surfaces at equilibrium are forced to adjust to these price ratios, no change will occur in them, except for $S_{e/1}$ when money assets are bought. The real relationships are homogeneous of degree zero in all prices, and will change only if affected from the outside.

From System [I–6, 7, 8] it will be seen that the money value of wealth and income will double if the stock of money, profits, and all prices except r rise proportionately. However, *real* wealth and income will have remained constant, because although money values have doubled so have prices: real wealth and income, that is, are homogeneous of degree zero in prices, profits, and money stock. If we return to [C'–2] now, knowing that $W_c + Y_c$ has doubled, we will find that the left-hand side of the relationship has also doubled. So, this expression will be homogeneous of degree one in prices, profits, and money stock or homogeneous of degree zero in real terms. [C–3] is unaffected by the changes being discussed by virtue of our analysis of [C–1], nor are the restrictions of [C–4, 5, 6] affected by the price and money stock changes.

Therefore, we may conclude that the interrelationships of the system, whose solution yielded System [I], are not affected in real terms by the stated changes. The only alterations that occur are changes in money values, which wash out in a real sense. This implies that the set of demand and supply functions in System [I] yields the same values for the variables under the changed conditions. The consumer would be indifferent between two situations in one of which all prices but r, his profit receipts, and his money stock were twice as high as the other. Were he to prefer the situation with higher money values he would be displaying a naive susceptibility to *money illusion*.

The Economic Nature of the Solution

Before we go further with our use of comparative statics to derive less obvious propositions about consumer behavior that inhere in our set of postulates, let us prepare the way by explaining in more detail than was necessary in Chapter 2 the economic meaning of some of the slopes we have used in the interrelationships.

THE SLOPES OF THE BUDGET CONSTRAINT

In Figures 2–12a and 2–12b we drew, in two dimensions, the configuration of the solutions for an interior maximum and a corner maximum. We have denoted the slope of the budget constraint $B_{2/1}$ in this simple two-dimensional case. What does it represent?

The equation of the budget line expresses the fact that the value of all baskets along it sum to the amount of wealth and income available, after provision for cash balances. That is, we have the following expression to represent the line algebraically:

$$X_1P_1 + X_1P_2 = (W_c + Y_c)(1 - K_{cu}r).   \tag{3–2}$$

Suppose we began at the basket $\mathbf{X}^1$ on the budget line, and suppose we added one unit of Y_1 to the basket. Then, in order to stay on the line we should have to reduce our purchase of Y_2 by a sufficient quantity so that just enough wealth-income was freed and only enough was freed to purchase this extra unit of Y_1. We may solve out to obtain what this amount would be:

$$(X_1 + 1)P_1 + (X_2 + \Delta X_2)P_2 = (W_c + Y_c)(1 - K_{cu}r)$$
$$(P_1 + \Delta X_2P_2) = 0$$
$$\Delta X_2 = -P_1/P_2   \tag{3–3}$$

A unit increase in the consumption of Y_1 implies that the consumption of Y_2 must be decreased by the amount P_1/P_2 if the consumer is to continue to consume all of his budget. A moment's thought will indicate the rationale of this result: if Y_1 costs $2 a unit and Y_2 costs $4 a unit, then a unit increase in the consumption of Y_1 adds $2 to the budget, which must be obtained by reducing Y_2 by $P_1/P_2 = .5$ unit.

This expression $-P_1/P_2$ is, of course, the slope of the budget line, whereas the position of the line has been determined so that the end points are those amounts of each good taken singly which the budget would buy, and therefore, given P_1 and P_2, reflect the size of the budget.

Economically, the slope of the budget line is a rate of transformation to the consumer: it indicates to him that he may transform good Y_2 into good Y_1 at the rate $-P_1/P_2$ via exchange in the market. It is therefore a *market rate of transformation*, and the fact that the rate does not change regardless of how much he so exchanges is a reflection of our environmental assumption (Consumer Postulate 7) that Consumer c has no power in the market. That is to say, the budget line indicates that no matter how much Y_1 he begins with, he may sell it and buy Y_2 at a fixed rate given to him among the data.

By our assumption of nonsatiation in Consumer Postulate 3 he will be led from the interior of AOB in Figure 2–10 to the budget line, and by our assumption of pure competition the consumer will be a powerless pawn in the market economy that will force him to move along the line in substituting Y_2 for Y_1 while searching for his optimum. If he were a power factor in purchasing Y_1 or Y_2, then as he absorbed more of Y_1 (and/or Y_2) its price would rise, so that as we moved on the X_1-axis toward the origin P_1 fell and/or P_2 rose, the slope of the budget line BB' would become less steep, as we have drawn it in Figure 3–1. Note the tendency that this type of budget line has of lessening the occurrence of corner solutions, because such solutions imply very high prices for one of the goods and very low prices for the other. We shall assume, however, that the straight line budget curve is most representative of realistic buying situations for consumers, and use it exclusively.

THE SLOPES OF THE INDIFFERENCE CURVES

Let us now ask, for the indifference curve of Figure 3–1, what the economic meaning of the slope at any point is. The indifference curves, reflecting our assumption that the preference function is globally strictly quasi-concave, do not have slopes that remain constant over their extents. As we move toward the left on the X_1-axis, that is, toward the origin of the goods space, the slope becomes steeper and steeper (compare it with the nonlinear budget line of Figure 3–1, which is becoming less steep along the same path, and the linear budget lines of Figures 2–12a and 2–12b, which remain constant in slope on the same path). We shall ask, therefore, (1) what the economic meaning of the slope of an indifference curve is at any point, (2) why it is not identical at all points of the curve, and (3) how we can justify our assumption concerning its continuous (absolute) increase as we move in the direction we have just discussed.

Because the slope is changing continuously, we shall have to make our changes in the contents of neighboring goods baskets very small, else we

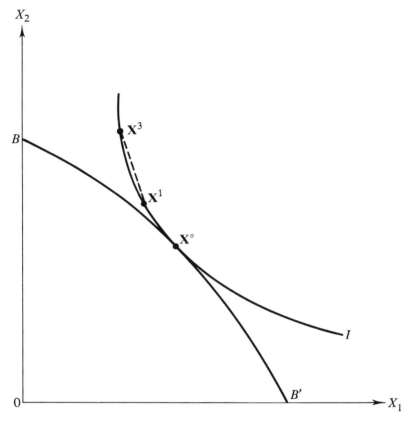

FIGURE 3–1. Equilibrium with a Nonlinear Budget Line.

should have the situation of baskets X^1 and X^3 on Figure 3–1 between which
the slope of the curve has taken many values; if we hope to summarize the
nature of the slopes of the indifference curve between these two baskets with
a single value, we should have to take some such average slope as the line
connecting them possesses, and this is unsatisfactory because it departs from
the curve by so much. However, if we move X^3 closer and closer to X^1 that
line will depart less and less far from the curve, and if we get very close
indeed the line will be closely approximated by the slope of the curve at X^1.
Therefore, if we change the consumer's holdings of Y_1 by very small amounts
in our analysis, we will be able to summarize the behavior of the slopes
between the new and old baskets of the curve by taking the slope of the
curve at the old basket (or the new, for because they are so close no perceptible
difference between them can be discerned).

Inasmuch as we may choose any point along the indifference curve to
illustrate the meaning of the slope at that point, we might as well choose the

solution point $\mathbf{X}^\circ$ of Figure 3–1. If we put the basket into the M_c function of [2–4], we would get a specific value of M_c, say M_c°, whose magnitude would depend upon the ordinal index selected. That is,

$$M_c^\circ = M_c(\mathbf{X}_c^\circ). \tag{3–4}$$

Now for very small changes in the amounts of Y_1 and Y_2 held by Consumer c—let us signify these changes' smallness by using dX_1 and dX_2 instead of ΔX_1 and ΔX_2—we can obtain the change in the preference index caused by such changes in the neighborhood of $\mathbf{X}^\circ$ by assuming a simple linear relationship:

$$dM_c^\circ = S_{m/1}^\circ \, dX_1^\circ + S_{m/2}^\circ \, dX_2^\circ. \tag{3–5}$$

That is, if we begin with the basket $\mathbf{X}^\circ$ and take any pair of small changes in its content of Y_1 and Y_2, the upward or downward movement on the hill of Figure 2–7 or Figure 2–8 may be approximated by (1) multiplying the slope $S_{m/1}^\circ$, or the rise in M_c for a unit rise in X_1 with X_2 constant, by the number of units X_1 rises, or dX_1; (2) multiplying $S_{m/2}^\circ$, or the rise in M_c for a unit rise in X_2 with X_1 constant, by dX_2, the number of units X_2 rises; and (3) adding these two products together to get the total rise in M_c, which, because it is very small, is designated dM_c.

But at the basket $\mathbf{X}^\circ$ in Figure 3–1, or, more accurately, in a very small neighborhood of it, we are interested in changing the composition of baskets in a specific way: in such manner that M_c° does not change, which is to say that $dM_c^\circ = 0$. This is just another way of stating we want to change the composition $\mathbf{X}^\circ$ in such a way that we remain on the same indifference curve. We therefore impose the restriction for our data changes that they sum to zero changes in M_c°, so we may rewrite [3–5] as

$$S_{m/1}^\circ \, dX_1^\circ + S_{m/2}^\circ \, dX_2^\circ = 0. \tag{3–6}$$

Then, we find the slope of the indifference curve at $\mathbf{X}^\circ$ to be

$$\frac{dX_2^\circ}{dX_1^\circ} = -\frac{S_{m/1}^\circ}{S_{m/2}^\circ}. \tag{3–7}$$

We find, therefore, that the slope of an indifference curve at any point is (1) negative, and (2) equal to the ratio of the slopes of the preference hill in the Y_1 and Y_2 directions. But, in an economic sense, what does this mean? The ratio on the right-hand side of [3–7] tells us the rate at which the consumer converts Y_2 into Y_1, in terms of equivalent satisfaction, for small changes in their quantities when he starts from the basket $\mathbf{X}^\circ$. It was obtained by requiring that for a given small change in X_1 as much X_2 be given him as would compensate him and only just compensate him for his loss in satisfaction. Therefore, the ratio of the two goods quantities in the equation reflects this need for preference equivalence. In crude terms, if $dX_2/dX_1 = -4$, then at the basket in whose neighborhood the relation holds, for small changes a loss of 4 units of Y_2 can be just balanced by the gain of one unit of Y_1. The rate at which the consumer's preferences transform the goods is $-4:1$, *when he starts* from the basket $\mathbf{X}°$ and makes only small changes.

As we move along the same indifference curve in Figure 3–1, therefore, and stop at each basket, the slope at that basket yields the relative desirabilities of small changes in the composition of the basket made so that total satisfactions remain constant. The indifference curve, viewed as a collection of slopes, is the set of *psychological rates of transformation* for the consumer in question. It reveals his ability to transform one good into another in such a manner as to obtain neutral impacts on his preferences as he starts with different initial collections.

But why is the indifference curve not a straight line? The simple response, of course, is that we shaped our postulate set so that it was not linear. Why, then, did we do so? The answer is that the economist believes that consumers do not find many goods to be perfect substitutes for one another. If the indifference curve were a straight line it would mean that for a given level of satisfaction, no matter how much Y_1 and Y_2 were contained in baskets that lay on the indifference curve, the consumer would transform them into one another psychologically *at the same rate*. If one had 10 glasses of beer and 1 dish of pretzels, or 1 glass of beer and 8 dishes of pretzels (assuming that these baskets yield the same level of satisfaction), taking one glass of beer away from the consumer's initial basket would require giving him the same number of pretzels to compensate his loss. This is intuitively implausible for most goods, and violates the most casual observation of consumer behavior.

Rather, the economist postulates that as a consumer gives up successive units of Y_1, Y_2 becomes a poorer and poorer substitute for the unit of Y_1 lost, so that more of Y_2 must be obtained to compensate. In terms of equation [3–7], as we move along the X_1-axis by small units from right to left, the slope of the hill in the M_c direction with respect to Y_1 becomes steeper relative to the slope in the Y_2 direction. This makes the slope of the indifference curve, dX_2/dX_1, grow larger in the absolute sense as we move in the same direction toward the origin along the X_1-axis, and yields the shape of the indifference curve we have called *convex*. The rate at which a consumer transforms Y_1 into Y_2 psychologically decreases as the amount of Y_1 decreases.

THE SLOPES OF THE BUDGET CONSTRAINT AND THE INDIFFERENCE CURVE AT THE POINT OF SOLUTION

The interrelationships of [C–3] require that the slope of the budget line and the slope of the indifference curve at $M_c°$, the value of the preference function at the solution, must meet certain restrictions. Condition [C–2] tells us, along with Consumer Postulate 3, that the budget line and the indifference curve at this point of equilibrium must come into contact, for otherwise the consumer would be failing to obtain his maximum satisfaction. Condition [C–4] further restricts this point of equilibrium and states the nature of the contact of the two curves. Conditions [C–3] say that at the equilibrium the slope of the budget line must be either (1) steeper or less steep in an absolute sense, depending upon circumstances, than the slope of the indifference curve, or (2) equal to the slope of the indifference curve at the point of contact.

If the first of these conditions holds, it means that at the point of maximum consumer satisfaction the psychological rate of transformation of the goods is greater than the exchange rate of transformation. For example, it means that although the consumer can exchange Y_2 for Y_1 at a rate of (say) 1 to 3 in the market, the consumer at the point of equilibrium finds them equivalent in psychological satisfaction at the rate of 1 to 4. If he gives up a unit of Y_2 he frees enough of his wealth to buy 3 units of Y_1, but, because 4 of these units would exactly equal his loss of pleasure from the sacrifice of Y_2, he would not profit by making the exchange and would actually lessen his total satisfaction level.

But how can this occur at a solution? For if this situation exists, as de-scribed, the individual can move along the budget line to a higher indifference curve and therefore cannot be initially at a basket in his maximal set—unless for some reason he is prevented from making such moves. The only reason debarring him from doing so is that he is at one end or the other of the budget line: he is at a corner of *AOB* of Figure 2–10, at which he bumps into a wall that prevents him from moving in the proper direction. We must, therefore, specify, if we are to assure ourselves an optimum in our solution, that when this inequality of slopes occurs we are indeed at a corner. This is the function of interrelationship [C–4], which excuses the inequality only when the relevant good is taken in zero quantity, and we are at a corner. That is, the first unit of the good whose quantity is zero requires the sacrifice of so much of any of the goods taken in nonzero amounts in equilibrium that it does not com-pensate in psychological satisfaction for any of the goods that could be given up to get it.

On the other hand, if the second of the alternatives holds at the point of equilibrium, the slopes of the budget line and the strategic indifference curve are equal, and, by virtue of Consumer Postulate 3, because the point on the (strictly convex) indifference curve must also lie on the (linear) budget line, the curves must be tangent at the solution. On the basis of the reasoning used in the previous case, this means that the rate of transformation of the goods by exchange exactly equals the rate of transformation psychologically, so that the consumer can get no net psychological gain by moving away from the point of tangency.

Although interrelationship [C–4] allows for the possibility that this tangency will occur at an end point—because if the slopes happen to be equal there the quantity taken might be zero without violating the constraint—we will ignore this improbable occurrence. We will, therefore, refer to the solution that occurs when all of the conditions in [C–3] rule as equalities as an *interior solution*, or a solution that occurs in the interior of the field of choice *X*, so that some of every factor service, consumer good, money stocks, and bonds is taken by Consumer *c* in equilibrium. On the other hand, the solution that occurs when one or more of the conditions of [C–3] are met as inequalities will be referred to as a *corner solution*, or a solution that occurs on at least one edge of the field of choice, so that all goods, services, money stocks, and bonds are not taken in positive amounts in the solution.

The corner solution is that which is most realistic. There seems no plausible reason why every consumer should be expected to demand some of every alternative good in the economy, even under conditions when we allow all such alternatives to be perfectly divisible. Rather, it would surprise us if every consumer did find himself at an interior solution. Moreover, in the case of the consumer submodel of Chapter 2, for the general price vector **P**, the consumer will choose to hold his wealth *either* as money stocks or capital goods—not both. We will view it, therefore, as the general case and the interior solution as the special case.

The Derivation of Propositions

The last conclusion of our analysis is somewhat embarrassing to us in view of our goals, for it introduces complications into a comparative statics analysis. Of course, if it were possible to work in two or three dimensions with our problems, and therefore to assume that there were two or three goods in the consumer's field of choice, we could remain with geometric techniques of finding new solutions with changes in the data and be able to handle corner solutions quite easily. Suppose, for example, we are at the corner solution depicted in Figure 3–2, and we postulate further that the price of Y_1 falls in the manner depicted by the movement of the budget line from *MN* to *MP*. In this case the fall in price is not enough to induce a departure from the corner, and the price change has no effect upon the equilibrium basket.

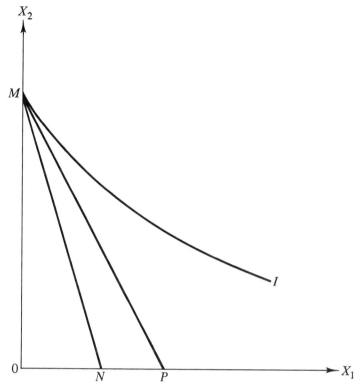

FIGURE 3–2. Displacement of a Corner Solution to Another Corner Solution.

Now, if we are given specific functions for M_c and the wealth-income constraint, so-called concave programming techniques will allow us to solve such problems, although the procedures are usually quite lengthy. To a more limited extent, so-called *parametric programming* techniques will allow us to make judgments concerning the numerical differences in the old and new solutions when the data are shocked, at least for functions that can be approximated by linear segments.[1] That is to say, we can apply comparative statics techniques in explicit situations, either by computing the numerical answers to the model for the old and the new sets of data, or by computing the differences between them directly. However, if we do not have specific functions, and we attempt to derive insights by such techniques using such a generalized representation of a function as M_c, we do not get very far. Too much depends upon the exact nature of the function and the exact degree of datum change.

[1] For a summary of parametric linear programming, see Walter W. Garvin, *Introduction to Linear Programming* (New York: McGraw-Hill, 1960), Ch. 15.

In our consumer analysis, therefore, let us deal wholly with interior maxima for our comparative statics displacements. We have asserted that it is wholly unjustified to ignore the realistic conditions that lead in most cases to a corner solution. We have not erred in our presentation of the interrelationships [C–1] through [C–6] by insisting upon the equalities holding in the solution, for this would be assuming illegitimately that we already knew characteristics of the solution before it was obtained. But let us now make some bold assumptions about the nature of the solution, once obtained, as we operate in a small neighborhood of it. Let us resolve at the outset to move only by very tiny steps, because we are interested only in qualitative movements of the variables, and given the smoothness and continuity of our functions these qualities should be revealed as well by small as by large shocks to the system.

Let us simply assume, therefore, that for all of the small changes in data we shall impose, none of those goods which are taken in zero quantities in the old equilibrium will be demanded in positive quantities in the new solution. Although not a wholly satisfying postulate in that it assumes information about the new equilibrium which is not justified deductively, nevertheless we are not as wholly ungrounded as we would have been if we assumed that only an interior solution could exist when we set out to get the first equilibrium. For we now have information that in the latter certain goods were not consumed. And we are resolved to displace the system only by very small disturbances. In both these respects we have some philosophical basis for assuming that the new equilibrium will show no changes from zero to positive or positive to zero quantities in any good.

Therefore, let us simply take out of the attainable subset all goods that were purchased in zero quantities in the initial solution. Then, for example, if the attainable set contained three goods in the original solution, and if in that solution one of the goods were taken in zero quantity, we eliminate that good and its dimension and reproduce the equilibrium as an interior solution in two dimensions as in Figure 3–3, where we have assumed $X_1^\circ = 0$ in the initial equilibrium.

The reader should, therefore, be warned of the limitations of the method of analysis we are now going to employ. It is applicable only to interior solutions for both the initial and terminal states. Except when we limit ourselves to geometric diagrams, as we shall in this book, because it relies upon information about the slopes of the indifference curve its use requires that the slopes be defined in the neighborhood of the initial equilibrium. And because it depends upon the use of these slopes to approximate by line segments the shape of the preference function between points on the indifference surfaces, it can be used only for small shocks that change equilibria so slightly that the new equilibrium is very close to the old equilibrium. When we treat this kind of analysis with two-dimensional geometrical diagrams we have more freedom because the shape of the curve between any two points is clearly displayed. Moreover, for purposes of clarity we must make large changes rather than small. But when we deal with larger systems that cannot be so conveniently handled, the three restrictions just mentioned are severe limitations.

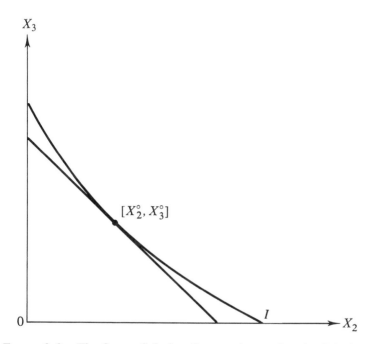

FIGURE 3–3.   The Corner Solution Converted to an Interior Solution.

Our justification is that it is a powerful method of gaining insights into qualitative changes in the equilibria for changes in the data when we do not have specifically defined functions. Practically speaking, it is the only body of methods we have at the moment for so doing. And because the whole purpose of modelbuilding is to obtain such propositions, if *generalized* modelbuilding—using nonspecific forms of functions—is to have any value we must fall back upon these admittedly defective methods.

THE SLOPES OF THE DEMAND FUNCTIONS

The propositions which we seek to derive concern the slopes of the demand functions in System [I] *at the initial solution*. Let us reproduce from that system the demand function for Consumer c for Y_2:

$$X_{c2}^{\circ} = D_{c2}(\mathbf{P}, \mathbf{Q}_c, K_{cu}, \boldsymbol{\alpha}_c, \boldsymbol{\pi}_v)$$
$$= D_{c2}(P_1, \ldots, P_n, P_{z_1}, \ldots, P_{z_m}, P_e, P_{Z_1}, \ldots, P_{Z_m}, r, Q_{ce}, Q_{cU}, K_{cu}, \boldsymbol{\alpha}_c, \boldsymbol{\pi}_v)$$
$$= D_{c2}(\mathbf{P}, Y_c, W_c). \tag{3-8}$$

Let us remove some of the clutter by ignoring the c subscript in the analysis to follow. Then, for any acceptable set of data (prices, wealth, and income) in the function, the amount of Y_2 taken by the consumer in the solution basket is yielded by this function, and we assume that it is positive.

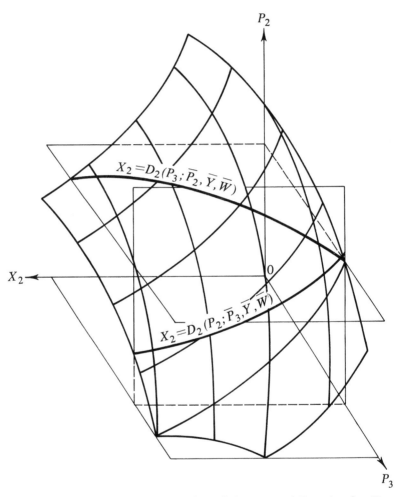

FIGURE 3–4.   The P_2- and P_3-Profiles of the Demand Function for Y_2.

There are three types of data changes that have an interest for us in trying to gain insights into the nature of this function. Let us list them before we try to derive some knowledge of their impacts:

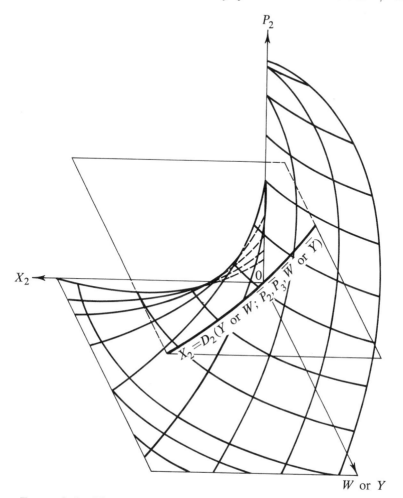

FIGURE 3–5. The *Y*- and *W*-Profiles of the Demand Function for Y_2.

1. *Own-Price Change.* One type of change we could impose would be to change P_2—the price of the good whose function we are studying—holding all other data constant. If we could find out whether the amount demanded of Y_2 rose, fell, or remained constant for a small change in P_2, all other data held constant, we would have information about the slope of D_2 at X_2° in the direction of P_2. In Figure 3–4 we have drawn the demand function for Y_2, with P_2 on the *z*-axis, P_3 on the *y*-axis, and X_2 on the *x*-axis. Of course, because we are operating in three dimensions, we must represent all other goods' prices by use of P_3 and we do not have room for Y_c or W_c.

If we hold P_3 constant at the value reflected in the initial equilibrium at X_2°, we have in fact taken our well-used piece of sheet metal and sliced the function at right angles to the base plane, so that we have a profile of the function showing how X_2 responds to price changes in P_2. This profile is labelled $X_2 = D_2(P_2; \bar{P}_3, \bar{Y}, \bar{W})$, which is our manner of indicating that P_2 is free to vary but that P_3, income, and wealth are not. At X_2° on that profile, we are interested in knowing in what direction we would move on the demand function if we moved up slightly on the P_2-axis. Would X_2 rise slightly, fall slightly, or remain the same? We have drawn it as falling, but that is, at the present point in our analysis, arbitrary.

2. *Other-Price Change.* Another change in the data we could impose is to change P_3 slightly—P_3 being taken as representing any other good's price except that of the good whose function is under analysis—holding P_2, Y, and W constant. This is done in Figure 3–4 by pushing the metal sheet into the demand function parallel to the base plane at the height of P_2 prevailing in the data set that yielded X_2°. We have labelled it $X_2 = D_2(P_3; \bar{P}_2, \bar{Y}, \bar{W})$, and once more we ask what its slope will be in the neighborhood of X_2°. We have drawn it to be negative, but once more this is quite arbitrary.

3. *Income and Wealth Changes.* The last change we might be interested in is the impact of a change in budget availability. Wealth changes might be accomplished by changing W slightly, whereas income changes would affect Y. On Figure 3–5 we have substituted W or Y on the y-axis, and have obtained a profile of the curve by holding P_2 constant. Our curve is labelled $X_2 = D_2(Y \text{ or } W; \bar{P}_2, \bar{P}_3, \bar{W} \text{ or } \bar{Y})$. Once more our questions concern the slopes of the demand function in the neighborhood of X_2°: we have drawn them as positive in arbitrary fashion.

THE IMPOSITION OF STOCK EQUILIBRIUM UPON THE CONSUMER

In seeking to evaluate these slopes let us make one further simplification: we do not yet have the basis for analyzing the consumer's approach to the future in a manner precise enough to consider his attitudes toward an increase in wealth. He may treat increases in the value of his stock of assets as quite different from an equivalent increase in the size of his income, depending upon his nearness to a stock equilibrium, his view of the future, and so forth. Let us for the present time, therefore, revert to the assumption that he begins the week in stock equilibrium so that the net investment $X_{ce}P_e + X_{cU} = 0$, and that no datum change makes this positive. Then we may rewrite, continuing to neglect the c subscript, the wealth-income constraint [C'–2] as the special case

$$\sum_j X_j^\circ P_j + \sum_i X_{z_i}^\circ P_{z_i} + X_u^\circ r - Y \leqq 0, \qquad [C'-2]$$

where the equality holds in the initial equilibrium for reasons discussed earlier. It should be clear that this implies that the small changes in the data which we impose upon the model will move the consumer to a new equilibrium where his value of assets is the same, no net savings being allowed. This will permit us a considerable amount of simplification in our analysis of the displacements. But the student should see that this abstraction from the problems of changes in the value of the stock of assets upon the consumers decisionmaking during the week is an omission of an important aspect of the real world.

THE DERIVATION OF THE PROPOSITIONS ABOUT THE SLOPES

Let us turn, therefore, to the search for information about the slopes of the demand curve for X_2 in the P_2, P_3, and Y directions. Because the functions of System [I] yield no information that will aid us, we must return to the set of interrelationships to see if we can obtain sufficient information about the slopes of the preference function in the neighborhood of $\mathbf{X}^\circ$ to give us the directions of the desired slopes of their solution.

The Own-Price Displacement. Let us suppose that our initial equilibrium $\mathbf{X}^\circ = [X_2^\circ, X_3^\circ]$ occurs at the point depicted in Figure 3–6. The *other* good, Y_3, may be viewed in several ways. We may simply accept it as another good among many, the remainder being out of view but whose quantities demanded are affected by any data shocks we administer to the system. Or we may assume Y_3 to be the only other alternative in the consumer's budget, either as a real good in itself, or as a fictitious good whose unit contains all other goods in amounts proportionate to their prices. Or, lastly, we may merely put Y, income, on the y-axis, treating dollars as a good with $P_U \equiv 1$.

Let us start our analysis with the first assumption, so that Y_3 is one good among many others. The budget line is tangent to the critical indifference curve at $\mathbf{X}^\circ$. Now, let us shock the system with an own-price displacement, which is meant to be small but which we will magnify for purposes of presentation. A fall in P_2 will be depicted in Figure 3–6 by an increase in the amount of Y_2 that the fixed money income of the consumer could buy if he were to purchase it exclusively; on the other hand he would not be able to purchase any more of Y_3. Thus, the income line pivots outward around the y-axis intercept, M, to intersect the x-axis at Q instead of N. This new budget line will be tangent to a higher indifference curve at $\mathbf{X}^*$, the new equilibrium.

The new income line MQ, with constant slope $-(P_2 + dP_2)/P_3$, with $dP_2 < 0$, is less steep in the absolute sense, and, therefore, must be tangent at a point on the new critical indifference curve, which also has a smaller slope than the old equilibrium point. If the new equilibrium basket lies to the

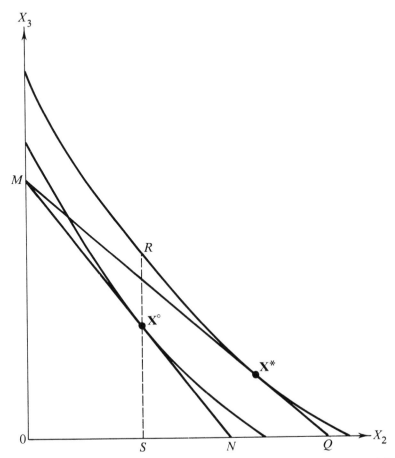

FIGURE 3–6. An Equilibrium Displacement of the Consumer Submodel.

right of the old it will include more Y_2 at the lower price than the old equilibrium included at the higher P_2. Let us extend the vertical line *RS* through the old equilibrium to intersect the new critical indifference curve at *R*. Is there any restriction contained in our postulates and therefore in the interrelationships that requires that $\mathbf{X}^*$ be to the left or right of *R*, or be directly over it?

The answer is no. Our restrictions require that the slope of all indifference curves be well defined at all points, be negative, and become less steep as we move from left to right along the *x*-axis. But the last restriction is wholly upon each indifference curve taken by itself, and does not restrict the behavior of slopes of different indifference curves. Thus, at *R* the slope of the critical indifference curve with the new equilibrium must be negative and well defined, but it may be greater than, equal to, or less than the slope of the old critical indifference curve at $\mathbf{X}°$.

This may be illustrated in the following manner. We have seen from [3–7] that the slope of the indifference curve at $\mathbf{X}°$, which we have denoted $S°_{3/2}$, equals the negative of the ratio of the slope of the hill in the Y_2 direction, $S°_{m/2}$, to the slope of the hill's height in the direction of Y_3, $S°_{m/3}$. The same relationship will hold, of course, at the point R. Therefore, by studying what happens to $S_{m/2}$ and $S_{m/3}$ as we move up the vertical line from $S°_{3/2}$ to R we may discern whether the indifference curves are becoming flatter or steeper.

Suppose as Y_3 rises by small amounts along the vertical line that $S_{m/3}$ gets steeper, indicating that an extra unit of Y_3 tends to make the next unit even more attractive. We may define our meaning here by saying that if Consumer c had a fixed amount of Y_2 and 3 units of Y_3, then if he were given one more unit of Y_3 he would give up (say) .5 unit of Y_4 to keep satisfactions constant. If, now, he were given a fifth unit of Y_3, he would be forced to give up (say) .7 unit of Y_4 to keep satisfactions constant, where we ignore the change in holdings of Y_4 upon the marginal valuations of itself. Suppose, also, that as Y_3 increases along the vertical line the height slope of the function in the Y_2 direction decreases, so that marginal units of Y_2 are less attractive. This is a sufficient condition for the indifference curves to become flatter as we rise from $\mathbf{X}°$ toward R.

On the other hand, suppose that in the same experiment, the height slope of the function in the Y_3 direction became flatter, so that as more of it was consumed marginal units had less attraction. Also, suppose that the acquisition of successive small units of Y_3 enhanced increasingly the successive marginal attractiveness of Y_2 along the line. This is a sufficient condition for the slopes of the indifference curves to become successively steeper as we rise along the vertical line.

Now, in the first case, a fall in the price of Y_3 means that the income line becomes flatter, and it is therefore possible for $\mathbf{X}^*$ to lie to the left of R as in Figure 3–7a. This implies that in the new equilibrium a *smaller* quantity of Y_2 is taken at a *lower* price—and if this happens we call Y_2 a Giffen good. In the second case, the new tangency of income line and indifference curve must occur to the right of R, and therefore more of Y_2 must be taken in the new basket. Under these conditions Y_2 is a *normal* good, because we should expect for most goods that a drop in price will lead to increased consumption, at least under conditions such as those in our model where the goods are infinitely divisible.

But—and this is our point—both of these sufficient conditions are possible, as well as many intermediate types of behavior of $S_{m/2}$ and $S_{m/3}$ along the

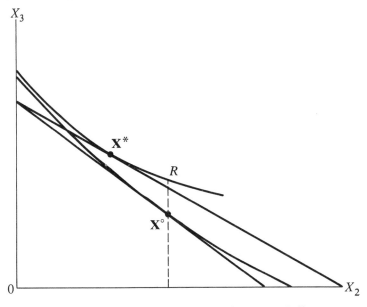

a. A Decline in Consumption With a Price Fall

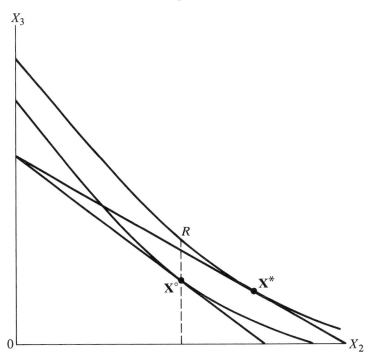

b. A Rise in Consumption With a Price Fall

FIGURE 3–7.   Consumer Equilibrium Displacements.

vertical line, which we have not discussed.[2] Our postulates are not sufficiently restrictive to prohibit an own-price displacement that moves the quantity of the good consumed in the same direction as the price change. Does this not contradict common sense and our own traditional treatment of the simple demand curve as sloping downward? To answer this let us attempt to go more deeply into the nature of the movement from $\mathbf{X}^\circ$ to $\mathbf{X}^*$.

The Income Effect of a Price Change. Let us come at the problem from a slightly different angle. In the analysis above we have studied the manner in which a succession of indifference curve slopes change as we travel a given path on the function. In essence, we have asked what the slope of a budget line would have to be to equal the slope at one of these positions on the line segment $\mathbf{X}^\circ R$, so that our budget line has to adjust to the slope of the indifference curve. Now, however, on Figure 3–8, let us freeze the slope of the budget line instead, and move it out in parallel fashion to touch the indifference curves along the locus of points *MN*. Then if indifference curves tend to become flatter as we mount a vertical line, the constant-prices variable-income budget line will be tangent to successively higher indifference curves at points that move toward the X_3-axis. That is, as Consumer *c*'s income rises *at constant prices* he takes less of good Y_2 in his equilibrium baskets.

The justification for this type of behavior is not difficult to explain. Such an *inferior* good tends, as we have seen, to have good substitutes that become even better substitutes when more of them are consumed. In terms of our first case, Y_2 has an excellent substitute in the sense that as more Y_3 is consumed the same amount of Y_2 is less attractive, while Y_3 becomes more attractive or does not diminish rapidly in desirability. Thus, for example, if a poor person were given 50 pounds of potatoes and no other food, but then were given successive increments of bread, as the latter were increased, its

---

[2] For those students familiar with the differential calculus, we present the following analysis. The slope of the function M_c at any point in the $X_2 X_3$ direction—that is, the degree of rise in X_3 for a unit rise in X_2—which we have symbolized $S_{3/2}$, is defined in [3–7] as

$$\frac{dX_3}{dX_2} = -\frac{\partial M_c}{\partial X_2} \bigg/ \frac{\partial M_c}{\partial X_3} = -S_{m/2}/S_{m/3}.$$

If we differentiate this slope with respect to X_3, we will obtain the behavior of the successive slopes as we climb a vertical line toward some point R. We obtain

$$\frac{d^2 X_3}{dX_2 \, dX_3} = -\left(\frac{\partial M_c}{\partial X_3} \frac{\partial^2 M_c}{\partial X_2 \, \partial X_3} - \frac{\partial M_c}{\partial X_2} \frac{\partial^2 M_c}{\partial X_3^2}\right) \bigg/ \left(\frac{\partial M_c}{\partial X_3}\right)^2.$$

We may simplify this equation in the following manner:

$$\frac{d^2 X_3}{dX_2 \, dX_3} = \left[\left(-\frac{dX_3}{dX_2}\right)\left(\frac{\partial^2 M_c}{\partial X_3^2}\right) - \left(\frac{\partial^2 M_c}{\partial X_2 \, \partial X_3}\right)\right] \bigg/ \frac{\partial M_c}{\partial X_3}.$$

When $d^2 X_3/dX_2 \, dX_3 < 0$, the curves become steeper along the vertical line, and when it is greater than 0 they become flatter. Obviously, we have not exhausted the possibilities in our two extreme cases.

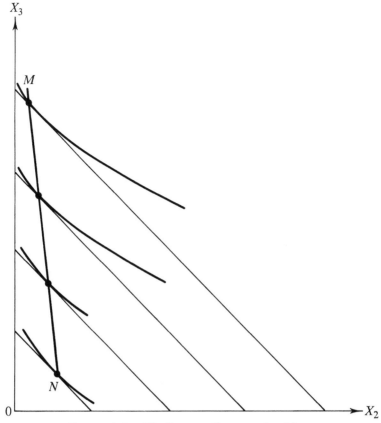

FIGURE 3–8. The Income-Consumption Line.

marginal satisfaction might for a time increase or at least not decline too rapidly, while it made potatoes less and less attractive. The consumer, who might not reduce his potato consumption if he were on a mere subsistence diet to begin with, would, given the limitations of the human stomach, begin to approach a limiting number of calories, and fill more and more of them with bread rather than potatoes.

To put the same phenomenon in terms of constant prices and varying income, we may say that if we held the prices of potatoes and bread constant but increased the poor person's income to allow him to buy more food, the same phenomenon would occur and for the same reasons. As he became richer, he would consume less of some goods like potatoes that are cheap but unattractive ways of getting calories. Therefore, we should *not* want to constrain our postulates in such fashion as to eliminate this case. Indeed, the proposition that the consumption of a good may decline with greater income yields a real insight into realistic consumer behavior.

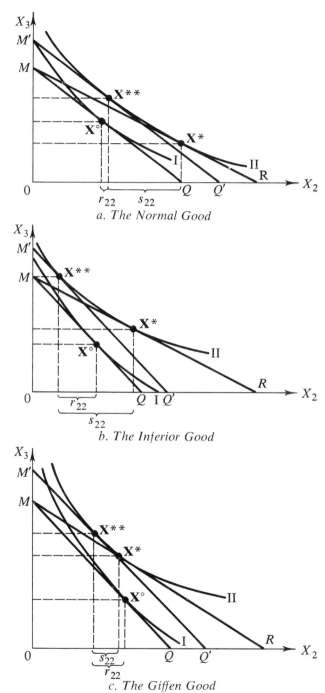

FIGURE 3-9.   Substitution and Income Effects of Price Changes.

But consider now this fact. Let us begin on Figure 3–9*a* with an equilibrium at $X°$ and shock the system by a fall in P_2, so that our new equilibrium occurs at X^*. At the latter equilibrium the consumer has attained indifference curve II, which represents, of course, a higher level of satisfaction than indifference curve I. Suppose, now, we had gotten Consumer *c* to indifference curve II not by a price change but by holding prices constant and increasing his income sufficiently. The increase in income just necessary is represented by MM' or Y_3 or QQ' of Y_2, and the equilibrium basket that would have been taken is X^{**}. From our analysis we know that this basket may lie to the left, right, or directly over the old equilibrium $X°$. However, the point X^*, the new equilibrium with the price change, will always lie to the right of X^{**}, simply because the new budget line MR is flatter than $M'Q'$ by construction. Inasmuch as our postulates of strict quasi-concavity for the function as well as its smoothness require that the slope of the indifference curves become smaller in the absolute sense as we move to the right, X^* must be tangent to a flatter income line further to the right.

Finally, however, note that we have not yet asserted any proposition about the location of X^* relative to $X°$. We know that X^* must lie to the right of X^{**} because both of these points are on the *same* indifference curve. However, we recall to the student's mind the point made earlier that nothing is implied concerning the slopes of indifference curves that are different at two points, except, of course, that they are negative.

We may view the move from the old equilibrium at $X°$ to the new equilibrium at X^* as a composite of two moves: a move from $X°$ to X^{**}, which is what the consumer would have done if he had been boosted to the new critical indifference curve by *income* change alone, and a move along the new critical indifference curve from X^{**} to X^*, which in some sense can be looked upon as a net result of the *price* change. Let us call the first component of the move the *income effect of the price change*, denoted r_{jj} to indicate that it is the income effect upon the consumption of Y_j (first subscript) associated with a change in the given P_j (second subscript). The income effect under analysis now is, therefore, the income effect of an *own-price* change, that is, a change in the given good's own price. The second component of the movement we shall term the *substitution effect of the price change*, symbolized s_{jj}, with the order of subscripts determined in the same manner as that of the income effect. Then the total change in the consumption of Y_2, or $\Delta X_2 = X_2^* - X_2°$, may be viewed as the sum of these two effects:

$$\frac{\Delta X_{2/2}}{\Delta P_2} = \frac{s_{22}}{\Delta P_2} + \frac{r_{22}}{\Delta P_2}, \qquad [3\text{–}9]$$

where the subscript behind the slash indicates that the change has occurred because of a change in P_2.

We know that s_{22} must always be negative, in the sense of moving in the direction opposite to the price movement, because of the diminishing marginal rate of substitution along any indifference curve. But we also know that r_{22} may be positive, negative, or zero, depending upon whether the consumer takes more, less, or the same quantity of the good when his income changes. Three cases are of importance to us:

1. The income effect is negative, in the sense that when price falls the real income of the consumer is increased and he increases his consumption of the good. If this occurs the income effect is negative because it moves consumption in the direction opposite to the price change, and it reinforces the substitution effect. The consumption of the good in question rises when price falls, falls when price rises. This case is illustrated in Figure 3–9a.

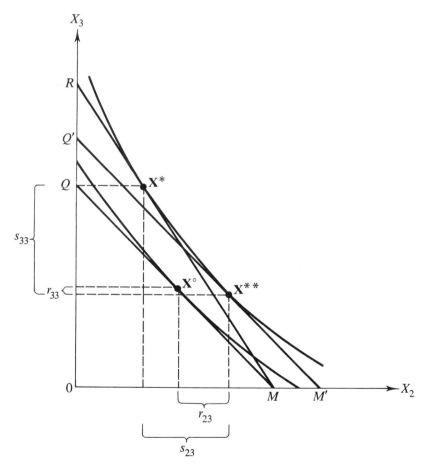

FIGURE 3–10.   The Other-Price Displacement.

2. The income effect is positive, offsetting the substitution effect to some extent, but the absolute value of the substitution effect is strong enough to override the income effect. Therefore, the consumption of the good once more increases with a fall in price, decreases with a rise in price, and the good is an *inferior* good. The case is illustrated in Figure 3–9*b*.

3. The income effect is positive, and so strongly positive that the substitution effect is swamped. In this case we get the perverse movement to lower levels of consumption of the good when its price falls and movement to higher consumption levels when its price rises, behavior that defines the *Giffen* good. This is illustrated in Figure 3–9*c*.

We may therefore state a proposition concerning consumer behavior:

PROPOSITION 1. For a small own-price change, consumption of the good in question will move in the direction opposite to that of price unless the income effect of the price change is (a) positive and (b) sufficiently large in the absolute sense to outweigh the substitution effect.

THE OTHER-PRICE DISPLACEMENT. What can we say about the change in the consumption of a good if a price other than its own changes? Suppose, for example, P_3 should fall in the present case, money income and P_2 remaining constant. On Figure 3–10, a fall in the price of Y_3, P_2, and Y remaining constant, is represented as a move of the budget line from MQ to MR. Once more, as in Figure 3–9, we may break up the total move from $\mathbf{X}°$ to $\mathbf{X}^*$ into an income effect, r_{23}, and a substitution effect, s_{23}, so that the total move may be represented by

$$\frac{\Delta X_{2/3}}{\Delta P_3} = \frac{s_{23}}{\Delta P_3} + \frac{r_{23}}{\Delta P_3}. \qquad [3\text{–}10]$$

The direction of the income effect will be the same as the sign of r_{22}, for no matter what the cause of the effective rise or fall in income, for equal effective changes in income the consumption of a given good will react the same way on this account. The *amount* of the effective change in income with a price change depends upon the amount consumed in the initial equilibrium of the good whose price has changed. The greater the amount of this good taken there, the greater the impact a fall in its price will have upon the consumer's purchases and the greater a rise in its price will restrict him. If a consumer purchases large amounts of Y_3 in $\mathbf{X}°$, then a fall in its price will move him to a higher indifference curve than if he consumed smaller amounts, and it will take a larger income to move him up to the new critical indifference curve.[3]

---

[3] Let $\partial X_2°/\partial Y$ be the marginal propensity to consume good Y_2 from income in the neighborhood of the equilibrium basket. The own-price income effect may then be written in exact form as $r_{22} = -(X_2° \, dP_2)(\partial X_2°/\partial Y)$. The expression in the first bracket depicts

But the sign of the substitution effect will be ambiguous. When we dealt with the own-price change we knew that the new income line with a lower price for P_2 must be tangent to the new critical indifference curve at a point farther to the right than the constant-price budget line drawn to determine the income effect. Because the difference between the tangency points of these two curves is the substitution effect, it was always negative.

Now, however, the situation is different, as Figure 3–10 makes clear. The new budget line with changed price must be tangent to the new critical indifference curve *to the left* of the tangency with the parallel budget line, **X****. However, because the latter can be to left, right, or over **X°**, the income effect can be negative, positive, or zero. We see that **X*** must always be to the left of **X**** on Figure 3–10, which implies that s_{23} is always positive. This however is not true in general, and holds only this rigidly for the case of two goods. With only two goods on the chart it appears as if all income must be spent upon Y_2 and Y_3, because the system is closed. When income changes of price movements are netted out $s_{33} < 0$, by our previous line of reasoning about own-price changes, and therefore $s_{23} > 0$ since it is measured from the same indifference curve. If the consumer is to get more of Y_3 and stay in the same indifference curve, he must get less of Y_2.

However, in systems with more than two goods, other-price substitution effects need not always be positive. If s_{23} is negative, so that a rise in P_3 leads to a fall in X_2, and a fall in P_3 leads to a rise in X_2, we say that Y_2 is a *net complement* of Y_3—net in the sense of netting out income effects. If s_{23} is positive, so that a rise in P_3 leads to a rise in X_2 and a fall in P_3 leads to a fall in X_2, we say that Y_2 is a *net substitute* for Y_3. In the first case—and neglecting income effects—a rise in P_3 leads to a fall in X_3, and if X_2 falls also it means that X_2 and X_3 tend to be consumed together. When the second case occurs, it means that a rise in P_3 reduces X_3, but X_2 expands because Y_2

---

the change in real income that results from a price change, for if P_2 falls by 5 cents and the consumer at the initial equilibrium consumed 100 units of the good, $-(100 \times (-.05)) = +\$5.00$ is a measure of the effective increase in real income obtained. If this increase in real income is multiplied by the marginal propensity to consume Y_2 from income, we obtain the rise or fall in consumption that can be ascribed to the income effect of the price change. Since the sign of the first expression in parentheses is under our control, the sign of r_{22} is determined wholly by the sign of the marginal propensity to consume Y_2 from income.

But also $r_{23} = -(X_3^\circ \, dP_3)(\partial X_2^\circ/\partial Y)$, and an exactly similar analysis of its make-up may be made. Its sign, too, will be dependent wholly on the sign of the marginal propensity to consume Y_2 from income. The expression in the first pair of parentheses merely determines the amount of the effective income change—dependent upon the amount of price change and the quantity taken of the good whose price has changed. Therefore, the sign of the income effect of a given good Y_2 will be the same—that of the marginal propensity to consume Y_2 from income—regardless of which price is changed, although, for a given cut in price, the quantitative level of the income effect will depend upon the amount of the good taken in the initial equilibrium.

is a substitute for Y_3. A *gross complement* and a *gross substitute* are goods that react in these respective ways when the income effect is added in.

We are led to the following proposition, because goods may be net substitutes or complements:

PROPOSITION 2. For an other-price change that is small, the substitution effect may be positive, negative, or zero, while the income effect may also move in these manners. Therefore, the quantity of the good taken in the new equilibrium may be more, less, or the same as in the old equilibrium basket.

THE INCOME DISPLACEMENT. We have already dealt at length with the nature of the possibilities for the movement of quantity demanded when income alone changes. We may merely record our conclusions for the sake of convenience:

PROPOSITION 3. For a given small income change, all prices remaining fixed, the amount demanded of a good may rise, fall, or remain constant.

A SUMMARIZATION OF CONCLUSIONS ABOUT THE SLOPES OF THE PROJECTIONS OF THE PROFILES OF THE DEMAND FUNCTION

Let us now return to Figures 3–4 and 3–5 and their arbitrarily drawn slopes for the profiles of the function to comment upon their up-to-now arbitrary construction.

THE PARTIAL DEMAND CURVE. The profile labelled

$$X_2 = D_2(P_2; \bar{P}_3, \bar{Y}, \bar{W})$$

is that slice of the demand function of System [I] which has received the greatest amount of attention in economic theory. It is, indeed, *the demand curve* for economists, which is to say that the behavior of the amount demanded of any good Y_2 when its own price changes, the prices of all other goods, income, and the stock of wealth remaining constant, has been the most interesting relationship for economists. It abstracts from what happens to $X_1, X_3, \ldots, X_n, X_{z_1}, \ldots, X_{z_m}, X_u, X_e, X_U$, as P_2 changes, although, of course, appropriate changes in these quantities are allowed to occur in the background.

The curve is called a *partial demand curve* or a demand curve that emerges from partial analysis because it takes into account only the changes in own-price, setting all the other arguments of the D_2 function in System [I–1] equal to fixed values. It is also partial in the sense that the analysis does not try to determine simultaneously for a change in P_2 what happens to the *whole* basket of goods, treating System [I] as a whole system rather than singling out only one equation in it. In both senses we lose the global or *general* outlook, and concentrate upon a narrow relationship.

There are, of course, very good reasons for doing so, which we shall develop now; but the student should be able to place this familiar body of analysis into the proper context of economic theory, to see what aspects of the consumer submodel are being abstracted from. That done, we shall leave the larger model for a time to spend some time with this bit of important partial analysis.

Of course, we should expect that, for given income and wealth, and given prices of other goods, the price of the good involved would exert a powerful impact on its consumption. The student should see that in determining the reaction of X_2 to changes in P_2 the reactions of X_3, X_4 *are* being taken into account, as our analysis of the price and income displacements above will make clear. It is the *prices* of these goods, not their quantities, which are held constant.

The Negative Slope. The negative slope of the demand curve which we have incorporated into the profile on Figure 3–4 does not now appear to be so arbitrary, for from Proposition 1, although it may slope positively in portions, we should expect such a configuration to be the departure from the normal. The positively sloped demand curve can occur only if the consumer would reduce his consumption of the good with a rise in income, and if the size of such reduction were great enough to outweigh the negative substitution effect. But once individuals in reasonably affluent economies are above the most primitive necessities, the chances are that such goods will have already left their equilibrium baskets: that is, they will be taken in zero quantities. Or, if consumed, they will not be the cheap staples they usually are when they are Giffen goods. For example, the American family consumes potatoes as a regular element in its diet, but the family is not so heavily dependent upon them for calories that a reduction in their price would cause fewer of them to be consumed.

A more frequent example of the occurrence of a backward-bending demand curve is that for leisure (we have included it in System [I] among the $X_{cz_i}^\circ$), which is also the obverse of the supply of labor. It was noted among poor colonial peoples whose value systems were not so permeated with the desire for material goods or whose field of choice was limited in its goods variety, that a rise in the price of labor led to a decrease in the amount supplied, which is to say that a rise in the price of leisure (the cost of not working) led to an increase in the amount demanded of it. Thus, a rise in its price within that segment of the demand curve for leisure revealing this perverseness would lead to an increase in demand for it. This is illustrated in the segment of the demand curve between P_1 and P_2 of Figure 3–11. This good reveals the income effect in its potent form. If his income were high enough to yield the laborer all of the material goods which his circumstances and culture led him to covet with any degree of intensity, a further rise in income might well lead him to choose more leisure to more goods. Nor would we look upon such behavior as intuitively irrational.

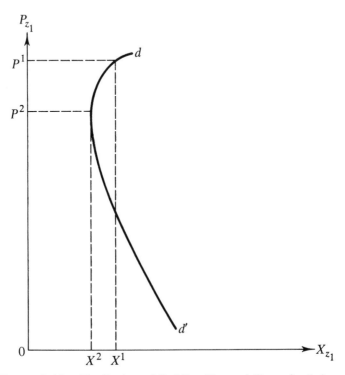

FIGURE 3–11. The Backward-Bending Demand Curve for Leisure.

Indeed, the same type of phenomenon may characterize the suburban American breadwinner. At a given level of income he and his family become accustomed to a certain basket that includes amounts of goods requiring fixed payments over time, such as life insurance, education costs, medical benefits, time payments for purchases, and so forth.[4] If the income tax rate

---

[4] In the analysis of footnote 2 let Y_3 be leisure and Y_2 the bundle of rigidly fixed goods of this type. Their rigidity implies that their marginal satisfaction is not much influenced by changes in X_3, so that we may suppose $\partial^2 M_c/\partial X_2\, \partial X_3 = 0$. We then obtain

$$\frac{d^2 X_3}{dX_2\, dX_3} = \left[\left(-\frac{dX_3}{dX_2}\right)\left(\frac{\partial^2 M_c}{\partial X_3^2}\right)\right]\Big/ \frac{\partial M_c}{\partial X_3}.$$

Since $dX_3/dX_2 < 0$, this expression will be negative if the marginal satisfaction of leisure is positive but diminishing as its amount increases, and the condition for flattening curves along the vertical line will not be met.

rises on such an individual, essentially reducing the price of his labor and of leisure, he may work harder to hold his income up rather than take more leisure. For him, too, leisure becomes an inferior good, and, indeed, with Giffen-good intensity.

There are exceptions to the rule, therefore, and our interrelationships help us to understand how they can occur. For example, in Figure 3–12, let us graph Y or income along the y-axis and X_{z_1}, the demand for leisure, along the x-axis. Let us assume the consumer's income is derived wholly from work. Because there are only 24 hours in a day, our units of leisure can go only from 0 to 24. The price of a dollar of income is obviously \$1 and the price of an hour of labor is P_{z_1}, the wage rate. Income will then represent the wage rate times the number of hours the consumer works, but let us also think of it as representing all other goods, a basket of such goods being priced at one dollar. Then, given his possession of 24 hours at a given wage rate, he might have the goods represented by the line OM with no leisure, or 24 hours of leisure with no goods at OQ, and his equilibrium choice will be at $\mathbf{X}^\circ$.

Now, suppose that the wage rate falls, so that in the new situation he could buy fewer goods if he worked 24 hours a day, but, of course, could still command only 24 hours of leisure. If the indifference contours tend to be sharply curved, approaching an L-shape in the limiting form, other goods and leisure tend to be complements. That is, the consumer tends to enjoy an extra hour of leisure in manners that require the use of goods: golf clubs, or tourist expenses, or theater tickets, for example. On Figure 3–12a we have graphed the preference map for such a consumer, and it will be seen that faced with a fall in his income by virtue of increased taxes, the consumer will take *less* leisure, not more, when its price falls. Assume that a tax on wages lowers the effective price of labor to that which is depicted in the slope of $M'Q$. That is, the slopes of the indifference curves along the vertical line $\mathbf{X}^\circ R$ get steeper as we rise and flatter as we fall, by assumption. Because the new income line is flatter than the old along the horizontal line through $\mathbf{X}^\circ$, it will tend to be tangent to the new critical indifference curve to the right of that line, meaning that fewer income goods will be taken: the consumer will not be wholly successful in preventing his income from falling. But, on the other hand, the new tangency will tend to be to the left of the vertical line $\mathbf{X}^\circ R$, which means that leisure will be reduced. Thus, income will be sustained somewhat and will fall less than it would if a positive income effect were not operating.

The income effect of this operation may be obtained by drawing $M'Q'$ parallel to the original income line and obtaining its tangency with the new critical indifference curve at $\mathbf{X}^{**}$. This depicts the necessary reduction in his income by a lump sum tax that would be necessary to reduce him to the new

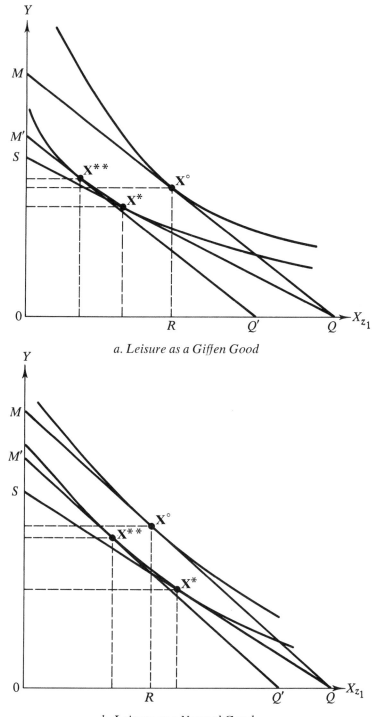

a. Leisure as a Giffen Good

b. Leisure as a Normal Good

FIGURE 3–12.   Leisure as a Giffen Good and as a Normal Good.

level of satisfaction without changing the price of leisure relative to the price of all other goods. Note that on Figure 3–12a if the income effect alone had operated, leisure would have been reduced even more than it was in order to sustain income, but that the substitution effect compensated to some extent.

On the other hand, suppose the consumer were one who found leisure and income to be substitutes. That is, he tended to spend leisure hours in activities that required few expenditures—watching television, visiting museums, or reading, for example. This implies that his indifference curves in Figure 3–12b are rather flat, and in this case we would find the consumer tending to consume more leisure with a fall in its price, as we have depicted on the figure. The substitution effect will be strongly negative, and although the income effect may be positive or negative, it will tend to be outweighed by the substitution effect, and leisure and all goods will tend to be gross substitutes.

In general, however, for a good that is more typical of the consumer's purchases and that does not consume large amounts of his income, so that a price change in it does not set up large income effects, we should expect the slope of the demand curve to be negative in the own-price direction.

The Elasticity of the Demand Curve for a Price Change. The degree of downward reaction of the amount demanded to a price rise or upward reaction to a price fall is measured by the economist at any given point on the demand curve with a concept called the *price elasticity of the demand curve.* Note at this stage that the concept of demand elasticity is related to a point on the demand curve, not to the entire curve itself or even segments of it. We define $e_P = (dX/dP) - P/X$, and specify further:

DEFINITION 1a. A demand curve is said to be of price elasticity greater than 1 at a point if, with a slight reduction of price at that point, the consumer's total expenditure on the good rises.

DEFINITION 1b. A demand curve is said to be of unitary price elasticity at a point if, with a slight reduction of price at that point, the consumer's total expenditure on the good remains constant.

DEFINITION 1c. A demand curve is said to be of price elasticity less than 1 at a point if, with a slight reduction of price at that point, the consumer's expenditure on the good falls.

We may illustrate these three modes of behavior by using the indifference curve analysis with income Y on the y-axis. On Figure 3–13a at a given initial equilibrium we have held income constant and reduced P_2 slightly. The consumer's selection of Y in the new basket $\mathbf{X}^*$ falls from OY° to OY^*. Therefore, because this good is income, the expenditure on good Y_2 must have risen from MY° to MY^*.

Now, of course, the value X_2° and the value X_2^* are quantities that lie on the demand curve for Y_2. Indeed, we may derive the whole demand curve

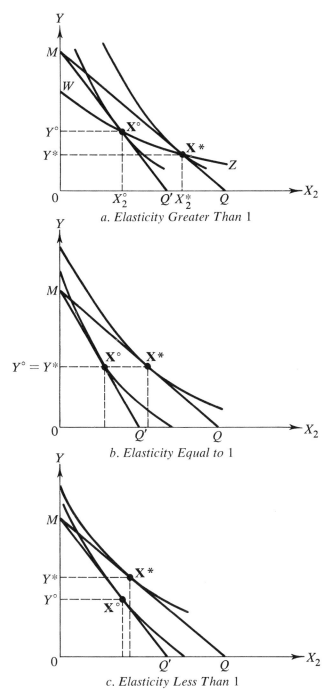

FIGURE 3–13. The Elasticity of Demand for Good Y_2.

from Figure 3–13a by a simple procedure. We simply fix Consumer c's income at M (while other prices are held constant in the background) and allow P_2 to take all allowable values the data-constraining postulates permit. The locus of tangencies of these income lines with the relevant critical indifference curves may be represented by the line WZ, and if we read the X_2 component from each such basket and graph it against the relevant price of Y_2 underlying the budget line, we will have the demand curve. By noting what happens to Y between two closely neighboring points such as Y° and Y^* on WZ, we can tell immediately whether the demand curve in this neighborhood is elastic (Figure 3–13a), of unitary elasticity (Figure 3–13b) such that $Y^\circ = Y^*$, or is price elastic to an extent less than unity (Figure 3–13c) such that $Y^\circ < Y^*$. Note that these elasticity concepts are all relevant to downward sloping demand curves; positively sloped portions of demand curve, are, of course, of elasticity less than unity with a vengeance.

We need not draw the indifference curves that lie behind the demand curve solutions in order to determine the elasticity of a demand curve at a point. For the amount of expenditure that a consumer makes on a good at the point X_2° is the product of price and that quantity:

$$E^\circ = P_2^\circ \cdot X_2^\circ, \qquad [3\text{–}11]$$

and the expenditure at the new basket is

$$E^* = P_2^* \cdot X_2^*. \qquad [3\text{–}12]$$

The change in expenditure, whose sign indexes what type of price elasticity the curve possesses at this point, is, when the change is very small,

$$\begin{aligned} dE = E^* - E^\circ &= P_2^* \cdot X_2^* - P_2^\circ \cdot X_2^\circ \\ &= (P_2^\circ + dP)(X_2^\circ + dX) - P_2^\circ \cdot X_2^\circ \\ &= X_2^\circ \, dP + P_2^\circ \, dX + dP \, dX. \end{aligned} \qquad [3\text{–}13]$$

If dP and dX are very small in magnitude, we can neglect their product as being very small indeed, so we have:

$$dE = X_2^\circ \, dP + P_2^\circ \, dX. \qquad [3\text{–}14]$$

Now, if we divide dE by $X_2^\circ P_2^\circ$ to get the percentage change in expenditure we will obtain

$$\frac{dE}{X_2^\circ P_2^\circ} = \frac{dP}{P_2^\circ} + \frac{dX}{X_2^\circ}. \qquad [3\text{–}15]$$

If the percentage change of expenditure equals zero, obviously the negative percentage change in price (which is opposite in sign to the change in quantity by virtue of the negative slope of the demand curve) equals (in absolute magnitude) the percentage change in quantity. If this percentage change is positive, quantitative changes must be greater relatively than price changes. And if this percentage change is negative relative price changes must be greater than the relative quantitative change.

The student is warned against identifying elasticity with the magnitude of the slope of a demand curve: indeed, it is because the slope of the curve varies with the arbitrary units in which the good is measured that the elasticity concept owes what usefulness it has. Obviously, the slope of a demand curve for apples measured in pounds will be quite different from that for apples measured in bushels: yet the underlying consumer preferences are not different, and by using a ratio of relative changes these slope differences can be neutralized. The result of this, however, is that slope is no longer a very

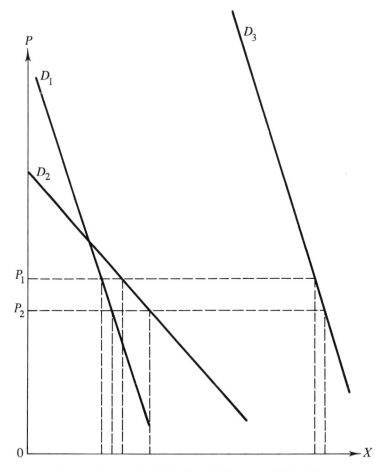

FIGURE 3–14.   The Relation of Slopes and Elasticity.
3–14

good visual index of elasticity except when the curves being compared are in the same general sector of the chart.

In Figure 3–14, for example, we have drawn two linear demand curves, D_1 and D_2, of different slopes in the same general location, and it can be seen that by virtue of the fact that quantities and changes in quantities are roughly comparable for identical prices and price changes, slopes will be relatively good indexes of which such curve is more elastic or inelastic at given prices. However, in the right-hand portion of the figure we have also drawn a linear demand curve, D_3, with slope equal to that of our steeper curve D_1 in the left-hand portion. Obviously, because of the extreme difference in position, the fact that the two curves are equi-sloped does not imply the equality of their elasticities. For equal initial prices and price changes, for example, equal absolute changes in quantities purchased will occur, but the quantity changes will be divided by much larger initial quantities for the curve on the right, and so its elasticity will be much smaller at every price.

Despite the fact that elasticity is a concept that relates to a point on the demand curve, or to a quite small region of it, if a given curve contains a large portion that is composed of points with elasticities greater than unity, the economist will frequently and loosely speak of the *curve* as *elastic*, and if it contains a large number of points that are less than unity in price elasticity, he will speak of the curve as *inelastic*. Be it noted that most smooth, continuous demand curves, linear and otherwise, change elasticities smoothly as the initial price falls toward zero, going from higher to lower elasticities. A flat curve, reasonably close to the price axis, therefore, will tend to have a large continuous portion whose elasticities are above unity, and is frequently spoken of as *elastic* (although the student is again cautioned about the proviso concerning the leftward position of the curve on the basis of our discussion above). Similarly, steep curves in this same general area or even farther to the right will tend to have large portions which have an elasticity less than unity, and are spoken of as *inelastic* curves.

The economic implications of elasticity are perhaps of more importance than these technical matters and *caveats*. A curve that is *inelastic* implies that the consumer (or all consumers if the demand curve is drawn for the whole market) for one reason or another does not respond very much to price changes. The commodity may be one like salt with very slight impact upon his budget, so that even if price rose or fell a great deal consumers would not change their demand for it by much. Or, again like salt, the good might have very few substitutes, so that if the consumer finds it hard to do without a rather fixed quantity of it—whether or not he spends much of his budget on the good—he tends to buy about the same quantity. If the consumer is a confirmed customer of a given firm's product, although many substitutes may in practice exist, he has been convinced of the great desirability of this brand and he may not switch purchases very quickly when prices rise. Generally speaking, for one reason or another, an inelastic demand curve reflects consumer immobility—keeping him attached to the product as price rises.

On the other hand, a curve that is *elastic* reflects a mobility of the consumer in these respects. The good may be one that absorbs large amounts of the consumer's budget and he may be quite able and anxious to spend on other things when price rises or buy more when price falls. The good may be a luxury, in the sense that he buys quickly at low prices but less quickly at high. Or the good—luxury or necessity—may have a great many substitutes, perhaps competing brands, and the consumer may not have a strong psychological commitment to any one of them.

This analysis points to a very important proposition: in general, the more the substitutes for a given product, the greater its elasticity. Frequently the product is not as readily defined as might seem at first glance. Is the product to be treated food, or bread, or pastry; is it Ford automobiles, or lower-priced automobiles, or all automobiles; is it all beverages, soda pop, or Coca-Cola? The greater the number of such similar products included in the definition, the more inelastic the curve becomes in general, because at every step of aggregation we exclude alternatives from the consumer's field of choice and restrict thereby his mobility.

The Elasticity of the Partial Demand Curve for Income Change. As we have seen, the partial demand curve also has a slope in the direction of income, indicating how purchases of the given good respond to the consumer's experience of an increase or decrease in income, all prices held constant. The income elasticity of such a good is derived for the same reasons as the price elasticity—because of the variability of slopes with the units in which income and the good are measured—and is defined in a quite similar way. We may symbolize the expression as e_y, and define it as the ratio of the percentage change in product consumed for a small percentage change in income:

$$e_y = \frac{dX_2/X_2^\circ}{dY/Y}. \qquad [3\text{--}16]$$

It is also useful to use unity as a benchmark, so that a curve that has an income elasticity greater than unity at some point is referred to as *income elastic* at that point; a curve that has unit income elasticity is termed *unit elastic* there; and an income elasticity of less than unity leads to the curve being called *income inelastic* at the point.

The income slope of the general demand curve of System [I] will, of course, determine the sign of this elasticity, the analysis of which we have already summarized in Proposition 3. Further, we may interpret the sizes of income elasticity in terms of the level of income from which the individual begins, the price structure that is frozen in the analysis, and the position of the good in the consumer's preferences. At lower levels of income, necessities probably will have quite large income elasticities: food, for example, in a subsistence economy will exhaust most of any increase in incomes enjoyed by the inhabitants, and any small amount not so spent probably will be applied to such basics as clothing and shelter. At higher levels of income, we may find that the rate of increase of food expenditures as income rises is quite small.

The Cross-Elasticity of Demand. Another measure of price elasticity for the partial demand curve may be defined for changes in prices other than the price of the good itself. We may construct the ratio of the percentage change in the amount demanded of the good at some point and the percentage change in the price of the other good:

$$e_{j/k} = \frac{dX_j/X_j^\circ}{dP_k/P_k^\circ},$$ [3–17]

whose value may be positive, negative, or zero, depending upon whether the goods Y_j and Y_k are gross substitutes, are gross complements, or are independent. Usually the size of the coefficient is of less interest than its sign, and consequently the concepts of unit elasticity or elasticity greater than or less than unity are not of importance.

The Elasticity of the Partial Demand Curve for Wealth Change. Lastly, we may convert the wealth-displacement of amounts demanded of goods to an elasticity concept by dividing the relative change in the amount demanded when wealth rises by the relative change in wealth. A change in $Q_{ce} + Q_{cU}$ or $Q_e + Q_U$ to denote a rise in the permanent income expected by the individual or community by virtue of a real change in wealth holdings can have quite different impacts upon the amounts demanded than income changes. Because income is treated as constant along with all prices, changes arising from price and income elasticities of the good in question will be neutralized. Nonetheless, certain specific goods may be quite sensitive to wealth changes. The individual might reduce his saving and indulge in more consumption if he feels wealthier, or he might be inclined to buy more of his own labor for use as leisure. He might increase his purchases of such luxury goods as resort services or restaurant meals. On the other hand it might stimulate him to accumulate more wealth, encouraging him to save and restrict consumption of luxury goods. The basic point is that changes in the value of the *stock* of assets he is holding can have important impacts upon his *flow* equilibrium.

A SUMMARY OF THE CONSUMER'S BEHAVIOR AS ANALYZED BY THE MANIPULATION OF THE SUBMODEL

We shall conclude by summarizing propositions concerning the behavior of the consumer as we can obtain them from our formal submodel. Our results are admittedly not unambiguous, but on the other hand neither are they meager, and, in many instances where they are ambiguous in the general analysis they can be made specific with the accumulation of some data or the making of informed guesses about strategic magnitudes for the functions concerned with given goods.

First, we have the direct predictions that are contained in the postulates themselves taken singly. The consumer is affected in his choice of a basket of goods only by his preexisting preferences, prices, income, and wealth, and his preferences are functions of the quantities of goods in the baskets only. He is, therefore, unaffected by what other consumers do, by advertising, or by snob appeal as reflected in prices. He is not a creature of habit to any great degree, being able to react rapidly to changes in prices and income so that his new choice of goods basket will reflect his basic preferences quickly. He is capable of adjusting his hours of work to the number that he wishes to work, being unbound by institutional arrangements, and consumes the services of other factors as well as his own labor. The reader will be able to judge for himself the poor correspondence of many of these to reality, but the ultimate purposes of these simplifications also must be judged.

To continue with this list of prima facie predictions, we insist that the consumer does not reveal the "drunkard's syndrome" of Figure 2–5, nor buy only one good and none of any other. Within the bounds of relevant reality, no good exists in his field of choice which he could receive in such quantity during a period that further amounts of it would yield nonpositive satisfaction. Presumably, these propositions are more realistic and will disturb few of our readers as descriptions—indeed, trivial descriptions—of consumer behavior.

Second, at an equilibrium point, if the own-price of a good changes the consumer may buy more, less, or the same amount of the good, depending upon the sign of the substitution and income effects of the price change, and, if they are opposite in sign, upon the relative magnitudes of the effects. In the normal case, both effects will be negative, and the consumer's demand will move in the direction opposite to that of the price change. If it does so, the partial demand curve will be negatively sloped, as it normally is assumed to be. We may further differentiate consumer behavior by the *degree* of responsiveness to price recorded in the price elasticity measure, which may be (in absolute value) greater than, equal to, or less than unity, reflecting basically the mobility of the consumer among goods.

If the income effect moves in the same direction as the price change, and by enough to swamp the substitution effect which *always* moves in the opposite direction from that of the price change, the good is a Giffen good. Our analysis leads us to predict that this phenomenon will occur relatively rarely on the demand side of the market, but may, when it occurs, affect rather important goods from the point of view of the value of them in the budget, because the income effect can become large usually only if much of a good is bought in the initial equilibrium.

If income is changed, we should expect most goods to reveal a movement of the amount demanded in the same direction as income, if any movement at all occurs. Further, the income elasticity can be (normally) positive or (abnormally) negative, and can have absolute values greater than, equal to, or less than unity, with interesting interpretations. And we have seen that we can also handle wealth changes in a like manner with those of income, obtaining an elasticity measure, but that our predictions of the direction of movement of amounts demanded of the good in question would be much less easily determined.

If some price other than the own-price is changed—a shock to the partial demand curve which, like that of income or wealth change, would shift the curve as it is usually drawn—it is impossible to predict a priori the direction of the total change in the amount taken, or indeed the direction of the substitution or income effect of such a price change. Relationships of net and gross substitutability and complementarity, as well as the complicating income effects, will dictate these results, and these will be quite different among the various goods considered. We have seen that we may define an elasticity concept to convert these results from absolute to relative magnitudes—the cross-elasticity of demand.

Lastly, under conditions of the model as we have described it—when money is used only as a transactions medium or as a capital asset with which to obtain future income by lending it for use as such a medium—the demand for it will be untouched by uncertainty of the future and its realistic function as the liquid hedge against imminent changes in the interest rate. Consequently, we have treated the demand for money services as linear in the value of goods demanded, and we shall handle the demand for money as an asset as a facet of the demand for capital goods and future earning power. In the monetary aspects of the economy, our model predicts that if all profits, money prices (except the interest rate), and the stock of money were to double, the consumer would not prefer the original to the changed situation, or vice versa. That is, all of his demand and supply functions would be unaffected in real terms by money illusion.

Selected Readings

1. G. C. ARCHIBALD, "The Qualitative Content of Maximizing Models," *Journal of Political Economy*, LXXIII (1965), pp. 27–36. The "conjugate-pair" limitation on fruitful results from displacements is discussed in depth.

2. GEORGE F. BREAK, "Income Taxes and Incentives to Work: An Empirical Study," *American Economic Review*, XLVII (1957), pp. 529–549. An empirical investigation of the impact of high marginal income tax rates on British professional men's attitudes to leisure. A good supplement to our theoretical analysis of this problem.

3. JOSEF HADAR, "Comparative Statics of Stock-Flow Equilibrium," *Journal of Political Economy*, LXXIII (1965), pp. 159–164. A short presentation of some displacements resulting from changes in wealth, particularly good because it stresses the similarities of the results of income displacements to them.

4. GEOFFREY S. SHEPHERD, *Agricultural Price Analysis* (Ames: Iowa State, Fifth Edition, 1963), Ch. 4, 5, 6. A close study of the derivation of demand and supply curves for agricultural goods from statistical data.

5. ELMER WORKING, "What Do Statistical 'Demand Curves' Show?," reprinted in G. J. Stigler and K. E. Boulding, *Readings in Price Theory* (Homewood, Ill.: Irwin, 1952), pp. 97–115. The earliest presentation of the "identification problem" involved in extracting demand curves from statistical observations.

CHAPTER 4

The Theory of the Firm: Fixed Output and Minimum Cost

WE MUST TURN now to the construction of our second group of submodels—those treating the behavior of the firm. Because we have gone into the data and postulate set of the consumer submodel in such detail, we will be able to save time and space by drawing freely upon that prior analysis and to exploit the symmetry of consumer and firm models. Similarly, we shall be able to refer the reader to the displacement-of-equilibrium analysis in Chapter 3 in order to shorten our explanations of the similar analysis of the firm's solutions. Let us turn directly to the specification of the set of data and postulates, derive the set of interrelationships from them, and obtain solutions to the first group of models. Following these tasks of construction, we shall then displace the models to obtain propositions concerning the firm's behavior.

The Set of Postulates and Data

As an initial vision of the problems that face the second decisionmaking unit in our model of the economy, it will be useful to highlight the similarities with and differences that distinguish them from the problems of the consumer. Both units may be viewed as *mechanisms* for the absorption of inputs and the production of outputs. In the case of the consumer the inputs are quantities of consumer goods, factor services, money services, and future income, and the outputs are of two types. First, there are outputs that are destined for use by other decisionmaking units in the economy, or *external* outputs; these are the supplies of factor services, money balances, bonds, or money stocks which the consumer sells. Second, there are outputs that remain *internal* to the system, which consist of the subjective satisfactions obtained by consumption of the inputs. The production and sale of the external outputs limit the production of the internal outputs and place the fundamental budget constraint upon the number of the latter outputs that can be produced.

The firm, too, may be viewed as a mechanism absorbing inputs and converting them into outputs. Further, it produces both internal and external outputs: the former are the intermediate types of product which the firm produces within its plant from the inputs it absorbs in order to make its final products for sale on the market, these latter constituting its external outputs. Whereas the internal outputs of the consumer are the ultimate products of that submodel, the external outputs of the firm constitute the be-all and the end-all of its existence. Moreover, we shall be happy to note that whereas the internal outputs of the consumer are subjective in nature, and give rise to all the problems of measurement discussed in Chapter 2, the internal and external outputs of the firm are objective and subject usually to measurement by easily derived cardinal indexes.

We shall find it convenient to ascribe maximization-minimization procedures to the firm, just as we have done to the process of consumer decision-making. There exists one most vital difference, as we shall see: the constraint placed upon the consumer in his maximization springing from the limited value of his external outputs does not exist for the firm. Because the firm buys its inputs and sells both its internal and external outputs, there is no income-wealth constraint upon its activities. It can therefore seek to obtain its maximum position without having to worry about remaining within some expenditure constraint.

With this initial unifying outlook upon the problems of both types of decisionmaking units, let us turn to the specification of the data and postulates of this submodel.

THE INSTITUTIONAL ENVIRONMENT

The firm in our submodel will enter markets on the Monday market day and make contracts to lease factors Z_i (that is, to hire factor services z_i), to hire cash balances u, to buy such goods Y_j as it needs in its own production (we shall designate such goods *intermediate* goods), and to sell its products Y_j and Z_i, or consumer-intermediate goods and capital goods. As in the case of the consumer, the firm makes contracts for these transactions at the prices fixed on the market day, and accepts and effects deliveries during the forthcoming week. Be it noted that the firm owns no resources of its own, hiring or buying all services and goods which it needs during the week and returning leased goods before the following Monday.

We shall simplify the analysis by assuming that each firm produces only one good, either a Y_j or a Z_i. This is not a necessary restriction but its adoption does allow us to present the firm's problems in their most straight-forward form.

The Assumptions of Economic Power. In the case of the consumer we adopted the assumption at the start of the analysis that no consumer had any power to affect price in any market in which he entered as buyer or seller, and we never abandoned that simple postulate. Moreover, we could defend the assumption as a realistic one in most instances. In the case of the firm, however, such an assumption is much less realistic, and, although we shall adopt it as an initial postulate for the submodel to be built in this and the following chapter, it must also be abandoned in the analysis of that chapter and of Chapter 6. Therefore, although important, the presence or absence of this assumption that the firm has no power to alter price in any market in which it enters as buyer or seller does not form the basis of the distinction between the models of Chapters 4 and 5 on the one hand, and Chapter 6 on the other.

As noted, the analysis of Chapter 5 will include cases where this zero-power assumption is violated. In our model construction we shall change the distinction on which models of the firm are categorized from the usual one of possessing no power to alter price to one of isolation from the feedback effects on the firm's own decisionmaking. We shall define *nonrivalrous competition* as an environment for the firm in which any decision that it takes concerning purchase or production of inputs and the sale of outputs is not felt sufficiently by any competitor to induce him to respond in manners that are felt by the initiating firm. That is, the firm is isolated in some manner from the consequences of its own decisions as they affect other decision-makers in the economy: there are no feedbacks of its own decisions upon itself via the reactions of other relevant production units in the economy. On the other hand, we shall define *rivalrous competition* as an environment for decisionmaking in which the firm, in making its decisions, must rationally take into account the fact that its decisions will affect the decisionmaking of other firms of the economy in ways that will force those firms to react in manners that will affect the original firm's decisions. The firm is not isolated from the consequences of its own decisionmaking in the way that it is in the first type of environment we specified.

Let us specify this distinction more finely. If a firm has the power to control the price of its product, and if it should raise that price, it must count upon the buyers' cutting back their purchases of it. This is, to be sure, a reaction to the firm's original action, and one that must be taken into account in determining the wisdom of the action. But if it results from the uncoordinated and foreseeable reactions to price change of many small units in the market for the product, it may be accepted as a predictable part of the environment by the firm, more or less to be accepted as it accepts the techno-logical implications of output decisions. In both cases, the firm is more or less involved in a game in which, ideally, it has complete information about the moves of its fellow players in reaction to its moves. The feedback of its own decision is taken into account fully and certainly in this ideal presentation at the time the original decision is made.

In the limit of this type of environment the firm's decision is not felt by any actor on the supply side of the market, which is alone relevant for a dis-cussion of competition, for when we deal with competition we always deal with actors on the same side of the market. That is to say, when the firm changes price for one reason or the other, no other firm feels the impact of the change upon its own profits and therefore does not react specifically and identifiably to the change. This, of course, implies that the original firm need not take into account in its decisionmaking the impacts of feedbacks from other firms—it is isolated from them on the supply side. We shall term this competition *nonrivalrous* because no other firm views itself as in direct, responding competition with this firm, and the original firm does not consider itself to be in such rivalry with other firms.

That is, we shall use the term *rivalry* to denote a type of competition in which firms are mutually aware of the impact of each other's decisions upon their welfares, react to each other's decisions, and are expected to so react by any rival in making his own decisions. This second type of competition—rivalrous competition—occurs when the environment is such that a firm cannot make a unilateral decision without affecting the welfare of other firms in a perceptible, identifiable manner, and these rivals are forced to react to the decision to protect their own interests. It need not imply that the firms involved are very large in some absolute sense: two automobile service stations at an intersection will also meet this criterion for being rivalrous competitors. The firm is in *nonrivalrous competition* when it makes its decisions in the spirit of the game of *solitaire*, playing the cards against the impersonal, nonresponding, and nonpurposive forces of nature. On the other hand, when the firm is in rivalrous competition, it is in a game of *poker* on the supply side of its operations, realizing that every decision it makes is noted by other members of the game, who are personal in their relations, purposive in their conflict with the player, and certain to make some response to his actions that may purposely include elements of bluff and uncertainty. We shall deal with environments in which the firm is in nonrivalrous competition in this chapter and the next, and turn to the problems of the firm in rivalrous competitive environments in Chapter 6.

A firm may be isolated from feedbacks of its initiating decisions in its product market on those decisions for two basic reasons: it may be lost in a crowd of competition, or it may be set in splended isolation, hermit-like in its fellowless firmament. That is, if a firm is producing a product that is exactly like the product of many other firms, or that is very much like the product of many other firms, then the impact of its own decisions will be spread over so many competitors as to be negligible in force upon any one of them, and therefore evocative of no response. We shall identify two cases of this type of isolation: the environments or *market structures* of *pure competition*, when the products of all of the many firms in the market are exactly alike, and of *monopolistic competition*, when the products of the many sellers are closely similar but not exactly alike, or when for other reasons a large number of sellers acquires some degree of control over the price of their products.

At the other end of the spectrum of nonrivalrous competition, it is possible to be isolated from other sellers because no other seller is close enough to the market which one monopolizes to feel the decisions of the monopolist. That is, if one firm produces a product whose nearest substitutes are quite far off in the space of products, then any changes in price or advertising which the producer effects will have negligible impacts upon the sellers of all other products and will evoke no response. This is the case of *pure monopoly* and it, too, may be put in the category of nonrivalrous competition.

We shall treat the case of pure competition as the starting point of our analysis, and then after building our submodel on its basis, turn to the cases of monopoly and monopolistic competition in that order.

THE FIRM'S TECHNOLOGY

The function that is analogous to the consumer's preference function in the theory of the firm is the *production function* and we shall proceed to its definition and restrictions on its shape. Let us first make the following assumptions.

PRODUCER POSTULATE 1. There exists a set of firms V, with elements $v = 1, 2, \ldots, o$, containing all existing and potential firms that could operate during the current week. These firms own no scarce resources, including the enterpreneur's skill in organizing, for the latter is assumed to be a free good under all conceivable circumstances, although his labor of management is a factor service like any other type of labor and may earn surpluses which we shall call *profits*.

As in the case of the consumer we shall blink the problems of group decisionmaking and of locating the locus of decisionmaking within the firm.

We shall simply assume that the firm acts in its decisionmaking as if it were a single person with consistent goals.

PRODUCER POSTULATE 2.   For every product that is capable of production in the economy— Y_j and Z_i—it is possible to partition the whole set of inputs in the economy into two distinct subsets. The first of these subsets—which we shall term the *irrelevant* set for the given commodity—contains all factor services z_i and intermediate goods Y_j that never enter the production of the good for any level of output. The second set contains all inputs that do at one or more levels of output enter production in positive amounts. We shall term the latter set the *relevant* set of inputs for the given commodity.

PRODUCER POSTULATE 3.   For each potential output Y_j and Z_i we construct its input space by choosing one axis for each input in its relevant input set. We may restrict ourselves for all goods to baskets of its relevant inputs that have zero or positive quantities of inputs, for the same reason that we restricted ourselves to such baskets for the consumer. We shall term these baskets *input mixes*.

The production function of each good maps such relevant input mixes, $\mathbf{X} = [X_{z_i}, X_j] \geqq 0$ into outputs $\bar{X}_J$ or $\bar{X}_{Z_i}$, which are nonnegative. (Let it be noted that when we must distinguish between Y_j or Z_i as an output and as an input we shall capitalize J or I to denote the good as output.) These outputs are defined as the maximum amount of commodity which the given input basket can yield under existing technology.

We may now proceed to the placing of some constraints upon the shape of the production functions.

PRODUCER POSTULATE 4.   The *relevant-input space* may be partitioned into two disjoint (that is, nonintersecting) subsets:

1. The set M contains all input mixes $\mathbf{X}$ that yield $\bar{X} = 0$—that is, it contains all input mixes that yield zero output. M contains $\mathbf{X} = 0$, or the input mix that has no inputs of any kind, and is bounded from below by zero for every input. M is *closed*, in the sense that it owns its boundaries, so that all baskets not containing every input are elements of M. Further, M has an interior—it contains baskets or mixes that possess positive amounts of more than one input. And M is *connected*—we may get from any basket in the set to any other in the set by paths of line segments in the set. The set M of input mixes is depicted by the shaded area in Figure 4–1.

2. The set M^* contains all input baskets $\mathbf{X}$ that yield $\bar{X} > 0$. M^* is bounded from below by M and is open, because it does not own its boundary. We assume it to be strictly convex—any two points in the set may be joined by a straight line and the whole line segment will lie in M^*. It is shown in Figure 4–1 as the unshaded portion of relevant-input space.

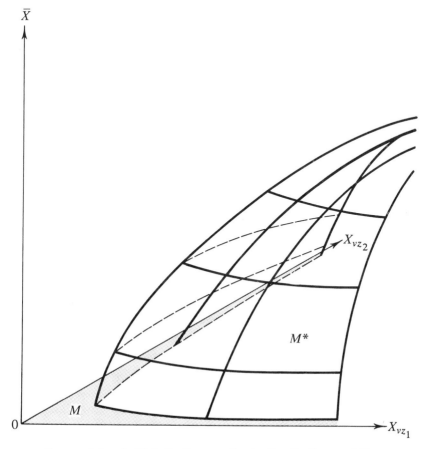

FIGURE 4–1.   A Globally Concave Production Surface on M^*.

What we are assuming with this partition of the firm's field of choice into subsets is this. Take any point on an axis of the relevant-input space and another basket in M^*, and connect the points with a line segment. We assert that the line will contain a finite length in M—in economic terms, it requires some minimal amount of all inputs in the relevant-input space to produce positive output.

PRODUCER POSTULATE 5.   The production function for each good, which we may define as $\bar{X}_J = T_J(\mathbf{X})$ and $\bar{X}_{z_i} = T_{z_i}(\mathbf{X})$, is assumed

1. to rise in a strictly monotonic fashion for all baskets in M^* to some maximum, and then fall continuously toward the base plane. That is, in the relevant input space where output is positive, the addition of more of one input with all others held constant always increases the total output up to

some maximum output, after which further additions of the input add negative increments of products;

   2. to be continuous on M^*;

   3. to be smooth;

   4. to be strictly concave on M^*.

In three dimensions the production function of a typical good would appear as is drawn in Figure 4–1. It arises abruptly from the base plane some distance from the axes, and has the familiar shape of the derby hat, complete with the falling portion of the hat.

PRODUCER POSTULATE 6. Profits for the firm on any output are defined as revenue minus cost, and the firm will choose one good to produce whose optimal output amount and minimum-cost expenditures will yield the firm the highest possible profit for the week.

PRODUCER POSTULATE 7. The firm's demands for cash balances during the week are some given positive fraction K_{vu} of its expenditures on inputs.

PRODUCER POSTULATE 8. Every firm possesses negligible amounts of power in every market in which it participates as buyer or seller, or could potentially so participate.

PRODUCER POSTULATE 9. The vector $\mathbf{P} \geq 0$ is specified to the firm.

With these postulates we have assured ourselves of the ability to get acceptable interrelationships for our model. Before turning to their derivation, however, let us state the set of variables for the model of the firm in pure competition.

The Set of Variables

In the complete producer submodel under pure competition, for which it will be the object of this chapter to construct cost curves, we shall determine values for the following variables in the solution:

   1. $\overline{X}_{vJ}$.   Firm v's output of goods Y_j this week.

   2. $\overline{X}_{vZ_i}$.   Firm v's output of goods Z_i this week.

   3. X_{vu}.   Firm v's demand for cash balances this week.

   4. X_{vz_i}.   Firm v's demand for factor service inputs this week.

   5. X_{vj}.   Firm v's demand for intermediate good inputs this week.

   6. π_v.   Firm v's profits this week.

The Interrelationships for Cost Curves

We shall derive the interrelationships among data and variables in a manner similar to that we used for consumers: the firm chooses a maximal-profit input-output mix [$\overline{\text{X}}$, X] from the technological opportunities open to it this week. We shall, therefore, draw rather extensively upon that prior analysis, not only to economize the reader's time but to emphasize the essential continuity of method and symmetry of approach between the consumer submodel and the derivation of a solution for the firm. We shall use the output of some Y_j to demonstrate the analysis, but it is to be understood that we might have chosen the output of a capital good, Z_i, equally well.

THE CASH-BALANCE DEMAND FOR MONEY BY THE FIRM

For reasons which we discussed at some length for the consumer submodel, we have assumed in Producer Postulate 7 that the demand for cash balances falls outside the production function, and is best determined as a simple linear function of the firm's expenditures on inputs for the week. Without further discussion, therefore, we assume that we are given a cash-balance coefficient for the firm, K_{vu}, whose value is independent of the good produced, and that the firm's demand for money this week if Y_j were produced would be

$$X_{vu/J} = \frac{K_{vu}(\sum_i X_{vz_i/J}P_{z_i} + \sum_j X_{vj/J}P_j)}{(1 - K_{vu}r)}. \qquad [F\text{--}1]$$

THE GEOMETRY OF THE INTERRELATIONSHIPS

We shall construct first a model of the firm's decisionmaking when it is operating under an output constraint. Formally:

PRODUCER POSTULATE 10*. The Firm v is constrained to supply a positive quantity, K_{vJ}, of a given Y_J, and zero quantities of all other goods.

This contraint is only a temporary one, but by imposing it we convert the firm's problem of maximizing profits to one of minimizing the cost of production of $\overline{X}_{vJ} = K_{vJ}$, for if both the quantity supplied and P_J are given, revenue is given, and only costs can be varied to maximize the difference. Let us define for present and current needs the firm's potential profits:

1. $\pi_{v/J} = \overline{X}_{vJ}P_J - \sum_i X_{vz_i/J}P_{z_i} - \sum_j X_{vj/J}P_j - X_{vu/J}r, \qquad J = 1, 2, \ldots, n$
2. $\pi_{v/Z_i} = \overline{X}_{vz_i}P_{z_i} - \sum_i X_{vz_i/Z_i}P_{z_i} - \sum_j X_{vj/Z_i}P_j - X_{vu/Z_i}r,$
$$i = 1, 2, \ldots, m. \qquad [F\text{--}2]$$

The *attainable set* of input mixes of the firm under such an output constraint is differently defined from that of the consumer. Because we have specified the level of output rather than expenditure as a datum constraining the firm, it is the *isoquant* for the given output level that bounds the attainable set of input mixes in M^*. An isoquant is an indifference curve for input mixes, depicting all input mixes which yield a given number of units of output. The firm can select any **X** in M^* which lies on or above the relevant isoquant, the inequality ruling if we assume that it may dispose of the excess output costlessly should it elect to use an input mix that produces a higher output than that required. (Note that we assume that the firm will use any **X** most efficiently in the sense of obtaining the maximum output available in the current technology defined by the production function.) Our piece of sheet metal, therefore, slices the production function parallel to the base plane at the given level of output, K_{vJ}; we may project the profile down onto that plane in order to remain in two dimensions; and we may work with the diagrams in Figures 4–2a and 4–2b.

Given P_J and $\bar{X}_{vJ}$, the revenue or amount of gross money receipts of the firm for the week is fixed. Because profits are merely revenue minus total costs, it follows that under the current constraints the firm will maximize its profits (which may imply minimizing losses) by minimizing its total costs. Therefore, the profit-maximizing motivation of the producer leads him to minimize costs, and our analysis becomes one of constructing the minimum-cost curve if, holding input and output prices constant, we vary the level of output over all values. That is, for each specified value of output, we will obtain the best input mix, and from our knowledge of the prices of the inputs we may obtain the minimum total cost of that output level by the definition:

$$C^\circ_{v/\bar{X}_J} = \sum_i X^\circ_{vz_i/\bar{X}_J} P_{z_i} + \sum_j X^\circ_{vj/\bar{X}_J} P_j + X^\circ_{vu/\bar{X}_J} r. \qquad [4\text{--}1]$$

The degree mark means that all values of the variables are relevant to the minimum-cost input mix for the specified level of output $\bar{X}_J$, and, as we have seen, this implies that the level of costs is that which maximizes profits for the given level of output.

In Figures 4–2a and b we have put two inputs on the axes, X_{z_1} and X_{z_2} (and we shall now drop the v subscript as unnecessary but understood). The input mixes capable of producing $\bar{X}_J$ and no more are then given by the isoquant labelled $\bar{X}_J = K_J$. At the given P_{z_1} and P_{z_2}, $K_{vu/J}$ and r, we may determine the slope of a set of expenditure lines of which we have drawn only E_1 and E_2. These are analogous to the consumer's budget constraint, in that they show at their intersection with the isoquants the input mixes that could be bought with a given expenditure that would produce the relevant output. But obviously, the firm will not be indifferent among the input mixes dictated by the expenditure lines, for they represent different total costs. The farther the expenditure line E is from the origin, the greater the total costs of production, as can be seen by reading from the intercept of E with either axis its equivalent in a single input. That is, for expenditure line E_1 the intercept on the X_{z_2}-axis is at OM, which indicates that the amount of money involved

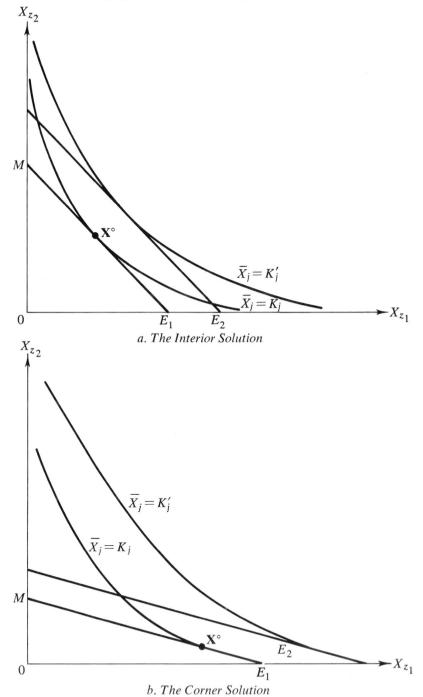

a. The Interior Solution

b. The Corner Solution

FIGURE 4–2.   Minimum-Cost Solutions for Given Rates of Output.

could purchase OM of input z_2. Therefore, as these parallel expenditure lines intersect that axis at higher and higher values, total money costs are growing proportionately.

As the student no doubt has determined, the maximum profit = minimum cost input mix will be that basket $\mathbf{X}^\circ$ on the isoquant where the latter is touched by the expenditure line nearest the origin. In the case of an interior solution, as in Figure 4–2a, this will occur at the point of tangency with the isoquant, for when this point is reached it is no longer possible to move the expenditure line farther toward the origin and remain on the isoquant. For the case of a corner solution, as in Figure 4–2b, it will occur when the input mix on the edge of the isoquant is touched. Note that we have not extended the isoquants to either axis, which differs from consumer theory where we either allowed them to intersect the axes or to approach them asymptotically. By terminating them before they reach the axes we depict geometrically our assumption that we need some of every input to produce any amount of output. A corner solution in the present case, therefore, is one in which only a *minimum amount* of one or more inputs is required to produce the given output. Except for this change, however, the corner solution may be described in the same fashion as that for the consumer.

By virtue of our assumption of strict global concavity of the production function over M^* (indeed we need only strict quasi-concavity because Firm v cannot move off the given isoquant if it wishes to minimize costs), we will receive unique equilibrium input mixes, as illustrated on Figure 4–2. Beyond these statements of differences, the geometry is exactly like that of our consumer analysis, and we may refer the student to it for a more extensive treatment.

THE ALGEBRA OF THE INTERRELATIONSHIPS

Once more we make the analysis brief by exploiting the theory of the consumer developed in Chapter 2.[1] We may symbolize the slopes of the production function in the direction of output for changes in X_{z_1} and X_{z_2} by S_{J/z_1} and S_{J/z_2}, and the slope of the expenditure line by E_{z_2/z_1}. Then, our slope conditions in equilibrium must be:

$$S^\circ_{z_2/z_1} \leqq E_{z_2/z_1}, \qquad\qquad [F^*\text{–}3]$$

[1] One difference in our derivation of systems [II′] and [II] from that of System [I] should be pointed out. Our method is a straightforward extension of the Kuhn-Tucker theorem for production functions globally concave on $M \cup M^*$ to those globally concave on M^*. At the present time the author can find no bar to such an extension, but until its nonexistence can be proved we must label the assertion that our [F] interrelationships are necessary and sufficient for the solutions of systems [II′] and [II] as a conjecture.

where, as in consumer theory, we always assume the slope is measured in the direction of a good whose amount demanded in equilibrium does not lie at a corner (i.e., is greater than minimal).

Next, and temporarily, we constrain Firm v to supply (not necessarily produce) exactly the quantity of output we require:

$$\bar{X}^{\circ}_J - K_J = 0, \qquad K_J > 0. \qquad [F^*-4]$$

Now, because our isoquants do not extend to either axis, an input mix will always contain some of both inputs. Let $X_{z_2/\bar{X}_J}$ be the minimum amount of z_2 that can be used in any input mix to produce $K_J = \bar{X}_J$ of output: then, this will be the value of X_{z_2} in that input mix which lies on the lower edge of the isoquant in the z_2 direction. Then, we must state the conditions when the corner solution may occur as follows:

1. $(X^{\circ}_{z_2} - X_{z_2/\bar{X}_J})(S^{\circ}_{z_2/z_1} - E_{z_2/z_1}) = 0.$ \qquad $[F^*-5]$

2. Output may exceed supply only if marginal cost is zero.

That is, if the slopes of the expenditure line and the isoquant are equal, greater amounts of z_2 than the minimal quantity may be bought; if they are unequal, only the minimal quantity can be bought. Also, since we will buy only K_J units of the good from the firm at P_J per unit, if the firm produces more than K_J it will not be maximizing profits—unless marginal cost is zero.

> All isoquants at all points are strictly convex, which is implied
> by the necessity of the production function to be globally
> strictly concave in its positive range. \qquad $[F-6]$

The nonnegativity requirements are set:

$$(X^{\circ}_{z_1} - X_{z_1/\bar{X}_J}) \geqq 0, \qquad X^{\circ}_{z_2} - X_{z_2/\bar{X}_J} \geqq 0, \qquad \text{Marginal cost} \geqq 0. \quad [F^*-7]$$

We may state for the sake of completeness the specific form of the cash-balance equation for this two-input case:

$$X_u = \frac{K_u(X_{z_1}P_{z_1} + X_{z_2}P_{z_2})}{(1 - K_u r)}. \qquad [F^*-1]$$

And, finally, we may restate the definition of profit in the specific case at hand:

$$\pi = K_J P_J - X^{\circ}_{z_1}P_{z_1} - X^{\circ}_{z_2}P_{z_2} - X^{\circ}_u r. \qquad [F^{*\prime}-2]$$

The generalization of this system to more than two inputs is so easily done that we shall list the conditions without comment. Note that we do assume that we are measuring the slopes in a direction of a good, z_1, which is taken in nonminimal quantity in equilibrium.

$$X_u^\circ = \frac{K_u(\sum_j X_j^\circ P_j + \sum_i X_{z_i}^\circ P_{z_i})}{(1 - K_u r)} \qquad [F\text{-}1]$$

$$\pi = K_J P_J - \sum_i X_{z_i}^\circ P_{z_i} - \sum_j X_j^\circ P_j - X_u^\circ r \qquad [F'\text{-}2]$$

1. $S_{j/z_1}^\circ \leqq E_{j/z_1}, \qquad j = 1, 2, \ldots, n$

2. $S_{z_i/z_1}^\circ \leqq E_{z_i/z_1}, \qquad i = 2, \ldots, m \qquad [F\text{-}3]$

$$\bar{X}_J^\circ - K_J = 0, \qquad K_J > 0 \qquad [F'\text{-}4]$$

1. $(X_j^\circ - X_{j/\bar{X}_J})(S_{j/z_1}^\circ - E_{j/z_1}^\circ) = 0$

2. $(X_{z_i}^\circ - X_{z_i/\bar{X}_J})(S_{z_i/z_1}^\circ - E_{z_i/z_1}^\circ) = 0 \qquad [F\text{-}5]$

3. Output may exceed supply only if marginal cost is zero.

The production function is globally strictly concave in its positive range. $\qquad [F\text{-}6]$

1. $(X_j^\circ - X_{j/\bar{X}_J}) \geqq 0,$

2. $(X_{z_i}^\circ - X_{z_i/\bar{X}_J}) \geqq 0 \qquad [F\text{-}7]$

3. Marginal cost $\geqq 0$.

The Solutions

From this set of conditions we may solve out to obtain the values of the variables as functions of the data solely; also, we now restore the subscript v to variables:

1. $X_{vj}^\circ = D_{vj}(\mathbf{P}, K_{vJ}, K_{vu}), \qquad j = 1, 2, \ldots, n$

2. $X_{vz_i}^\circ = D_{vz_i}(\mathbf{P}, K_{vJ}, K_{vu}), \qquad i = 1, 2, \ldots, m$

3. $X_{vu}^\circ = \dfrac{K_{vu}(\sum_j X_{vj}^\circ P_j + \sum_i X_{vz_i}^\circ P_{z_i})}{(1 - K_{vu} r)}$

4. $C_{vJ}^\circ = \sum_i X_{vz_i}^\circ P_{z_i} + \sum_j X_{vj}^\circ P_j + X_{vu}^\circ r. \qquad [II']$

For fixed levels of output as data, therefore, we can derive the demands for inputs and the minimum cost of producing that output from our interrelationships. Inasmuch as the cost curve is of major interest to us in this system, we shall confine our search for propositions to it, although the reader should understand that we might shock the solution in the same manner we did for consumers to see how the demands for inputs reacted. Because we have done this for consumers and the analysis will be exactly analogous, and because our major interest is in the model with output variable of which the cost curve is a most important part, let us economize the student's time by restricting ourselves to its consideration.

The Derivation of Propositions About Cost Curves

THE POSITIVE SLOPE OF THE TOTAL COST CURVE

One proposition about the total cost curve of System [II′–4] is that it is positively sloped throughout its length. If we hold input prices constant and vary the fixed levels of output by successively increasing K_{vJ}, we should be moving the expenditure line outward in a parallel manner on Figure 4–2a and 4–2b. We could touch higher isoquant curves, therefore, only with expenditure lines farther from the origin, so that at positive prices for the inputs the total cost of the higher output must rise as we produce more. We are not in the Land of Cockaigne where we can obtain product for nothing.

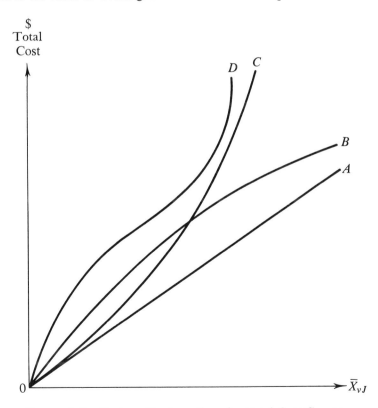

FIGURE 4–3. Various Configurations for Total Cost Curves.

On Figure 4–3 we have drawn four idealized shapes for cost curves that would meet this condition, *while we ignore for the moment the limitations on the shape of the production function contained in Producer Postulate 4 and the global concavity requirement of Producer Postulate 5 and their implications for the shape of the total cost curve.* We shall do this because while our production function aims at greater realism, the presentation of cost theory can be simplified by working with homogeneous functions which rise from the origin. After we develop the theory of costs in terms of such functions, it will be easy to return to the cost functions implied by Producer Postulates 4 and 5. It will be well to discuss each of these cost curves in turn and their implications concerning the shape of the homogeneous production function that produced them.

THE CONFIGURATIONS OF THE TOTAL COST CURVE

The restriction concerning positive slopes is a mild one and allows many types of configurations for the curve, of which we have chosen four idealized types.

LINEAR TOTAL COSTS. In Curve *A* of Figure 4–3 we have depicted a total cost curve which rises from zero when no output is produced (as do all our curves that spring from our submodel because firms have no fixed costs, owning no resources) in linear fashion. If prices of inputs are held constant, as is done in deriving a cost curve, every output will be produced with input mixes whose relative structure remains constant: that is, every quantity of output uses an input mix that has inputs in the same proportions. In Figure 4–4 we have shown the successive equilibria for representative outputs under such circumstances. Note that each solution input mix lies on a straight line through the origin, which implies that the input mixes retain the same structure although the absolute quantities vary by a common factor. That is, if the optimal input mix to produce 10 units of output is [5, 7], then because 12 units of output equals 1.2 times 10 units, the optimal input mix for 12 units will be the values in the first mix multiplied by 1.2, or [6, 8.4].

Let us first expand upon the reason why the firm undergoes no expense if it chooses not to produce. This is because in our model the firm owns no property and, as we have seen, leases all of its factor resource inputs and buys its intermediate good inputs or manufactures them. It has, therefore, no *fixed costs* which it must bear regardless of its decision on output; all of its costs are *variable costs*, in the sense that costs vary only with level of output.

Besides the total cost (= total variable cost) curve, we may define two other cost curves that are derivative from the total cost curve: (1) the *marginal* cost curve and (2) the *average variable* cost curve.

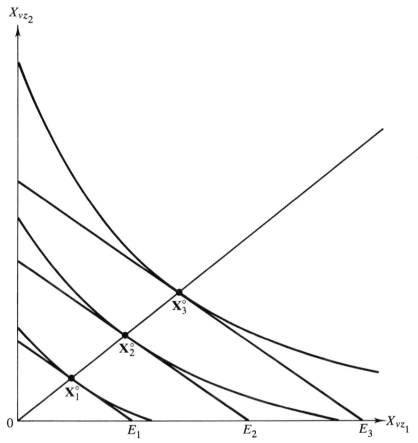

FIGURE 4–4. Successive Input Equilibria for Various Levels of Output with a Linear Homogeneous Production Function.

Marginal Cost Curve. On Figure 4–5, where we have reproduced the linear total cost curve, we have also drawn in the horizontal line at a *height* that equals the *slope* of the total cost curve. We define marginal cost at some given quantity of output to be the additional cost of a unit of output. For example, on the figure, if we are at output $\bar{X}_{vJ} = K_{vJ}$, at the fixed prices for input services, and if we wish to increase output to $\bar{X}_{vJ} = K_{vJ} + 1$, total costs will rise from the amount C_{vj}° to C_{vj}^{*}. This increment, $C_{vj}^{*} - C_{vJ}^{\circ}$, is marginal cost, or the additional cost of another unit on the present edge or margin of production, when the costs of both old and new quantities (and therefore the incremental quantity) are minimized.

In the present case of linear total costs, a feature of the curve is its constant slope. This is merely another way of saying that the marginal cost of producing an extra unit of output at *any* initial output is constant. This, of course,

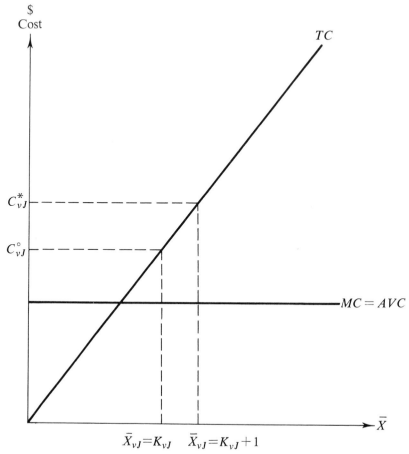

FIGURE 4–5. Total, Marginal, and Average Cost Curves for the Linear Homogeneous Production Function.

follows from the fact that if the firm wishes to halve its output, it halves every input quantity; if it desires to double its output, it doubles every input quantity. With prices of inputs constant and every additional unit of output produced with the same dose of all factors, considered as a tiny bundle of inputs with the same relative structure, the extra costs of production must be the same anywhere.

Average Variable Cost Curve. We have also drawn on Figure 4–5, coincident with the marginal cost curve, the average variable cost curve. This is defined as the variable cost of producing any output divided by that output, which yields the average variable cost per unit of that output quantity. Now, because the total cost of producing a zero output is zero, and because the additional cost of producing every unit is the same (that is, marginal cost is constant), it follows that the average variable cost must (1) remain constant (2) at the level of marginal cost. This equality of average variable and marginal cost will occur when optimal factor proportions are independent of output size, given a set of input prices. Geometrically, this implies that the tangencies of successive expenditure lines of constant slope with isoquants fall along a ray from the origin, as illustrated in Figure 4–4.

We have assumed that these results spring from constant input prices and a smooth, continuous, globally strictly *quasi-concave* production function (we recall to the student's attention that we are at present ignoring the restrictions of Producer Postulates 4 and 5 on the production surface). Let us now ask what other restrictions on the production surface are necessary to yield (1) isoquants that have the same slope along any straight line from the origin, (2) linear total costs, (3) constant marginal costs, and (4) constant average variable costs at the level of marginal costs.

Let us look at Figure 4–6, where the x- and y-axes depict amounts of z_1 and z_2 used respectively, and where $\bar{X}_{vJ}$ is depicted on the z-axis. Now place a pencil or other linear object with one end at the origin. If the reader moves the pencil within the nonnegative octant of the space as it makes some positive angle with the base plane, the pencil will trace out a surface. Note that the student might move the pencil with great abandon, but because we have set the requirement of global strict quasi-concavity, we restrict him to moving the pencil so that the isoquants are convex everywhere, which means that he will rotate the pencil about its pivot at the origin so that it sweeps in smoothly toward himself and then smoothly away on its travels from starting point to stopping point on the base plane (if we impose smoothness of the isoquants as a further quality).

Now consider the surface traced out by the pencil's movement. It was formed by rotating a straight line through space, so that, if we now consider that surface to be made of metal, the pencil will touch the surface at all points along a ray from the origin if it is laid on the surface. Let us so lay the pencil at some position on the surface, and then move it in a small arc on the surface. Obviously, the pencil will describe the same arc at every point on its length, and if the arc is small enough we can approximate it with the slope of the surface along the pencil. Therefore, we have met the conditions (1) stated earlier. And, of course, we have seen that the conditions (2), (3), and (4) follow from them for fixed input prices.

This type of function is called a *linear homogeneous* production function, and in our case it is smooth and continuous. It is homogeneous because the function begins at the origin of input-output space, and it is linear because it is traced out by a linear generator of the pencil type that we discussed. If we slice it parallel to the base plane at specific product levels, and project these

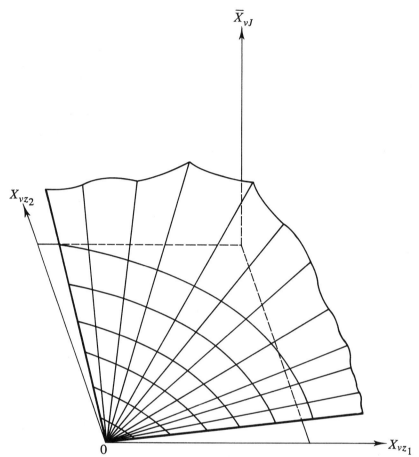

FIGURE 4–6. A Strictly Quasi-Concave Linear Homogeneous Production.

profiles down onto the base plane, we obtain the convex isoquant contours of Figure 4–4 which we require, because we have in addition imposed the condition that the surface be globally strictly quasi-concave.

Suppose now, as in Figure 4–7, we slice the function at some constant value for the input z_2, and study the profile that shows the variation of output as X_{vz_1} changes. Under our assumptions the profile of the hill may appear as it does in the figure: beginning to rise at some positive value for X_{vz_1} (with some fixed amount of X_{vz_2}), rising by decreasing amounts from the beginning to a maximum output, and then falling by increasing amounts toward zero output. We may use this profile to discuss the law of variable proportions for inputs.

The Law of Variable Proportions. The curve under discussion we shall call a *product curve,* and it depicts what happens to output when all inputs

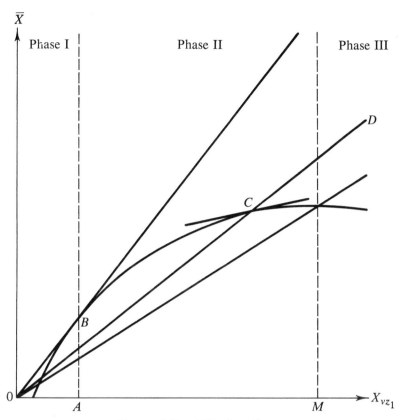

FIGURE 4–7. A Product Curve.

but one are held constant at some level and the variable input is allowed to take all nonnegative values. We may typically divide up such a *diminishing-returns-to-variable inputs* function into three parts or *phases*, as we have done in Figure 4–7, each of which has an important economic significance.

1. Phase I. Positive Marginal Products Greater Than Average Products. The *average product* of a quantity of variable input, given the quantities of fixed inputs, may be obtained by drawing a line from the origin to the curve at the given value of variable input, and determining the slope of this line. This slope is the total product (for example, AB in Figure 4–7) of the given number of variable input units divided by the quantity of factor (OA in Figure 4–7). On the other hand, the *marginal product* of any quantity of variable factor—or the additional product added to the total output by one more unit of variable factor at some given quantity of X_{vz_1}—will be the slope of the product curve at that point, or more exactly, the slope of a tangent to the curve at that point. We may, therefore, compare the average product and

the marginal product of a given X_{vz_1} by comparing the slope of a ray from the origin to the product curve over the input quantity with the slope of a tangent to the product curve at that point. If the slope of the ray is greater than that of the tangent, the average product is greater than marginal product; if they are equal, average product equals marginal product; and if the slope of the ray is less than that of the tangent, the average product is less than marginal product at that point.

Let us find on Figure 4–7 that ray which, when drawn to a point on the product curve, will have the greatest slope: the value X_{vz_1} under the curve at this point is the amount of variable input that (given the fixed levels of other inputs) will achieve the greatest average product. This quantity on the figure is OA. Notice that to the left of this point as we have drawn the curve the slopes of the product curve are greater than the slope of the ray. This means that the marginal products of X_{vz_1} are greater than the average products up to the ray's contact with the product curve. Because as we have drawn the functions the ray will be the maximal average product ray only if it is tangent to the product curve at the point in question, the slope of the ray and the slope of the product curve will be equal where average product is a maximum, so that average product at this point will equal marginal product.

We will designate as Phase I of the product curve that portion of the curve (if it exists) in which the marginal product of the variable factor is positive and greater than the average product.

2. Phase II. Positive Marginal Products Less Than Average Products. Beyond the maximum-average-product factor quantity marginal products remain positive, so that each additional unit of variable factor service contributes to total product a positive amount of product, until factor quantity OM is reached. However, these marginal products are less than the respective average products, as a comprison of the slope of ray OD with the slope of the tangent to the product curve at C will demonstrate. The phase ends at M where the marginal product of the quantities of variable factor service becomes zero.

3. Phase III. Negative Marginal Products. In Phase III the marginal product of each quantity of factor service is negative, which implies that production with factor service quantities beyond M actually results in a smaller total product than with smaller amounts of the variable input. That is, the absolute maximum of product that can be obtained with the given amounts of fixed inputs and any quantity of variable input is reached at M, where the marginal product of the variable input is zero. Beyond that point, so much of the variable input is involved in production that it actually worsens output in an absolute sense. Average product, which began to

decline at the start of Phase II, continues to decline with a vengeance throughout Phase III, of course.

The Product Curves of Linear Homogeneous Functions. Now consider the linear homogeneous production function for a moment. The point on the product curve which we have labelled *B* and at which maximum average product occurs is at the input mix $[OA, X_{vz_2}]$, where X_{vz_2} is being held constant. We know that there is a straight line ray from the origin of Figure 4–6 through this point on the production function, such that if we multiplied the input mix by $\theta > 0$, the output would also be multiplied by θ. But the same thing is true for every point on the product curve in Figure 4–7: if we multiplied the input mix that yields the point by θ, the point would lie on the ray from the origin through that point on Figure 4–7 at a position θ times the output away. That is to say, the entire product curve would be displaced in a proportionate manner and average products also would be equal. For example, the maximum average product ray would touch both curves at the maximum average product point and where marginal product was equal to average product.

What we are in effect saying, therefore, is that the product curve in Figure 4–7 is an accurate depiction of the product curve that could be obtained by slicing the production function at any fixed value for X_{vz_2}, except that every comparable point on the X_{vz_1} axis will be shifted over by θ, the value of the new X_{vz_2} divided by the old, and the height of the curve over such comparable points will be shifted up by the factor θ. That is, if we divide every value of X_{vz_1} by the fixed quantity of X_{vz_2}, and every value of output by X_{vz_2}, so that we have put every curve on the surface in *relative* terms, and if we reinterpret the product curve of Figure 4–7 in such relative terms, we would get the standardized product profile in that figure for every slice through the $X_{vz_2} > 0$ portion of the z_2 axis.

The economic significance of this fact—and it holds true only for linear homogeneous functions it must be emphasized—is that average and marginal output is a function of the *proportions* in which the fixed and variable inputs are combined only: the absolute amounts of these inputs are important only in determining the absolute amount of output.

Because this is true, a very interesting interpretation of Phase I and Phase III can be made in Figure 4–7. In Phase I the marginal products of the input mixes are greater than the average products, which means that each additional unit of variable factor in Phase I adds more to product than the average of all previous units of the input. This is an indication that the ratio of variable input to fixed input is too low, in this sense that further units of the variable input add more to output than the average of previous units, or that the variable input is not yet efficiently employed with the given amounts of fixed factor because the average output per unit is rising. But, because the only important consideration is the proportion in which the factors are combined, we could have gotten the same factor proportions by holding the variable input constant at some absolute amount in Phase I of Figure 4–7 and subtracting units of the fixed input, which in our example implies that we approach the desired proportions by subtracting units of z_2 and observe the marginal product of z_2 *rise*. But this means that the relative presence of z_2 in the input mixes of Phase I must have been too great—indeed, its contribution to output was a negative one. For the fixed quantity of z_1 we have postulated, X_{vz_2} must have been located in the Phase III portion of the z_2 product curve.

That is to say, Phase I and Phase III are really reflections of the *same* phenomenon in product curves derived from a linear homogeneous production function—relative overabundance of one input. Phase I of the product curve for z_1 occurs because the relative presence of z_1 in combination with a fixed amount of z_2 is too small. But because of the all-importance of proportions only, and the unimportance of absolute quantities of inputs in explaining the shape of the profile, this means that the relative amount of z_2 was too great, such that a reduction of one unit of z_2 would reduce the marginal product of the fixed amount of z_1. But the marginal product of z_1 can fall only by total product increasing, so that a reduction of one unit of z_2 must increase product. Therefore, the original X_{vz_2}, considered as variable with a level of z_1 fixed temporarily at X_{vz_1} in the Phase I portion of the product curve in Figure 4–7, must be in the Phase III portion of the z_2 curve. Thus, Phase I input quantities for the variable input imply Phase III input quantities for the fixed input, and result when one input is present in too small a proportion relative to the other, or, equivalently, when one input is too abundant relative to the other.

It follows, therefore, that if Phase I is merely a reflection of a Phase III for some input, and if Phase III is a portion of the product curve for some input in which total product is actually declining, the firm would never find it optimal to operate in Phase I any more than in Phase III to produce a given output if all its inputs were freely variable and it could sell all the product at a fixed price. For if it were in Phase I, and the firm could freely vary all inputs, it would prefer to buy fewer inputs of the type in relative overabundance and thereby escape its contribution of negative marginal product.

It should be pointed out that if the product curve of Figure 4–7 begins at zero output to the right of the origin, the curve must have a segment of Phase I characteristics. That is, in terms of our interpretation, if some finite minimum amount of z_1 is required before any output is forthcoming, then the fixed factor will always be in excess supply for a segment of production.

On the other hand, if the curve goes through the origin, or it intersects the z_2-axis, average product will be highest for $X_{v z_1} = 0$, and Phase II will begin immediately. In either case, obviously if z_2 taken by itself yields some output, even with no z_1, or even if it yields zero output when no z_1 is present, it cannot be in excess supply in the sense of possessing a negative marginal product.

The Marginal and Average Cost Curves Reflected in the Product Curve. To this point, and as depicted formally in System [II'], we have assumed that the firm has had the ability, for any given level of output we impose on it, to vary *all* of the inputs—to move from one product curve to another—in order to produce that output at minimum cost (= maximum profit). The total cost curve that would result when prices are held constant but output levels are changed in System [II'–4] assumes this full degree of freedom.

But in the product curve of Figure 4–7 we have arbitrarily assumed one (or a group) of the factors to be held constant in order to obtain a side profile of the production function. The fact is that under certain conditions the firm must produce on such a product curve: that is, it is constrained to vary one or more inputs and hold one or more inputs constant at a fixed level. The reader should see this as another constraint added to our interrelationships: the firm is constrained not only to produce a given output (which we vary to obtain costs for all outputs) but to produce it using a fixed amount of one or more factors.

This is quite likely to be the case of the firm in the short run, where our specific assumption that the firm in our environment can hire as much as it likes of all inputs during the week is violated in the real world. It will be recalled that we adopted this postulate in order to introduce long-run aspects into the week's solution. Realistically, however, the firm cannot increase the size of its plant in a short-period analysis: it can merely employ and purchase other inputs and combine them with the fixed amount of the plant. Let us therefore associate z_2 with plant—including buildings and other rather difficult-to-vary types of capital or experienced management—so that the product curve of Figure 4–7 may be viewed as that which results when plant is of a given size, $X_{v z_2}$. At this point, then, for the first time, we shall step out of the confines of the environment of our models and deal with some aspects of economic reality we cannot handle within them. We shall discuss cost curves as derived only from Phases I and II of the product curve, because Phase III introduces backward bending or discontinuous curves with no realistic relevance.

The total cost curve for a given plant size must always be at least as high at every level of output as the total cost curve when all factors are freely variable. It can never penalize the firm to be able to vary all factors and inputs rather than be forced to hire some in fixed amounts, and should normally allow it an ability to achieve lower costs. Moreover, total costs will include now a fixed cost component, shown in Figure 4–8 as $TFC/\bar{z}_2$ (total fixed costs when X_{vz_2} is fixed) and horizontal over all levels of output to reveal its unchanging character as the level of output changes. We have also indicated with a slash and a $\bar{z}_2$ subscript that it depicts fixed costs for a fixed level of plant.

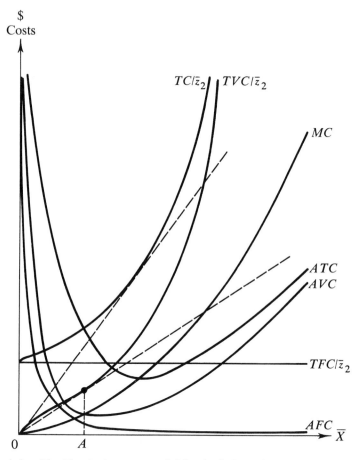

FIGURE 4–8. The Total, Average, and Marginal Cost Curves for the Product Curve of Figure 4–7.

The total variable cost curve for the fixed plant, $TVC/\bar{z}_2$, now represents the manner in which the costs of inputs that are variable—in our case z_1—rise as output rises. Let us state the relationships between average and marginal products and average and marginal costs, and relate these latter two costs to the total variable cost curve.

We may state, of course, that total product equals average product times number of units of variable input producing it. That is,

$$\bar{X}_{vJ} = \frac{\bar{X}_{vJ}}{X_{vz_1}} X_{vz_1}.$$ [4–2]

Total variable costs will be

$$TVC/\bar{z}_2 = X_{vz_1} P_{z_1},$$ [4–3]

and average variable costs will be

$$AVC/\bar{z}_2 = \frac{TVC/\bar{z}_2}{\bar{X}_{vJ}} = \frac{X_{vz_1}}{\bar{X}_{vJ}} P_{z_1}.$$ [4–4]

Thus, average variable cost is equal to the reciprocal of average product per unit of variable factor times the price of a unit of z_1. Then, when average product of the variable input rises, average variable costs must fall, and when average product falls, average variable costs must rise. Therefore, we may say that because average product rises steadily up to $X_{vz_1} = OA$ on Figure 4–7, average variable costs will fall to that critical input quantity, and then begin to rise, and rise continuously thereafter.

Marginal cost may be represented as the reciprocal of marginal product times the price of the input:

$$MC/\bar{z}_2 = \frac{\Delta X_{vz_1}}{\Delta \bar{X}_{vJ}} P_{z_1},$$ [4–5]

and, more exactly, where we allow the increments of product and of inputs to shrink down to very small amounts:

$$MC/\bar{z}_2 = \frac{dX_{vz_1}}{d\bar{X}_{vJ}} P_{z_1}, \qquad \frac{dX_{vz_1}}{d\bar{X}_{vJ}} \geqq 0.$$ [4–6]

Marginal cost is positive when the marginal product is positive and undefined (or infinite) when marginal product is zero at the point OM of Figure 4–7 where output achieves a maximum for this plant. It is negative when marginal product becomes negative, since cost increments are positive even if output increments are negative, but we have restricted the definition to nonnegative marginal products.

Because, from [4–6], the slope of the marginal cost curve is $(d^2 X_{vz_1}/d\bar{X}_{vJ}^2)P_{z_1}$, and because the product curve of Figure 4–7 rises by decreasing amounts throughout its length, we can say that the marginal cost curve must rise throughout its length for this example. This permits us to draw it as we have done in Figure 4–8, although we have been arbitrary in assuming that marginal cost rises by increasing amounts. On the other hand, the slope of the average product per unit of variable input is, from [4–4],

$$\frac{dAVC}{d\overline{X}_{vJ}} = \frac{P_{z_1}}{\overline{X}_{vJ}} \left(\frac{dX_{vz_1}}{d\overline{X}_{vJ}} - \frac{X_{vz_1}}{\overline{X}_{vJ}} \right).$$ [4–7]

Therefore, average variable cost falls to the point A, where the slope of the product curve and of the ray from the origin to that point are equal, then rises indefinitely thereafter, Here, too, we have been arbitrary in assuming that the average cost curve falls by decreasing amounts over the falling portion.

Lastly, we may draw in the average fixed cost curve, $AFC/\bar{z}_2$, which is derived by dividing the fixed costs by units of output. It will fall steadily until the point OM is reached on Figure 4–7, then begin to climb again until it reaches infinity where output reaches zero.

The Relation of the Plant Curves and the Cost Curves When All Factors Are Variable. We have seen that when all inputs are variable the linear homogeneous production function will yield a linear long-run total cost function through the origin and a constant average total cost and marginal cost curve that coincide. How are these related to the short-run *plant* curves, for we may now term the former *long-run* cost curves, with the implication that only in the long run can the firm make adjustments in its plant, and the latter *short-run* because in that length of period the plant is fixed?

We have seen that two input mixes that have the same input proportions and differ only by a scalar multiple will yield outputs on a linear homogeneous function that differ by that same scalar multiple. The average total cost of producing with a given input mix will be the same regardless of the scale of its usage. But consider now the same phenomenon holding output constant and viewing the cheapest average cost at which every size of plant could produce it. By slicing the production function parallel to the base plane we obtain an isoquant depicting all input mixes that would yield the absolute level of output desired. Its interpretation is close to that we gave the indifference curve in our consumer submodel, if we substitute level of output for level of satisfaction and input mixes for consumer goods baskets. Now, if we continue to view z_2 as plant, then the isoquant shows for every size of plant the amount of z_1 the firm would have to employ to produce the given output.

Every size of plant (X_{vz_2}) will require a different amount of z_1 to produce a fixed level of output, and, therefore, at a fixed **P** will yield different short-run average variable and total costs. This is true even though we have a linear homogeneous production function, for this quality of the function becomes important only when we can freely vary *all* inputs. Because for every size of plant the average variable and average total cost curves are U-shaped, if the profiles are as we have drawn that of Figure 4–7, a plant of given size is most efficiently used when average total costs are a minimum. That is to say, because we have a linear homogeneous production function, whenever the marginal product of the variable factor is greater than its average product, the marginal product of the fixed factor must be negative, and where the average product of the variable factor equals its marginal product, the marginal product of the fixed factor must be zero. Because the short-run cost of the plant is zero, when it is used to the point where its marginal product is zero, it is being used most efficiently. By taking all possible plant sizes and adjusting the variable inputs to reach this minimum, we are allowing all inputs to be freely varied. The linear homogeneous characteristic of the function asserts itself, then, in the phenomenon that these minimum average total costs will be at the same level for all firm plant sizes, because variable inputs will be employed until the factor proportions reach the values that lie along the ray from the origin which touches the production function at all points over the line of the base plane depicting that factor proportion.

The long-run average total cost curve for the firm, therefore, consists of points on different short-run average total cost curves. That is, the long-run average total cost of producing a given output is the cheapest input mix for a given **P** when all inputs can be varied, which is to say when any level of plant can be chosen. Therefore, we may draw, as on Figure 4–9, the average total cost curves for every possible plant size, of which we have drawn three, and for every possible output choose that cost level which lies on the lowest plant curve (or short-run average total cost curve). The long-run average total cost curve considered as the succession of points lying on different short-run average total cost curves is known as the *envelope* of the short-run cost curves. We have labelled it *LRAC* on Figure 4–9 and have labelled the average short-run cost curves *PC* (plant curves).

The peculiarity of linear homogeneous functions which we have discussed is now apparent graphically: the envelope curve is a horizontal straight line. This depicts the fact that if variable inputs are adjusted freely, every plant will ultimately reach that structure of input mix which yields the minimum average cost. We will be travelling along the ray from the origin on the surface over the optimal input mix proportion line on the base plane. This is to say that for the firm to produce any output at a given **P** when it can vary the size of its plant, under such conditions it will produce most efficiently (not necessarily most profitably) by using the same input mix at different scales. This implies, however, that the long-run marginal costs of production will equal long-run average costs of production, because any extra unit of output is obtained by building a slightly larger plant and using other inputs such that the extra unit is produced with the same input mix as all previous units

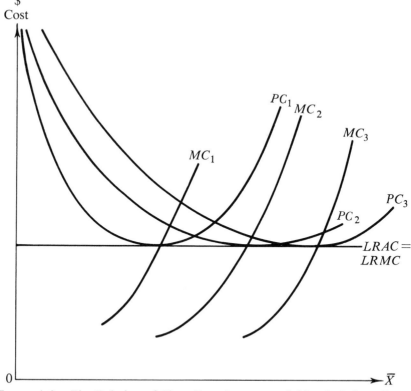

FIGURE 4–9. The Relation of Short-Run Average and Marginal Cost Curves to Long-Run Average and Marginal Cost Curves for Linear Homogeneous Production Functions.

of output. We have labelled the long-run marginal cost curve on Figure 4–9 as *LRMC* and made it coincide with *LRAC*. It can also be looked upon as the succession of plant curve marginal costs relevant to each level of output on the *LRAC* curve, so that *LRMC* consists of the plant curve marginal costs for all segments of the plant curves lying on the *LRAC* curve.

On Figure 4–10 we have drawn the relationships between the short-term *total* cost curves and the long-run *total* cost curve. Once more each point on the latter curve may be viewed as a point on the short-run total cost curve where average total cost reaches a minimum. The short-run total cost curves lie wholly above the long-run curve except at this one point of tangency.

The requirement that the linear homogeneous production function be globally strictly quasi-concave has been assumed throughout. Let us now remove the restriction that the production function be linear homogeneous and discuss cases where the restriction that it be strictly quasi-concave does not imply linear average costs in the long run.

Total Costs Rising by Decreasing Amounts. On the whole set of input mixes let the reader now imagine a smooth and continuous production function shaped like the bell of a trumpet which has been halved longitudinally, rising from the origin of relevant-input space and tilted back over that space. Note that the function will be globally quasi-concave, so that the isoquants will be convex. The singular characteristic about this function, however, is its feature of increasing returns to scale. By this we mean that if we multiply the components of some input mix by $\theta > 0$, output will rise by a factor greater than θ. On Figure 4–11 we have sliced such a function at levels of output which are rising by a constant amount: on the diagram, each isoquant represents an output level that is 50 units greater than the previous one. Note that when this is done with such a surface, the isoquants get closer

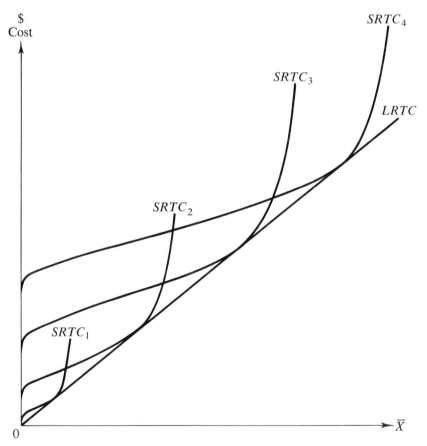

FIGURE 4–10. The Relation Between Short-Run Total Costs and Long-Run Total Costs for a Linear Homogeneous Production Function Yielding U-Shaped Short-Run Average Cost Curves.

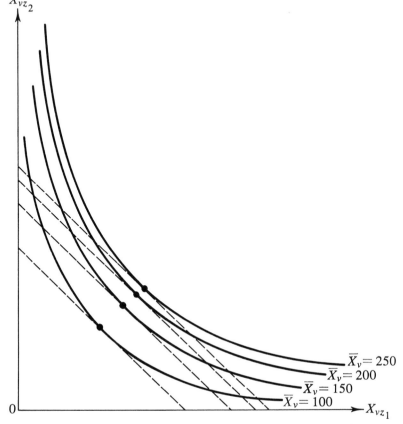

FIGURE 4–11. Isoquants of a Production Surface Revealing Increasing Returns to Scale.

and closer together, indicating a greater steepness of the production hill as we rise from the base plane.

This fact that the surface rises increasingly steeply over input mixes as we move out from the origin along any ray implies that if we increase expenditures by some constant amount, we get the greater-than-proportionate increase in product denoted by the diagram. It follows, therefore, that long-run total costs must rise by less than constant amounts. On Figure 4–11 we have drawn in expenditure lines and indicated the optimal input mixes for the specified levels of output. On Figure 4–12 we have drawn the total cost curve as rising by decreasing amounts for outputs shown on the figure.

Now, let us slice this production function at some constant level of input z_2 and derive the product curve as we did for the linear homogeneous function. We omit Phase III of the curve and depict merely Phases I and II. The curve is zero until some positive amount of X_{vz_1} is reached, and rises by increasing amounts and then by decreasing amounts until it reaches its maximum. We know, therefore, that marginal product will rise by increasing amounts before it passes through a phase in which it rises by decreasing amounts, while it will remain above average product in Phase I before the latter attains its maximum, then fall below average product in Phase II. Marginal costs, therefore, will fall before they begin to rise below average cost, equal average cost where the latter reaches a minimum, then rise and remain above average cost as the latter rises up to the output that marks the end of Phase II. We have shown this behavior in Figure 4–13.

The total cost curve rises by decreasing amounts and is related to the total cost curves for various levels of plant as shown in Figure 4–14, while the long-run average cost curve of the firm is the envelope of the plant curves

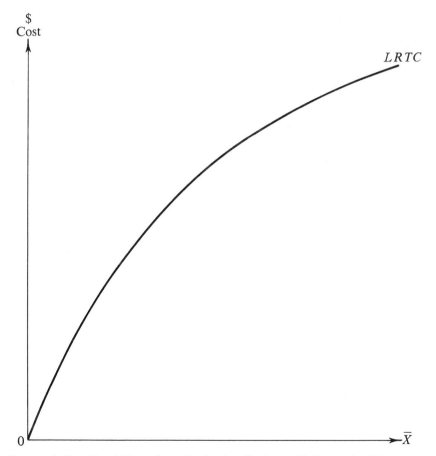

FIGURE 4–12. Total Costs for a Production Surface with Increasing Returns to Scale.

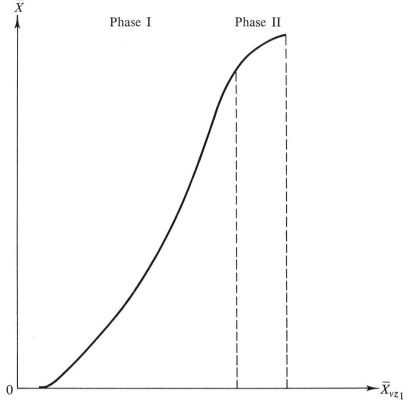

FIGURE 4–13. The Product Curve Profile of a Production Function Strictly Quasi-Concave with Increasing Returns to Scale.

as shown in Figure 4–15. Marginal cost in the long run consists of the relevant segments of the plant curves' marginal costs—that is, the short-run marginal cost segments for those outputs of the short-run average costs which lie on the long-run average cost.

Therefore, when the production function possesses this shape and the firm is told to maximize profits *subject to some specified output level,* long-run cost curves when all factors are variable reflect continuously increasing returns to scale until some point before the function's maximum is reached. Plant curves, however, possess a U-shape for outputs up to a maximum set at the boundary of Phases II and III.

Total Costs Rising By Increasing Amounts. Suppose now that we have a globally strictly concave production function rising from the origin of relevant input space, The difference between the configuration of this type of function and a linear homogeneous function is quickly shown in this manner: if the piece of sheet metal is laid on the surface of the linear homogeneous function, it will touch the function everywhere along a straight line and at all other points lie above it. On the other hand, by definition the metal plane will touch the globally strictly concave function only at one point and lie above it at all other points.

The distinctive feature possessed everywhere by the globally strictly concave function is illustrated in Figure 4–16. The isoquants for successive increments of product of the same amount become increasingly farther apart as we rise up the hill. This indicates decreasing returns to the scale of activity: if we multiply all quantities in some input mix by $\theta > 0$, output expands by less than a factor of θ. For any given product curve, the configuration will be that of a curve with no Phase I, beginning at or above the origin with a general

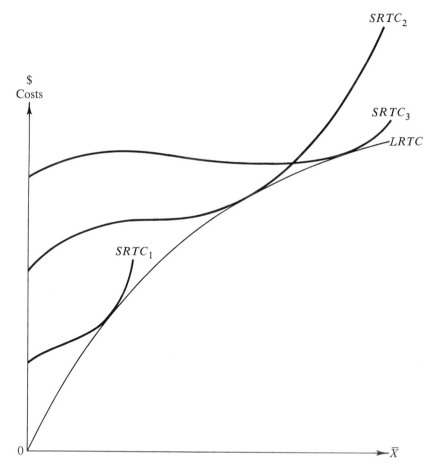

FIGURE 4–14. The Relation Between Short-Run and Long-Run Total Cost Curves Under Increasing Returns to Scale When the Production Function is Strictly Quasi-Concave.

shape like that for the linear homogeneous production function as drawn in Figure 4–6, but it may not now be used as a representative in relative terms for all slices of the production function through the z_2-axis. The absolute levels of employment of factor services now do make a difference, just as they did for the function exhibiting increasing returns to scale—and it is impossible to standardize a product curve using relative inputs and output.

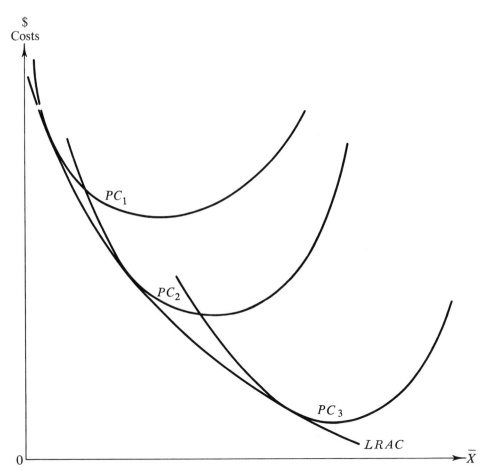

FIGURE 4–15.   The Relation Between Plant Curves and Declining Long-Run Average Costs When the Production Function is Strictly Quasi-Concave.

The Phase II and Phase III of the product curves correspond exactly with those that existed for linear homogeneous functions except that they are clouded by the fact that part of the reason for the decline from an absolute maximum is due to the effects of absolute amounts of factors. A proportion of 5 to 1 for factors z_1 and z_2 may be acceptable when output is 20—in the sense of placing us in Phase II—but may be unacceptable when the output is 100. Proportions alone no longer dictate whether input mixes are in Phase II or III. The short-run average variable, average total, and marginal costs which we get from this type of product curve rise uniformly. The long-run total cost curve, which must reflect the diminishing returns to scale of output, must appear as Curve C of Figure 4–3 rather than Curve A. Because expenditure curves that jump by constant amounts will yield less than constantly increasing amounts of product, long-run costs, depicted on Figure 4–17, must be rising by increasing amounts.

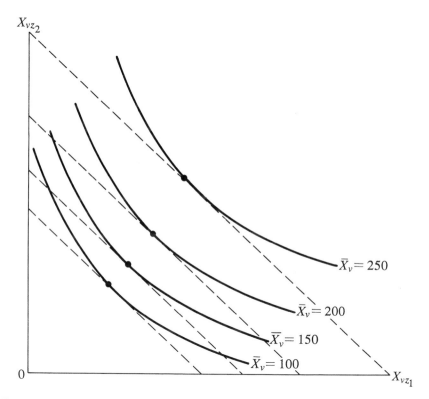

FIGURE 4–16.   Isoquants of a Production Surface Revealing Decreasing Returns to Scale.

A COMBINATION OF THE THREE CONFIGURATIONS FOR THE PRODUCTION FUNCTION.   We may combine the three types of function we have considered —the trumpet-shaped, the linear homogeneous, and the strictly concave— defined over the whole relevant-input space. Then the set M of input mixes, if it exists, consists of all mixes lying on rays from the origin over which output is zero. Over any ray from the origin with positive output we assume that output rises from zero by increasing amounts for a time, passes through a linear homogeneous phase, and then passes into a phase in which it rises by decreasing amounts. We have depicted the function in its rising range in Figure 4–18.

The long-run total cost function for such a production function is shown on Figure 4–19. It rises by decreasing amounts from the zero output point, reflecting the initial increasing returns to scale of the function, then for a very

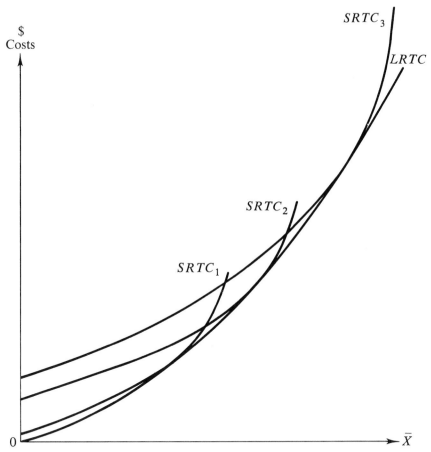

FIGURE 4–17. The Relation Between Short-Run and Long-Run Total Cost Curves Under Decreasing Returns to Scale.

brief segment of output it rises by constant amounts, after which it passes from the linear homogeneous segment to rise by increasing amounts in the manner of the globally strictly concave function. Average total cost declines in the first phase, moves sidewise in the second, and rises in the third, reflecting the reflex performance of average product.

Marginal product rises first by increasing, then decreasing, amounts, by constant amounts in the linear homogeneous phase, and by decreasing amounts in the concave phase: therefore, marginal cost in the long run will be falling, constant, and rising, equalling average cost in the linear homogeneous phase where the slope of the function equals the slope of a ray from the origin just touching the function at that point.

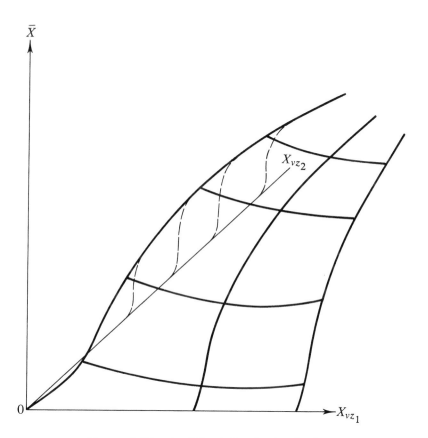

FIGURE 4–18.   An Eclectic Production Surface.

The product curves will also reflect these three segments: Phase I will end after a concave portion at a brief linear portion, and will be followed by a concave phase II. The relations among long-run and short-run average cost curves are shown in Figure 4–20, and, once more, as we should suspect, the former are made up of long-term segments of the latter.

AN ECONOMIC JUSTIFICATION FOR U-SHAPED COST CURVES.   One interesting aspect of the relation between the U-shaped short-run plant average total cost curve and the U-shaped long-run average cost curve is important. Note that

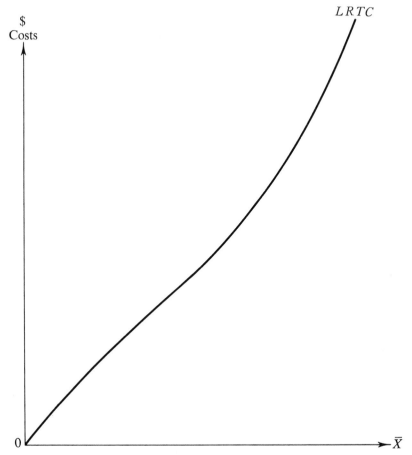

FIGURE 4–19. The Long-Run Total Cost Function for the Eclectic Production Function.

to the left of the long-term average cost minimum the short-run plant curves are tangent to the curve to the left of their own minima, whereas to the right of the minimum point of the long-term average cost curve the plant curves are tangent at points to the right of their own minima. Only at the minimum point of the long-term curve does the minimum correspond to the minimum of a short-run curve. This implies several interesting insights: as we have already noted, the use of a given plant optimally in the sense of producing at its output of lowest average cost is a different thing from producing a given output optimally when all factors and inputs are variable. To produce any given output most cheaply when all inputs are variable, one would use a given plant curve at less than or more than its minimum-cost output, except at the minimum-cost point on the long-term curve.

Economic theorists have ordinarily taken these U-shaped long- and short-run average cost curves to be typical of long-run and short-run plant cost behavior in the realistic economy. Some practical reasons for this choice will become apparent as we go forward with our profit maximization analysis with variable outputs. But some degree of justification can be put forward on technological and economic grounds. First, in the short run, the firm's plant and equipment are held fixed in quantity. At very low outputs, therefore, to the extent the physical layout is not divisible and removable from the scene, it will probably be in excess presence compared with inputs variable in the short run, and because it is not a perfect substitute for those inputs, average costs of small outputs will be large. However, as variable inputs are added to the fixed plant and equipment, average costs may be expected to decline for two reasons: (1) in terms of factor *proportions* the excessive presence of the fixed factor is reduced and therefore costs must fall, and (2) the greater absolute amount of the variable factors allows certain reorganizations of their

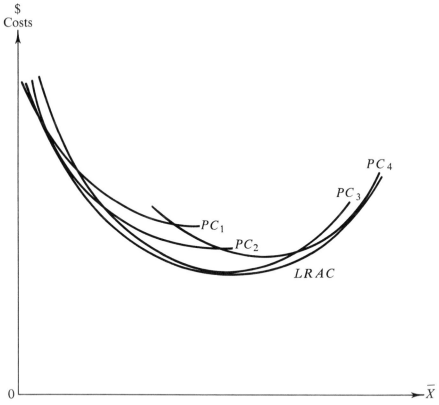

FIGURE 4–20. The Relation of Short-Run and Long-Run Average Total Cost Curves when Average Costs Are U-Shaped.

productive relationships to be realized, which further enhance output. With one bricklayer employed, he must stop bricklaying, get the bricks and mortar, and start bricklaying again; with two men employed, one can remain at the site of the bricklaying and the other carry materials to him. The result may very well be more work accomplished than if the second man were set to work in the same manner as the first.

After a time, however, such internal economies to the firm with a fixed plant and equipment become exhausted and the average variable cost stops declining and starts to rise. Meanwhile, average fixed cost continues to decline and carries average total cost with it for a time before the latter turns up when the average variable cost rise outweighs the average fixed cost fall. Why, however, does not the elimination of these internal economies lead to a mere flattening out of the average variable cost curve into a straight line? Indeed, the economist believes this may frequently happen over some range of outputs; but he asserts that ultimately as more and more variable factors are added to the fixed plant and equipment, efficiency begins to decline, and the variable factors become less and less substitutable for the fixed factor. This turns the curve upward to complete the U-shape.

In the long run, however, we cannot fall back upon a fixed plant and equipment to explain the U-shaped average total (= average variable) cost curve. How then does the economist justify it? Here again he finds one factor that is not perfectly divisible and variable, although it is no longer plant and equipment. Usually he believes that management and coordination become increasingly efficient for a time as plant size rises along with output, that there is an optimum size of plant and output for management to co-ordinate most efficiently, that beyond that plant size inefficiencies begin to creep into the overseer process, and costs begin to climb. One cannot simply go into the market and buy more management as one would buy more labor, and even if one could there would be no guarantee that the new larger management would be as efficient as the old for higher output levels and larger plants.

For these reasons we shall adopt the U-shaped cost curve, with the possibility of a linear segment at its minimum, as typical for all of the firms which we shall analyze. Although such cost curves are implied by the hybrid homogeneous function we have just discussed, they are also implied by the nonhomogeneous production function defined in our postulates, although by requiring that it be strictly concave over the set M^* we have eliminated the possibility of linear segments. At this point of our analysis, therefore, we shall revert back to the restrictions of Producer Postulates 4 and 5, using the U-shaped long-run and short-run average cost curves it yields, and its rising marginal cost curves.

The Derivation of Propositions About Input Mixes

We have spent a great deal of time going back to the interrelationships of the model to find out the alternatives that the various cost curves could approach in configuration. This aids us in discerning information about the cost curves of System [II'–4]. Let us now see if we can glean any information about what happens to the various demands for inputs as we shock the system by (1) an own-price change, other prices and output fixed; (2) an other-price change, own-price and other prices as well as output being fixed; and (3) an output change, all prices fixed. Our discussion will be able to draw upon the analogous displacement analysis for the consumer and thus we will be able to move more rapidly. We assume an interior solution on an isoquant whose level is fixed by the data. We shall then shock the system in the manners mentioned to determine the relevant slopes of a typical input demand function in System [II'].

THE SLOPES OF THE DEMAND FUNCTIONS FOR INPUTS

Let us once more remove some of the clutter by eliminating the subscript v for the firm, although its implicit presence will be understood. Then we may turn to Figure 4–21, which finds the firm at an initial equilibrium $\mathbf{X}^\circ$ on a fixed isoquant at a fixed set of prices for z_1 and z_2.

OWN-PRICE CHANGE. Suppose now P_{z_1} falls by a small amount. The expenditure line would shift from MN to $M'N'$, but the constraint that the firm relocate on the *same* isoquant means that the analogue of the income effect cannot arise in this situation. The income effect of a price change on the consumer was a result of that consumer's budget constraint: if we had indeed placed a total expenditure constraint upon the firm rather than an output constraint it would have occurred in this case too. But because we did not place an expenditure constraint on the firm, we may eliminate the complication of the income effect from the analysis, so that the only effect operating on the firm's new equilibrium choice at $\mathbf{X}^*$ will be the substitution effect, s_{11}.

The evaluation of this effect is peculiarly easy, inasmuch as we are constrained both before and after the price change to be on the same isoquant. Because the slope of the total expenditure line is less steep after the price change, it must be tangent to the isoquant to the right of the old equilibrium. Therefore, $s_{11} = (\partial X^\circ_{z_1}/\partial P_{z_1})\, dP_{z_1} < 0$. That is, a fall in the input price must always lead to an increase in the amount purchased of that input, output remaining unchanged.

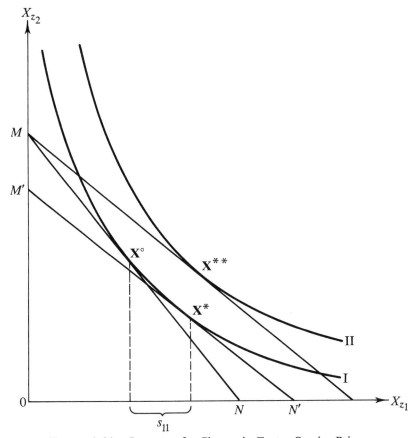

FIGURE 4–21.   Impacts of a Change in Factor Service Price.

OTHER-PRICE CHANGE. From this conclusion it must follow from the figure that $(\partial X^{\circ}_{z_2}/\partial P_{z_1})\,dP_{z_1} = s_{21} > 0$, for the isoquant's slope in the interior is always negative. We are travelling down the same isoquant, which must mean a reduction of other factors when one is increased. This result, however, as in the case of the other-price substitution effect for the consumer, follows only because there are two goods and no more in the problem. For more than two inputs, however, some may rise in usage, others fall, and others remain constant.

OUTPUT CHANGE. Suppose we now move the total expenditure line outward to a small degree holding prices constant. Once more we may draw upon our analysis of the consumer to see that although the new equilibrium at the new specified output level must have the same slope as the old, that may occur to the left or the right of the value $X^{\circ}_{z_1}$. This possibility set is shown in Figure 4–22. Therefore, a rise in output may lead to a rise, fall, or

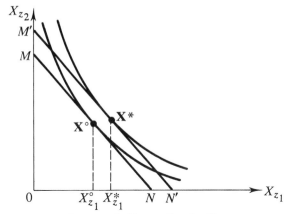

a. Increase in Factor Service Usage

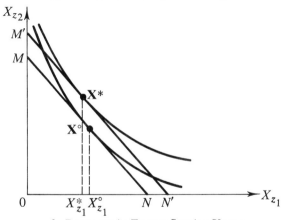

b. Decrease in Factor Service Usage

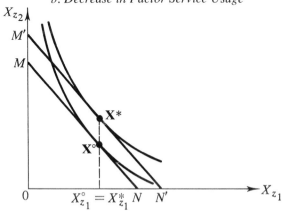

c. No Change in Factor Service Usage

FIGURE 4–22. Possible Impacts on Factor Usage of a Rise in Output.

constancy in the amount of input taken. We shall refer to this change in demand for an input by virtue of a change in output levels as the *expansion effect*, and denote it $e_{z_1 J}$ to symbolize the impact on input z_1 of change in the output of $\overline{X}_J$.

What this implies is that there may exist inferior inputs, similar to inferior consumer goods, which are more suitable to production at lower levels than to outputs at higher levels. We can be a bit more explicit concerning its causes than we could be in consumer theory however. Consider the vertical lines through $X_{z_1}^\circ$ in Figure 4–22. As we rise along it, X_{z_1} remains constant while X_{z_2} increases as the variable factor. We are, then, following the product curve for z_2 at this fixed value of X_{z_1} and the straight line is in fact that product curve viewed directly overhead. Because the production function is globally strictly concave over M^* by Producer Postulate 5, we know the marginal product of z_2 rises by decreasing amounts. We may apply the analysis of footnote 2 of Chapter 3 to see that since this implies that $\partial^2 T_J / \partial X_{z_2}^2 < 0$, in order for $X_{z_1}^* < X_{z_1}^\circ$ it will be necessary that the marginal product of z_1 fall as z_2 increases its presence. That is, the presence of more z_2 must make the constant amount of z_1 smaller in productivity at the margin.

Conclusion

Our analysis of the decisionmaking of the firm in the current model has operated under the constraint that output is fixed. It is, as we have shown, a model that minimizes the costs of production of any given output level. Therefore, because no firm that is maximizing profits in any environment can do so unless its costs are minimal, the current System [II'] is applicable to all forms of rivalrous and nonrivalrous competition.

On the basis of strictly convex isoquants (implied by the strict concavity of the production surface over M^*) we have seen that own-price substitution effects are negative and other-price substitution effects are nonevaluable. However, we noted the lack of complicating income effect in the analysis, which made it simpler than displacement work in the consumer model.

When the level of output was changed, however, in an equilibrium displacement, we noted perhaps the most interesting result of the analysis: the possibility of inferior inputs characterizing production. The fact that our production function is strictly concave over M^* merely implies that the marginal product of an input falls continuously as it increases in quantity, but this does not constrain the behavior of the marginal products of other inputs in any simple way as this one increases. Consequently, the expansion effect of an output change upon any input is not evaluable.

Selected Readings

1. D. V. T. BEAR, "Inferior Inputs and the Theory of the Firm," *Journal of Political Economy*, LXXIII (1965), pp. 287–289. Further discussion of the inferior input.

2. CHARLES J. HITCH and ROLAND N. MCKEAN, *The Economics of Defense in the Nuclear Age* (New York: Atheneum, 1965), pp. 105–142. An application of least-cost reasoning to a military problem.

3. RICHARD H. LEFTWICH, *The Price System and Resource Allocation* (New York: Holt, Rinehart and Winston, Third Edition, 1966), pp. 111–116. A very good arithmetic and geometric presentation of the symmetry of Phases I and III for the linear homogeneous production function.

4. OM P. TANGRI, "Omissions in the Treatment of the Law of Variable Proportions," *American Economic Review*, LVI (1966), pp. 484–493. This short article is valuable because it shows the shapes of cost curves in Phase III of the product curves.

5. JACOB VINER, "Cost Curves and Supply Curves," reprinted in G. J. Stigler and K. E. Boulding, *Readings in Price Theory* (Chicago: Irwin, 1952), pp. 198–232. A classic presentation of the derivation of supply curves from cost curves.

CHAPTER 5

The Theory of the Firm in
Nonrivalrous Competition: Variable Output
and Maximum Profits

OUR ARBITRARY assumption in the first model we constructed for Firm v that it was constrained to maximize profits subject to a supply constraint was valuable in that it allowed us to derive the optimal cost curves for the production of every product for each firm. These minimum cost curve solutions are those that will rule for all firms regardless of the rivalrous or nonrivalrous environment in which they find themselves, because these aspects of their environment as reflected in product markets do not affect their best input mixes for producing any given output.

The Determination of Output

We must now move, however, to the next stage of our modelbuilding and will assume the existence of pure competition where no individual or firm has any impact upon the price of any good or factor service. In it we shall allow the firm perfect freedom to select that output level which maximizes its profits. That is, it will select that output which, when it is produced at the minimum total costs (long-run or short-run depending upon the assumptions we make) and sold at the price given by the market for the firm's output, yields the firm its highest attainable surplus over those costs. We substitute the following for Producer Postulate 10*:

PRODUCER POSTULATE 10. The producer is capable of producing any Y_j or Z_i, but must in the event produce at most one of the goods in the positive amount he deems best.

This postulate means that we have freed the firm to vary its output, that it may hypothetically produce any output of any good to see what profits it may make on it, but that when it produces it must choose only one good.

This last requirement is not an essential one, but we have made it in order to simplify the analysis.

The maximization procedure under the new freedom proceeds exactly as the model of the previous chapter proceeded, and obtains the cost curves for every level of output for every good for Firm v. But it then goes one step farther. Instead of assuming the profit function contains a given amount of a given good, as we did in $[F'–2]$, we must now define a profit function for the firm for every good in the economy as a potential output and for variable quantities of inputs *and output*. Let us write these functions into the inter-relationships as substitutes for $[F'–2]$, as we have already done in the definition of $[F–2]$ on page 145.

SHORT-RUN OUTPUT DETERMINATION

Now, taking these products one at a time and successively, we must deter-mine that point in input-output space $[\overline{X}, \mathbf{X}]$—or that level of output and that input mix—which will maximize the firm's profits in $[F–2]$. For sim-plicity we may decompose this simultaneous determination into two steps. We already know, for the short run, the minimum total, variable, average total, average variable, and marginal costs for each level of output of the firm and for each product. Using our deduction of the U-shaped average variable cost curve, we have drawn the total cost curve for some typical product on Figure 5–1, with total fixed and variable costs drawn in as well. Also, we know from the set of data the price P_J or P_{Z_i} of the good in question. From this information, it should be rather simple to determine that output which yields the maximum profit when the given good is produced. From knowledge of the best output and profits for this product and every other product, it will be an easy matter to work back to the optimal or maximal-profit point $[\overline{X}^\circ, \mathbf{X}^\circ]$.

We may draw on Figure 5–1 a *total revenue function*, TR, to depict the manner in which the firm's receipts vary as total output rises and is sold at the given price. The assumption of our present environment is that the firm can sell any quantity of output at the given price: it is so small a factor in the sale of the product that its quantity offered to the market does not make any perceptible impression on it. Therefore, the average revenue the firm gets for any quantity of sales of the product is equal to the *marginal revenue* it gets, because each additional unit of output sold yields the same revenue as every previous unit. Moreover, average revenue and marginal revenue must equal price, because every unit is sold at that value. Therefore, the total revenue curve is a straight line through the origin, the latter point of course depicting

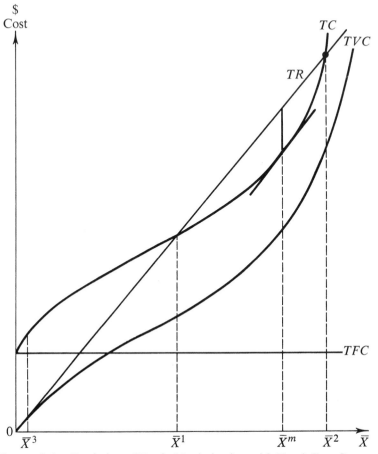

FIGURE 5–1. Depiction of Profit Maximization with Total Cost Curves.

the fact that revenue will be zero for zero output, and with slope equal to the price of the product.

The difference between the total revenue curve and the total cost curve, *TC*, at any output depicts total profit $\pi_{v/J}$ for that amount of that product produced in the optimal short-run fashion. We seek, then, by Producer Postulate 6, to maximize this difference for the firm, selecting that good to produce, that quantity of that good, and that short-run manner of producing that quantity of that good, which yield the desired maximum. For any given good, how can we be assured that the output level we choose yields the highest possible profit figure available under the circumstances in which the firm finds itself?

First, we can say that if there is a segment of the total revenue curve that lies above the total cost curve the maximum profit output (if it exists at all) must occur in that segment. Suppose this is the case. Where in the interval of output quantities corresponding to that segment of the total revenue curve does the maximum profit point occur? On Figure 5–1, the outputs along the interval $\bar{X}^1$ to $\bar{X}^2$ yield positive profits, so the maximum output must occur for some output in this interval. Consider the outputs to the left of $\bar{X}^m$: in this interval profit grows as we move from lesser to higher outputs, as is evident from a study of the difference between the total revenue and total cost curves. This difference continues to grow until the point $\bar{X}^m$ is reached, beyond which it declines, indicating that profits shrink. For a very brief time in the neighborhood of $\bar{X}^m$ total profits are neither rising nor falling, but are remaining constant. At $\bar{X}^m$ therefore the slope of the total cost curve (*TC*) is equal to the slope of the total revenue curve (*TR*), inasmuch as the curves are neither approaching one another nor diverging from one another. At this point we have reached maximum profits. Before that point is reached in the interval of nonnegative profits every unit of output is adding profit—marginal profit is positive—and after that level of output is reached every unit adds negative profit: at $\bar{X}^m$ marginal profit is zero.

We may put this same analysis in terms of average and marginal curves, as we have drawn them on Figure 5–2. The average and marginal revenue curves, as we have indicated earlier, coincide and we have marked them *P*, which is in fact the constant level of both these magnitudes and the price of the good in the market. Marginal cost (*MC*) and average total cost (*ATC*) we have drawn in also. Our criterion from the analysis of Figure 5–1 for the maximum profit output is that marginal profit be zero. Because marginal profit is merely marginal revenue *minus* marginal cost, marginal profit will be zero where marginal revenue equals marginal cost; however, profits will be maximized at such a point only if, when we increase output, marginal cost lies above marginal revenue. This last qualification must be added to eliminate an equality between the two that occurs when marginal cost is falling, as at $\bar{X}^3$, for if marginal cost is falling while marginal revenue is constant, profits cannot have reached a maximum. This is true because at the equality marginal profit is zero, but to the right of the point marginal profit is positive. Therefore, obviously, it cannot pay the firm to stop at the equality point. This point may be located on Figure 5–1 where the slope of the total cost curve equals the slope of the total revenue curve and where the total cost curve lies above the total revenue curve.

The amount of profit may be determined from Figure 5–2 by determining average profit for the maximal output and multiplying it by that amount of output. The average profit is the difference between average revenue (or price) and average total cost for the optimal output, and this times output equals the profit rectangle *ABCD* shown on the diagram.

Note several characteristics about this profit magnitude. First the maximum profit need not be positive: it may be zero or even negative. This situation is shown in Figure 5–3, and the minimum loss or negative profit is *PABC*. That is, the maximization of profit may imply the minimization of losses in the short run when, contrary to our model, fixed costs exist for the firm. The basic

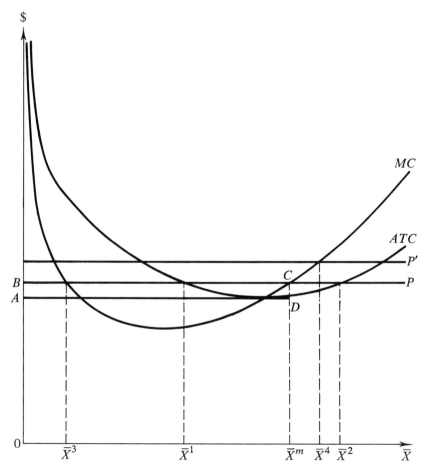

FIGURE 5–2. Depiction of Profit Maximization with Average and Marginal Cost Curves.

explanation of this is that in the short run fixed costs springing from the existence of the plant and equipment burden the firm, and must be met whether or not the firm produces output. Therefore, if the marginal cost— which is the change in total variable costs as well as total cost—is less than price, the unit of output contributes all of the cost that could be escaped by not producing it, and if marginal cost is above average variable costs, the unit adds something that can be used to pay the fixed costs. Only if the inter-section of the price and marginal cost curves lies below average variable cost can that output never be produced, for then the unit would not recover the variable costs that could be avoided by not producing it.

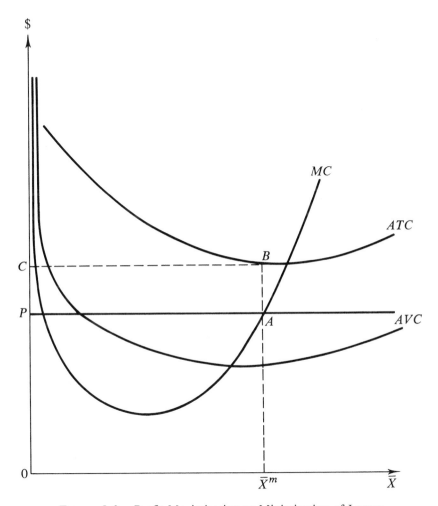

FIGURE 5-3. Profit Maximization as Minimization of Losses.

LONG-RUN OUTPUT DETERMINATION

In the long run the determination of output under pure competition will proceed in similar fashion. The given price for the product will yield a total revenue function, the analysis of Chapter 4 will yield a minimal total cost curve when all inputs are variable—including plant and equipment—and long-run output will fall where marginal cost equals price if marginal cost is rising at this output. Because there are no fixed costs, in order for the firm to produce this output profits to the firm must be nonnegative.

We have seen that each average cost figure on the long-run curve implies a given size of plant that yields the lowest average cost for that output level. Therefore, a determination of a long-run output implies that if the firm in pure competition would expect the price of the product to remain at a given level, it would build that size of plant which yielded the long-run maximum profit and use it in the short-run maximum profit manner. This is true because the long- and short-run prices would be the same, and therefore average revenue curves would be identical, and because at the critical point where long-run marginal cost equals price, short-run marginal cost for the relevant plant does too, inasmuch as the long-run marginal cost is merely a point on that short-run marginal cost curve. Thus, the long-run and short-run profit motivation is in perfect accord: the firm does not have to sacrifice short-run profits to make maximum long-run profits. Because the long-run analysis is used primarily to decide the optimum size of plant and equipment the firm should build, the long-run average cost curve has been called the *planning curve.*

Note that because the price in the long run must be expected to be at least as high as the minimum average point on the long-run average cost curve, the firm will build a plant just large enough to produce at its own lowest average cost if the expected price is at the long-run minimum average cost, or, if expected price is above that point, will build a larger plant than that which yields the desired output at its short-run minimum and overutilize it. However, as we shall see, there are good reasons, external to the firm in pure competition, why it will in fact produce that plant whose minimum average total cost occurs at the minimum point of its long-run average cost curve.

In our model we are operating in a long-run environment even in the short-term week; the paradox occurs, of course, because of our assumption that every week the firm may purchase just that input mix of all factors and produce any one output that it wishes to. It owns nothing at the beginning of the week and nothing at the end. These simplifying assumptions allow us to study long-run phenomena even within a short-run matrix. We shall, then, state our additional interrelationships resulting when we add output as a variable for the case when all inputs are variable, or, as it is usually referred to, the long run.

First, we assume that the firm has undertaken to compute all of its hypothetical maximum profit potentials through the production of every good and has derived a maximum profit figure for each good in [*F*–2]. Then we require that it select that maximum profit figure which is the greatest over all goods as a reflection of Producer Postulate 6:

$$\pi_{v/k}^{\circ} = \underset{Y_J, Z_i}{\text{maximum}}\ (\pi_{v/1}, \ldots, \pi_{v/n}, \pi_{v/Z_1}, \ldots, \pi_{v/Z_m}). \qquad [F\text{--}8]$$

Because the firm has the option of not producing—having no fixed costs that might induce it to produce at negative profit—it must make at least zero profits. If profits are negative for its best choice of output in [F–8], we require that its output be zero, whereas if profit is zero or positive, it may produce positively.

Now let $\bar{X}_{vk}^{\circ}$ symbolize the maximum-profit output of the maximum-profit good. Then we require that the firm, if it produces any good, produce only its best good, and that the following replace our interrelationship [F'–4]:

$$1.\quad \bar{X}_J^{\circ}(\pi_{v/k}^{\circ} - \pi_J^{\circ}) = 0.$$

$$2.\quad \bar{X}_{Z_i}^{\circ}\ (\pi_{v/k}^{\circ} - \pi_{Z_i}^{\circ}) = 0. \qquad [F\text{--}4]$$

But in order to determine the very best profit opportunity we must first determine the maximum-profit output of *every* good. To [F–3] we add the condition (continuing to use Y_J as the example) that marginal revenue from the hypothetical sale of the good not exceed marginal cost (symbolized MC_J):

$$3.\quad P_J - MC_J \leqq 0. \qquad [F\text{--}3]$$

To the conditions of [F–5] we must add the constraint that if the inequality rules in [F–3–3] the optimum output is zero:

$$4.\quad \bar{X}_J^{\circ}(P_J - MC_J) = 0. \qquad [F\text{--}5]$$

And, to [F–7] we must add nonnegativity constraints on output and profit:

$$4.\quad X_J^{\circ} \geqq 0.$$

$$5.\quad \pi_J^{\circ} \geqq 0. \qquad [F\text{--}7]$$

We may now solve out interrelationships [F–1] through [F–8] to obtain the new set of solutions which includes the variable-output assumption:

$$1.\quad X_{vj/J} = D_{vj/J}(\mathbf{P}, K_{vu}), \qquad j = 1, \ldots, n, \quad J = 1, \ldots, n$$

$$2.\quad X_{vz_i/J} = D_{vz_i/J}(\mathbf{P}, K_{vu}), \qquad i = 1, \ldots, m, \quad J = 1, \ldots, n$$

$$3.\quad X_{vj/Z_i} = D_{vj/Z_i}(\mathbf{P}, K_{vu}), \qquad j = 1, \ldots, n, \quad i = 1, \ldots, m$$

$$4.\quad X_{vz_i/Z_i} = D_{vz_i/Z_i}(\mathbf{P}, K_{vu}), \qquad i = 1, \ldots, m, \quad i = 1, \ldots, m$$

$$5.\quad \bar{X}_{vJ} = S_{vJ}(\mathbf{P}, K_{vu}), \qquad J = 1, \ldots, n$$

$$6.\quad \bar{X}_{vZ_i} = S_{vZ_i}(\mathbf{P}, K_{vu}), \qquad i = 1, \ldots, m$$

$$7. \quad X_{vu/J} = \frac{K_{vu}(\sum_j X_{vj/J}P_j + \sum_i X_{vz_i/J}P_{z_i})}{1 - K_{vu}r}$$

$$8. \quad X_{vu/Z_i} = \frac{K_{vu}(\sum_j X_{vj/Z_i}P_j + \sum_i X_{vz_i/Z_I}P_{z_i})}{1 - K_{vu}r}$$

$$9. \quad C_{vJ} = \sum_j X_{vj/J}P_j + \sum_i X_{vz_i/J}P_{z_i} + X_{vu/J}r$$

$$10. \quad C_{vZ_i} = \sum_j X_{vj/Z_i}P_j + \sum_i X_{vz_i/Z_i}P_{z_i} + X_{vu/Z_i}r$$

$$11. \quad \pi_{v/J} = \bar{X}_{vJ}P_J - C_{vJ}$$

$$12. \quad \pi_{v/Z_i} = \bar{X}_{vZ_i}P_{Z_i} - C_{vZ_i}$$

$$13. \quad \overset{\circ}{\pi}_{v/k} = \max_{i,J} (\pi_{v/J}, \pi_{v/Z_i})$$

$$14. \quad X^{\circ}_{vj} = X_{vj/k}$$

$$15. \quad X^{\circ}_{vz_i} = X_{vz_i/k}$$

$$16. \quad X^{\circ}_{vu} = X_{vu/k}$$

$$17. \quad \bar{X}^{\circ}_{vk} = \bar{X}_{vk}$$

$$18. \quad \bar{X}^{\circ}_{vJ \neq k} = \bar{X}^{\circ}_{vZ_i \neq k} = 0. \tag{II}$$

Despite the complex appearance of these functions they are quite straight-forward in their interpretation. Under the assumption that the specific good behind the slash is produced, System [II–1, 2, 3, 4, 7, 8] defines inputs that yield minimum costs for the best output levels, which are given by System [II–5, 6]. System [II–9, 10] defines these minimum costs, System [II–11, 12] defines the implied profits, and System [II–13] explicitly yields the highest obtainable amount of profits and implicitly names that good (if any) which is to be produced by the firm. System [II–14, 15, 16, 17, 18] defines the equi-librium levels of inputs and outputs. This completes the construction of the submodel of firm behavior in the purely competitive environment when production functions are of the form postulated in Producer Postulates 4 and 5, or, alternatively, meet any other restrictions that yield U-shaped average total costs and rising marginal costs.

Displacing the Equilibrium

We have in this complete solution to the firm submodel for pure competi-tion one new relationship or function that is not transparently simple: the supply curve of output. Note that, in the space which contains all $n + m$ possible goods outputs, we have a corner solution in that the firm is allowed to produce only one good; but even were we not to impose that restriction the firm would not in general produce some of every good in the economy. Therefore, we assume that such changes in the data that we impose will not be large enough to lead the firm to change its production to another type of good. Moreover, we assume that the firm we choose to analyze is producing *some* positive output in the initial equilibrium. Let us then analyze the slope of the functions for input demand and output supply in the own-price and other-price directions.

AN ANALYSIS OF THE DEMAND FOR INPUTS

In our displacement of the minimum-cost submodel of Chapter 4 we changed prices on the assumption that the amount of output was fixed, and we changed output with the assumption that the prices of inputs and of that output were fixed. We shall shock the present system by varying only the prices of inputs and of the product.

OWN-PRICE CHANGE. On Figure 4–21, assume that P_{z_1} falls, shifting the equilibrium from its initial value $\mathbf{X}°$. Now, *if* the firm were constrained to produce as much output as it could with the fixed expenditure of its initial position, then it would move *à la* the consumer to a new equilibrium at $\mathbf{X}^{**}$. But we have emphasized that under the perfect freedom the firm has, it is not so constrained. Rather, with the new input-price situation it will move to a new output level that maximizes its profits, and no reason exists why that new equilibrium will be at $\mathbf{X}^{**}$ on the isoquant labelled *II* in the figure. Therefore, our simple analysis with diagrams that was so useful for illustrating displacements of the consumer's equilibrium fails us for the firm.

A fall in the price of an input may be seen to set off two independent effects on the absorption of the relevant input. First, it will induce an expansion or decline in the consumption of the input because the level of output will change if marginal costs change, and, second, a substitution toward or away from the input whose price has changed may occur, even if we abstract from the induced change of output. If the price of an input rises, we may state without proof that its use by the firm will always decline, under the assumptions that the firm is maximizing profits and that it has a globally concave production function over M^*.[1]

The sum of both of these effects will never result in a movement of the demand for the input in a direction opposite to that of the own-price change. On Figure 5–4 we have illustrated this result for the case of a rise in P_{z_1}.

---

[1] For a proof see Robert E. Kuenne, *The Theory of General Economic Equilibrium* (Princeton: Princeton University Press, 1963), pp. 172–175.

We have broken up the movement from $X^{\circ}_{z_1}$ to $X^{*}_{z_1}$ into two components: (1) the movement from $X^{\circ}_{z_1}$ to X'_{z_1}, which would have resulted if output had been constant, and which will always be negative or opposite to the sign of the price change; and (2) the movement from X'_{z_1} to $X^{*}_{z_1}$, which represents the (negative in this instance) expansion effect. We have no way of knowing

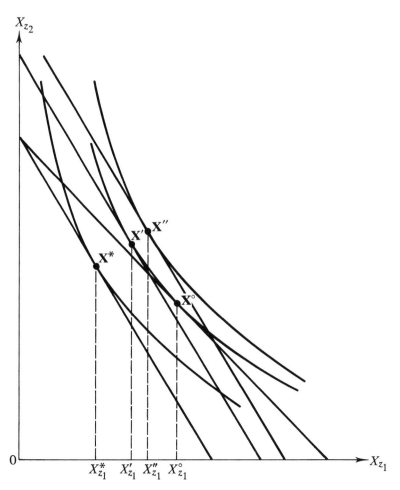

FIGURE 5–4.   Possible Effects of a Rise in Factor Service Price When Output Is a Variable.

which isoquant this new equilibrium will fall upon, and have merely assumed that it will be the one used in the figure. We do know, however, that the new equilibrium expenditure line must be tangent to the new isoquant to the left of $X^{\circ}_{z_1}$ by virtue of our unproven assertion. But this could mean that the new critical isoquant might be below the isoquant of the original equilibrium or above it. That is, this restriction is not sufficient to guarantee that output will *fall* when the price of an input rises, or rise when the price of an input falls. Both possibilities are illustrated on Figure 5–4 at $X_{z_1}^*$ and X_{z_1}'' respectively.

OTHER-PRICE CHANGE. Once more, the amount demanded of an input with a change in price of another input will be the sum of an expansion effect and an other-price substitution effect of the type we have just described. However, the latter will not be determinate, because the input in question may be a substitute or a complement of the input whose price changed, and this indeterminateness will be compounded by an ambiguous expansion effect. Therefore, the total change may be positive, negative, or zero in terms of the direction relative to the price change.

PRODUCT PRICE CHANGE. Suppose, now, that the price of the product were to rise: what will happen to the demand for the typical input? Because marginal costs are rising at the old equilibrium, the sign of the change in input demand will depend upon what happens to the demand for the input as output expands, prices constant. But, we may draw upon our knowledge of what happens to the demand for consumers' goods as income expands, prices constant, to see that although we expect the normal case to be one where the amount demanded for the input rises when output rises, the opposite may occur. The *expansion effect* of an output rise—which is analogous to an income effect for the consumer—may be negative in the abnormal case, and we may refer to such an input as an *inferior* input.

We have seen in Chapter 4 that the economic meaning of input inferiority is that the amount demanded of it may be reduced as the firm expands in size of plant and equipment or in production with a given plant and equipment. For example, it may well be that when the firm is small or producing relatively small quantities of output, it will employ large amounts of trucking services to deliver its product, but that when it grows larger it may reduce them in favor of rail services. In these circumstances, trucking services would be an inferior input.

We must note here for further reference that global strict concavity of the production function over M^* implies that the marginal cost of producing the output rises as output rises. That is, as we travel up the production function, the hill must rise by decreasing amounts in every uphill direction. Our consumer theory did not contain this restriction because we could not travel on the preference function at will: we could go no higher than the budget line. In the case of the firm, however, it is capable of going anywhere on the hill that it desires, and consequently we must take into account the shape of the hill in *every* direction.

In the case of the consumer, when we displaced the equilibrium we went from one budget plane to a new budget plane. At both the old and the new equilibrium—very close together by design—we had to worry about the shape of the function only at the relevant slices made by the respective budget planes. At neither point could the consumer get off the budget plane. Thus, for example, if the preference function were shaped like the bell of a trumpet, because the consumer would be in the old and new situations at two different levels of the hill, he could not go higher and would not go lower, and the shape of the hill in the sideways direction at both equilibria was what counted. Thus the quality of quasi-concavity was sufficient to guarantee us that the consumer was at a *constrained* maximum.

The same thing was true of the firm when we arbitrarily imposed the necessity that it produce at *fixed* levels of supply. This meant that it was forced, when marginal costs were positive, to locate at one isoquant, and the shape of the production function above and below that level was unimportant. The firm could minimize costs by being assured that at its chosen input mix it could not reduce costs by moving sideways. Therefore, by imposing the assumption of global quasi-concavity in the strict sense upon the production function at every output for each firm, we assured the possibility of minimum costs at the tangency of expenditure line and isoquant.

But now we have freed the firm to produce whatever level of output it chooses: it can roam at will over its production surface. Thus, the shape of the function in the uphill direction becomes important. For example, if the production function rises by increasing amounts in the product direction the firm obtains increasing returns to scale of output. If its long-run marginal cost curve intersects the price of the product in the former's falling portion, we have seen that maximum profits cannot have been attained, for further units of output will bring positive marginal profits to the firm. Therefore, our initial position will not be a true profit maximum.

Indeed, suppose the production surface is linear and homogeneous. Providing only that it is strictly quasi-concave, we know that short-run marginal costs will be rising, so that if we are constrained to produce with a fixed amount of some input, we will have rising marginal costs at the equilibrium. But suppose all inputs are variable: then marginal costs are constant for any given set of input prices. That is to say, if we walk up the hill following any ray from the origin, our path will be linear, indicating that marginal costs are constant because total costs are rising by a constant amount. But in this situation it may be (1) impossible to get marginal cost to equal marginal revenue at any point, so that either there is no finite maximum-profit output if marginal revenue is above marginal cost, or that maximum-profit output is zero if marginal revenue is below marginal cost, or (2) the two curves may coincide throughout their length so that the firm's maximum-profit output is indeterminate, unless we can find some manner of restricting the output of the firm by such phenomena as capacity limitations.

We insist, therefore, that marginal cost be rising at our points of equilibrium. This means that the shape we imposed on the preference function in the sideways direction, which was such that we got a Phase II side profile, with its implied fall in marginal product, must be imposed on the function *in all directions*. As we expand any input or group of inputs, up to and including all inputs, we must get decreasing returns to those inputs. As a minimum this condition must hold true in the immediate neighborhood of the old equilibrium, because for small displacements from it we shall find the new equilibrium within such a small neighborhood, and the condition of rising marginal cost will be met there whatever is true outside of that neighborhood. However, we have been more restrictive in requiring this condition to hold at all points on the production surface.

A SUMMARY OF THE SLOPES OF THE INPUT DEMAND FUNCTION. We may summarize our findings about the relevant slopes of the demand functions for inputs by the firm. The slope in the direction of own-price will always be negative, even when output is a variable in the analysis. The slope in the direction of other-prices is ambiguous, either substitutability or complementarity among inputs being possible. Lastly, we should suspect the ordinary case of a change in product price to reveal a slope in the positive direction, because with rising marginal cost, a rise in product price under pure competition will induce a rise in output, and we should suspect the typical input to expand its role under such circumstances. However, the slope may in fact be negative if the input is inferior.

AN ANALYSIS OF THE SUPPLY OF OUTPUT

OWN-PRICE CHANGE. With a rise in the price of the product, under pure competition, with marginal cost rising in function of amount produced, output must expand; similarly, with a fall in price, the output must fall. This may be illustrated on Figure 5–2: when the price rises from P to P' output rises from $\bar{X}^m$ to $\bar{X}^4$ in order to reequate marginal costs and price.

OTHER-PRICE CHANGE. Suppose an input price changes: what will be the effect upon output? Normally, we should expect that a fall in the typical input price will induce a fall in marginal cost and thus induce an expansion in output. However, if the input is an inferior input, it is actually possible for a fall in its price to bring about a *rise* in marginal cost and so induce a *fall* in output. Suppose, for example, to use the illustration of trucking services we employed in the previous section, the price of trucking services falls to the firm. This would lead to an increase in the number of trucking services used by the firm. But, by assumption, trucking services are best adapted to smaller scale operations. Thus, let us assume, the marginal product of railroad services to the firm falls, and the firm reduces its demand for said services, which entails reducing output, in the abnormal case, below its previous level.

We may therefore state that under conditions of pure competition, a change in the price of the product will induce a change in the amount supplied in the same direction as the price change. A change in the price of an input will be expected normally to change output in the opposite direction, although the possibility exists if the input is inferior that the change in amount supplied will be in the same direction as the price change.

With this last proposition we have completed the building of the submodel of the firm under conditions of pure competition for smooth and continuous production functions. One of the drawbacks of the submodel is that it does not allow us to assume linear average short-run cost curves to exist, because we have seen that the failure of such functions to yield rising marginal costs makes it impossible to set size limitations on the plant, and when one or more firms become sufficiently large, the assumption of pure competition is no longer tenable. Also, we know that the short-run cost curves of many firms tend to exhibit linear portions in reality, and our model fails to take this fact into account.

Is there no way to salvage linear plant curves for the firm and provide a model explaining firm behavior under conditions of constant cost which meets conditions frequently found in the real world? Modern developments in economics have succeeded in providing a linear model that contains an alternative to the smooth production functions we have used. Moreover, because the production function assumed is linear and homogeneous, it may frequently be fitted to realistic data, and practical problems of optimum product mix be solved for the firm. Let us develop this alternative model at length for the firm in pure competition, once more stepping outside the bounds of Producer Postulates 4 and 5.

A Linear Model for the Firm in Pure Competition

We have seen that under the regime of linear homogeneity, with all inputs variable, constant average and marginal costs of production occur, and the firm will produce either nothing if profits are negative, an indeterminate amount if profits are zero, or an infinite amount if profits are positive. In the latter two cases nothing exists to provide barriers to further production. But, realistically, at least in the short run, barriers do exist, which we have recognized in the shape of our short-run product curves, even in the case of linear homogeneity. Each firm has certain capacity restrictions that cannot be violated over periods of quite substantial length. In our analysis of smooth production functions we have assumed these resources to be in fixed supply and viewed them as exerting a gently upward push on costs as output expands, with average and marginal costs rising over the relevant output domain.

But let us go to the other extreme in our interpretation of the manner in which these capacity constraints exercise their restricting influence. We may view each of them as exerting their force in the manner of a group of tethers: as long as no one of the capacities is used up there is no restriction imposed upon production, but as soon as one of them is exhausted, an absolute bar to further output occurs. That is, instead of the outlook we adopted in our smooth-function models through which we viewed the influence of the fixed factors as being exerted continuously and smoothly, we shall now view it as being totally ineffective over an interval of output, and then suddenly being totally restrictive once a critical value is reached.

We shall introduce this outlook by adopting a linear model whose solutions will be corner solutions. In so doing, we may not only present a modern method of approaching the firm's problems that has been gaining increasing favor recently, but we may also illustrate incidentally our contentions in the presentation of the consumer and firm submodels that the searching out of a maximum of this variety presents interesting problems of a markedly different character from the location of an interior maximum.

THE DERIVATION OF THE FIRM'S PRODUCTION FUNCTION

For the short run, let us assume that Firm v has two fixed inputs, say z_2 and z_3, available this week in the quantities Q_{vz_2} and Q_{vz_3}. In addition to these fixed inputs it employs, let us assume, one variable input, z_1, purchasable from the market in any quantity desired at the price P_{z_1}. By combining these inputs the firm produces outputs of Y_j to the amount $\overline{X}_{vJ}$. Its problem is to find, at the given price P_J for its output, the maximum profit output and optimal input usage for the coming week.

For the production of the given good let us assume the firm has three *productive activities*. By a productive activity we mean a method of combining given amounts of the fixed and variable inputs to produce one unit of output. That is, we define an activity $\mathbf{A}_k$ as a schedule of inputs required for the production of one unit of output, which we may write as follows:

$$\mathbf{A}_k = \begin{bmatrix} a_{2k} \\ a_{3k} \\ a_{1k} \end{bmatrix}, \qquad [5\text{--}1]$$

where a_{2k} is the amount of z_2 required to produce a unit of Y_j using activity A_k, a_{3k} is the amount of z_3 required, and a_{1k} is the amount of z_1 required by that activity. We shall assume that Firm v has three such activities, each yielding a unit of product, which it may use to design its output program in Week 1. Let us give them numerical definition for illustrative purposes:

$$\mathbf{A}_1 = \begin{bmatrix} 2 \\ 3 \\ 4 \end{bmatrix}, \qquad \mathbf{A}_2 = \begin{bmatrix} 4 \\ 3 \\ 3.5 \end{bmatrix}, \qquad \mathbf{A}_3 = \begin{bmatrix} 6 \\ 5 \\ 2 \end{bmatrix}. \qquad [5\text{--}2]$$

That is, we may assume that Firm v is a bakery, that z_1 is labor, z_2 is the flow of services from a stock of ovens, z_3 is the flow of services from a fixed stock of delivery trucks, and that $\overline{X}_{vJ}$ is loaves of bread produced. Then activity 1 $(\mathbf{A}_1)$ requires per loaf of bread produced 2 units of oven capacity, 3 units of delivery truck capacity, and 4 units of labor service, this week, and activities 2 and 3 may be similarly interpreted. Inputs z_2 and z_3 are owned by the firm and not available through the market: because they are neither bought from nor sold on a market, they are not priced by the market. However, both the product and the variable input are so priced: let us assume that $P_J = .25$ and $P_{z_1} = .05$, where the unit of labor service might be measured in minutes.

With these price data we may immediately calculate the unit profit on each activity: let π_k be the profit earned on $\mathbf{A}_k$. Then, with a revenue of .25 from all activities, we may subtract the labor costs to obtain

$$\pi_1 = .25 - .20 = .05, \quad \pi_2 = .25 - .175 = .075, \quad \pi_3 = .25 - .10 = .15,$$
$$[5\text{--}3]$$

which are the net revenues received from the operation of each productive activity at an intensity level of unity.

Because the variable inputs are available from the market in unlimited quantities at fixed prices, once we have taken account of them in calculating the unit profit of the activities we may ignore them, and identify our activities wholly by their inputs of the fixed capacities. This will allow us in our geometrical presentation to limit our input space to capacity space, with one axis for each capacity, and thus, in our illustration, to reduce the dimensions of the input-output space to three instead of four.

We shall now make three assumptions concerning the nature of the production relations holding for the firm, in order that we may once more obtain a continuous, real-valued production function under these conditions of production.

LINEAR PRODUCTION POSTULATE 1. Suppose $\mathbf{A}_k$ is an activity contained in the technology. Then $\theta \mathbf{A}_k$ for $\theta \geq 0$ must also be in the production set available to the firm. This assumption accomplishes several purposes. First, by accepting $\theta = 0$, the assumption implies that the *null activity*, A_0, which absorbs no fixed or variable inputs and yields no output, is an element of the technology. This implies we get nothing for nothing, and only finite amounts of output for finite input. We have graphed this activity as the origin of capacity-output space in Figure 5–5.

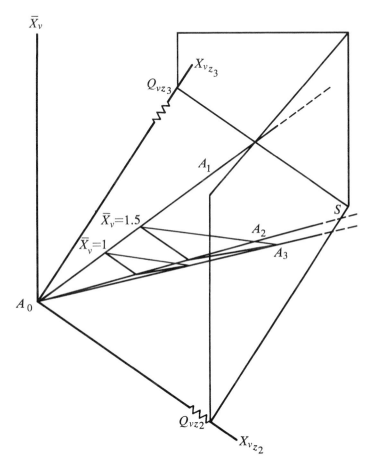

FIGURE 5–5. The Production Surface as a Convex Polyhedral Cone.

Secondly, the postulate implies that all inputs and the output are indefinitely divisible, because θ can take any nonnegative value.

Thirdly, the assumption asserts that the technology has the appearance of a cone with vertex at A_0, for if we draw a line in output-capacity space through any activity and thereby obtain the *process* which employs that activity at any nonnegative intensity level, that line will lie in the technology set throughout its length. Thus, there can be no economies of scale in using any single process forming part of the technology. If we multiply all inputs in a process by a factor of 2, output must rise by a factor of 2 as well. We already have become familiar with this restriction in our discussion of linear homogeneous production functions in Chapter 4 and the fact that the pencil which we used to generate that surface would lie on the surface over its entire length when one end rested at the origin of the space (that is, at A_0).

A difference between the linear homogeneous function now being postulated and that discussed in Chapter 4 is that the number of *lines* or fundamental processes that project out into the space in the current model is finite —presently the three lines defined by the processes based upon the A_k of [5–2]—whereas in the smooth function of the former chapter they could be considered infinite. But we can fill in the production relations between the fundamental processes by combining them, and we must restrict the results of such operations. By *combining* the fundamental processes we mean merely that the firm employs more than one of the productive processes at positive levels.

LINEAR PRODUCTION POSTULATE 2. If A_k and $A_{k'}$ are processes in the production set, then $A_k + A_{k'}$ must also be in the production set. This is called the *additivity-of-processes* assumption, and it assures us that no economies or diseconomies will occur when two or more processes are combined. In terms of geometry, it means that our cone now has flat sides or facets obtained by joining the lines of neighboring fundamental processes by passing planes through them. We have pictured the three-faceted cone of production for the baker's problem on Figure 5–5.

Linear Production Postulates 1 and 2 define a continuous linear homogeneous production surface with flat sides, and, as we have drawn it, it reveals all of the combinations of capacity inputs and outputs which the firm could employ technologically to produce bread. From the three *fundamental* productive activities defined in [5–2] the firm may—wholly from the view of technological considerations—multiply any number of them by any nonnegative constants and combine such processes into a production program.

It will pay us, however, in terms of computational convenience, to extend the number of fundamental activities contained in the cone. We do this by defining another assumption:

LINEAR PRODUCTION POSTULATE 3. The firm is capable of disposing of its capacity services and output costlessly; that is, without absorbing other resources.

Let us define two more processes—D_2 and D_3—to be called *disposal processes* as distinguished from *productive processes*, whose activities contain inputs of zero amounts of all but one capacity input and zero output. In other words, the processes at unit level are

$$\mathbf{D}_2 = \begin{bmatrix} 1 \\ 0 \\ 0 \end{bmatrix}, \qquad \mathbf{D}_3 = \begin{bmatrix} 0 \\ 1 \\ 0 \end{bmatrix}. \qquad [5\text{--}4]$$

We may then plot these activities as we did the productive activities, and they will fall on the input axes and remain in the base plane, because they yield no output. They give rise to processes that coincide with the relevant input axes, and the convex polyhedral cone is modified by possessing the entire base plane as a facet, as well as by new facets obtained by passing planes between the input axes and their nearest productive process. Then our production set is completely and finally defined.

We may derive isoquants from this cone as we did for our smooth functions, by slicing the cone parallel to the base plane and projecting the profiles onto the base plane. They consist of linear segments—convex combinations of the relevant processes—and give the rough appearance of approximations to our smooth isoquants. Indeed, we may view our smooth isoquants as being derived from such linear segments by allowing the number of processes in the analysis to approach infinity. Further, we may define a production function by choosing for every vector of capacity usage the greatest possible output of the good.

We may now return to the main stream of our analysis, having derived a production surface. How would we determine minimum costs and maximum-profit input mixes for such a function? This is not our purpose, of course, because we have assumed that no prices exist for the inputs involved. However if we had assumed that z_2 and z_3 were variable inputs with market prices, we could find that expenditure curve which touched the specified isoquant at the lowest possible level. Observe an interesting set of characteristics: (1) in general, the expenditure line will touch at a vertex or corner point of the isoquant, which means for our two-input case that in general it would be profitable to use only two of the activities—productive or disposal—at positive intensity levels; (2) even when the expenditure line coincides with a whole linear segment of the isoquant, we may use one or the other of a pair of the generating processes instead of the combination of them without sacrificing profit; and (3) in order to maximize profits (which implies minimizing of cost) it will not prove necessary to use more than two processes in this two-capacity problem.

Let us now move on, however, after this brief diversion to study the manner in which we might apply this method to standard minimization of cost procedures for variable inputs. We are not able to obtain from the data prices for the two capacities z_2 and z_3, because they are fixed in quantity and nonsaleable in the short run. How, then, does our bakery proceed to determine its best process mix? That is (1) what activities does the bakery choose to employ, and (2) at what levels of intensity does it operate them, in order to maximize profits?

Let us draw on Figure 5–5 the capacity restrictions on output. We place a vertical line through Q_{vz_2} and Q_{vz_3} and thus bound the feasible production set—as depicted by the quantities of capacities used—within the rectangle $A_0 Q_{vz_2} S Q_{vz_3}$. Any input mix within the rectangle or on its boundaries will be feasible from the viewpoint of capacity restrictions. Note that the only input mix in the entire set that uses both capacities to the full is at S: at any other point along $Q_{vz_2}S$ capacity z_3 is not fully used, at any other point along $Q_{vz_3}S$ capacity z_2 is not fully used, and everywhere else neither capacity is fully used.

SOLVING THE PROBLEM OF MAXIMIZING PROFITS

Let us state our problem in terms of the interrelationships that spring from our data and postulates. We seek to maximize a *criterion* variable called *profits*, Z_v, as the *objective* of the firm, where profits are defined as

$$Z_v = \pi_1 x_1 + \pi_2 x_2 + \pi_3 x_3 + 0d_2 + 0d_3, \qquad [5\text{–}5]$$

where x_k is the *intensity level* at which the activity A_k is employed and where d_2 and d_3 are the intensity levels at which the disposal activities are employed. The profits on the disposal activities are zero, of course, and we add them to the definition of Z_v merely for completeness.

We are constrained to choose a mix of activity intensity levels that maximizes Z_v subject to the constraint that we do not use more than the amount of capacities available to us,

$$a_{21}x_1 + a_{22}x_2 + a_{23}x_3 + 1d_2 + 0d_3 = Q_{vz_2}$$
$$a_{31}x_1 + a_{32}x_2 + a_{33}x_3 + 0d_2 + 1d_3 = Q_{vz_3}, \qquad [5\text{–}6]$$

and are also subject to the constraint that we choose nonnegative activity levels:

$$x_k \geqq 0, \quad d_2 \geqq 0, \quad d_3 \geqq 0. \qquad [5\text{–}7]$$

Let us fill in these equations in [5–5] and [5–6] with the values contained in our data set, and further assume that $Q_{vz_2} = 100$ and $Q_{vz_3} = 50$. Then, we may write [5–5] as

$$Z_v = .05x_1 + .075x_2 + .15x_3 + 0d_2 + 0d_3 \qquad [5\text{–}8]$$

and [5-6] as

$$\begin{bmatrix} 2 & 4 & 6 & 1 & 0 \\ 3 & 3 & 5 & 0 & 1 \end{bmatrix} \begin{bmatrix} x_1 \\ x_2 \\ x_3 \\ d_2 \\ d_3 \end{bmatrix} = \begin{bmatrix} 100 \\ 50 \end{bmatrix}, \qquad [5-9]$$

using the matrix form for writing equations. By this usage we are employing a more convenient way of displaying the data, and the rules of matrix multiplication tell us to multiply each item in the row of the large matrix to the left of the equality sign by its corresponding item in the column and to sum these products, making this sum equal to the value of the right-hand side in the given row.

The matrix notation is more convenient because each column in the matrix of [5-9] depicts the capacity requirements of one of our five fundamental activities. Each one, then, yields a process ray in Figure 5-5, as we have seen. Because we have plotted those activities in the two-dimensional space with the firm's scarce capacities on its axes, we may refer to this as *capacity-space*, every point of which depicts a combination of two amounts of capacity. Also, on the right-hand side, the amount of capacities available to the firm also appears as a pair of coordinates in capacity-space, and we may plot it too as a ray from the origin terminating at that point, which we have denoted **K** on Figure 5-6. Let us refer to all of these directed line segments as *vectors*, which for our purposes may be viewed merely as pairs of coordinates or points in the two-dimensional capacity-space.

To begin our analysis we must assert a most important proposition: that any point in the capacity-space can be derived as a linear combination of any *two* independent vectors in the space. That is, any point in capacity-space —and we are interested by virtue of [5-7] only in positive weights—can be obtained by weighting any two vectors that contain the point within the angle they distend at the origin. If the point falls outside the angle, one of the weights will be negative, and because the weights are the x_k and d_2 and d_3 in [5-9], this would violate [5-7].

Indeed, we may frame this statement more generally. Let us term a set of vectors in capacity-space *independent* if we cannot derive any of them as a weighted sum—or, in mathematical terminology, a *linear combination*—of the others. Let us view, for example, the vector $\mathbf{A}_1$ as a first set: that is, assume the set of vectors we consider contains only it. If we weight this vector by positive, negative, or zero weights, we are able to move along only the ray through it and the origin. With one vector in a two-dimensional space we cannot get off the line regardless of the weights we employ. Suppose we are

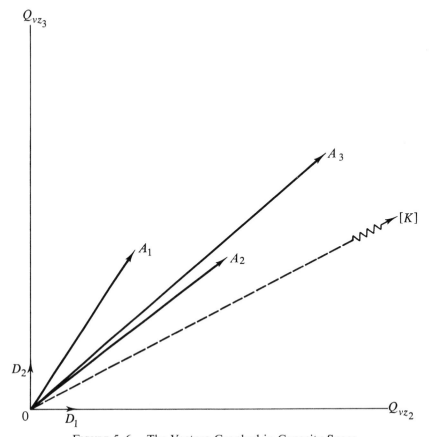

FIGURE 5–6. The Vectors Graphed in Capacity-Space.

given a second vector, say $\theta \mathbf{A}_1$. This second vector does not help us because it is not independent of $\mathbf{A}_1$. It has been obtained as a linear combination of $\mathbf{A}_1$. Thus, the new vector will not help us to get elsewhere in the space because it is not independent of $\mathbf{A}_1$.

Consider, however, $\mathbf{A}_3$, and let us include it in the set of vectors under consideration. Now $\mathbf{A}_3$ is independent of $\mathbf{A}_1$, because it cannot be derived from $\mathbf{A}_1$. We may show this in the following way. Let us seek the weight, x_1, which, when used to multiply $\mathbf{A}_1$, will yield $\mathbf{A}_3$. But we know such a weight will merely take us along the ray through $\mathbf{A}_1$, and $\mathbf{A}_3$ does not lie along that ray. Therefore, we cannot derive $\mathbf{A}_3$ from $\mathbf{A}_1$. Finally, consider also $\mathbf{A}_2$: let us add it to the set of vectors being considered.

Now these three vectors give us an ability to move about anywhere in the two-dimensional capacity-space. For example, let us take the vector $\mathbf{K}$ as an example of *any* vector in the space that does not lie along one of the rays of the three vectors. Then, we may seek the set of weights which, when applied to the three activity vectors, will yield **K**:

$$x_1\mathbf{A}_1 + x_2\mathbf{A}_2 + x_3\mathbf{A}_3 = \mathbf{K} \qquad [5\text{-}10]$$

or, in specifics,

$$\begin{bmatrix} 2 & 4 & 6 \\ 3 & 3 & 5 \end{bmatrix} \begin{bmatrix} x_1 \\ x_2 \\ x_3 \end{bmatrix} = \begin{bmatrix} 100 \\ 50 \end{bmatrix}. \qquad [5\text{-}11]$$

Now, because we have two equations in three unknowns, there are in general an infinite number of solutions. For example, the weights $x_1 = -20.8$, $x_2 = 16.7$, and $x_3 = 12.5$ will, when substituted in [5-11], yield a solution vector. That is, this set of weights will, when applied to the relevant vectors, and the results are added, get us to the point in capacity-space **K**.

We say that the set of vectors $\mathbf{A}_1$, $\mathbf{A}_2$, and $\mathbf{A}_3$ *spans* the capacity-space, meaning by this that we can get to any point in that space by weighting these vectors and adding. Let us pause to interpret this in a slightly different way. Each column of the matrix in [5-11] is a point in capacity-space: it is a point associated with the capacity input requirements of the three productive activities. So, we have seen, is the column vector on the right-hand side a point in capacity-space, for it is the vector that tells us how much of the capacities are available. The only vector unaccounted for in [5-11], therefore, is the vector of unknowns containing the desired activity levels.

This last vector, when filled with any trio of real numbers, is a point or vector in *productive activity-space*. That is, imagine a three-dimensional space such as that whose nonnegative octant is drawn in Figure 5-7, along each of whose axes is graphed respectively x_1, x_2, and x_3. Then, any point in that space consists of a vector of numbers such as those in the solutions to [5-11]. Our equation system, therefore, consists of relationships between two spaces, or, rather points in two spaces.

For example, instead of specifying the right-hand vector, let us allow it to be determined by the equation system of [5-11] and put into the x-vector values of our own choosing that represent points in productive activity-space. What does the system do? For example, let us put in the vector [1, 0, 0], which is the point in productive activity-space that depicts the operation of $\mathbf{A}_1$ at unit level and $\mathbf{A}_2$ and $\mathbf{A}_3$ at zero levels. Let us call it the *unit vector* $\mathbf{v}_1$ of productive activity-space, and, of course, it falls on the x_1-axis in that space at the point [1, 0, 0]. If we multiply the large matrix by this unit vector, what do we get? We obtain the vector [2, 3] or the vector $\mathbf{A}_1$. What does this mean?

We may view this matrix, whose columns are vectors in capacity-space, when multiplied by a vector in activity-space, as *mapping* a point in activity-

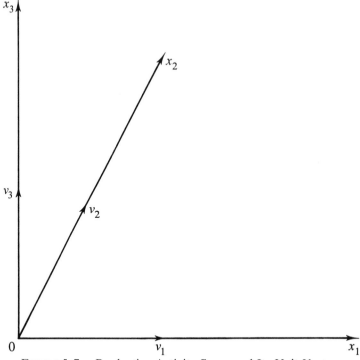

FIGURE 5-7. Productive Activity-Space and Its Unit Vectors.

space into a point in capacity-space. That is, the multiplication transforms any point in activity-space into its image in capacity-space. In what sense? In the important sense that the capacity needs of any activity intensity vector are determined, and this is that vector's image in capacity-space. In our example, the operation of A_1 at unit intensity level implies the use of 2 units of z_2 and 3 units of z_3, which is exactly what our mapping tells us. The same would hold true, of course, if we choose unit vectors v_2 and v_3 to be mapped into capacity-space—the mappings would be the column vectors that correspond to the given activity.

It follows, therefore, that the vectors of inputs for each activity depicted in the columns of the matrix are the images in capacity-space of the unit vectors of productive activity-space. Now, any vector in productive activity-space can be viewed as being obtained by multiplying each unit vector in productive activity-space by an appropriate factor and adding the weighted unit vectors. Thus, for example, the vector [5, 4, 9] can be viewed as

$$
\begin{bmatrix} x_1 \\ x_2 \\ x_3 \end{bmatrix} = 5 \begin{bmatrix} 1 \\ 0 \\ 0 \end{bmatrix} + 4 \begin{bmatrix} 0 \\ 1 \\ 0 \end{bmatrix} + 9 \begin{bmatrix} 0 \\ 0 \\ 1 \end{bmatrix}, \qquad [5-12]
$$

so that in capacity-space the image of this point is obtained by similarly weighting the images of the unit vectors of productive activity-space:

$$\begin{bmatrix} x_1 \\ x_2 \\ x_3 \end{bmatrix} \rightarrow 5\begin{bmatrix} 2 \\ 3 \end{bmatrix} + 4\begin{bmatrix} 4 \\ 3 \end{bmatrix} + 9\begin{bmatrix} 6 \\ 5 \end{bmatrix} = \begin{bmatrix} 80 \\ 72 \end{bmatrix}. \qquad [5\text{--}13]$$

Therefore, we may view the process levels as the weights that are applied to the images of the activity-space unit vectors in order to get the image in capacity-space of a point in activity-space.

Now, let us go back to [5–11] and interpret that system of requirements. The large matrix we know contains, column by column, the images of the unit vectors of productive activity-space in capacity-space. That is to say, in our example, the matrix $[A_1, A_2, A_3]$ maps the point in productive activity-space $[-20.8, 16.7, 12.5]$ into the point $[100, 50]$ in capacity-space. These weights are the activity intensity levels which, when applied to the images of the unit vectors of productive activity-space, will get us to the point that just represents the capacity levels available to the firm.

In general, returning to [5–9], we will be dealing with an *activity*-space whose unit vectors span the space, and a capacity-space with unit vectors that span the space. Any point in activity-space can be viewed as a linear combination of the unit vectors that span the space, and any point in capacity-space can be viewed as a linear combination of its unit vectors. In our case, the activity-space is a five-dimensional space—counting in the disposal activities—and the capacity-space is a two-dimensional space. If we map each of the unit vectors of activity-space into capacity-space, then the values in the vector $[x_1, x_2, x_3, d_2, d_3]$ may be viewed as the weights that are applied to these images to obtain a weighted sum of image vectors that yield the capacity vector. We may draw in Figure 5–6 the images of the unit vectors in activity-space corresponding to the disposal processes.

Now, let us make a most interesting point. Although we may obtain a set of weights x_1, x_2, and x_3 to apply to the images of the unit vectors of activity-space to obtain the capacity vector, as we did in [5–11], we do not *have* to use three vectors to obtain this point in two-dimensional space. Indeed, the result of [5–11] we obtained yields one negative activity level, which makes the solution infeasible, but even if all of the values were positive we would note that we *need* not employ three vectors to get our linear combination. Indeed, one of these three vectors can be obtained from the other two. That is, let us solve for the set of weights applied to A_1 and A_2 which will yield A_3:

$$\begin{bmatrix} 2 & 4 \\ 3 & 3 \end{bmatrix}\begin{bmatrix} x_1 \\ x_2 \end{bmatrix} = \begin{bmatrix} 6 \\ 5 \end{bmatrix}, \qquad [5\text{--}14]$$

and if we solve we obtain $[x_1, x_2] = [.33, 1.33]$. Therefore, the vectors $\mathbf{A}_1$, $\mathbf{A}_2$, and $\mathbf{A}_3$ are not independent. How many vectors are needed to get anywhere in a two-dimensional space? This is the problem, for what has occurred here is that we have gotten to the $\mathbf{A}_3$ point in capacity-space by judiciously weighting vectors $\mathbf{A}_1$ and $\mathbf{A}_2$. Could we get to $\mathbf{A}_2$ by weighting judiciously $\mathbf{A}_1$, or vice versa? Only if the one were on the same ray from the origin as the other. In general, we may not, for having only one vector in a two-dimensional space, as we have seen, does not allow us to get off the ray it defines.

In general, in order to get anywhere in an n-dimensional space, we must be provided with n independent vectors, so that in a sense each one adds an ability to move in another dimension. In the case at hand, we need as a minimum only two independent vectors in order to get anywhere in capacity-space. The minimum number of vectors needed to span a space is called a *basis* for that space, and the weights applied to the images in capacity-space of the minimum number of unit vectors of activity-space in order to get to the capacity vector is called a *basic solution*. For example, if we eliminate $\mathbf{A}_3$ from our set of vectors, we have $\mathbf{A}_1$ and $\mathbf{A}_2$, and because they are independent they constitute a basis for capacity-space. Now, let us assume $x_3 = d_2 = d_3 = 0$, and solve out for the solution to the system if that solution is a set of weights applied to this particular basis of capacity-space. We have from [5–9]:

$$\begin{bmatrix} 2 & 4 \\ 3 & 3 \end{bmatrix} \begin{bmatrix} x_1 \\ x_2 \end{bmatrix} = \begin{bmatrix} 100 \\ 50 \end{bmatrix}, \qquad [5\text{--}15]$$

and we obtain as a solution $[x_1, x_2, x_3, d_2, d_3] = [-16.7, 33.3, 0, 0, 0]$.

This is indeed a basic solution but it is not a *basic feasible* solution to the system because it violates the nonnegativity constraint for activity intensity levels in [5–7]. Therefore, we limit our search to those basic feasible solutions to the system [5–9], and from them we seek to extract that one which maximizes profits. This may be viewed as the nature of our problem: in a capacity-space of two dimensions, if we had only two images of the unit vectors of a two-dimensional activity-space to use as a basis, there would be a unique solution that would be basic and might be feasible. When we have a set of linear equations equal in number to the set of unknowns, if there are a finite number of solutions that are nontrivial there is a unique solution. But in a linear programming problem of the type we now face, the introduction of a disposal process for each of the capacities guarantees that there will be more activities than capacities, and therefore, that the images of the unit activities of the activity-space will be greater in number than the number of the capacities.

Consequently, there will be a large number of basic solutions to the problem, and usually a quite large subset of the basic solutions which are feasible. Therefore, in the linear programming problem we must somehow proceed from one basic feasible solution to another, moving if possible always in the direction of worse to better profit solutions.

But can we eliminate nonbasic feasible solutions from consideration? Suppose we find a basic feasible solution that yields the highest profit of any basic feasible solution: can we be sure that there is no nonbasic feasible solution containing more nonzero activity intensity levels than dimensions in capacity-space that will yield higher profits? Or must we study them too? Our analysis allows us to answer the question already. A nonbasic feasible solution is a point in activity-space that is also a set of weights applied to the image vectors in capacity-space of the unit vectors in activity-space. But if a point in capacity-space has been obtained by weighting a number of vectors greater than the number in a basis, that same solution can be obtained by weighting two or more basic solutions in a *convex combination,* or a weighted sum with weights that are nonnegative and sum to unity.

Let us put this in another way: imagine the set of basic feasible solutions, and plot each as a point in activity-space. There will be at most only one such solution for each basis of vectors. Now, draw a straight line connecting any two basic feasible solutions: it will be, as we have seen, a convex combination of the two solutions, and, because at least one vector will be contained in one basic solution and not the other, the convex combinations will be nonbasic. But these nonbasic solutions will also be feasible solutions to the problem. Conversely, any nonbasic feasible solution can be obtained from some convex combination of basic feasible solutions.

Therefore, any nonbasic feasible solution can at best be only as profitable as the optimal basic feasible solution. To get the nonbasic feasible solution, either the basis containing the optimal basic feasible solution was used in the convex combination or it was not. If the optimal basic feasible solution was not used, obviously the nonbasic solution was obtained by weighting nonoptimal basic feasible solutions, and the weighted average of such solutions must be less than optimal. If the optimal basic feasible solution was used, a nonoptimal basic feasible solution was also used, and the weighted average of these two can at most be equal to and will usually be less than the optimal basic feasible solution. *Therefore, if we find the optimal basic feasible solution, we are assured that we need search no farther.* We shall, therefore, begin that search.

FINDING AN INITIAL BASIC FEASIBLE SOLUTION.   We shall start with any basic feasible solution, test to see if it can be bettered, and if so move from it to a better basic feasible solution. Only when we are assured that no better basic feasible solution exists will we stop this iterative procedure. One possible basic feasible solution which we may adopt initially is that one which consists wholly of weights applied to the images of the disposal activities; that is, we shall merely assume as an initial hypothesis that the firm decides to produce nothing and lets its capacities run completely to waste. The solution is trivial and immediate, but we shall set up the problem as we would do if the solution were not so easily obtained:

	v_4	v_5	**K**	v_1	v_2	v_3	u_1	u_2
u_1	1	0	100	2	4	6	1	0
u_2	0	1	50	3	3	5	0	1

[5–16]

This *tableau* is explained in the following way. The first two column vectors will be taken as the vectors in the current basis, and in our case they are the unit vectors v_4 and v_5 in activity-space. We have, from the equation system in [5–10], the images of these unit vectors of the basis in capacity-space. That is, for example, the first column may be viewed as the weights that have to be applied to u_1 and u_2, the unit vectors in capacity-space, in order to get the image of v_4 in that space. We may interpret v_5 in the same way, as well as **K**, the capacity vector, and the unit vectors of those activities which have been currently eliminated from the basis (v_1, v_2, and v_3). Also, for reasons that will be made clear as we proceed, we shall put the unit vectors of capacity-space themselves into the tableau.

Now, the vectors in the columns are images in capacity-space: that is, all of the vectors listed at the top of the tableau are expressed in the basis formed by the unit vectors of capacity-space. What we truly want, however, as a solution, is the image of **K**, not in its own space—capacity-space—but in a subspace of activity-space containing only the disposal processes. We want to know the point into which **K** is mapped in that disposal activity-subspace, for that will tell us what linear combination of the basis vectors in capacity-space is equivalent to **K**, or, in economic terms, what combination of the basis vectors will just use up the given economic capacities. Let the student turn back to [5–9] and see that this is the meaning of such a system, for the column vector of unknowns will be, in the solution, a mapping of the column vector of given capacities into activity-space. We are seeking the *equivalent vector* in basis activity-space to the capacity vector in capacity-space.

In the case of the tableau of [5–16] it so happens that we already have what we are looking for, which is what makes this case so trivial. The disposal activities were chosen so that their images would be identical to the unit vectors in capacity-space, and, therefore, all of the vectors in that tableau being expressed in the terms of the unit vectors of capacity-space, they are also expressed in the unit vectors of the activity-subspace containing only the disposal activities. Let us therefore rewrite the tableau by putting the unit vectors of the activity-subspace on the left to indicate that all vectors are expressed in that basis. This we have done in [5–17].

TESTING THE INITIAL FEASIBLE SOLUTION. This "new" tableau tells us

	v_4	v_5	K	v_1	v_2	v_3	u_1	u_2
v_4	1	0	100	2	4	6	1	0
v_5	0	1	50	3	3	5	0	1

[5–17]

that now all of the column vectors have been put on the basis of the unit vectors in activity-space whose relevant activities are included in the current basis. Thus, for example, to obtain the unit vector v_4 in that activity-subspace whose unit vectors are v_4 and v_5, it is obvious that we must weight the first of these unit vectors by 1 and the second by 0. More interestingly, in order to obtain the image of K in this same activity-subspace, we must weight the unit vector v_4 by 100 and v_5 by 50. And all other vectors may be so interpreted.

Now, this interpretation of the vectors in terms of the activity-subspace leads to several interesting conclusions. First, because K is equivalent to the first disposal activity being operated at a level of 100 and the second at a level of 50, we may put these values of $d_2 = 100$ and $d_3 = 50$ into [5–8] to obtain the value of profits, Z_v, for the firm. Of course, if the capacities of the firm are used up with these two activities, profits are zero. Can the firm do any better than this with its capacities?

To answer this question, let us look at the vectors v_1, v_2, and v_3, and interpret what their values in [5–17] mean. We have said that these are the unit vectors in activity-space for the productive activities expressed on the basis of the remaining two unit vectors of that space. What does this mean in economic terms? It means that in terms of the capacity inputs absorbed, the unit vector in one of these three columns is the equivalent of the number of units of the basis vectors indicated in that column. For example, the column under v_1 indicates that the operation of activity A_1 at the unit level absorbs as much of capacity z_2 and z_3 as v_4 operated at a level of 2 and v_5 operated at a level of 3. That is, the *excluded vectors*—those vectors which are currently excluded from the basis in which all other vectors are expressed—appear in the tableau as equivalent combinations of the basis vectors, equivalence being defined in terms of capacity usage.

But this gives us the ability to answer the question whether the firm could do better to use another basis for its basic feasible solution, in terms of getting more profits. For we may reason in this manner: if we operate A_1 at unit intensity we will gain π_1 in profit. But to introduce this, we will have to take capacity inputs away from the activities currently in the basis. In fact, we will have to reduce the operations of D_2 by an intensity level of 2 and of D_3 by an intensity level of 3. We will therefore sacrifice the profit earned on 2 units of operation of D_2 and 3 units of D_3. Therefore, the net gain or loss by substitution of one unit of A_1 (that is, v_1) for its equivalent combination in basis activities may be computed:

$$\Delta Z_{v/1} = \pi_1 - 2\pi_4 - 3\pi_5 = .05. \qquad [5\text{--}18]$$

In exactly similar fashion, we can compute what the change in profits would be if we introduced a unit level of operation of A_2 and A_3 into the solution and obtained the capacities to do so by reducing the levels of operation of the basis activities. We obtain, of course,

1. $\Delta Z_{v/2} = \pi_2 - 4\pi_4 - 3\pi_5 = .075$

2. $\Delta Z_{v/3} = \pi_3 - 6\pi_4 - 5\pi_5 = .15.$ $[5\text{--}19]$

SHIFTING THE BASIS. We may conclude, therefore, that it would benefit the firm to introduce any one of the three excluded activities into the basis, because if it were introduced (1) the capacity constraints would not be violated, and (2) profits would increase. Although we may introduce any of the three candidates into the basis, let us follow the convention of choosing that one whose use would increase profits the most per unit level. But if it pays to introduce one unit of A_3—in our example it has the greatest unit profit increment—it will pay to introduce A_3 to the limit of the intensity level which the capacity limitations will allow, for our system is a linear one, and we may substitute units of A_3 for units of D_2 and D_3 at constant rates.

We are resolved, then, to eliminate one of the current activities from the basis. But which? The determining consideration here is the need to keep activity intensity levels nonnegative. Consider the requirements of A_3 for capacities as reflected in the ability to substitute for the activities in the basis. From [5–17] we can see that we could introduce $100/6 = 16.67$ units of A_3 for the first activity's intensity level in the basis and $50/5 = 10$ units of A_3 for the second activity's intensity level in the basis. Our rule for determining which of the existing basis activities to remove is simply that we remove that one for which this ratio, if positive, is a minimum, and for a simple reason. If we chose D_2 for removal and left D_3 in the basis, it would be necessary to operate the latter at negative levels, because its z_2 requirements relative to the availability of z_2 would allow A_3 to be introduced at such a high intensity level that the z_3 requirements would be insufficient to support it. Therefore, the basic solution would not be feasible. If we assure that we substitute always for that activity in the basis whose elimination would allow the *lowest* intensity level of the new basis vector to occur, we will guard against such occurrences.[2]

In our case, the minimum-ratio rule leads to a substitution of A_3 for D_3 and we accomplish this procedure by revising the tableau of [5-17] to read as follows:

	v_4	v_3	K	v_1	v_2	v_5	u_1	u_2
v_4	1	6	100	2	4	0	1	0
v_5	0	5	50	3	3	1	0	1

[5-20]

We have now lifted v_3 out of the excluded sector of the tableau and placed it in the included-activity portion, while we have lifted v_5 out of the included-activity portion of the table and placed it in the excluded portion.

Now, for the same reasons as those explained in connection with the first tableau, what we desire is to express every vector in the tableau on the basis of v_4 and v_3, the unit vectors of the subspace containing D_2 and A_3. We know that when we have done this, the first two column vectors will consist of a unity value in each diagonal position and zeroes elsewhere, for two vectors expressed in terms of themselves as a basis must be so represented. Let us try to obtain this result following these two rules: (1) we may multiply a row by any nonzero value if we are sure to multiply every value in the row by that number, and (2) we may add or subtract a row thus treated to or from any other row if we are sure that every item is added to or subtracted from its corresponding item in the other row.

First, let us multiply the second row by -1.2 and add it to the first row:

	v_4	v_3	K	v_1	v_2	v_5	u_1	u_2
v_4	1	0	40	-1.6	.4	-1.2	1	-1.2
v_5	0	5	50	3	3	1	0	1

[5-21]

---

[2] In determining this minimum ratio, we eliminate negative ratios, for these can occur only if introduction of the excluded activity would lead to an *enhanced* ability to employ the relevant included activity. Thus, it can never set the limit to introducing the new activity. Infinite ratios are excluded for the same reason. If all ratios are negative or infinite, the problem has no finite solution, for one of the activities can be substituted indefinitely for the basis activities. If the minimum ratio is zero, the substitution of the new activity for the indicated activity may not result in an increase in profits, and theoretically a cycling could result, leading to an indefinitely recurring sequence of solutions. In practice, however, the technique usually leads out of the cycle and toward the solution.

Next, divide row 2 by 5:

	v_4	v_3	**K**	v_1	v_2	v_5	u_1	u_2	
v_4	1	0	40	-1.6	.4	-1.2	1	-1.2	[5–22]
v_3	0	1	10	.6	.6	.2	0	.2	

Our tasks for this step are now completed, for we have put the entire tableau on the new basis. Let us repeat quickly the interpretation we gave the tableau in [5–22]. Each column vector has now been put in terms of its capacity-usage equivalent in basis activities. A_1, for example, operated at unit intensity, uses the same amounts of capacities as v_4 operated at the level -1.6 and v_3 operated at the level .6. Let us check to assure ourselves that this equivalence is true:

$$A_1 = -1.6D_2 + .6A_3 = -1.6\begin{bmatrix} 0 \\ 1 \end{bmatrix} + .6\begin{bmatrix} 5 \\ 6 \end{bmatrix} = \begin{bmatrix} 3 \\ 2 \end{bmatrix}, \qquad [5–23]$$

and our result does check. Again, **K** expressed in the new basis asserts that capacities would be just used up if A_3 were operated at the level 10 and D_2 were operated at the level 40.

Let us now check again to see if the firm can do any better in terms of profit-making. Were it to introduce a unit intensity level of operation for A_1, Firm v would obtain .05 of gross profit, would gain 1.6 units of D_2, which adds nothing to profits, and would lose the profits from .6 units of A_3, or .09. Net, therefore, a unit intensity level substitution of A_1 would increase profit initially by .05, but the *opportunity cost* of .09 would make this a loss of .04. A unit intensity introduction of A_2 would increase profit initially by .075, but this would be offset by reductions of .6 × .15 and .4 × 0, or .09, for a net loss of .015. Lastly, the introduction of the disposal process D_3 might be expected to reduce profits, for it introduces no gross profits, and forces us to reduce the level of operation of A_3 by .2 units, which loses .03 gross and therefore net. Thus, we may conclude that none of the excluded activities could be introduced with profit into the basis and that therefore we have found the optimal basic feasible solution to the problem. The firm should employ A_3 at the intensity level $x_3 = 10$ and D_2 at the intensity level $d_2 = 40$, while $x_1 = x_2 = d_3 = 0$. The optimal point in activity-space is [0, 0, 10, 40, 0]. Profits will be a maximum at the value

$$Z_v^\circ = .05(0) + .075(0) + .15(10) + 0(40) + 0(0) = \$1.50. \qquad [5–24]$$

We are also assured from our analysis that no nonbasic solution can yield more profit than this. This is an extremely important theorem in linear programming problems, for we are assured before we begin the analysis that the optimal activity mix will contain positive activity levels for no more than the number of activities equal to the dimension of capacity-space, and, in all but the occasional exception, the number of nonzero activity levels will be *exactly* equal to the dimension of the capacity-space.

Let us also point up the lesson that was merely mentioned in Chapters 2 and 3. When we have maximum (or minimum) problems in which corner solutions occur, wherein some of the variables receive zero values, there are no analytic techniques to solve directly for the optimum. Rather, we must feel our way around the functions, and test combinations to see if we have, by trial and error, arrived at the optimum or whether we must travel on. Such techniques make general analysis—in the sense of striving for results in the absence of specific data—quite hard to obtain. If the price of bread were changed and the price of inputs were varied, we should have to attack the problem anew to find the optimum activity level mix.

PRICING THE CAPACITIES.   But we may derive some very interesting implications from our analysis. Consider, for example, the last two columns of the tableau in [5–22]. We included in our analysis the unit vectors of capacity-space without explanation, and it is time now to see what we have obtained. Following the lines of our previous interpretation, the two columns show the image of the unit vectors of capacity-space in the optimal activity-subspace: that is, in that portion of activity-space containing only those activities with positive levels in the optimal solution. But $\mathbf{u}_1$ depicts one unit of capacity z_2 and zero units of capacity z_3, while $\mathbf{u}_2$ depicts one unit of capacity z_3 and zero units of capacity z_2. Therefore, the unit vectors of capacity-space really depict one unit of each capacity.

The vector showing $\mathbf{u}_1$ on the basis of optimal activities is, therefore, the equivalent combination of optimal activities that uses up one unit of z_2 and none of z_3. This turns out to be operation of $\mathbf{A}_3$ at zero intensity and of $\mathbf{D}_2$ at an intensity level of one. In other words, a unit of capacity z_2 is equivalent in the optimal solution to the operation of a disposal process at unit level. We may put the implication in recognizable language by saying that the marginal physical product of a unit of z_2 in the optimal solution is zero, for if we had one more unit of it, we would be able to put it into only one unit of an activity that yields no product.

On the other hand, consider the marginal physical product of z_3. Were we to obtain one more unit of z_3, we could increase the level of $\mathbf{A}_3$ by .2 units and would have to decrease the level of $\mathbf{D}_2$ by 1.2 units. The increase in activity level x_3 would yield .2 extra units of product, while the decrease in the level d_2 would sacrifice no product, so that the net marginal physical product of a unit of capacity z_3, reflected in the image of $\mathbf{u}_2$ in optimal activity-subspace, is .2 units of product.

What of the *marginal value product* of these two capacities? We may obtain these merely by multiplying the optimal activity intensity equivalents of the unit vectors of capacity-space by the value of the product forthcoming from each. Because each productive activity yields one unit of output by construction, and because the price of bread is .25 by assumption, the marginal value product of z_2 is 0 and of z_3 is .05. Thus, once more we may obtain an economic magnitude that has a direct resemblance to economic variables we shall deal with at length in our discussion of the laws of markets.

Lastly, the marginal value products cannot be viewed as the net contributions of the capacities to profits because variable factors are involved in the productive activities. Therefore, we may obtain the *marginal net value product* of each capacity by multiplying the marginal products by the profit value of each activity. This yields a value of zero for z_2 and of .03 for z_3.

We have seen that the firm cannot price the two capacities through a market, but suppose we *impute* prices to them on the basis of these marginal net values. That is, from our economic analysis we know that factor services in the market tend to receive their marginal net revenue products as prices, as we shall see in Chapter 7. Anticipating this result, suppose we set $P_{z_2} = 0$ and $P_{z_3} = .03$. Can we justify this set of imputed *shadow* prices? How can a capacity that is used at positive levels in the optimal productive activity be imputed to be worthless to the firm? Of course, we must recall the role of the marginal concept in economic analysis. Inputs receive prices determined by the value of their contributions in their *last* employment, not the value of their average products, and if these inputs must always be hired with some other input in fixed proportions, their contribution to revenue at the margin must be reduced by the cost of the cofactor service.

Therefore, the firm is correct if it imputes a zero price to capacity z_2, for at the margin it is a free good. That is, it is in such abundant supply that oven capacity does not become an effective constraint upon the bakery's operations. The factor which in fact sets limits to the ability of the firm to make profits this week is the firm's delivery capacity. Therefore, this week oven capacity is a free good, in that an excess supply exists, and its rational price to the firm is zero. For similar reasons, we may value the only scarce factor owned by the firm—z_3—at its net marginal value product.

The total value of the firm this week—considered as the sum of the product of shadow prices times amounts of capacities available—is therefore

$$V = P_{z_2} Q_{vz_2} + P_{z_3} Q_{vz_3} = 0(100) + .03(50) = \$1.50. \qquad [5\text{--}25]$$

Note a most interesting result: V, the value of the firm, equals Z_v°, the total profits of the firm when the capacities are used optimally. We can show that this result will always hold in our solutions. If we value the capacities at the imputed shadow prices, the profits of the firm will be completely accounted for. That is, our method of solving for the optimal activity level mix yields a set of prices for the capacities which, when applied to the quantities of capacities, will just distribute profits over the capacities. This is a most interesting result, for it tells us that when we set about to find the maximum-profit activity mix, we are simultaneously engaged in the determination of a set of shadow prices for the capacities which, when used to value the stocks of those capacities, will just exhaust the profits of the firm. Further, we could show that these prices for the capacities are derived from an implicit *minimization* analysis that seeks those prices which will minimize the value of the firm subject to the requirement that the values of activities at those prices be greater than or equal to the profits earned from them. That is, when the prices of the capacities are optimal, all activities at those prices must be worth more than the profits they derive—and therefore will not be used—or must be just equal to that profit, in which case they will be used. Thus, employed activities will be priced so that profits on them after deducting imputed costs of capacities are zero.

A FINAL WORD ON THE LINEAR PROGRAMMING MODEL

It is the great virtue of the model, whose production function for the firm is assumed to be that implied by Linear Production Postulates 1, 2, and 3, that the analysis may be taken into the real economy and be used to attack the problems facing the firm. Many types of processes used in modern manufacturing do seem to lend themselves to the kind of cook-book treatment that our linear, noninteracting, activities require. It has long been known, for example, that many firms view their average total costs as essentially linear in most relevant sectors, or at least view their average variable costs as constant. Consequently, this model and this body of techniques for solving it have given the economist a great increase in his ability to analyze real-world problems, and have brought the economic theory of the firm much closer to reality.

Further, we have used merely one type of problem—and that a simple one to illustrate the potentialities of the technique. It is also useful in determining a firm's optimal product mix if it has a set of productive activities that produce different products, and it has been applied to decisions concerning optimal warehouse location, optimal deliveries from given warehouses to given demand points, and many others. Further, the techniques have been extended, though with less success, to solving problems in which the objective function is not linear in the variables but is concave, and which is constrained by concave restraints not necessarily linear.

The Firm's Decisionmaking in Nonrivalrous, Nonpure Competition

There remains but one step for us to take in our construction of entrepreneurial decision models under conditions of nonrivalrous competition. This consists of considering the cases where the firm is large enough relative to the size of the market for the good it sells to have an impact upon price as it varies its supply, but where such impacts on the sales of other firms' goods are sufficiently small to permit competition with those firms to be nonrivalrous.

The existence of such an environment is reflected in two conditions: (1) the sales curve of the firm, showing the amounts of the product it can sell at varying hypothetical prices, exists, and (2) the sales curve of the firm is downward sloping rather than horizontal, as it is in pure competition. The first of these conditions indicates the absence of rivalrous competitors—or at least rivalrous competitors who have not yielded up their freedom to react in unpredictable, nonforeseeable ways to the firm's price decisions. For if the firm had nonnegligible impacts upon the sales of another firm, and if that second firm had not made clear the pattern of its reactions by agreement or past actions, the original firm could not gauge the results of its own price actions upon its own sales. They would be dependent upon the reactions of the rival, which are by hypothesis unknown.

Given this first condition, it is the second that spells the difference between this case and the one we have just analyzed. In the cases of pure competition —both for the smooth production functions we constructed and for the linear programming convex polyhedral cone we built—it was assumed that the firm could sell any feasible amount of product at a fixed, unchanging price. Most particularly, the postulate was that the price of the product did not fall as the firm produced more of it, so that in order to sell more product the firm did not have to offer lower prices. Let us turn to analyze the impact upon the firm's decisionmaking when price does fall if the firm increases output.

THE NONCOINCIDENCE OF PRICE AND MARGINAL REVENUE

For Producer Postulate 8 we substitute the following:

PRODUCER POSTULATE 8*. Every firm possesses negligible amounts of power in every market in which it participates as buyer, but for every good which the firm can produce potentially there exists a *sales curve* $X_{vJ} = D_{vJ}(P_J; \mathbf{P}^J, \mathbf{Q})$ or $X_{vZ_i} = D_{vZ_i}(P_{Z_i}; \mathbf{P}^{Z_i}, \mathbf{Q})$, for which dX_{vJ}/dP_J and $dX_{vZ_i}/$

dP_{z_i} are negative, and where we define $\mathbf{P}^k$ to be the vector containing all prices but P_k.

In Figure 5–8 we have drawn the sales curve of the firm, dd', under conditions which we have assumed above. The downward slope indicates, of course, that it can sell larger quantities of output only if it reduces prices to induce the marginal buyer to purchase the last unit of the larger output. Inasmuch as all units must sell at the same price, all units must suffer a price reduction.

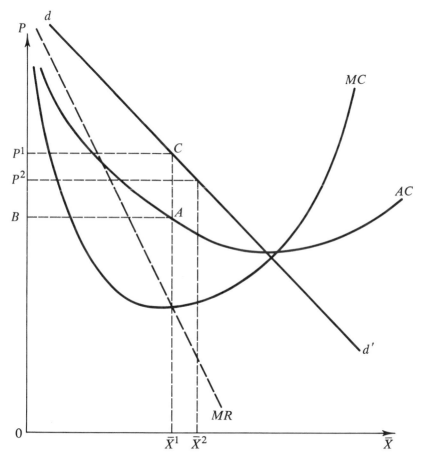

FIGURE 5–8. The Price-Output Solution for Pure Monopoly.

Consider, for example, the point $\bar{X}^1$ for which level of output the firm would obtain the price P^1. Now, the sales curve informs us that if the firm wishes to sell the larger output $\bar{X}^2$ it must consent to see price fall to P^2. One conclusion we may arrive at immediately on the basis of the postulates we constructed for the firm: the profit-maximizing firm will never move from

$\overline{X}^1$ to $\overline{X}^2$ if it means leaving the elastic portion of the sales curve, for this implies both an increase in total costs (because output rises) and a decrease in revenue, and therefore must mean that profit has fallen. Consequently, the firm will always operate in the elastic portion of the curve.

Marginal revenue is defined as the net increase in total revenue that results from a small change in output and sales. When the sales curve of the firm is downward sloped, marginal revenue must always be less than the average revenue (or price) at which a given output can be sold. Consider, for example, what occurs between the two points $\overline{X}^1$ and $\overline{X}^2$: by lowering the price from P^1 to P^2, a *gross* increase in revenue consisting of the new sales $(\overline{X}^2 - \overline{X}^1)$ times the new price accrues, but against this must be netted out the reduction in price suffered on the amount $\overline{X}^1$, which could have been sold for P^1. Thus, we may depict marginal revenue as total revenue at the new price minus total revenue at the old price, this increment consisting of the increment of sales at the new price minus the price reduction times the old quantity. The marginal revenue curve will, therefore, lie below the sales curve or average revenue curve, as we have shown on Figure 5–8.

THE NEW MAXIMUM-PROFIT CONDITION FOR THE FIRM

This complication introduces only one major change into the interrelationships of our firm submodel. The long-run and short-run cost curves are unaffected: obviously, they reflect only technological conditions and the conditions of supply for inputs, and the presence of monopoly power in the market in which the firm sells cannot affect these. The only interrelationships to be affected are [F–4] and [F–5].

Under conditions of pure competition, the determination of the profit-maximizing output, as depicted in Figure 5–2, when the minimum-cost curves are given, occurred when the firm brought about the equality of price and marginal cost with appropriate side conditions. What the firm was doing was assuring itself that marginal profit was zero: that is, that it was producing every additional unit of output that added more to revenue than to costs. As we pointed out there, the essential point about this equality of price and marginal cost was the fact that marginal revenue was being equated to marginal cost, for these are the relevant variables in determining marginal profit. Under conditions of pure competition the average revenue or price line happened to coincide with the marginal revenue curve.

Now that this coincidence no longer is true, it is the marginal revenue curve that possesses major interest for us in profits analysis. We must now equate it with marginal cost to determine the firm's best output—and for the same reasons as those we gave in our analysis of the firm in pure competition

—and must check to see that in fact we do have a profit maximum, by assuring ourselves that marginal cost lies above marginal revenue at higher outputs.

The equality of these two magnitudes occurs at the intersection of the curves and yields the best profit output for the firm. The price at which this output can be sold is determined by extending a straight line perpendicular to the output axis through this point to the sales curve, striking it at P^1 on Figure 5–8, which is the price at which the market will absorb the output. Profits, as in the case of the purely competitive firm, will be average revenue less average cost times sales, and are depicted by the area P^1CAB on Figure 5–8.

With this alteration, the analyses of profit maximization in conditions when the sales curve slopes downward and when it is horizontal are formally identical—at least until we introduce two additional complications, as we do subsequently. That is, the monopolist and monopolistic competitor (each of whom has a sales curve that slopes downward) do not seek to do anything different from the pure competitor in our submodels. Each attempts to maximize profits. The basic distinction is that the environments in which they function make these aims true at different relations between price and marginal cost. The implications for the market will be developed in Chapter 7 and for social welfare in Chapter 9.

Therefore, in the cases where sales curves are not horizontal, interrelationship [F–3–3] must be altered to read as follows:

$$MR_k^{\circ} - MC_k^{\circ} \leq 0, \qquad\qquad [F'-3-3]$$

where MR_k°, of course, is the marginal revenue for the good in question and the degree mark indicates as usual values at the solution. In like manner, we must write

$$\bar{X}_k^{\circ}(MR_k^{\circ} - MC_k^{\circ}) = 0. \qquad\qquad [F'-5-4]$$

That is, output can be positive only if the equality holds in [F'–3–3].

DISPLACEMENT OF EQUILIBRIUM

If the equilibrium of the firm with sloping sales curve is disturbed, the movements of variables will be constrained not by product price remaining constant but by the given sales curve, or, if the displacement involves it, the change will be not an alteration of product price but a shift of the sales curve. Obviously, the propositions that held for the slopes of the input demand functions for given output amounts in the case of the horizontal demand curve for product will not alter.

When outputs are variable, because we continue to insist that each firm produce only one output in equilibrium, the choice of output will be made in a fashion similar to that of the pure competitor. The good yielding the maximum of the maximum-profit levels will be selected. We shall again assume that for all displacements none is so great that it would render some other good more attractive for production.

The propositions concerning the impact of a change in product price on input demands and output supply will hold true of the firm with sloping sales curve, when we substitute shifts in the marginal revenue curve in the same direction for shifts in the price of the product under the assumption of horizontal sales curves. A rise in the marginal revenue curve for the firm may induce a reduction in the amount of an input if it is inferior. Usually, however, it may be expected to expand that input's presence. It must also expand the amount of the good supplied, because the new marginal revenue curve intersects a rising marginal cost curve. And, a change in the price of an input would normally be expected to change marginal cost in the same direction and move output in the opposite direction. However, the unusual case of the inferior input may reverse these movements.

TWO NEW VARIABLES FOR THE FIRM

A last complication occurs for the firm with a downward-sloping sales curve. The firm that finds itself so large a factor in the market for such a good as to have this impact upon price may also be able to affect the sales of its product in two ways that were not open to the firm with a horizontal sales curve. Let us look at each of these new variables in turn.

SELLING COSTS AS A VARIABLE. One of the possibilities that emerges when the firm is in one sense or another isolated from other firms, so that its product can be identified with it, is that the producer may find it to his advantage to advertise his product, to send salesmen on the road to intensify its sales, to offer discounts or other inducements to customers, or wholesalers, or retailers to stock the product, and so forth. All such expenditures that are aimed at affecting the sales curve of a given product are termed *selling costs*. They are distinguished from production costs, with which we have been dealing to this point, in that production costs are independent of the sales curve whereas selling costs cannot be so taken because their very aim is to affect the sales curve.

Such expenditures will not be made when pure competition prevails, for in these conditions the sales curves of the firm are horizontal, which implies that the firm can sell all it wishes to sell at the prevailing price. It has, therefore, no incentive to pay for selling efforts under the prevailing market structure. However, it might be that a strong effort in the selling cost line would be capable of convincing consumers that the producer or his physical product or service was preferable to that of other producers in the industry. If the firm were successful in such an effort, for the current week and presumably for an indefinite number of weeks to follow, the sales curve of the firm would be tilted upward in the negatively sloped direction, away from the horizontal. That is, we mean by the statement that the firm is successful in differentiating itself or its product from the industry that it succeeds in making its sales curve less than infinitely elastic, so that, if it chose to raise its prices, it would not lose all of its customers, but some who were convinced that its product at a higher price was better than the rest of the industry's at a lower price would remain with the firm. Then the successful firm would no longer be a pure competitor and would remain in the sloped-sales-curve class.

If the pure competitor could not hope to achieve such results—for example, if he were a wheat farmer in Kansas producing No. 1 Manitoba wheat, and if he could have no hopes that he could convince the Chicago Pit that John Jones's No. 1 Manitoba wheat was better than that of all other producers—then selling expenditures would imply nonmaximization of profit. Because firms can sell all they wish at the going price, and because any success their campaign achieves would benefit all producers in the absence of an ability to differentiate the advertiser from the crowd, it could not raise the going price by an amount sufficient to repay the selling costs.

Selling costs, therefore, imply sloping demand or sales curves to the firm. The goals of selling costs are probably best stated as two: (1) for a given price and quantity solution, to decrease the price elasticity of the sales curve, and (2) for a given price to increase the sales of the product. The first goal is a means of saying that the firm's selling costs succeed in giving it more power over price by virtue of increasing the attachment of consumers to the product. Thus, if selling costs affected only the elasticity of the sales curve in the region of the equilibrium, it would allow the firm to increase price, reduce sales, and increase profit. But profit can be increased in a second way, which probably in a dynamic world of uncertainty has more attraction. This is to increase the sales potential of the firm at the going price and all prices, even though this could raise the price elasticity of demand and in this sense reduce product loyalty.

A word of caution is in order here, however: we have treated price elasticity of demand as a rough measure of consumer loyalty to product, and so it may be considered when the sales curves being compared are in roughly similar portions of the graph. However, elasticity measures lose their ability to perform this comparison when the relevant sales curves are widely separated. For example, for a sales curve close to the price axis, an elasticity of

−.5 indicates that a rise in price of 1 per cent will cause a fall in sales of only .5 per cent, which might imply a fall in absolute terms from 10 units to 9.95 units, at some given initial price. Suppose, however, that the firm engages in a great selling cost campaign, and at the same price the elasticity of the new sales curve is −1. Then a 1 per cent rise in price will reduce sales by 1 per cent, but in absolute terms this might mean a fall in sales from 1,000 to 990 units. Who is to say that the first situation, with the lower elasticity, denotes a stronger consumer loyalty than the second? Two markets with very large differences in numbers of customers present different problems in retention of consumer loyalty and they can be lost sight of in such relative comparisons. Therefore, price elasticity of the sales curve, especially when the absolute sales levels are not in the same neighborhood, cannot be used as the only dimension in gauging consumer loyalty.

Actually, of course, the firm attempts to accomplish both goals: to convince consumers that its product should be purchased in greater numbers at all prices, and to convince them of the greater attractiveness of the product, even at higher prices.

The firm faces two new decisions in its attempt to maximize profits, therefore. What amount should be expended in all types of promotional efforts, and what should be the allocation of this amount among all the various selling media? Of course, the two decisions are interdependent and simultaneous. We should add to our interrelationships, therefore, a number of conditions that will tell us when optimal amounts and distribution of selling costs have been achieved, and from them we should derive additional functions in System [II], which indicate the amounts of each type of selling cost medium's service taken in function of the data.

We shall not in fact do this because the knowledge concerning the decisions of firms in these areas is not yet complete or reliable. Indeed, to judge by such evidence as is available, firms tend to handle their advertising expenditures in a kind of linear, rule-of-thumb manner similar to that we have adopted for their determination of money balances in the environment of our model. In many cases they seem to allocate a fixed percentage of their gross receipts in one period to the next period's advertising campaign, and decide where to spend it on the basis of their judgments as to effectiveness. This implies that when sales fall, advertising expenditures fall, at the very time when the firm might maximize profits by increasing such expenditures. In any event, such evidence as is available concerning actual practices of deciding selling cost budgets does not reveal a very sophisticated profit-maximization approach. In view of this, we shall not build the variable into our variable set, or the relationships determining it into our set of interrelationships. However, if we cannot say much concerning what *is* done, we may spend some time seeing what our framework of profit-maximization says *should* be done, and then see if any important objections can be raised to the analysis.

Selling Costs as Investment. A first characteristic of selling costs that strikes the investigator as he considers their nature is that they have many of the aspects of investment. First, a selling cost program cannot be considered outside of a time context, which is to say that it must be viewed for some period in the future. Expenditures made this week in attempting to influence the consumer must be expected to shift the sales curve in future weeks as well as this week; the influence upon the sales curve must be expected to be revealed for a number of weeks in the future. The sales curve does not jump over to the right with the expenditure in Week 1, and then, in the absence of expenditures in Week 2, resume its old position. Consumers' experiences with the greater amount of the product sold in Week 1 will presumably alter their preferences for the product, so that the experience will not be reversible.

Second, if the impact upon receipts can be considered only over a period of weeks, so must the plan of expenditures be considered for a period of time. There is no inherent reason why the best manner of spending a given amount on selling costs is to do so in one large lump sum in one week. Rather, the more plausible pattern of expenditure would seem to be one which is more evenly phased through time.

From both of these aspects of the problem—the fact that the expenditures on selling costs will be in the nature of a pattern of costs through time for a given number of weeks in the future, and the fact that the returns from the campaign will be a pattern of increased revenues expected over a given number of weeks—it would seem that the firm should approach the problem of determining the amounts and allocation of selling costs as it approaches the decisions it makes on investment. In Week 1's market day, the firm must form some expectations for Week 2, Week 3, . . . , Week *h*, of how given amounts of expenditures in Week 1 and each of these future weeks would affect the potential sales of its product at all hypothetical prices. Note that this means it must form expectations of the extent to which $10,000 of selling costs expenditure in Week 5 will affect the sales curve at all prices in Weeks 6, 7, 8, . . . , *h*, and so forth for every week in the horizon.

The firm would then discount all receipts and expenditures over the entire horizon at the rate of return, $1/P_e$, expected to rule over this period (or at the various rates of return expected over the whole horizon if they are not expected to be constant), and these expectational discounted functions will be added to the interrelationships of the model. The profit-maximizing solution will yield values for the amounts and types of advertising and other selling cost expenditures to be made in each week over the horizon of weeks, and the interrelationships from which these solution functions are determined will include the condition that the discounted marginal dollar of selling costs each week in each type of selling cost medium used equal the discounted stream of marginal revenues over the time horizon expected to accrue from it. Each week, of course, the expectations and plans will be revised according to the experience of the previous week.

The naive logical implication of this, of course, is that the firm should go into the long-term bond market and borrow in order to obtain the wherewithal to finance such an investment program. Of course, in our simple economy, the firm would be unable to do so, because it would not have the wherewithal to redeem the bonds at the end of the week, but let us blink this difficulty in order to get closer to the real economy for a moment. Certainly, we do not find firms doing this. Rather, as we have indicated earlier, the evidence seems to be that advertising campaigns are treated as expenditure on current account, although, of course, they are planned over time. Why should this be true? Should not the economist point out that the desirable thing would be to include these activities as part of the firm's capital expenditures?

Of course, the greatest deterrent to the firm's consideration of selling cost expenditures in this light—and most particularly, to borrowing at long term to finance them—is the uncertainty involved in such programs. The success or failure of selling costs in affecting sales curves is probably the most unpredictable of phenomena, subject to all the whims of consumers, the creative imagination of the advertising profession, and so forth. Experience probably builds up slowly in the field, and even the greatest amount of it cannot yield guesses sufficiently reliable to warrant an increase in the firm's fixed indebtedness or a dilution of its equity capital. It is the nature of wise decisionmaking to include uncertainty in the analysis of flows of receipts over time by raising the rate at which one discounts receipts in the future, and this implies that expected receipts that are not quite close in time will be of almost negligible weight in the firm's planning.

However, even after these sharpest features of the analysis have been softened, it is likely that the view of selling costs in this light will have some value for firms. Certainly from the review of the evidence, no such sophistication exists in these directions, and even introducing the basic concepts may allow firms to approach the problems in a more fruitful way.

PRODUCTS AS VARIABLES. Another complication that exists in the analysis of firms' decisionmaking under conditions of sloping demand curves is that of product differentiation. Realistically, firms do not sell corn flakes: they sell Kellogg's Corn Flakes, Post Toasties, and a host of others. Moreover, Kellogg's Corn Flakes can be made more or less sweet, larger or smaller in size, darker or lighter in color, with or without vitamin supplements, and so forth for a very large number of dimensions. Further, they can be packed in a larger or a smaller box, a white or a green box, with or without coupons to be redeemed for silverware, with or without offers of bathtub-worthy diving submarines to be obtained for 50¢ and one box top, and so forth. Beyond this, they may be sold in chain stores only, or in chain stores and independent stores, and so forth.

In the realistic sense, therefore, the product sold by a retailer or a manufacturer is a bundle of qualities, each with a given intensity value, many of which are not concerned physically with the product. The location of the store in which the good is bought, the personality of the salespeople, the atmosphere of the store, the prestige of its name, and many other such qualities, enter into the appeal of the product. By making decisions concerning the outlets to sell his product in, the manufacturer is in a sense varying the product he is selling in such a way as to maximize his profits. More directly, he is taking the same steps when he attempts to find the optimum package in which to sell the product, the optimum degree of sweetness, and so forth, for it.

When these dimensions are added into economic analyses, it may be seen that it would be difficult to find many products exactly like others. Thus, one of the conditions for pure competition would be most difficult of being met. Location, for example, will usually introduce important quality differences into products: two service stations, selling exactly the same brand of gasoline in a city, are not selling the same products in this extended sense if they are located at different points in the city.

The problem of the firm is not only to choose that genus of product that maximizes profit, as we had it do in the beginning of this chapter, but to vary product in all of the dimensions under its control in order to get the highest profit possible. This may imply putting out various models of the product, different colors, different brands of it, and so forth. If we imagine a quality-intensity space in which every potential quality of the product can be measured with indices going from 0 to 1, with noncontinuous attributes receiving index values of 0 if the quality is not possessed and 1 if it is, we may depict the firm as including this space in its data. Its task, then, for expected prices over products described in such bundle-of-quality-intensity terms, is to find that product which maximizes profits, simultaneously with the best input mix and best allocation of an optimum total selling cost.

The difficulty of analyzing these problems—important as they are—in general terms is apparent, and we shall not try to incorporate them in our model in more rigorous form. This is not to imply, however, that they do not constitute some of the most important problems in the decisionmaking of the firm, nor that firms do not devote massive resource efforts to determining values for them.

A Summary

In the analysis of this chapter, we have presented submodels of firm behavior in conditions of nonrivalrous competition under the assumption that minimum cost curves have been determined. Beyond this cost-minimization procedure, firms must, if they are in pure competition, decide upon the maximum-profit output of their standardized good, and, if they face downward-sloping demand curves, they must do this for a product whose qualities may be varied in many directions, as well as deciding upon a maximum-profit selling cost expenditure. We have dealt with these profit-maximization decisions, as well as those for the pure competitor with linear activities, in more or less detail.

Our emphasis in this chapter has been upon the similarities and symmetries of the decisionmaking for firms in the environment of nonrivalrous competition. The linear programming model may always involve corner solutions and the smooth-function models may only occasionally permit them or frequently require them, but the economic reasoning of the models employing these postulate sets is identical. And, again, the sales curve of the firm may be horizontal or slope downward, but given a product and given selling costs (if any), the maximum-profit output reasoning is the same in both cases. Only in the case of selling costs and product differentiation do we encounter basic differences where firms with negatively sloping sales curves differ qualitatively in their decisionmaking.

We must now essay the next task in our concern with building submodels of firms' decisionmaking: the problems of the firm in rivalrous competition.

Selected Readings

1. Kenneth E. Boulding and W. Allen Spivey, *Linear Programming and the Theory of the Firm* (New York: Macmillan, 1960), Ch. 1, 2, 3. A good presentation of linear programming and related concepts from a different viewpoint than that presented in this book.

2. F. Fisher, Z. Griliches, and C. Kaysen, "The Costs of Automobile Model Change Since 1949," *Journal of Political Economy*, LXX (1962), pp. 433–452. An attempt to cost the variation of product in an industry that has come to depend upon it for competition among firms. Some of the techniques used may be more advanced than the student can handle, but the study will still be found valuable.

3. Robert E. Kuenne, "Quality Space, Interproduct Competition, and General Equilibrium Theory," in Robert E. Kuenne, editor, *Monopolistic Competition Theory: Studies in Impact* (New York: John Wiley, 1967). An attempt to build quality differences and product differentiation into the economic model.

4. Lester G. Telser, "How Much Does It Pay Whom to Advertise?," *Papers and Proceedings*, *American Economic Association*, LI (1961), pp. 194–205. A theoretical attempt to account for the varying amounts of selling costs applied to different consumer goods.

CHAPTER 6

The Theory of the Firm in Rivalrous Competition

WITH INTERRELATIONSHIPS [F–1] through [F–8] and their implied System [II] of general solutions we have obtained a determinate submodel of the firm's behavior, at least conceptually. That is to say, the elements that enter into the derivation of values for the variables can be given a formal statement within the confines of the nonrivalrous and purely competitive environment as there defined. Further, we have altered the set of relationships to include nonpure competition of the nonrivalrous sort. In terms of interrelationships of firm with firm, the keynote of that environment was its anonymity. The ramifications of one firm's impacts were lost in a crowd or in the insulating separation of space.

Now we must deal with an environment where these insulations are not present—where a firm must take into account the fact that competitors will feel the impacts of its policies and will react to them. We shall see that in order to obtain determinate solutions for such environments we shall have to introduce postulates of a different sort into the analysis—postulates that are much more specific in content, and that insist upon the specification of certain behavioral attributes of the reacting competitors. But no longer may we conduct our analysis with the faceless mass of competitors possible in Chapters 4 and 5.

Let us return to the starting point of the models for nonrivalrous competition to begin anew in the analysis of the new environment. We assume therefore that relations [F–1], [F′–2], [F–3], [F′–4], [F–5], [F–6], and [F–7] hold for firms, and from them System [II′] is given. That is, at the start of our modelbuilding for this environment, we have for every firm minimum total cost curves.

The Phenomenon of Rivalry

We have consistently defined the crucial distinction between environments in which the firm operates to be that concerned with whether or not the firm feels the repercussions of its own strategies via reactive strategies of its competitors. If it does, these competitors we have defined to be *rivals*, and the competition to be *rivalrous* or *oligopolistic*. The mutual interdependence of decisionmaking within such a group of rivalrous competitors or *oligopolists* ("few sellers") is recognized by each, and each is aware that whatever decision he makes in the profit-maximizing price-and-output, product, and selling cost areas will be felt by his rivals and reacted to.

One important implication of this phenomenon is that the individual firm may not be able to define its sales curve as it did in Chapter 5. The sales curve of the firm for a given product and a given level of selling costs expenditure depicts the amount of the product the firm expects to sell in a domain of relevant prices. Implicitly, as we have seen from our consideration of the demand curve for the individual consumer upon which the sales curve is based, the sales curve assumes that the prices of all other goods (among other data) are held constant at some predetermined level. Now, if a firm has rivals, when the firm changes its price the rivals must be expected to react with price-output, selling costs, or product variation changes of their own. The exact nature of these three potential types of strategy, taken singly or in combination, and their expected success for their adopters may be only vaguely ascertainable from the vantage of the firm originally contemplating a change in its own policies. This uncertainty means, therefore, that on both counts—possible inability to foresee the exact nature of competitors' reactions and, if they are foreseen, to judge their success—the original firm may be unable to define the sales it expects of a given product with given selling costs at a given price.

The ability to define or at least have some ideas concerning the firm's sales curve depends upon the existence of *reaction patterns* that characterize rivals' strategies within the group. That is to say, it may be that rivals have agreed formally to act in concert in jointly determining their strategies. Such cooperative policy formation may range from the tightest agreements that allocate production among the various firms—perhaps closing some down in the interests of joint maximization of group profits—through agreements to divide markets, or set identical prices. We shall term all such groups of rivals, or oligopolists—which term as we have seen recognizes that there is a fewness of sellers in the market so that each rival's action affects each member of the small group—*cartelized rivals*. By this term we mean that there is a formal, active, effective decisionmaking machinery whose result is to remove the oligopolists' autonomy of decisionmaking and subordinate it to the group's interests. This may in fact redound to the benefit of each member of the agreement—indeed, it may be impossible to hold the group to the agreement if any member of it is disaffected, and feels he could do better if his autonomy were restored. Nevertheless, the reactive patterns of the industry under such cooperative agreements are defined for the firm by group-regarding formal procedures.

A second group of reactive patterns we shall term *collusive*. These reactive patterns are those which result when each firm acts independently in the design of its strategies, but where formal contact among the rivals exists such that communication and bargaining among them occur. In the most straightforward case, for example, one rival may attempt to bribe another into acceptance of its policies by offering to coordinate strategies or by making side-payments. These latter might be in the form of money or in the way of favors, positive or negative. The original firm might agree to leave or not enter the other firm's market areas, or not to start a new product line that would interfere with the second firm's established brands, or to license valuable patents it controls to the second firm, and so forth. In the negative sense the first rival might threaten price cuts in strategic areas of the second firm's product line or spatially important markets, or it might threaten to launch a punishing selling cost campaign that would damage the second firm in established areas of product dominance, and so forth. We could illustrate these and many more types of inducements and threats from the rich annals of American oligopolistic competition in the last quarter of the nineteenth century.

The defining characteristic of collusive oligopoly, therefore, is the formal contact of oligopolistic rivals with one another and the bargaining from positions of strength using side-payments of one kind or another to induce other firms to respond in the manner desired to the originating strategy of one firm or group of firms. It differs from cartelized oligopoly in that there is no formal group-regarding, joint decisionmaking procedure that sets firms' policies essentially simultaneously and that makes of the firm's reaction pattern a group-determined response.

A third type of oligopolistic reaction pattern we shall term that of *tacit collusion*. By this phrase we wish to denote those types of industrial structure in which cartel action and cooperative bargaining among autonomous firms do not occur, but in which the inner logic of the structure of production among the rivals and, perhaps more importantly, the experience gained by all firms in coexistence over a rather long period, lead each rival without any formal contact with his peers to follow a pattern of strategy that is strongly predictable by his fellows in their strategic decisionmaking. That is, the mores and folkways of the industry, as they have evolved over its history, and as they reflect the personalities of the leaders of the industry over its history, decide in as definite a way as a more overt collusion would have, which firm is the price leader and which firms are the price followers, which firms will be allowed a price differential on their products, which firm will be allowed to dominate certain market areas, whether or not an industry will permit any one plant to be built in a plush market or whether that market is one in which all will have an opportunity to sell with no special advantages, and so forth.

The institutional bars in the United States to the first two types of oligopoly —at least for domestic markets—make the third type of oligopoly peculiarly important. The recognition of mutual or circular interdependence by each member of a group must lead to utter anarchy of decisionmaking unless each can form *some* idea of how his rivals will react to his own decisions. The very structure of his environment forces each member of the group to search for consistent patterns of his rivals' behavior, at the same time that a desire for order puts something of a premium upon consistency in his own reactions. The result is that the *effects of collusive action* can be obtained even in its absence. Close price followership of one or two large firms in the industry, or similarity in price bids on contracts, or failure to exploit spatial opportunities in locating new plants or entering new markets, may occur without any formal consultation among the rivals.

Lastly, and more or less to provide a theoretical analogue at the other extreme to the case of cartelization rather than to pursue a realistic case, we may specify an enrivonment of *complete uncertainty*, in which each rival has absolutely no idea how his fellows will react to his own strategies. Again, it would be very difficult to find an oligopolistic market in which prior experience with and knowledge of the controlling individuals in the industry did not give rivals a more or less good idea of the actions that might follow feasible decisions of their own. However, it does give us a theoretical starting point where each firm cannot draw its sales curve except on the basis of some subjective probability reasoning concerning its rivals' behavior. In such situations as these—even if they are pure theory—we may gain valuable insights into the behavior of realistic markets. As in the case of pure competition in Chapter 5, using it as a starting point may prove to be convenient.

In this chapter we shall present a variety of models and of less rigorous analyses designed to obtain certain patterns that are possible or likely to be met in reality. We emphasize that the phenomenon of rivalry makes a solution on the basis of information obtained from the data and postulate sets of Chapters 4 and 5 impossible to attain: we must add to them specific information about the reaction patterns of rivals if known. There is an infinity of possible ways in which a group of rivals can react to strategic moves by one or more of their number, and consequently we cannot hope to present one or two neat models that fit all realistic cases. Profit maximization under the conditions of rivalry is not easily defined, so that the heavy use made of such extremum reasoning in determinate economic theory is modified in a large number of ways. Therefore, the reader is cautioned that although we are dealing with the most frequently occurring type of competitive environment in the real world, we can rely upon formal techniques of reasoning that are generally applicable to a very small extent indeed—except to gain insights into the nature of the decisionmaking.

The Environment of Complete Uncertainty

Because it presents the fundamental problems of rivalry in full if unachievable purity, let us see what actions the firm might take in its decisionmaking if it were completely in the dark concerning the reactions of its rivals to its moves. For convenience sake, let us assume that there are only two producers in the industry, each of whom recognizes the interdependence of its decisionmaking with the other, but each of whom has no knowledge of the other's basic reactive tendencies. We shall assume, therefore, that no cartelization is possible, no cooperation or tacit collusion is yet achievable although no doubt each rival hopes they will come, and, therefore, that each acts independently.

Under such circumstances, the problem that would be uppermost in the minds of both rivals probably would be that of the potential instability of the competitive solution that might destroy them both. Let us first, therefore, use an interesting economic technique to illustrate the nature of this difficulty.

POTENTIAL INSTABILITY—THE PRISONERS' DILEMMA

In Table 6–1 we have constructed a tableau that lists an exhaustive set of the strategies available to Firm B during the coming week in the columns, and a similar exhaustive set of strategies available to Firm A in the same period. Let us suppose the following simple situation: a price was arrived at last week in the market for the good produced by both firms, and the only strategies in the strategy sets of both of them in the current week is to hold price constant at last week's level or to lower price by 10 per cent. Each firm, therefore, in the absence of the other firm's strategic decision, must make a decision on Monday, the market day, and is committed to that decision for the entire week.

TABLE 6-1: A TABLEAU FOR THE PRISONERS' DILEMMA

		FIRM B'S STRATEGY SET	
		1. Constant Price	*2. Lower Price*
FIRM A'S STRATEGY SET	1. *Constant Price*	1,000; 1,000	−2,000; 1,500
	2. *Lower Price*	1,500; −2,000	100; 100

In each of the cells of the tableau we have listed the payoff to A first and to B second, if the relevant combination of strategies were selected. If A and B both decide to keep prices constant this week at their level last week, each will earn $1,000 in profits. However, if A holds price constant and B lowers his price, A will suffer losses of $2,000 while B will enjoy larger profits of $1,500. We have assumed that the same payoffs will be reversed if B decides to hold price constant and A lowers his price. On the other hand, if both firms lower prices, each will make only $100 in profits for the week.

This situation has been called *the prisoners' dilemma* because it can be interpreted in the following manner, which helps to bring out the inner logic of the problem. Two suspects are picked up by the police independently on suspicion of having jointly committed a burglary. They are kept apart from each other by the police and, in an attempt to get confessions, the police offer inducements to each man. Both men know that if neither confesses they will both get off with 30-day sentences for disturbing the peace—trumped-up charges by the police. If either confesses and the other holds out, the informer gets off scot-free while the latter gets five years for burglary. If both confess, they each get 3-year sentences.

This is the kind of dilemma faced by each of our duopolists. Both are well-off if the status quo is maintained. However, each is tempted to disturb it because (1) if he does and his rival does not, his profits will be higher, and (2) if he does not and his rival does, severe losses will be inflicted upon him. Each is led, therefore, to lower his price, and they both are severely penalized. This is a situation in which the structure of the game imprisons the participants, because each of the duopolists' actions can be made to seem quite rational under reasonable assumptions. Consider, for example, Firm A: if it chooses the first strategy, it will be aware of the temptation facing Firm B to inflict a severe loss upon it or to avoid the same severe loss being inflicted upon Firm B. The same reasoning holds true for Firm B. Therefore, juggling these "if I, then he" propositions in the predecision phase of the market day, each firm may be led through a rational process to select a joint solution that is quite below what is possible if they both could be assured of the other's reaction.

Note that this uncertainty results in a lower price to the public and therefore some basis for reducing all types of nonindependent action as a policy measure exists. But, on the other hand, this can be gained at the cost of extreme instability in the market for the firms' product, to the extent of endangering a positive supply of it. Price wars may be a result of such a structure, although, as we shall see, when we put this *game* on a continuing basis, with participants playing it week after week, we should expect some type of tacit cooperation to result. But even under these conditions each participant may be tempted now and again to seek the short-run gain by lowering his price, upsetting the stability of the market, and possibly leading the other rival to take punitive action.

We have in this paradigm, therefore, not so much a realistic presentation of the day-by-day problems of decisionmaking in the oligopolistic industry, as the core problem of their existence, although the defense mechanisms that have been developed to prevent its emergence may be so effective that its immediacy is not so great. Potentially, however, the upsetting of the current equilibrium with consequent losses for all or most of the participants must threaten the oligopolistic industry.

A FIRST REACH FOR ABSOLUTE CERTAINTY: COURNOT-TYPE SOLUTIONS

Another type of reaction that is capable of adoption by a rival in such conditions of absolute uncertainty is to formulate a hypothesis about the other rival's behavior and cling to it, even in the face of its demonstrated invalidity, perhaps in the hope that the rival will ultimately see its value and adopt this procedure. More realistically, again, we may present this type of action as an initial introduction to the problem of reaction curves, frankly recognizing its limitations as a representation of rational firm behavior.

THE COURNOT MODEL. Let us assume that three *symmetry* conditions hold true for our pair of rivals: (1) that they are producing exactly the same product measured in exactly the same units, and that the maximum output of each is one-half the amount which would saturate the market; (2) that consumers are absolutely indifferent between them if their products sell at the same price; and (3) that both firms have identical cost structures. These assumptions are not neutral in their implications for rivals' behavior, needless to say, and we shall point out some of their bearings later.

For even greater simplicity let us assume that the sales curve for the product is a straight line with intercepts on both axes, as illustrated in Figure 6–1, and also that total, average, and marginal costs of production are zero. That is, let us assume that each firm can obtain its product at real costs of zero,

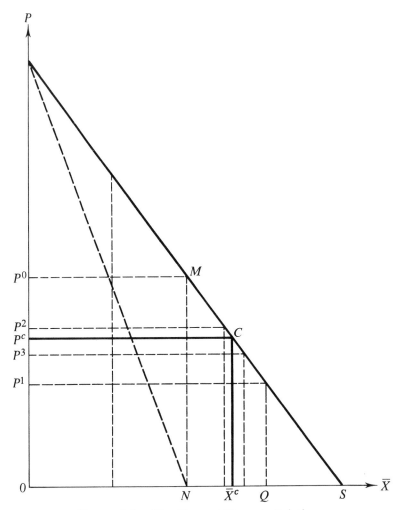

FIGURE 6-1. The Cournot Duopoly Solution.

perhaps by selling mineral water directly from the springs. These two assumptions are not as restrictive as they may appear to be at first sight—given the symmetry assumptions—and if they were lifted they would not affect our solutions vitally.

Let us now assume that in the absence of knowledge concerning the manner in which Firm B will react, Firm A assumes that this week Firm B will continue to produce the same amount of output as it did last week. We shall assume that Firm B's decisions are made upon the same hypothesis concerning Firm A's reactions. Let us begin by assuming that Firm A initially in Week 0 has the entire market to itself as a monopolist; then, for a linear sales curve and a marginal cost of zero, it is easily shown that marginal cost will equal marginal revenue will equal zero at the output level ON that is halfway between zero output and the output that would be sold at a zero price.[1] Throughout our analysis we shall term this latter output *saturation output*, and denote it S.

Assume now that Firm B arrives on the scene in Week 1 and, in the absence of any knowledge concerning the nature of the impact on Firm A of its own decisions, assumes there will be none. Specifically, let us assume that Firm B will assume that in Week 1, regardless of what it does, Firm A will continue to sell ON in output. What Firm B does essentially is to truncate the aggregate sales curve at the point M, and treat the remainder of the sales curve as its own. Therefore, it essentially treats the segment MS as its sales curve and, on the basis of the same type of reasoning as that in which Firm A engaged, it will set the output at NQ, which is halfway between N and S. This will be $\frac{1}{4}$ of the saturation sales, so that with Firm A's initial $\frac{1}{2}$, the market will be supplied with $\frac{3}{4}$ of the saturation output. Price, therefore, which must be the same for the outputs of both producers, will fall from P^0 to P^1.

But, in Week 2, each firm can make a readjustment, because the expectation of each firm may not have been fulfilled in Week 1. Firm A, ignoring the output reaction of Firm B the previous week, now assumes that the rival will continue to supply $\frac{1}{4}$ of S, and thus, subtracting out that amount from S, it decides to produce $\frac{1}{2}(S - \frac{1}{4}S) = \frac{3}{8}S$. In similar fashion Firm B continues to assume that Firm A will continue to supply its previous output, or $\frac{1}{2}S$, and does not alter its output, so that total output in Week 2 is $\frac{3}{8}S + \frac{2}{8}S = \frac{5}{8}S$. This is a fall in total output and causes P to rise to P^2.

In Week 3, however, Firm B's expectations have been disappointed. It now assumes, ignoring experience, that Firm A will continue to supply $\frac{3}{8}S$, and chooses the output $\frac{1}{2}(S - \frac{3}{8}S) = \frac{5}{16}S$, while Firm A continues to supply $\frac{3}{8}S$. Therefore, total supply reaches $\frac{11}{16}S$, and price falls to P^3. This process will continue until a limiting price and output is reached—if ever— for the firms. In fact, if both firms continue to react in this myopic way, such

---

[1] Given a linear sales curve, $P = a - bX$, the total revenue curve will be $PX = aX - bX^2$. Marginal revenue will then be

$$MR = \frac{d(PX)}{dX} = a - 2bX. \tag{1}$$

Thus, the marginal revenue curve will be a straight line with the same price-axis intercept as the sales curve and will have one half the algebraic slope. Therefore, because the profit-maximizing (equals revenue-maximizing) output will be determined where this marginal revenue equals a marginal cost curve that is coincident with the quantity axis, it will cross this axis halfway from the origin to the intercept of the sales curve with the quantity axis.

a limiting position will be reached, and a stationary solution to this dynamic model will emerge. In equilibrium, because both firms are symmetrical in every way, it can be shown that profit maximization by the firms requires that they be supplying equal amounts of product[2]: each firm will be maximizing profits only if it supplies one half of S minus the other's supply when the latter is equal to its own supply. That is,

$$\bar{X}_v = .5(S - \bar{X}_v) \qquad [6\text{–}1]$$

for either firm in equilibrium, while total supply will be

$$\bar{X} = 2\bar{X}_v = S - \bar{X}_v = S - .5\bar{X}$$
$$\bar{X} = .67S, \qquad [6\text{–}2]$$

and so,

$$\bar{X}_v = .33S. \qquad [6\text{–}3]$$

Indeed, these results can be generalized for n oligopolists instead of two. Total supply will be[3]

$$\bar{X} = \frac{n}{n+1} S, \qquad [6\text{–}4]$$

[2] Price is a function of the total supply of product, $\bar{X}$,

$$P = F(\bar{X}), \qquad (1)$$

where total supply is the sum of the firms' separate supplies:

$$\bar{X} = \bar{X}_a + \bar{X}_b = \Sigma \bar{X}_v. \qquad (2)$$

Revenue (and therefore profits) for the individual firms are defined as

$$\pi_v = \bar{X}_v \cdot F(\bar{X}), \qquad (3)$$

in our zero-cost conditions. Under appropriate restrictions on the shape of the profit function, which are met in the linear demand case, profits will be a maximum for the firm when

$$\frac{d(\bar{X}_v \cdot F(\bar{X}))}{d\bar{X}_v} = \bar{X}_v \cdot F' + P = 0, \qquad F' < 0 \qquad (4)$$

or

$$\bar{X}_v = -\frac{P}{F'}, \qquad (5)$$

which is the same for both firms. Total output is, then,

$$2\bar{X}_v = \bar{X} = -\frac{2P}{F'}, \qquad (6)$$

or, in general, when there are n firms,

$$n\bar{X}_v = \bar{X} = -\frac{nP}{F'}. \qquad (7)$$

[3] In footnote 2 we have shown that $\bar{X}^\circ = -(nP^\circ/F')$. Let us prove now that for the case of the linear sales curve, $P = a - bX$, this implies that $X^\circ = (n/n + 1)S$. It is simply shown that $F' = -b$ and $S = a/b$. We may rewrite the sales curve in the form $P = bS - b\bar{X}$ and the expression for equilibrium output as $\bar{X}^\circ = (nP^\circ/b)$. From the linear sales curve, at equilibrium quantities, therefore, $P^\circ = b(S - \bar{X}^\circ)$, or $\bar{X}^\circ = n(S - \bar{X}^\circ)$, from which the desired relationship follows directly.

and individual supplies will be

$$\bar{X}_v = \frac{1}{n+1} S.$$ [6–5]

Thus, with every entry of a new firm, supply increases and approaches the purely competitive level S. Indeed, if we allow n to increase indefinitely, $n/n + 1$ will approach 1, and thus the purely competitive result is obtained as we go to the limit. This solution for the rivalrous environment, where n is relatively small, is the *Cournot* point $C = [\bar{X}^c, P^c]$, as graphed on Figure 6–1.

THE COURNOT MODEL WITH ONE KNOWLEDGEABLE RIVAL. It is, of course, unrealistic to assume that as the weeks go on the rivals will not become aware of the irrationality of their assumptions that the other's outputs will be held constant as they adjust their own. Sooner or later, therefore, we would expect to pass out of the case of complete uncertainty—which we have assumed led to the initial tacit assumption of constant rival supplies—to that of mutual interdependence recognized. For example, suppose that Firm A realizes that Firm B is not keeping its output constant in response to Firm A's actions, while Firm B continues to be unaware of the reaction of its rival.

In such a case Firm A will be able to define the reaction curve of its rival. Let us return to Week 1, in which Firm A begins as a monopolist supplying $.5S$ as a maximum-profit output. When Firm B enters and supplies $.25S$, it will now pay Firm A to hold its output constant, for in this case price will fall to P^1, but Firm A will be selling 67 per cent of the market and Firm B only 33 per cent. As a monopolist, Firm A received $P^0 \times .5S$ in profits; now, as a duopolist, it is getting $.5P^0 \times .5S = .25P^0S$, which is half of what it got before. But this will be better than what it would receive if it continued under the delusion concerning the constancy of its rival's supply behavior, for the final price under this assumption would be $.67P^0$ with a consequent higher total profit for both firms, but Firm A would receive only $.67P^0 \times .33S = .22P^0S$. This more sophisticated level of knowledge on the part of Firm A would not be detrimental to the interests of the public, because a larger amount of product would be supplied at a price closer to its marginal social cost (of zero). But the determinateness of the case depends upon one of the rivals making an unrealistic assumption concerning the reaction curve of the other.

THE COURNOT MODEL WITH TWO KNOWLEDGEABLE RIVALS. Even though we pass out of the type of oligopolistic environment where both rivals seize upon a rigid assumption concerning their opponents' reactions by virtue of a lack of knowledge, into an environment of certain knowledge of these patterns, let us complete our consideration of this case by assuming that Firm B realizes that Firm A will vary its output in response to Firm B's decisions.

We then leave the world of determinateness. For if Firm A adopts the policy of rigidly producing .5S, Firm B must find it most profitable in the short run to produce .25S. It might, therefore, follow the policy of being an *output follower*: that is, it would recognize Firm A as the *output leader* of the industry, and, when Firm A set an output, take that as a datum and adjust. We would then eliminate the fear of instability in the industry, and move up into the third of our oligopolistic environments, in which tacit cooperation restores determinateness. But note that the willingness of Firm B to play this role depends upon such specifics as the personalities of the men in charge of Firm B and Firm A, the costs of not accepting this imposed role, and so forth: facts, in short, that could not be obtained except by study of the specifics of the industry, and which are not readily generalizable.

For example, if Firm B were not satisfied with producing .25S, it might produce, say, .5S. This would force both firms to accept zero profits, and it might, if Firm A were unwilling to fight, lead it to accept the followership role and produce .25S. On the other hand, and probably more realistically, after a period of sharp conflict some intermediate solution might be arrived at, perhaps the joint-profit maximization output ON. The basic importance of the analysis is to see that if both parties adopt more realistic outlooks upon the rationality of their rival, the division of output and its total becomes indeterminate and dependent upon many specific factors not capable of ready generalization.

THE COURNOT-TYPE MODEL WITH PRICE RATHER THAN OUTPUT POLICIES. The Cournot solution—and indeed, all of the variants of it with which we have dealt—may be viewed as unrealistic in quite another sense. All of them involve rivals setting output policies—that is, each rival decides to produce a fixed amount of output and throws it on the market to obtain the price for it which the market dictates. However, a much more common practice for oligopolies to follow is to set a price, and to offer to sell as much at that price as the market will take.

One reason why oligopolies are much more apt to adopt a price policy than an output policy is that with the former the effects of miscalculating are much less apt to disturb a stable oligopolistic situation. If it turns out the firm produced so much that a fall in price is necessary to sell it, that fall in price might very well touch off a price war in which all rivals would suffer large losses, even when the firm had no intention of disturbing the status quo. On the other hand, if prices are held rigid, miscalculations will merely result in losses or fewer profits as well as the carryover of inventories than might have been obtained if correct foresight had been enjoyed, but without unsettling competitive price wars.

This asymmetry of the potential destabilizing impacts of price and of output policies is an important one in understanding modern industrial policy, and must be emphasized. If we retain the assumption of the Cournot model that total market demand is perfectly known and if we convert the Cournot model into a system with price policies being followed by rivals, the potential solutions are much less favorable to all parties than when output policies are followed. It is true that this result depends upon the assumption that demand is perfectly foreseen, for in the absence of this certainty, output policies could result in fluctuating prices, which could be misinterpreted as price-cutting. That is, of the two possible policies—a price and an output policy—the former has the immediate impact of signalling to competitors the desire or lack of desire to upset the stable solution then ruling, whereas the latter, in being unknown to rivals, can only be guessed at through its impact on prices. Therefore, in a situation where rivals are concerned to maintain the perhaps hard-won status quo ruling in the industry, a direct control over price would seem preferable.

Suppose, now, in the original Cournot solution, both rivals are capable of supplying the entire market, and that both rivals make the assumption that their opposite numbers will keep their *prices* constant when they adjust their own prices. In Week 0 let Firm A be a monopolist and set P^0 as the monopoly price. Then, in Week 1, when Firm B comes on the scene, under the assumption of a fixed price for Firm A, it will pay Firm B to set a price slightly under P^0, for this will take the entire market away from Firm A and therefore maximize Firm B's profits. But, of course, it will then pay Firm A in Week 2 to cut price slightly under this price set by Firm B, and so forth, until price is bid down to the competitive level of zero.

Price competition, therefore, in the sense of setting prices as a policy, is more destructive of the rivals' welfare than output policy, under the unrealistic assumptions of each firm that his rival will not alter his behavior. Moreover, if one of the rivals becomes knowledgeable concerning the reaction patterns of his opposite number, there is no strategy he can employ that will have hopes of restoring stability, short of his abandoning production, for his rival will always seek to capture the whole market no matter what price he sets. If both rivals become knowledgeable, we are once more in the area of indeterminateness where some sort of tacit collusion may be expected to emerge over time, for utter price war of a blundering type may be expected in situations (where costs are not zero) to carry price below cost and to inflict actual losses upon the participants. Consequently, unless one or more controlling personalities are peculiarly obstinate, we must expect the actors to struggle through to some type of stable price solution. But, again, this takes us into the area of our third type of environment—tacit collusion—and we shall reserve further comments for that discussion.

The Attempt to Foresee a Spectrum of Rival Reactions— Game Theory

THE ZERO-SUM GAME

Let us now drop the postulate that in his lack of knowledge each entrepreneur makes the rigid assumption that his rival has a 100 per cent probability of following one strategy out of a large number in his strategy set, and let us suppose that each rival selects a finite number of strategies that are potentially capable of being used by his rival. We have reentered the world of the prisoners' dilemma in defining a set of alternative strategies, which we shall assume to be exhaustive in setting bounds on potential behavior.

For example, let us return to the Cournot type of situation with each rival adopting an output policy, but each doing so in full knowledge that the other can react with any one of a set of such policies. To make our example concrete let us assume that the sales curve to the industry is the following,

$$\bar{X} = 1,200 - 10P, \qquad [6-6]$$

so that $S = 1,200$ in our previous examples and on Figure 6–1. Now, let us view the problem from the viewpoint of Firm A, and to make it simple let us assume that Firm A views its own strategy set as consisting of four strategies:

A.1. Producing $.5S$
A.2. Producing $.33S$
A.3. Producing $.25S$
A.4. Producing $0S$.

Further, we shall assume that Firm B has and is assumed by Firm A to have exactly the same exhaustive strategy set. Let us display in the tableau of Table 6–2 the profit payoffs to Firm A for every combination of its own and Firm B's pure strategies.

Now we shall make an initial assumption: in the absence of further knowledge, Firm A believes that Firm B is a perfectly malevolent opponent, in the sense that Firm B interprets every dollar of loss to Firm A as a dollar of gain to itself. This is admittedly quite unrealistic, because it makes Firm B's gains the mirror image of Firm A's losses, without even considering the earnings that the combination of strategies in the cells imply for Firm B.

TABLE 6–2: A PAYOFF MATRIX FOR FIRM A

	FIRM B'S STRATEGY SET, B			
	B.1 = .5S	B.2 = .33S	B.3 = .25S	B.4 = 0S
FIRM A'S A.1 = .5S	0	12,000	18,000	36,000
STRATEGY A.2 = .33S	8,000	16,000	19,950	32,000
SET, A A.3 = .25S	9,000	15,050	18,000	27,000
A.4 = 0S	0	0	0	0

Nevertheless, despite the rather self-centered, paranoid outlook of Firm A, we shall assume it as an initial postulate concerning Firm B's behavior in an uncertain world.

Note that our state of *uncertainty* includes a good deal of knowledge. We know all of Firm A's strategies, all of Firm B's strategies, and all of the payoffs to Firm A of any combination of strategies, with, under our assumption, the index of satisfaction derived from the outcomes by Firm B. This type of game—where the rivals are assumed to be at utter and complete loggerheads, in that each one's loss is an exact index of the other's gain, so that for any cell the net payoff over both rivals is zero—is called a *zero-sum* game. Although it is the type of game that is most amenable to analysis by current game theory techniques, one can see that the assumption frequently violates the nature of the payoffs in oligopoly, and therefore that the zero-sum game is not readily applicable. Nonetheless, as an initial introduction to the techniques of game theory, we shall use it.

Firm A views Firm B as a rational, calculating, knowledgeable opponent whose own best interest lies in making Firm A fare as badly as it can. This situation might indeed be approached when two rivals are bent on eliminating their opponent from the industry, and where the money losses of an opponent are linearly related to his survival capacity.

Consider Firm A's train of thought. First, it will never play strategy A.4, which consists of producing nothing at all. We can see this because A.4's payoffs are dominated in the strict sense by strategies A.2 and A.3, in that column by column the firm does better with each of these latter strategies; and A.4 is weakly dominated by A.1, in that the firm earns at least as much by playing it whatever the opponent does as it earns with A.4. If a strategy is strictly or weakly dominated by at least one other, we can eliminate it from the strategy set, because it will never be played by a rational profit maximizer.

Which, then, of the three remaining strategies should Firm A play under the assumptions it is making about Firm B's motivation? Firm B, under these projected assumptions, will select a strategy from its set in the absence of knowledge as to Firm A's choice, and it will find its own strategy B.4 dominated too. That is, were Firm B to produce nothing Firm A would get at least as much (and therefore Firm B at most as little) as it would from any of the other three strategies. Indeed, Firm B's B.1 dominates the other three strategies in its set, because by playing this strategy, Firm B can hold Firm A to no more than it could hold its opponent to if it played B.2, B.3, or B.4. Consequently, Firm B must be expected to play strategy B.1. Firm A, then, reasoning in this projective fashion about Firm B's behavior, would rationally argue that it should select that one of its own three nondominated strategies which would yield the maximum profits obtainable under the constraint that Firm B plays its dominating strategy. The maximum payoff to Firm A is $9,000 in column 1, occurring for A.3, and therefore we would predict that Firm A will choose to produce .25S and Firm B, .50S.

Such a neat solution to zero-sum games may not always exist, in which case we will follow a train of reasoning discussed below. In general, we can test to see whether such a determinate point exists, and, if it does, what strategy pairs are involved, in the following fashion. On the right-hand side of the tableau of Table 6–2, next to each row, write the minimum payoff obtainable from Firm A's play of that strategy. Firm A, being a conservative decision-maker who grants his opponent the compliment of being extremely farseeing and intelligent, assumes that Firm B will play its own best strategy, and therefore that Firm A will have to be defensive against it. This argues for Firm A's playing that strategy which would yield it the *highest minimum* payoff in the table. That is, under this assumption of Firm B's behavior, Firm A decides to choose that strategy which would provide a guarantee that Firm B could not reduce its payoff below that minimum level by playing any of the four strategies listed. If Firm A plays that strategy which yields the highest minimum payoff in the table, no matter what Firm B does in playing the four strategies discussed, it cannot reduce Firm A's payoff below that value.

In Firm A's projective vision, Firm B views Firm A as a knowledgeable, intelligent opponent, who will try to do as well as he can. Therefore, by writing the maxima of the columns beneath the respective columns, Firm B will attempt to limit Firm A's gains by playing that strategy which keeps its gains at the minimum of those maxima. That is, by playing the strategy that yields Firm A at best the lowest maximum, Firm B can guarantee that Firm A will not do better and can do worse if it selects from its given set of four a strategy other than the one giving that maximum.

Now, if the value of the maximum minimum in the rows (the *maximin*) equals the value of the minimum maximum of the columns (the *minimax*) we have a *saddle point* for the pure strategies. That is to say, neither opponent, on the basis of this train of reasoning, will have any inducement to change his strategy. Firm B, in our case, obviously will not change because, regardless of the choice of strategy of Firm A, it can never keep Firm A's profits at levels less than those in column 1. And Firm A will not be enticed to change because whatever strategy it chooses makes its outcome worse. Therefore, each firm, given the actions of the other, is doing as well as it can do. However, as we have indicated already, this simple situation may not in fact exist, in which case we must use another technique.

Before we turn to this, however, let us comment upon the results obtained. It will be noted that under the conditions we have stated, this strategy induces a quite conservative result for Firm A: it leads the firm to an output followership solution of the type we have discussed in the case where one rival becomes knowledgeable in the Cournot model. That is, this type of solution is that which would result if Firm B realized that Firm A was not keeping its output constant in response to Firm B's actions, and therefore went to the monopoly point and let Firm A adjust as best it could. This is an excellent example of the basic point that maximin strategic reasoning is extremely conservative, in that it expects the opponent to be completely knowledgeable concerning the set of his own and one's own strategies, to know the payoff outcomes of each cell in the table, to be completely rational in his decisionmaking—in short, its employer expects the worst.

We have seen that over a series of weeks this might not be the best strategy in some higher sense: indeed, it is the most passive strategy the firm can adopt short of going out of business. It may pay Firm A to raise its output to show Firm B that it will not passively accept the followership role, or even try to force the role upon Firm B itself. In a dynamic world, the options of the firm are much greater than the narrow set defined in the strategies and the rationality of the firm in two person, zero-sum game theory.

To illustrate the method of solution for the game if we do not get a saddle point for the pure strategies, let us suppose that the government, hoping to get Firm A to produce as much as the strategies allow, gives it a subsidy of $13,000 if both it and Firm B produce $.5S$ each, and obtains the subsidy by taking $13,000 from Firm B. Then the payoff in the cell of row 1, column 1 of Table 6–3 becomes $13,000 instead of the zero value it had in Table 6–2. Firm A's effective strategy set is again that containing A.1, A.2, and A.3, while Firm B's set now contains B.1 and B.2, because the second column is no longer dominated by the first. We reproduce the new situation below, eliminating dominated strategies.

Suppose Firm A played its maximin strategy A.1, and Firm B played its minimax strategy B.1. This pair of strategies could not lead to a steady state if a time dimension existed in the solution. For example, if this were the solution for Week 1, in Week 2 Firm B would find that as long as Firm A

TABLE 6–3: THE PAYOFF MATRIX WITH SUBSIDY TO FIRM A

		FIRM B'S EFFECTIVE STRATEGY SET		
		B.1 = .5S	B.2 = .33S	Row Minima
FIRM A'S	A.1 = .5S	13,000	12,000	12,000
EFFECTIVE STRATEGY	A.2 = .33S	8,000	16,000	8,000
SET	A.3 = .25S	9,000	15,050	9,000
Column Maxima		13,000	16,000	

plays A.1, it should play B.2, and let us assume that it does. But having done so, it affords Firm A the opportunity in Week 3 to play A.2, its best option under the assumption Firm B plays B.2. But then in Week 4 Firm B will shift back to B.1, and so forth indefinitely with no stable solution occurring.

Now when we interpret the game as being played through time it is possible to attain a different type of saddle point: one in which so-called mixed strategies are used by both firms. Let us adopt this viewpoint: suppose that Firm A considered the choice of a strategy as a drawing from a lottery in which the probability of selecting each of the three strategies had been set in some optimal fashion. That is, let us define a *mixed strategy* as some convex combination of the three pure strategies, where the weights are the probabilities of drawing the relevant pure strategy and playing it. For example, one such strategy for Firm A might be

$$(.5 \, A.1 + .3 \, A.2 + .2 \, A.3), \qquad [6\text{--}7]$$

which means that the probability of playing A.1 this week is .5, of A.2 is .3, and of A.3 is .2. Operationally, we may imagine the firm to draw at random from a universe that contains slips of paper with A.1, A.2, and A.3 printed on them in these proportions. Let us assume that the firm will value the outcomes of these mixed strategies at the value obtained by applying the same weights column by column to the payoffs and summing over the columns. For example, if Firm B played its B.1, the payoff to Firm A of the mixed strategy in [6–7] would be

$$.5(13,000) + .3(8,000) + .2(9,000) = 10,700. \qquad [6\text{--}8]$$

Now consider the problem from the viewpoint of Firm B. It also may play its two strategies in convex combinations to obtain mixed strategies. On Figure 6–2 we have labelled the horizontal axis as the probability of Firm B playing B.1, running from 1 to 0. Any point on the axis is a choice by Firm B of a proportion in which to play B.1 and the implied proportion to play B.2.

Thus, for a probability of 1 of playing B.1, Firm A can get a maximum payoff of 13,000 by playing its A.1. By playing B.2 with certainty (the probability of playing B.1 is 0) Firm B allows Firm A to obtain a maximum payoff of 16,000 by the latter playing A.2. However, by playing mixed strategies and by accepting probabilistically-weighted payoffs in the same manner as the payoffs to pure strategies, Firm B can gain a considerable protection against Firm A's pure strategies.

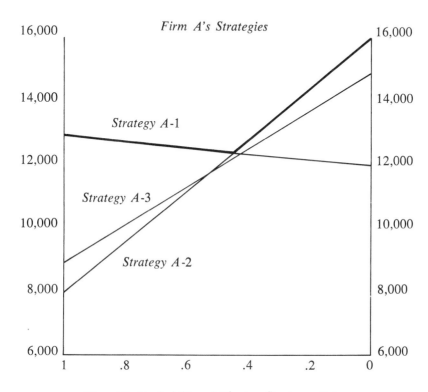

Firm B's Probability of Playing Strategy B-1

FIGURE 6–2.   The Effectiveness of Firm B's Mixed Strategies Against Firm A's Pure Strategies.

For example, if Firm B plays the mixed strategy consisting of a .8 probability of playing B.1 and a .2 probability of playing B.2, then it can assure that the maximum payoff that Firm A can get will be 12,800 (.8 × 13,000 + .2 × 12,000) if Firm A plays Strategy A.1. We have drawn in heavy lines the maximum expected payoff that Firm A would receive from any of the three strategies in its pure strategy set for every possible mixed strategy available to Firm B.

The minimax strategy for Firm B—that mixed strategy which yields the smallest maximum payoff to Firm A—occurs at the intersection of the lines for A.1 and A.2, at the probability value of 4/9 = .44 for the play of B.1. Therefore, as a protection against the pure strategies of Firm A the optimal strategy for Firm B is to play B.1 44 per cent of the times and B.2 56 per cent of the times. This yields a *maximum expected payoff* to Firm A of 12,440, and no matter what Firm A does in the matter of choosing a pure strategy to play each week, it can get no more than this, even if it played the same pure strategy each week and Firm B did not catch on to the pattern of play and take advantage of his knowledge. Indeed, this strategy of Firm B's makes the two effective pure strategies for Firm A equally profitable, so that the latter could play either with indifferent preference, except for this one joker of giving valuable information to Firm B. If Firm A were to play strategy A.1 or A.2 all the time, Firm B would soon realize it and alter its mixed strategy to be either a probability of 0 or of 1 respectively in playing its own B.1.

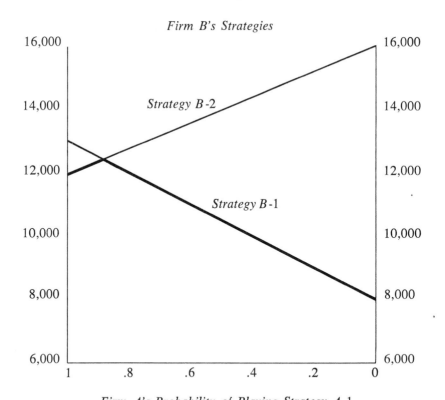

Firm B's Strategies

Firm A's Probability of Playing Strategy A-1

FIGURE 6–3.   The Effectiveness of Firm A's Mixed Strategies Against Firm B's Pure Strategies.

Therefore, Firm A too must randomize its strategies in order that Firm B cannot guess which it will choose on any particular play of the game. But that is about all we can say at the moment, except that Firm A may be seen from Figure 6–2 to be able to eliminate A.3 from its effective strategy set. This is because it lies wholly below the maxima traced out by the line segments formed from A.1 and A.2. Whatever Firm B does, Firm A will always do better playing one of these two. However, although we know Firm A must randomize between these two effective strategies, it does not follow that the best probability of selecting A.1 is .5. Let us therefore study Figure 6–3, which shows the payoffs to Firm A for any mixed strategy of Firm A involving A.1 and A.2 against the two pure strategies B.1 and B.2.

We have drawn in heavy lines the *minimum* expected payoff that Firm A would receive for any of its mixed strategies against either of Firm B's pure strategies. Note that the maximum of these minima (the maximin) occurs at the value of about .9 for the probability of playing A.1. Therefore, the optimum mixed strategy for Firm A against the pure strategies of Firm B is to play, on a random basis, A.1 90 per cent of the times and A.2 10 per cent of the times. The expected payoff to Firm A if it does this—that probabilistic payoff below which Firm B cannot lower it—is $.89 \times 13,000 + .11 \times 8,000 \cong 12,440$, or the same payoff which we obtained as the minimum of the maximum payoffs. Indeed, this value is called *the value of the game* and it will be the same for both mixed strategies, just as it is for the solution when a pure-strategy saddle point exists. Further, it was the great contribution of von Neumann to prove that if mixed strategies are allowed into the game, such a saddle point will *always* exist.

One difficulty with the mixed strategy in game theory is that it is difficult to interpret its meaning in a game in which only one play is made. In this situation there can be no worry about the opponent's guessing one's strategy from previous plays. On the other hand, if the game is a continuing one, as in our case, with a new choice of strategies each week, the mixed-strategic game does lend itself to interpretation as we have done.

We may summarize our conclusion concerning the modified Cournot-type situation, in which one rival is viewed as having no interest in his own profits but only in minimizing the profits received by his opponent. This allows us to interpret the rivalry in so-called zero-sum game terms. In this situation, the profit-maximizing rival will follow the most conservative policy of becoming an output-follower when no outside payments or other collusion is permitted. When we altered conditions to give Firm B a second undominated strategy, Firm A was seen to have an optimal mixed strategy of producing .5S about 90 per cent of the weeks and .33S about 10 per cent of the weeks for an expected payoff of about 12,440 per week, while Firm B's best interference strategy consists in producing .5S about 44 per cent of the weeks and .33S about 56 per cent of the weeks. The supply of output to the public fluctuates between .66S to S over the weeks, with a mean expectation of about .89S per week.

THE TWO-PERSON, NONZERO-SUM GAME

We must now take another step toward reality, however, and in so doing reveal how much of game theory is disqualified as giving close approximations to it by virtue of the lack of relevance of the zero-sum assumption. We obtained our outlook of total rivalry by assuming that Firm B was interested only in minimizing Firm A's profits. But in economic reality, this is quite unlikely except in the most exceptional circumstances when *guerre à outrance* is being waged. Rather, to use our Cournot-type example, each cell in Table 6–2 should contain not only a profit entry for Firm A, but one for Firm B as well, and it will be closer to the truth to expect Firm B to choose strategies designed to maximize its own payoffs rather than to worry overly about minimizing Firm A's profits.

When we do this, however, the game becomes immediately more complicated, and one for which it is more difficult to define a solution. For the case at hand, because both firms are symmetrical in relevant respects, under our assumptions the payoff matrix is identical for both rivals when the strategies are reversed. We shall define an equilibrium pair of strategies in the same way we did for the zero-sum game: a pair of strategies is an equilibrium pair if and only if neither rival can do better, given the other's choice of strategy in the pair. Thus, for the mixed-strategy case we have just investigated, we can see from the analysis that neither rival can do better, given the other's playing of the mixed strategy we assigned him, than the mixed strategy we derived for that rival. Moreover, it is possible to assert that for every noncooperative nonzero-sum game with finite numbers of strategies in the strategy sets of the players, at least one mixed-strategy equilibrium will exist.

But though an equilibrium pair might possess an intuitive plausibility in zero-sum theory—even as a mixed-strategy result interpreted as a play of the game over time—the difficulties that arise when both parties are not at complete loggerheads frequently make the equilibrium pair unsatisfactory in this respect. To illustrate this, let us return to the case of the prisoners' dilemma discussed previously. We may now point out that the peculiar feature of the nonzero-sum game there depicted is that Strategy 2 dominates Strategy 1 for *both* rivals. Therefore, the maximin strategies of both rivals yield an equilibrium for the pure strategies [A.2, B.2] in that game, because given that the other rival plays his second strategy, the first rival always does better if he plays his second strategy as well.

But is this a solution in the sense of being the selection of strategies that we would expect to emerge realistically? Imagine that two rivals are in the "hold price constant-lower price" dilemma of Table 6-1, with Strategy 2 dominant for both. Were the game to be played week after week, the game-theoretic reasoning we have used would lead us to predict that week after week the rivals would engage in price war. Even if, through the pattern of their play (and no direct collusion), each rival revealed to the other the desire to choose a hold-firm policy, and thus attempted to induce the other to be nonrational and choose the first strategy, if this choice [A.1, B.1] is made each knows that the rival will always be under the temptation to double-cross and gain the temporary advantage.

Indeed, under the regime of our reasoning, each rival would be nonrational if he did not play Strategy 2 at all times. For suppose the game were to be played for two weeks; then, one may reason in this manner. Even if on Week 1 both players decide to play their first strategy, each must, rationally, decide to play Strategy 2 in Week 2, for in this way he will protect himself against his rival's temptation to do the same thing and benefit in the last week if his rival plays status quo, and at no cost, because the game is not continued in Week 3. Therefore Week 2—the terminal week—is decided. But this in effect means that Week 1 is the new terminal week, and the same reasoning holds for Week 1! No matter how long the finite period we choose, by such chain reasoning we may reason that it will always be the rational choice of both rivals through time not to deviate from their equilibrium pair.

But somehow, from our knowledge of human behavior, few of us would accept this as the solution that would actually emerge: human beings do muddle through to tacit understandings; price wars do not continue forever, even if rivals are not driven out of business; one firm's refusal to defect from tacit bargains does deter rivals from exploiting their best short-run advantage, and so forth. The game theorist's response is that if all of this is true, then the payoffs in the matrix should reflect it, and the equilibrium pairs will be different, but that as long as the conditions are as determined, the rational behavior would be perennial price war in the absence of cartelization or cooperation. We may accept this as just, but not helpful, because in reality we will have to play games whose objective payoffs are net profits, and in this sense we may doubt the realistic relevance of equilibrium strategy pairs in many instances.

Another aspect of nonzero-sum game theory that differs from zero-sum game theory, besides the lessened plausibility of equilibrium strategy pairs, is the fact that communication of one's proposed strategy may in fact be to one's advantage. This is never true in zero-sum game theory: in that environment, if one played a strategy other than the optimum one, the opposing rival would benefit from knowing it, and therefore the original player would lose by divulging his intention to play it, whereas if one played one's optimum strategy one neither gained nor lost by communicating intent. However, in our present game, if rival 1 communicated to rival 2 before the game began that he intended to play Strategy 1 no matter what rival 2 did, and if rival 2 were convinced of his sincerity, rival 1 could benefit by the choice of [A.1, B.1].

Even more importantly—and with consequences of great complexity for the construction of a formal theory of nonzero-sum games—in a nonzero-sum game rivals may benefit *mutually* by collusion. This is never true in zero-sum game theory. That is, it is a valuable insight to see that whenever rivals' interests are not completely antagonistic they usually can do better by cooperating. Because, in the economic sphere (and most other social spheres as well) the nonzero-sum game is the rule, there must always be a tendency inhering in the logic of the game for rivals to get together cooperatively to benefit mutually, and quite frequently this implies conspiracy against the public or other interested parties.

Now, let us return to our Cournot-type game of Table 6–2. Because there is a complete symmetry concerning rivals' payoffs when strategy choices are reversed, the new payoff matrix would be as produced in Table 6–4. We are

TABLE 6–4: A TWO-PERSON, NONZERO-SUM GAME
PAYOFF MATRIX

		FIRM B'S STRATEGY SET, B			
		B.1 = .5S	B.2 = .33S	B.3 = .25S	B.4 = 0S
FIRM A'S	A.1 = .5S	0; 0	12; 8	18; 9	36; 0
STRATEGY	A.2 = .33S	8; 12	16; 16	20; 15	32; 0
SET, A	A.3 = .25S	9; 18	15; 20	18; 18	27; 0
	A.4 = 0S	0; 36	0; 32	0; 27	0; 0

now explicitly recognizing that Firm B is playing the game not to interfere with Firm A's profits except insofar as this is entailed in its own profit-maximization. The complications of this more realistic case have already been mentioned, but it is worth our while to probe them more deeply.

The maximin strategies for Firm A and Firm B are A.3 and B.3, for these guarantee them a best minimum return below which the opposing rival cannot reduce them. It would imply that each rival plans to produce .25S, so that together they produce the monopoly output and share the joint maximum profits equally. This is indeed a happy result of their conservative policies, for it means that with each rival granting his opponent a giant quota of rationality and intelligence (which in all probability he does not possess to such full measure) the structure of the game allows them to set that output which results in the highest total profits on the board, and, by virtue of the symmetry with which we have endowed the firms, to split it equally. This would seem to offer the prospect of obtaining a highly plausible solution, because this might well have emerged from the formation of a cartel or from collusion. Note the fact that the introduction of assumptions that recognize that Firm B is not a total and unremitting opponent of Firm A in the sense of having no other goal but the maximizing of Firm A's embarrassment, has allowed Firm A to double its prospective profits—if, in fact, this strategy pair is a solution to the game.

But, unfortunately for the participants, the maximin pair [A.3, B.3] is not an equilibrium point, for it does not provide the optimal strategy for the other rival's choice. Consider, for example, Firm A. If in Week 1 Firm B does indeed play B.3, it would pay Firm A to play A.2 in Week 2. But if Firm A plays A.2 in Week 2, it will pay Firm B to play B.2 in Week 3. Once this pair of strategies is reached, we do have an equilibrium pair, for in Week 4 Firm A finds that there is no better strategy than A.2 against B.2, and consequently the solution remains at this equilibrium point—the Cournot point! For in this position, each firm produces .33S and the market receives .67S, as we saw the Cournot solution yielded.

Thus, the Cournot model's result, which we criticized before as having been achieved by a reasoning process that was not very perceptive, may receive greater intellectual support by being shown to be the end-result of a rationale that does face up to the fact that the opponent's output may change and that endows him with the greatest of rational powers.

Note also that a milder version of the result of the prisoners' dilemma has occurred. The jointly desirable result in which the rivals share equally the monopoly profit is sabotaged because of the potential short-run benefit each rival may enjoy by leaving the position and by the uncertainty each rival feels about the other's adhering to the tacitly-arrived-at "bargain." Uncertainty concerning the rival's "honorableness" leads each rival to accept smaller profits than those the most conservative policy would allow them to enjoy. But if this game were played over many weeks—and by this game we mean the one depicted in the payoff matrix of Table 6–4 specifically—could we not expect that the solution would indeed be the equilibrium point rather than the joint-profit maximization point?

Our own answer would be no, for in the present example if the firms were doublecrossed they would not suffer great disadvantages, and the potential losses might well be worthwhile to attempt to establish the joint-profit result. For example, suppose Firm A saw the possibility of trying to obtain this solution, adopted A.3, and firmly adhered to it for a succession of weeks even though Firm B followed its short-run interests and adopted B.2. With this failure of Firm B to cooperate, Firm A makes only 3,000 less than it would receive under the joint-maximization result, and it still earns 15,000. This might well warrant the attempt to establish for all time the joint result. Suppose, for example, Firm A followed this strategy for four weeks, while Firm B showed no sign of adopting B.3. Then, Firm A might punish Firm B in the fifth week by adopting A.1, which reduces Firm B's profits to 8,000 at the cost of only another 3,000 to itself. Then, after one week of such punishment, Firm A could go back to its A.3 policy, hoping that Firm B would begin to get the idea.

Whether one agrees with the possibility of this type of behavior or not, this example does point up the fact that in the real world with dynamic games of this type being played over time, rivals who mutually recognize the interdependence of their strategies can arrive at joint profit maximization results, or at least at results better than equilibrium strategy pairs, by such methods of indicating their desires and intended responses by the pattern of their play. In nonzero-sum games, therefore, which is another way of saying that the rivals' interests are not at complete odds, equilibrium strategy pairs may not provide a satisfying approach to reality. By such surmises as that we have just engaged in, we can show that rivals may over time evolve a method of cooperating that is just as effective as explicit cartelizing or collusive behavior without any such formal agreement. That is, a cartel or collusive policy is not proof of cartel or collusive agreements.

But inasmuch as we have reached a favorable stage of our analysis, when we may fruitfully tackle the problems of cartelization and collusion, let us turn to them to see their potentials for the rivals.

Cartelization as a Solution

Let us ignore for the moment institutional barriers to such formal agreements among rivals as cartel and collusive covenants, and analyze their potential utility for the rivals. In cartelization, the reader will recall, the individual firm agrees to subordinate its policy to the dictates of a decision-making power, which presumably decides firms' policies in such manner as to maximize joint profits and effect a mutually satisfactory division of profits among the firms. For example, in the present case, the cartel would impose the monopoly solution upon the two firms, and then divide the profits equally, effectively choosing the strategy pair [A.3, B.3].

However, there are good reasons in reality why firms might balk at such cartelization agreements, even in the absence of legal or cultural barriers. In our example, we have retained the simplifying assumption of symmetry between our two firms, which may imply that each firm has equal bargaining power and will settle for equal profit shares. But consider the more realistic picture. Different firms will have, at the time of consideration of the desirability of a cartel agreement, different shares of the market, different costs, more or less aggressive managements and selling campaigns, differentiated products, and so forth. Consequently, the nondominant or weaker firms may very well believe that their bargaining power in such cartels would be poor and that the cartel's decisionmaking power would discriminate against their interests in terms of profits and a voice in the strategy of the cartel.

Indeed, weaker rivals might fare very badly, for if their costs were higher than the other members' costs the cartel might order them to close down one or more of their plants, or even to close out the firm completely, in return for compensation payments. These actions may very well be nonreversible for the firm: that is, the firm would have to break up its production team, losing its experienced personnel, stop its research programs or development of other products, abandon its daily contact with markets and prospects, and so forth. Any firm that lacked confidence that the stronger members of the cartel would honor its commitments to pay compensation once the firm was out of existence, or more generally, was uncertain about any stronger member of the cartel defecting and thereby destroying it and all of its commitments, would think long and hard about totally subordinating its policies to a cartel board in which its bargaining position was weak. Indeed, the cartel's promises might be suspect because its own life might be threatened by rivals not yet on the scene, given the future development of other products or producers and the possible reluctance of the latter to enter the existing cartel.

Uncertainty, therefore, concerning the sincerity, intentions, and ability of the stronger members of a cartel to honor its agreements—agreements that may severely penalize the smaller firm's ability to survive in the cartel or to leave the cartel should it think it to its advantage—militates against the formation of tight combinations that sacrifice most of the firm's autonomy, even in the absence of institutional restrictions.

Indeed, it may be true that cartels are most readily formed when the component firms are of about equal bargaining power on the one hand, or when the firms are so unequal in power that the weaker firms have no real option. In the intermediate cases—when one or two largest firms coexist with several medium-sized but by no means weak firms—the disincentives are too strong.

Collusion as a Solution

From the viewpoint of the objection just raised to a surrender of autonomy as a means of eliminating conflict among rivals, it would seem that a much more acceptable means of accomplishing this task would be by the technique of autonomous firms making firm and binding commitments with other firms to set certain prices, limit advertising or product variation, refrain from invading certain markets, set output restrictions, submit agreed-upon bids, and so forth.

As soon as we admit this new dimension into the analysis we open up Pandora's box of strategic considerations in attempting to guess what the solution will be. The profits received by each firm in such collusion are a function of its bargaining ability, the psychological makeup of its negotiators, the state of public opinion and the industry's concern about it, and so on for a lengthy catalog. Once more, our discussion cannot hope to be exhaustive in any sense, but will aim merely at giving a flavor of the problems and a glimpse of their infinite variety.

SIDE-PAYMENTS IN THE NONZERO-SUM GAME

Suppose that the game played in Table 6–4 settled down at the equilibrium pair [A.2, B.2], and now let us open the possibility of collusion among the rivals. Consider Firm A's possibilities: if it could induce Firm B to cease production (adopt B.4), Firm A could adopt A.1 and make the monopoly profit. To do this, however, it would have to offer a side-payment of at least $16,000 to Firm B, because that is what it is earning at the equilibrium pair. Suppose Firm A offered Firm B $17,000; then, Firm A would retain $19,000 or $3,000 more than the equilibrium payoff, and Firm B would be $1,000 better off than it is at the equilibrium. Consequently, if the possibility of collusion or cooperation were open to the firms, Firm A might press Firm B to accept such a settlement.

On the other hand, and particularly given the symmetry assumptions underlying this analysis, Firm B is motivated to try the same bribe to Firm A to cease production. If Firm A hesitates for the reasons we pointed out above concerning the cessation of production, Firm B might compromise with its desire to get its highest possible payoff and try to induce Firm A to accept

A.3, in which case it would play B.2, and make side-payments of perhaps $1,500 to Firm A. But, again, it is also to Firm A's advantage to induce Firm B to do the same.

In the case of symmetry, the pair which we previously signalled as reasonable might well be the compromise; each firm, in realization of the equality of bargaining strengths, might settle for an even split of monopoly profits, and for this prospect be willing to undergo the risk of the other's defecting now and then to A.2 or B.2.

More generally, we may approach the negotiations among the players in the following fashion. By playing his maximin strategy, each firm can guarantee a profit value of $9,000: therefore, let us begin with the assumption that no series of final payoffs in which one party receives less than $9,000 is feasible. On this basis we may eliminate the following strategy pairs from consideration: [A.1, B.1], [A.1, B.2], [A.1, B.4], [A.2, B.1], [A.2, B.4], [A.3, B.4], [A.4, B.1], [A.4, B.2], [A.4, B.3], [A.4, B.4]. Only those remaining afford the opportunity of bettering the maximin solutions through collusion. Therefore, as originally formulated, in two-person nonzero-sum games, the search for solutions was limited to the designation of the pure strategies and their convex combinations that would yield to each rival the maximin payoff or more.

We have drawn on Figure 6–4 the payoffs of the pure strategy pairs of Table 6–4, the lines representing the maximin payoffs of both firms, and the triangular feasible payoff set contained in the area between the maximin lines and the frontier of the set. We may draw upon our discussion of vectors in Chapter 5 to point out that any payoff-pair in the triangular set *J* may be obtained by weighting one or more pairs of strategies in *J* by positive or zero weights, or, indeed, by employing strategy-pairs that lie outside the feasible set *J* in the same manner to get a payoff-pair within it. However, these non-negative weights in analysis are the proportions of times strategy-pairs must be played to get a desired joint-payoff, and consequently they must sum to unity. That is, we must obtain desired payoff-pairs only by *convex combinations* of the pure strategy-pairs in the table. By suitable weightings we may obtain any payoff-pair in *J* by agreements among the rivals to play strategies certain proportions of the times. However, let us use the reasoning introduced in our discussion of consumer theory to argue that such agreements should always move the rivals to the frontier of the set *J*, or the hypotenuse of the triangle formed by it. Just as the consumer would always find it to his advantage to move out of the interior of his attainable set, so would the rivals always be able to find some point on the frontier that is superior to any payoff-pair in the interior of *J*. Therefore, what we may call the *strategy negotiation subset* of the feasible set of payoff-pairs is the line that bounds *J* from above, which

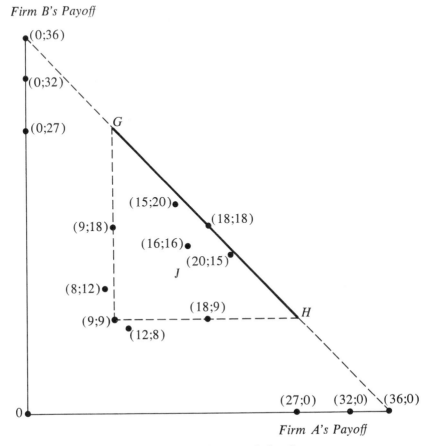

FIGURE 6-4. The Negotiation Set.

we have labelled *GH* on Figure 6–4 and have drawn in heavy line. If rational firms collude by agreements to play strategy-pairs certain proportions of the times in order to obtain desired payoff-pairs over time, we would expect that such agreements would involve *convex combinations* of pure strategies which yield payoff-pairs on this boundary. In our case, convex combinations of [A.1, B.4] and [A.4, B.1] or [A.1, B.4] and [A.3, B.3], or [A.4, B.1] and [A.3, B.3] would permit such payoffs to be attained.

But the analysis to this point assumes that firms are limited in their negotiations to agreements about the proportions of times firms will play agreed-upon strategies. But firms may make non-monetary *side-payments* that are not received via the market. Further, if we introduce more than two players in the game we introduce the complicating factor of coalition-formation in collusive bargaining. That is, it becomes possible for two or more rivals to form coalitions against one or more other rivals, and a new dimension is added to the struggle for a solution. Very little work has been done on general game theory for the n-person game, zero-sum or otherwise.

The Contribution of Game Theory to Oligopoly Submodels

We have presented much of our oligopolistic rivalry theorizing within the framework of game theory. What conclusion should we arrive at concerning its usefulness in gaining insights into realistic oligopolistic behavior? Our conclusion must be that the theory is most useful in providing a framework for organizing our thinking, for gaining insights into the core characteristics of rivalrous competition, and for understanding the reasons for the multiplicity of potential solutions. This is a valuable contribution to our understanding: it allows us to achieve a certain unity of treatment and progression from one level of complexity to another. However, it must also be said that game-theoretic models provide us with few pat solutions, and when they do they are usually for situations that do not approach sufficiently closely the phenomena of reality.

We have seen that that portion of game theory that is most fully developed and yields determinate solutions is zero-sum or strictly competitive, whose characteristic is the completeness of the competition among rivals. Indeed, as we have seen in the simple type of Cournot model that formed the basis for our approach, this assumption implied that a rival Firm B was much more interested in harming its rival Firm A than in obtaining profits for itself. Obviously, the realistic relevance of this assumption of perfect antagonism must be quite restricted.

Abstracting from this important point, however, formal zero-sum game theory assumes that every strategy of one's own and one's opponents' strategy sets is known to every player, and that every outcome of every constellation of strategy sets for the play of a game is known. Practically speaking, also, it assumes that the preferences of firms among outcomes is a linear transformation of the profits earned, which is subject to doubt. Most importantly, perhaps, the approach to the decisionmaking in such a framework endows the rivals with perfection of cognizance and rationality, and leads each rival to adopt the most conservative type of policy—conservative to a degree that may be unrealistic in terms of its implied sacrifice of opportunities that a bit more daring and a less formidable view of one's opponents' abilities would permit.

We found also that many and perhaps most zero-sum games will have equilibrium points only if the concept of the mixed strategy is introduced into the game. In economics we have a greater ability to interpret the meaningfulness and operational character of the assumption than in other fields. We may interpret it as dictating random drawings from universes of specified composition to determine which pure strategy to play week by week. But in using this interpretation we have adopted a dynamic outlook upon the game, which means that the original assumption that rivals selected their strategies completely independently of one another without any knowledge concerning the others' predilections is altered. With a continuous playing of the game the rivals reveal information through their patterns of play, and this leads us to view the equilibrium points with some skepticism as true solutions.

When we abandon zero-sum game theory for its more realistic counterpart, nonzero-sum or nonstrictly competitive game theory, we face up to the likelihood that rivals' interests will not be strictly antagonistic, but with this added reality we receive our full share of complications. It becomes more difficult to accept as intuitively plausible equilibrium points through time when the ability to move to mutually advantageous positions exists. More importantly, however, in such an environment it always becomes possible for all parties to bargain collusively to agree upon strategies that yield bargaining solutions. These specific solutions are determined, however, by the specifics of each situation, *ad hoc*. The possibilities are further compounded by the existence of the ability to make side-payments. When we recognize the possibility that rivals will be able to gain or lose through nonmarket means, a whole new dimension arises. And, finally, the ability that exists when more than two rivals face one another to form coalitions complicates the search for solutions even more. Not much has been done in these areas of analysis to produce a generalized set of conclusions.

Game theory, therefore, has not succeeded in introducing into the body of oligopoly submodels any great degree of generalization in terms of solutions, procedures, or types. It is, of course, as highly dependent upon specific situations and additional assumptions as existing models. What it does give us, however, is a framework of organization that allows us to unify treatment, as well as a specific strategic way of thinking (the *maximin*) that may have some explanatory power in certain situations.

Some Concluding Reflections on Rivalrous Competition

Our broad conclusion is that rivalrous competition affords the potentiality for an infinity of methods and types of price-selling cost-product variation solutions and that the specific solution applicable to a situation can be obtained only by the addition of a wealth of further information in the general case.

Our analysis must end, therefore, by offering not a unified and rigorous submodel of the types we constructed in Chapters 2 and 5, but, given the minimum cost curves of Chapter 4, some more or less valuable insights into the competition afforded by such weak tools as we have to study it.

THE DE-EMPHASIS OF PRICE COMPETITION

One insight that our use of such simple models as the Cournot model gave us was the fact that most disastrous results could occur if rivals used an aggressive type of price competition. Rivals who undercut the current market price for the product not only telegraph their strategies immediately, but they endanger a market structure stability that may have been attained only painfully, and they force rivals to react very quickly. This is particularly true in pure oligopoly—few sellers of an undifferentiated product—or even in differentiated oligopoly where the degree of consumer's loyalty to brands is not great, as in competition among the national brands of gasoline in the United States. In such cases the *only* manner of meeting the "price chiseler's" nefarious challenge is to lower the price of each rival's product, setting off the most disastrous type of warfare, which continues until the offending rival comes to his senses. After that event has occurred, it may be very difficult for the industry to reachieve the original price level once more, and the losses may continue for some time after the war is over.

We might suspect, therefore, that firms will adopt a price policy rather than an output policy, and, once having adopted it, will tend to keep price relatively constant. We may depict this rationale by the so-called *kinked demand curve* dKD' shown on Figure 6–5. This analysis is not an analysis of how the price now ruling came to be P_j°: the process by which that price was decided upon by the firm has been abstracted from. Rather, the kinked curve offers some explanation of why P_j° will not be readily changed once arrived at. Firm v believes that if it lowers price below the existing level its rivals will be forced to engage in price war and lower their own prices, so it would gain sales only as new consumers are drawn into the market. This is depicted along the sales curve DD', which is drawn on the assumption that all rivals lower prices as Firm v lowers its price to the levels shown. Therefore, the sales curve will be inelastic along this lower portion, total revenue may well decline as total costs increase, and rational policy will dictate that no price cut be made.

On the other hand, if Firm v raises its price it may believe that its rivals will not follow course, preferring instead to receive Firm v's customers at the going prices. Therefore, Firm v believes that if it raises price it will lose sales very quickly—that is, along an elastic sales curve dd'. Therefore, revenue will decline faster than costs, and the firm desists. Both points of view may lead the firm to adopt a very stubborn price policy, and help to explain the observable stability of prices in real-world oligopolistic groups.

As a consequence, the emphasis in competition may shift into the product variation and/or selling cost areas. These types of competition are not so apt to inflict acute distress upon rivals or to induce reactive policies by rivals that upset the stability of the industry, probably because rivals tend to be

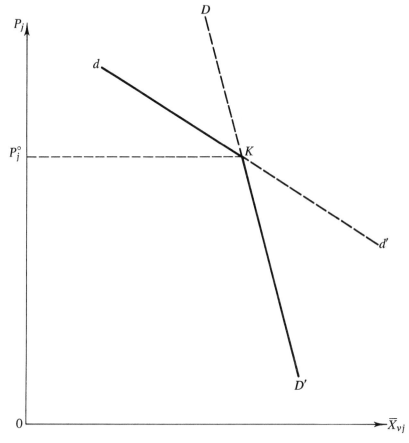

FIGURE 6–5. The Kinked Sales Curve.

relatively symmetrical in their abilities to compete in these areas as they are not where prices differ markedly. Even the most successful advertising campaign, presumably, does not prove disastrous to rivals, and generally they will be able to offset it at least partially without employing such expensive expedients as price reductions. Again, even the most successful of package or product differentiations seldom inflicts grievous wounds on other rivals, because consumer loyalties are not so fickle in these respects as they are in the price dimension.

This means that the gains of technological progress that permit total costs to be reduced are likely to be passed along to the consumer not as price decreases, but as products with improved quality at the same price, or at least as products with more expensive features whether or not they can be construed as improvements in quality. Also, it means that such cost reductions will be passed along to the consumer as a greater variety of products or models, giving him a greater choice rather than narrower choice at lower prices. Some of the reduction may be spent as selling costs. Where price competition in a vigorous fashion is denied the rivals effectively, great stress will be placed upon building up consumer loyalties to brand names and toward attempting to differentiate in the consumer's mind the undifferentiated. All of these aspects may be observed in modern oligopoly.

THE EMERGENCE OF LEADERSHIP-FOLLOWERSHIP PATTERNS

The phenomenon of the kinked demand curve is an excellent example of the third type of rivalry pattern which we discussed—the case of tacit collusion. Each firm may never be in actual contact with other firms, yet each may come independently to the conclusion that its sales curve in the upper and lower segments has the appearance of that in Figure 6–5. But much more sophisticated patterns based upon the same sort of phenomenon may arise in an industry.

Over time, one or a few firms may be viewed by the rest of the rivals in a group as price setters, and the followers may fall in behind the leaders when prices are changed in a rather firmly set manner. For example, one or more of the larger national refiners of gasoline may be accepted as price setters in a region, and once set, all nationally known brands in the region and all local brands may fall in behind the change with a differential accepted by usage.

A Summary of Rivalrous Competition

In terms of our ability to construct rigorous sets of interrelationships among all the data and variables of the problem, and of deriving from them general solutions to all of the variables' values, our analytical power over rivalrous competition is very weak. The fact that in reality very large sectors of the industrial economy are characterized by rivalrous competition, and, indeed, when location and other product-differentiating factors are taken into account, it may be taken as characterizing most market structures, it follows that much of the complexity and richness of reality escapes our wide-meshed net of generalizable theory.

However, we have succeeded in gaining insights into some of the implications of the analysis at the general level. Probably this is the most we can hope for: it will always be necessary to handle oligopoly as a specific analysis. But this surely should not be discouraging: it may lower the level of the analysis in its generality, but it promises a richness of variety and spiciness of detail that is lacking in the stereotyped models of determinate nonrivalrous forms.

Selected Readings

1. WILLIAM FELLNER, *Competition Among the Few* (New York: A. Knopf, 1949), Ch. 1, 4, 5, 11. An excellent statement by a distinguished economist of the inner logic of oligopoly.

2. ROBERT F. LANZILLOTTI, "Pricing Objectives in Large Companies," *American Economic Review*, XLVII (1958), pp. 921–940. A valuable empirical study of the criteria used in the pricing policies of very large American firms.

3. KURT W. ROTHSCHILD, "Price Theory and Oligopoly," in G. J. Stigler and K. E. Boulding, *Readings in Price Theory* (Homewood, Ill.: Irwin, 1952), pp. 440–464. A good essay on the meaning of determinateness and indeterminateness in oligopoly theory.

4. THOMAS C. SCHELLING, *The Strategy of Conflict* (Cambridge, Mass.: Harvard University Press, 1960), Ch. 2. The application of strategic thinking to the problems of bargaining among rivals, with some important implications for oligopoly market structure.

5. MARTIN SHUBIK, *Strategy and Market Structure* (New York: John Wiley, 1959). An imaginative application of game theory to oligopoly.

6. WILLIAM S. VICKREY, *Microstatics* (New York: Harcourt, Brace, and World, 1964), pp. 342–367. A compact presentation of basic game theory.

CHAPTER 7

The Theory of Market Behavior

To THIS POINT we have studied in some depth the individualized decision-making of the action units of the market economy: firms and consumers. Whether or not we could obtain determinate solutions from generalized submodels for each of these units depended essentially upon whether or not the external impacts of its decisionmaking reacted back upon it through the agency of other action units. Where they did not, we had the ability to treat the unit as an isolated cell in a tissue of cells, to speak paradoxically; that is, although the unit was acting within the matrix of a social process of decision-making, it was self-contained in the sense of being able to take into account only its own direct impact upon its own welfare in making its decisions. For consumers we have the set of general solutions containing demands for goods and supplies of factor services for each c, $c = 1, \ldots, s$, given the assumptions of amounts of factor endowments for each of them, a cash balance coefficient, receipts of profits, and a fixed value for each price in the economy, $\mathbf{P}$. For firms we have the set of general solutions for input demands and costs (for firms in both rivalrous and nonrivalrous competition), and for output supplies and profits (for cases in nonrivalrous competition) for each v, $v = 1, \ldots, o$, given the assumptions of a fixed price in $\mathbf{P}$. These general solutions are contained in Systems [I] and [II] respectively.

We have reached the point, now, where, in the language of Chapter 1, it is time to step up the level of ambition of our models by one level: to select a given product or factor service, remove its price from the data set (holding all other prices in the data set at fixed levels), and place it in the variable set. We wish to show, that is, how the price at which a product sells or for which a given factor service exchanges is arrived at in a free economy *on the assumption that all other prices have already been determined and remain fixed throughout our analysis at their complete equilibrium levels.* By *complete*

267

equilibrium levels we mean that if we bring the one market we are analyzing into equilibrium the values of al¹ the variables that rule will form a complete or general equilibrium for the whole set of markets.

Note, therefore, the limited nature of this enhancement of our ambition: our data and postulate sets contain all of the data and postulates of the consumer and firm submodels that led to Systems [I] and [II] except that the price of a specific good or factor service—Y_j, Z_i, z_i, E, or u—is no longer fixed. Moreover, except for that one price, we assume that all prices are at those levels which are compatible with every market being in full or general or complete equilibrium simultaneously with every other.

We are, therefore, going to study the result of the *interaction* of decision-makers whose individual goals have been determined in cell-like independence but who, in order to attain them, must function in an organ-like competitive-cooperative environment with other like cells. If we may continue the analogy we used in Chapter 1, and regard the *market*—the real or fictional arena in which these action units interact to effect their selfish aims—as the organ of the organism whose structure and functioning it is our ultimate goal to depict, we may make the following points. It is the function of the organ to produce a ratio for the goods or services exchanged in the market, which meets certain conditions imposed by a data and a postulate set. That is, we want a *solution* value for the ratio in which two goods exchange in the market. To say this is to say that we wish to have, for any given set of data reflecting the external environment in which the market functions, an anatomical chart of the market at rest, with the results of its steady-state functioning. Further, we are interested in the *physiology* of the organ: how does it relate the inputs and outputs of its functioning to arrive at a result, and how does it react to its own states when it is out of its steady-state solution?

Note, to start, that every market is a place where two goods exchange, and therefore its function is to produce a solution with relevance to *two* goods. In the real world, and in our models, because the *other good* is always money, we tend to forget this aspect of the mechanism. The money price of a commodity, therefore, is a ratio of transformation into money of a product or service; that is, a price which tells every person in the economy the rate at which it is possible to *transform* a given amount of the good into money and vice versa.

We shall develop our analysis of markets for products first and then turn our attention to service markets.

The Product Markets

We shall choose a typical intermediate-consumer good, Y_j, and examine the structure and functioning of the market that determines its money price.

THE CONSUMER-INTERMEDIATE GOOD MARKET

Let us recall our specific environment. On Monday of the given week, demanders of the good Y_j and suppliers of it meet in a market and by the end of the day an equilibrium price P_j° emerges for the good (assuming all other equilibrium prices are already attained) from the interaction of buyers and sellers, at which the equilibrium relation between the quantity demanded and supplied is achieved.

THE MARKET DEMAND FUNCTION. We may interpret this result as an equilibration of the desires of buyers and sellers. From Systems [I] and [II] we may determine the *market demand curve*, or the function that shows the *desire* of all consumers and firms to use the product this week as a function of its own price (all other prices being held fixed at their general equilibrium levels). From System [I] we may write for each consumer the demand function,

$$X_{cj} = D_{cj}(P_j; \mathbf{P}^j, \mathbf{Q}_c, K_{cu}, \boldsymbol{\alpha}_c, \boldsymbol{\pi}_v) \qquad \text{[I–1]}$$

where, it will be recalled, we define $\mathbf{P}^j$ to be the vector of all prices except that one whose symbol appears in the superscript. Note that we have dropped the degree mark from X_{cj} because the function no longer always gives us the solution value in this larger system consisting of the market.

Because we have assumed that every consumer's demand is independent of every other's, in that the set of consumer postulates takes no notice of a given consumer's choices being influenced by what other consumers are choosing, we may simply add these consumer demand functions over all consumers to obtain the *aggregate consumer demand function*:

$$X_j' = \sum_c X_{cj} = D_j^c(P_j; \mathbf{P}^j, \mathbf{Q}, \mathbf{K}_{cu}, \boldsymbol{\alpha}, \boldsymbol{\pi}_v) \qquad \text{[7–1]}$$

where $\mathbf{Q}$ is a matrix containing as columns the $\mathbf{Q}_c$, or vectors of asset endowments, for all c, $\mathbf{K}_{cu}$ is a vector of cash balance coefficients for all c, and $\boldsymbol{\alpha}$ is the matrix of profit shares for all c.

Because entrepreneurial demand exists for Y_j too, to be used as intermediate product, we must go to System [II] to obtain

$$X_{vj} = D_{vj}(P_j; \mathbf{P}^j, K_{vu}), \qquad \text{[II–14]}$$

and we may simply add over all firms to get the *aggregate entrepreneurial demand function*

$$X_j'' = \sum_v X_{vj} = D_j^v(P_j; \mathbf{P}^j, \mathbf{K}_{vu}). \qquad \text{[7–2]}$$

Finally, in order to get the *market demand curve*, we must combine the total consumer demand curve with the total entrepreneurial demand curve, and we obtain

$$X_j = X'_j + X''_j = D^c_j(P_j; \mathbf{P}^j, \mathbf{Q}, \mathbf{K}_{cu}, \alpha, \pi_v) + D^v_j(P_j; \mathbf{P}^j, \mathbf{K}_{vu})$$

$$= D_j(P_j; \mathbf{P}^j, \mathbf{Q}, \mathbf{K}_{cu}, \alpha, \pi_v, \mathbf{K}_{vu}). \qquad\qquad [7\text{--}3]$$

THE MARKET SUPPLY FUNCTION.   It is a bit more difficult to derive the *market supply curve*, for it will depend upon (1) the rivalrous or nonrivalrous nature of the environment, (2) whether the sales curve faced by the firm is horizontal or negatively sloped, (3) whether we treat the short-run or long-run period for our analysis, and (4) whether the firm receives any advantages or suffers any disadvantages in the cost of operations from a change in the level of the *industry*'s operations. We shall consider these combinations of elements in some detail.

Supply Functions in Nonrivalrous Environments: Pure Competition.   Let us consider first the case of the short run and also assume that there are no economies or diseconomies of operation external to the firm and internal to the industry in which the firm produces. In this last connection, it must be pointed out that we have eliminated one source of such economies or diseconomies by holding all prices faced by the firm fixed. This assumes, therefore, that the raw material and primary input prices will not vary as the industry buys more or less of them. For example, in the real world, as one industry expands its output it may buy more and more of some raw material whose production requires increased applications of inputs or of inputs of lesser efficiency. Therefore, the price of the input will increase to all firms in the industry as the latter's output rises, and this rise in prices will affect every firm's costs.

Because we have eliminated such occurrences (by holding the prices of inputs constant as the industry varies its outputs of the good in question), the nature of industry economies and diseconomies operating in our market models are wholly real rather than monetary. That is, as an industry expands its output in the short run, there may arise certain efficiencies or inefficiencies based wholly on such output expansion from which every firm may benefit or suffer in the way of experiencing lower or higher costs. For example, as all firms in an industry that is highly localized geographically expand outputs in the short run, the railroad servicing them may be able to increase the number of train arrivals and departures per day. This might allow firms more frequent deliveries of inputs and shipments of outputs, which may permit all firms to reduce the level of their inventories of inputs and outputs, and thereby lower costs. In the long run, the growth in number and size of firms may lead to the establishment of a pool of skilled labor needed by the industry and readily available to fill its needs, so that even if the wages of labor are held constant its efficiency rises and lowers the cost of the output of every firm in the industry.

The Short Run with No Industry Economies or Diseconomies. Let us first assume that the industry does not enjoy any such economies or suffer analogous diseconomies as its output alters. Then, if we set successively all

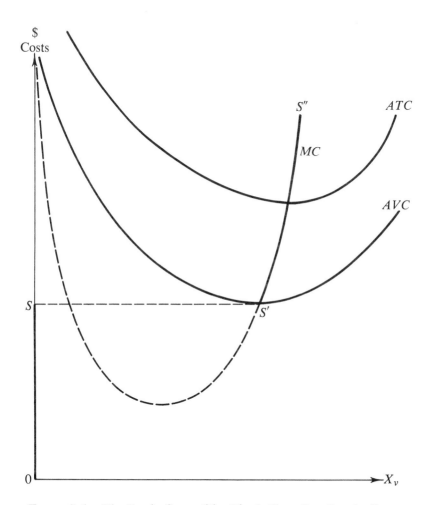

FIGURE 7–1. The Purely-Competitive Firm's Short-Run Supply Curve.

allowable prices which the product yielding maximum profits can attain for every firm producing it, and see how the industry's desire to supply is determined, we would find that each firm's desire to supply is zero until the minimum point of its average variable cost curve is equal to the price, and that from that point the firm determines its desire to supply at the intersection of the price line (sales curve) with its (rising) marginal cost curve. Therefore, the supply function in System [II–5] or [II–6] in these circumstances is seen to be the firm's marginal cost curve above its intersection with the average variable cost curve, and to follow the price axis below that critical price. We have depicted this supply curve for the firm in pure competition for the short run with no industry external effects on Figure 7–1, where it is labelled $OSS'S''$.

Because there are no interaction effects of firm with firm, we may derive the supply curve of the industry by adding these firm supply curves horizontally; that is, price by price, we merely add the amounts that every firm producing the good would be willing to supply to the zero amounts firms not producing the good are desirous of supplying. We then obtain

$$\bar{X}_J = \sum_v \bar{X}_{vJ} = \sum_v S_{vJ}(P_J; \mathbf{P}^J, K_{vu})$$

$$= S_J(P_J; \mathbf{P}^J, \mathbf{K}_{vu}). \qquad [7\text{--}4]$$

The Short Run with Industry Economies or Diseconomies. If the individual firm's supply curve is dependent on the level of industry output, then we should have to rewrite System [II–5] or [II–6] in the following manner:

$$\bar{X}_{vJ} = S_{vJ}(\mathbf{P}, K_{vu}; \bar{X}_J), \qquad [\text{II}'\text{--}5]$$

where, of course, the industry output $\bar{X}_J$ is given as a datum. This explicitly recognizes the fact that Firm v's marginal cost curve (as well as its average variable and total costs) is functionally dependent on the level of industry output taken as a datum. This means, as shown in Figure 7–2, that a different set of these curves exists for every hypothesized level of industry supply. If the industry's expansion induces *economies* of operation for the firm, the average cost curves shift to the right or fall, and the marginal cost curves do likewise. If the expansion of the industry raises costs and induces diseconomies, the average cost curve will shift to the left or upward, as will marginal cost curves. Then, to obtain the market supply curve, the curves of System [II'–5] must be added over all firms to obtain [7–4], which will contain the explicit impact upon its own cost levels of the size of industry supply.

The Long Run with No Industry Economies or Diseconomies. In the long run, every firm will have sufficient time to adjust its plant and equipment to produce the optimal supply in the optimal manner. Now, inasmuch as new firms are able to come into existence with optimal quantities of plant and equipment, and existing firms are able to go out of business, this optimal amount and optimal manner for each firm will occur at the very lowest average total cost consistent with all firms earning just enough to remain in the industry. This will be at the minimum average total cost of the plant curve whose minimum average total cost is the lowest for all possible plant curves. From Figure 7–3 we see that this will be at the minimum point of the firm's long-run average total cost curve. Every firm—previously existing and new ones—will build the plant that corresponds to this minimum average cost point on its long-run average cost curve, which we have labelled $LRAC_v$,

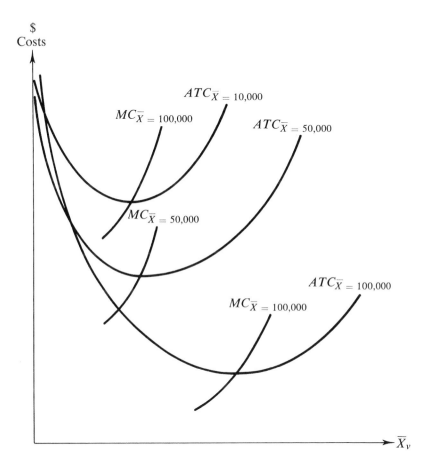

FIGURE 7–2. The Firm's Cost Curves as Functions of Industry Output.

$LRAC_{v'}$, $LRAC_{v''}$, and so forth. Moreover, the minimum average total cost will be at the same dollar level for such firms: this is true because the time period will be long enough so that all factors whose efficiencies allow lower costs to be attained by favored firms will have their prices bid up to include the payment for those greater efficiencies. Inasmuch as we are holding all other prices constant at their equilibrium levels, therefore, it must be true that locations that allow more sales to be made will receive higher payments through competition to just neutralize this greater advantage; the more able plant manager, whose greater ability allowed short-run costs to be lower than the average in the industry, will be bid for by other plants and will have his salary raised to include the greater earnings he is responsible for, and, if competition is thorough, the salary will rise by only enough to offset them. If the labor force of a plant is more efficient than another labor force, com-

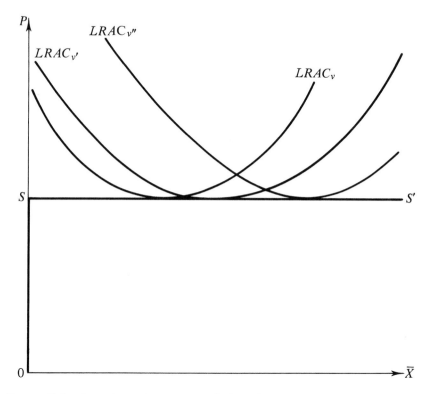

FIGURE 7–3. Long-Run Average Total Cost for the Firm and the Industry Supply Curve.

petition should seek out its causes and reward them with the differential advantage. When all such payments are made, each firm will have an average cost plant curve tangent to the long-run average total cost curve at the latter's minimum, and that minimum will be at the same level for all firms. The payments to *all* factors required to equalize their cost-efficiency are payments that are not necessary to induce them to remain in the industry, and therefore they take on the nature of surpluses or *rents*. We will discuss them more fully when we consider the behavior of product service markets.

Every firm, with the plant that has a cost curve tangent to the long-run average cost curve at the latter's minimum point, would determine its supply in the short run by following the marginal cost curve for the plant. However, in the long run, it never leaves the intersection of marginal cost with price that occurs at the minimum point of that short-run average total cost curve. This is because when price does rise above this point, in the short run the firm follows its marginal cost curve to determine output and earns positive profits, but these profits tempt in firms from the outside, which build plants with the same minimum average cost level, increase supplies, and force price down again to be tangent to average total costs at the minimum.

Effectively, with all other prices given (and, in our case, although this is not important in the present context, at their equilibrium values) this means that the market supply curve will be a horizontal line, *SS'* on Figure 7–3, with a height equal to the cost level of the minimum average long-run cost. That is, effectively, even though each firm is assumed to be operating with a production function that is not linear and homogeneous in inputs, the industry is in fact so operating in the long run because all of the increases and decreases in output that constitute its response to market forces will be made by entry and exit of firms operating at the same minimum average cost level. We have, then, the effect of linear homogeneity, which is to say constant average and marginal cost, but with a determinate output for every firm in the industry.

Let us, therefore, take any firm producing Y_j, and define c_{vJ}^* as the minimum average total cost of producing this product:

$$c_{vJ}^* = \min_{\bar{X}_{vJ}} \frac{C_{vJ}^\circ}{\bar{X}_{vJ}}. \qquad [7\text{--}5]$$

Then, we may define the industry supply function in the following manner:

$$P_J^\circ = c_{vJ}^*. \qquad [7\text{--}6]$$

That is, in equilibrium, the price of the commodity must be at this critical cost level.

The market demand curve for the product will intersect this price-cost line and determine the equilibrium amount exchanged, but in this type of cost situation the price is determined by costs.

The Long Run with Industry Economies or Diseconomies. The short-run difficulties we encountered with reference to the firm's average costs and marginal costs must also be built into the long-run analysis to take account of the industry's impact upon the firm's costs. The complication is depicted on Figure 7–4, where the firms' minimum average cost levels c_{vJ}^* are shown as rising or falling as a function of $\bar{X}_J$, total industry output; if industry economies occur, the locus of minimum-cost points (drawn as the dashed line of

Figure 7–4) falls as output of the industry expands, and if diseconomies occur the locus of points rises. At every level, however, all firms have plant curves tangent to the price line drawn through the average cost ruling at that level.

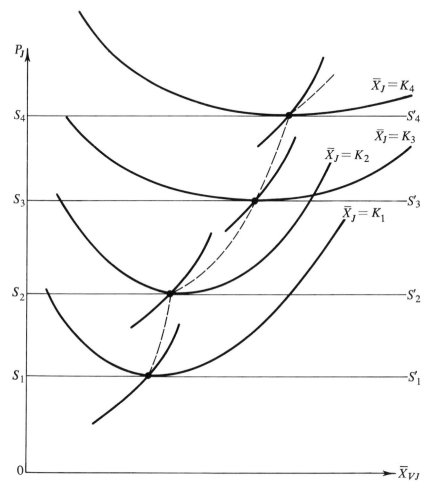

FIGURE 7–4.   The External Effects of Industry Output on the Firm's Long-Run Average Cost Curve.

As in the short-term case, these complications are best dealt with by including in the definition of the firm's production function an argument that contains the industry's output. Then, before the firm's production relations can be defined it is necessary to know what the industry's total output is. In this way, the value of c_{vJ}^* will include the effect on costs of industry output, and the relation of [7–6] will include the phenomenon explicitly.

Supply Curves in Nonrivalrous Environments: Negatively Sloping Sales Curves. We are somewhat more fortunate in handling the supply curves of firms whose decisionmaking is made in the face of downward-sloping sales curves, because, under conditions which dictate that the firms are in non-rivalrous competition, the firm's and the industry's output coincide. This means that any economies or diseconomies of the type we have discussed that are internal to the industry are also internal to the firm. They are, therefore, implicitly included in the firm's production function. We may, therefore, deal only with the short-run and the long-run supply curves without these complications. This outlook is somewhat forced in that market structure which we shall call *monopolistic competition*, because although each firm produces a different product there is a great deal of product similarity, which may mean that the type of industry external effect on the firm which we discussed for the case of pure competition is present. In this case the same type of inclusion of industry outputs in the production function of each firm would be required, presumably including the output of *every* different variety of the product in question. In this section, however, we shall assume that the firm produces a product whose nearest substitutes are distant enough so that no such external effects are experienced.

The Short Run. In the short run, the firm with a downward-sloping demand curve in the nonrivalrous environment will be operating with a given plant curve, and, as we have seen, will, under our assumptions, seek to determine its output where marginal cost and marginal revenue are equal. Having done this, the firm may do either of two things which, if it has fore-seen perfectly the actions of consumers, will come to the same thing, but which if it is operating under conditions of some uncertainty as to consumer reactions may not.

The firm may determine an *output policy*, in which case it produces a given amount of output—given by the intersection of marginal cost and marginal revenue—and throws it on the market to obtain the price at which the market will absorb it. If the firm is correct, the price will be the profit-maximizing price its analysis determined. In this case, the supply curve during the week for the firm will be that shown as S_oS_o' on Figure 7–5, or the vertical line through the hopefully profit-maximizing output:

$$\bar{X}_J = \bar{X}_{vJ}^\circ. \qquad [7\text{--}7]$$

And, again, if the sales curve has been correctly foreseen, this output should sell at the profit-maximizing price on the sales curve that helped determine it.

On the other hand, the firm has the option of setting the price of the product and offering to sell as much as the market desires during the current week at that price. Of course, the price will be that determined by extending

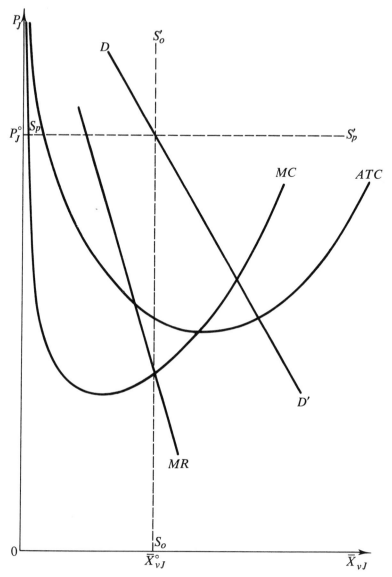

FIGURE 7–5. The Monopolist's Supply Curve: Output and Price Policies.

a vertical line upward through the intersection of marginal cost and marginal revenue to the expected sales curve, or S_oS_o' in Figure 7–5. Once more, if the firm has guessed correctly, this price will result in the optimum output being absorbed by the market. If the firm has not gauged the sales curve properly, the set price will result in fewer or larger sales than were foreseen, and the firm will have failed to maximize its product's profits. The supply curve would then be S_pS_p' as drawn on Figure 7–5, or

$$P_J = P_J^\circ. \tag{7-8}$$

It is, of course, a horizontal straight line through the estimated profit-maximizing price on the sales curve.

The Long Run. Fortunately, in the case of pure monopoly, we need change very little of this previous analysis to accommodate the long run. The only change is that in this longer period the firm will be able to change its plant curves optimally, so that it will seek to equate its *long-run* marginal cost with the marginal revenue. This determines the optimal plant which the firm will design for its operation. Beyond this, however, our analysis is unchanged. The supply curve will be one whose nature is that of [7–7] or [7–8] period after period.

For the firm in monopolistic competition, however, our analysis is changed in one important respect. Because other firms can enter the production of close, if not identical, goods, the sloping sales curve of the firm will shift to the left, so that marginal costs will equal marginal revenue for outputs whose average cost equals or is only slightly less than price. Thus profits are eliminated or greatly reduced in the long run. However, the firm will follow a price or output policy, with attendant guesses at an uncertain sales curve.

It is worth noting that in the environment we have detailed for the operation of our models this uncertainty concerning consumer and entrepreneurial demand for products cannot exist, for the process of reaching a market equilibrium each Monday assures that only the equilibrium output will be produced. Therefore, the firm may be viewed in these circumstances as having *either* type of supply curve.

It is important to point up the distinction between supply curves in the purely competitive environment and in the nonpurely competitive, nonrivalrous environment, for many economists deny that supply curves exist in the latter case. However, we shall define the supply curve as the *desire to supply*, and its depiction in pure competition relates a *quantity desired to be supplied* at every possible price, by the firm or industry. On Figure 7–1 the supply curve for the firm in the short run is $OSS'S''$, and on Figure 7–3 the supply curve for the industry in the long run is OSS', portions of which curves coincide with the price axis.

In the nonpurely competitive cases, however, the depiction of the desire to supply in the current week is at once more simple and more complex. If the firm follows an output policy it desires to produce and sell a given amount of output regardless of the price it brings on the market this week. Of course, it has its hopes and expectations of what that price will be, and were it to expect a price to rule other than the one its analysis leads it to expect, the output would be different. But this does not alter the fact that its desire to supply this week is depicted by the vertical line S_oS_o'. In the real economy, once the firm has decided upon the period's output, if the price in the market takes any value along the P_J axis the firm's desire to supply remains at the constant output depicted. In the purely competitive case, should this occur, the desire to supply would respond with changed output, and the supply curve reflects this variability, but it would not occur in the nonpurely competitive market and the supply curve reflects this with equal faithfulness.

If the nonpurely competitive firm follows a price policy, the same interpretation holds. The supply curve $S_pS_{p'}$ of Figure 7–5 depicts the desire to supply any amount of output the market desires at the fixed price P_J°, the desire to supply is undefined at any other price, because effectively no other price can rule. The firm does not desire to supply at any other price, which is not the same thing as saying that it desires to supply zero at any other price. Faithful depiction of the desire to supply in the current period requires that the supply curve be as drawn in Figure 7–5.

Supply Curves in Rivalrous Environments.   Finally, what will the supply curve of the oligopolistic firm be? It will not surprise the reader to learn that we have no way of determining it. Its shape will be either that of [7–7] or [7–8]: having a decision to make, the firm must decide upon a given output or a given price during the period, and then face its market with that policy. But what it is that determines either of these *values* is not generally determinate on the basis of cost curves alone, given the basic uncertainty concerning the definition of the sales curve of the firm. We have emphasized, for example, that the kinked demand curve analysis is not one of the manner in which price is determined but an explanation for the stickiness of price once it has been determined in some fashion. It follows, therefore, that if costs change, we cannot use the kinked sales curve to determine where the new price will be, for this analysis implies that the figure may be used for determination by costs of price changes, when it is originally impossible to determine price by such means. In realistic pricing it is logically possible that such a procedure is followed, but then this is a specific form of reaction pattern for the industry in question, and is not generally valid.

We must, therefore, disqualify our general techniques from an ability to determine the level at which the price-policy or output-policy supply curve is set. If these supply curves are used in our analysis of market behavior, therefore, they must be given among the data set of the model.

THE INTERACTION OF MARKET DEMAND AND SUPPLY CURVES TO DETERMINE PRICE AND QUANTITY EXCHANGED.   Given the market demand for a consumer-intermediate good Y_j, and given a supply curve for it derived in

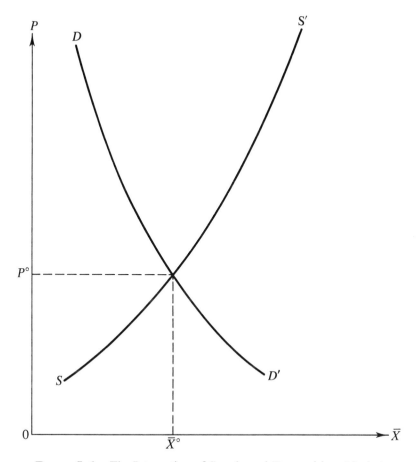

FIGURE 7–6.   The Interaction of Supply and Demand in a Market.

any of the above manners for short run or long run, the normal confrontation of buyers and sellers may be depicted by the interaction of these two curves, as we have drawn them in Figure 7–6. On the market day of Monday, buyers seek to acquire the units they desire as prices are set in the market and sellers seek to dispose of the various outputs they desire to sell at the prices that materialize in the market. If the market supply curve is a horizontal line at some price—so that the long-run zero-external-effect purely competitive solution prevails or sellers can and have set a price policy—then equilibrium price in the market must be set at that level and the interaction of buyers and sellers can determine only the equilibrium amount exchanged. If the market supply curve is a vertical line through an output, reflecting sellers' output decisions, the amount exchanged must be the given volume of output offered, and only the equilibrium price is free to vary. Lastly, if the market supply curve has neither zero nor infinite slope, both price and amount exchanged are determined by interaction of the decisionmaking units as depicted by the two curves.

Behind the market demand curve, by virtue of our analysis of Chapter 2, we know that individual consumers are striving to attain their consumption goals, and by use of the analysis of Chapters 4 and 5 we know that firms are effecting purchases in an overall profit maximization goal. Underlying the market supply curve, in the case of nonrivalrous competition at least, we assume from the analysis of Chapters 4 and 5 that the firms are attempting to maximize profits in their sales of product. An *equilibrium* of these conflicting motivating forces can be defined as a price and an amount exchanged which, once reached, shows no tendency to change. This implies that no actor in the market has reason to bid a higher or lower price for the good by virtue of the fact that he cannot buy or sell as much of it as he desires at the ruling price.

Our conditions are that at every price each buyer be able to effect his desires, and at positive prices every seller be able to effect his desires. The market demand curve depicts the *desire* of buyers to purchase goods, and the market supply curve the *desire* to sell goods by sellers. Only when these desires are thoroughly satisfied—in game-theory senses, only when, simultaneously, buyers are playing their best strategy given that played by sellers and all other buyers, and when sellers are playing their best strategy given that played by buyers and all other sellers—do we have a mutual satisfaction of desires and a status quo that does not tend to change.

It is this chain of reasoning that leads us to state the simple interrelationship that defines the relations between variables and data for this market submodel:

$$X_j^\circ \leqq \bar{X}_j^\circ, P_j^\circ(X_j^\circ - \bar{X}_j^\circ) = 0, \qquad P_j^\circ \geqq 0. \qquad [7\text{–}9]$$

These conditions state that market demand must be no greater than market supply at the equilibrium price, that price must be nonnegative, and that if the inequality holds, that equilibrium price must be zero. It is most important that the student understand that demand means *desire* to buy, and supply means *desire* to supply. Then this manner of stating the equilibrium conditions takes into account the possibility of corner solutions, for it is possible that in equilibrium the configurations of Figure 7–7 *b.* or *d.* may occur, and the good is a free good. The normal equilibrium of Figure 7–7*a.* and the somewhat unusual corner solution of Figure 7–7*c.* are also depicted.

Suppose in the process of competition in the market the equilibrium price or quantity is temporarily attained, but, by virtue of the dynamics of the competitive process, these values are departed from instead of stopped at. Will the equilibrium be reattained, or might the market go through the entire

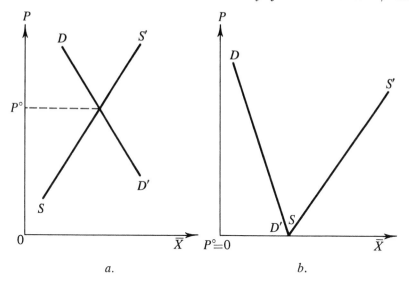

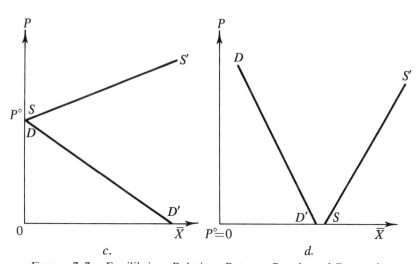

FIGURE 7–7.   Equilibrium Relations Between Supply and Demand.

market day without reachieving the equilibrium? To broach these questions is to enter the area of the physiology of the market—the manner in which the states of the market emerge from previous states and give rise to future states. More specifically, to ask such questions is to pose the problem of dynamics which we termed *the stability of equilibrium* in Chapter 1, and we shall violate our decision there not to build dynamic models long enough to present a simple dynamic model of the market's functioning.

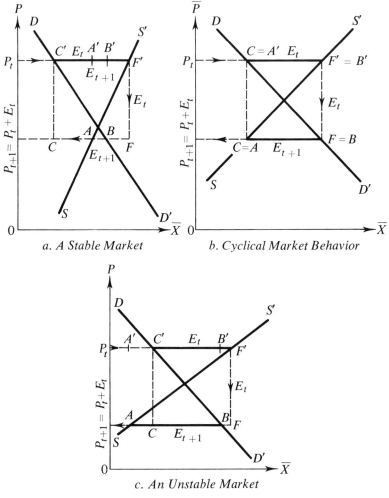

a. *A Stable Market* b. *Cyclical Market Behavior*

c. *An Unstable Market*

FIGURE 7–8. Stable and Unstable Markets.

The Stability of Market Equilibrium. Let us investigate some of the more important features of the market's anatomy and functioning that would cast some light on the problem posed. To keep the analysis simple, let us assume that the market demand and market supply curves are linear, as shown in Figures 7–8*a.*, *b.*, and *c.* We must also specify certain features of the behavior of buyers and sellers in the market which we have not yet specified, to wit, the manner in which they react as groups when the market is not in equilibrium.

We may approach this task in either of two ways. First, we may go back to Chapter 2 and build a model of consumer response to situations when the individual consumer has not yet attained his desired maximal basket. That is, we should have to specify the direction and rate of speed with which the consumer moves his purchases of goods and supplies of services when, at fixed prices, he is not spending his desired amount of income and/or he is not spending it on the goods in the amounts that are equilibrating for him. We mentioned such relationships in our discussion of the complete model in Chapter 1 on p. 21. Also, we can go back to Chapter 5 and define, for the firm, the direction and rates of reaction it will evidence when it is not producing the equilibrating amounts of output and/or absorbing the equilibrium amounts of inputs which we also discussed in Chapter 1. Then, from these two sets of dynamic analyses for the *individual* consumers and firms we may build market reaction functions for buyers and sellers and so specify our dynamic model in this way.

Second, we may ignore these microscopic analyses for each individual unit in the market and seek to summarize them by specifying directions and rates of reaction for the aggregate of consumers and firms. We may, in short, seek to describe the movements in reaction of the mass without bothering to cope with the movements of each of the atoms. This second approach is much more promising, both in the simplicity with which it can be constructed and manipulated, and in the fruitfulness with which it may be possible to describe realistic market behavior.

Let us specify the following reaction patterns for the group of consumers and firms. We shall break up the market day into a succession of small periods—say, of 5 minutes' duration—and thus attempt to portray the physiology of the market for good Y_j as it strives to attain an equilibrium solution through this succession of tiny time intervals. We may refer to these time intervals as $t = 0, 1, 2, \ldots$, and we shall suppose that at $t = 0$ the price of the good is given among the data at P^*.

Now, if price is above the equilibrium price, P°, in any time interval, supply will exceed demand, or, we may say, excess demand, which is demand minus supply at the given price, is negative. Let us hypothesize that when this occurs suppliers compete among themselves to bid price down. On the other hand, if price is below the equilibrium price, demand will exceed supply, so excess demand will be positive, and we shall assume that buyers will bid price up by competition. Therefore, we may summarize by saying that we shall assume that the *direction* of price movement possesses the sign of the excess demand:

$$\text{sign}\,(P_t - P_{t-1}) = \text{sign}\,(X_{t-1} - \bar{X}_{t-1}), \qquad [7\text{–}10]$$

where we have eliminated the *j*-subscript as unnecessary but understood.

But let us make the further assumption that the *amount* of the price change is also a function of the amount of the *excess* demand; that is, that the price will change in the indicated direction to a greater extent if excess demand is greater in the positive or negative direction than if it is closer to zero. We will make the simplest assumption along these lines and postulate that the relationship is a simple linear one. That is, for a given constant, K,

$$P_t - P_{t-1} = K(X_{t-1} - \bar{X}_{t-1}), \qquad K > 0. \qquad [7\text{--}11]$$

But consider the value of K in [7–11]: if we change the physical unit in which Y_j is measured, it will be possible to reduce K to unity, and we may therefore eliminate this troublesome constant. Because K is positive, its conversion to the value $+1$ will affect no sign in [7–11]. Therefore, with the understanding that we have effected such a change in units, we may rewrite [7–11] as follows:

$$P_t - P_{t-1} = X_{t-1} - \bar{X}_{t-1}. \qquad [7\text{--}12]$$

By our previous assumption demand and supply curves for the market are linear, or may be approximated in reasonable fashion by linear functions. We may measure in units from the equilibrium price, $P°$, and write these functions in the following fashion:

$$1. \quad X_{t-1} = X° - D'(P_{t-1} - P°)$$

$$2. \quad \bar{X}_{t-1} = X° + S'(P_{t-1} - P°), \qquad [7\text{--}13]$$

as they are drawn on Figure 7–8. The values D' and S' are, of course, the slopes of the demand and supply curves respectively, and we note for future reference that D' is positive for the normally-sloping demand curve as we have written the demand equation.

If we substitute the functions of [7–13] into [7–12], we obtain

$$P_t - P_{t-1} = -(D' + S')P_{t-1} + (D' + S')P° \qquad [7\text{--}14]$$

which we may abbreviate to

$$P_t = AP_{t-1} + BP°, \qquad [7\text{--}15]$$

where $A = (1 - D' - S')P_{t-1}$ and $B = (D' + S') = 1 - A$.

We will state without proof that the particular solution to this dynamic equation in terms of the data consisting of the original price P^* and the equilibrium price $P°$, may be written as follows:[1]

$$P_t = A^t P^* + BP° \left(\frac{1 - A^t}{1 - A} \right). \qquad [7\text{--}16]$$

Because $B = 1 - A$, this simplifies to

$$P_t = A^t(P^* - P°) + P°. \qquad [7\text{--}17]$$

---

[1] For a development and proof see Samuel Goldberg, *Introduction to Difference Equations* (New York: Wiley), 1961, pp. 63–67.

It may be seen that if the absolute value of A is less than unity, the first term on the right-hand side will disappear and the equilibrium will be approached as time goes on. From [7–14] it may be seen that $A = (1 - D' - S')$. Let us restrict ourselves to the case where the demand curve is negatively sloping and the supply curve is positively sloping, and recall that under these conditions $D' > 0$ as noted earlier. Then, for

$$D' > 0, \qquad S' > 0, \qquad\qquad [7\text{–}18]$$

the condition for stability may be written

$$|1 - (D' + S')| < 1, \qquad\qquad [7\text{–}19]$$

which yield the condition for [7–18] that $D' + S' < 2$.

The rationale of this condition can be easily demonstrated. Let us define the excess demand at period t as $E_t = X_t - \bar{X}_t$: then it may be seen from [7–13] that

$$E_{t+1} = [1 - (D' + S')]E_t. \qquad\qquad [7\text{–}20]$$

The condition that $P°$ be reached from any initial value $P*$ is that the absolute value of E_{t+1} be less than the absolute value of E_t, which implies that the absolute value of the term in brackets be less than 1, as written in [7–19]. Therefore, the rather mysterious conditions in this last expression are seen to be necessary and sufficient to guarantee that excess demand converge toward its equilibrium value of zero.

We have illustrated this graphically in Figure 7–8. On Figure 7–8a. the case where $|E_{t+1}| < |E_t|$ is illustrated. The value $D'E_t$ of [7–20] is the distance $CB = C'B'$, and the value $S'E_t$ is drawn as $AF = A'F'$. The value $B'F'$ is the algebraic sum of a negative excess demand E_t and positive $(-D'E_t)$ term, and $A'B'$ is the final result of adding to this partial sum the positive $(-S'E_t)$. The result is $A'B' = E_{t+1}$ which is less in absolute value than E_t, and so the system is stable. On Figures 7–8b. and 7–8c. we have illustrated cases of cyclical behavior with no tendency to equilibrium and of instability respectively, and their geometric interpretation follows that of the case of stability.

THE CAPITAL GOOD MARKET

We have developed the theory of market behavior for a good that is both a consumer good and an intermediate good. The other type of produced good in our model is the capital good, Z_i, whose market treatment is a bit more difficult inasmuch as we do not have an explicit demand curve for each type of capital good. We have supply curves for them, of course, and we may obtain the market supply curves in exactly the same manner as we did for goods Y_j. With all the complications discussed in our derivation of supply functions for goods Y_j, consequently, we may hypothesize the existence of the analogues of [7–4], [7–6], [7–7], or [7–8] for every type of producible asset Z_i.

But we may not yet derive the demand curve for the good. Suppose we had an equilibrium net value of savings originating from the consumer sector, $X_e^\circ P_e^\circ$. We have assumed that the prices of all capital goods, P_{Z_i}, except the one in question are fixed. However, from the fact that the equilibrium value of all investment in new capital goods is given, we cannot derive a demand curve for the capital good in question. We simply do not yet have a sufficient number of conditions to determine the allocation of the fixed amount of savings among the various choices of capital goods. These will have to be supplied by the nature of the determinants of demand for capital goods and by the conditions that we must place upon the relations of capital goods prices and services when we come to treat the economy as a whole in Chapter 8. We must, therefore, postpone further treatment of the demand functions for individual capital goods; however, if we may anticipate that analysis, it must be true for each capital good Z_i, $i = 1, 2, \ldots, m$, that its supply equal or exceed its demand, that its price be nonnegative, and that if the good is in excess supply that its price be zero:

$$X_{Z_i}^\circ \leqq \bar{X}_{Z_i}^\circ, \quad P_{Z_i}^\circ(X_{Z_i}^\circ - \bar{X}_{Z_i}^\circ) = 0, \quad P_{Z_i}^\circ \geqq 0. \qquad [7\text{–}21]$$

The Paper Asset Markets

THE LONG-TERM BOND MARKET

Again, in discussing the equilibration conditions in the long-term bond market, we shall assume that all other prices except P_e are held fixed at their general equilibrium levels. Then, from our discussion in Chapter 2, we have for each individual a demand curve for changes in his holdings of bonds:

$$X_{ce} = D_{ce}(P_e; \mathbf{P}^e, \mathbf{Q}_c, K_{cu}, \boldsymbol{\alpha}_c, \boldsymbol{\pi}_v) - Q_{ce}, \qquad [\text{I–3}]$$

where $i_k^\circ \geqq r^\circ$ among the data.

The supply of bonds, of course, is the obverse of the supply of capital goods, other than those issued by consumers, which will be netted out of the market demand for bonds:

$$X_e = \sum_c X_{ce}. \qquad [7\text{–}22]$$

Then, drawing upon the supply curves for capital goods discussed in the preceding section, we may define the firm's supply of bonds:

$$\bar{X}_{ve} = \sum_i \frac{\bar{X}_{vZ_i} P_{Z_i}}{P_e}, \qquad [7\text{–}23]$$

which we may sum over all firms to get the market supply curve for bonds:

$$\bar{X}_e = \sum_v \bar{X}_{ve}. \qquad [7\text{--}24]$$

In the determination of P_e° and the amount exchanged of bonds, X_e°, we impose the condition that supply be no less than demand at the end of the market day, that the price of bonds be nonnegative, and that if bonds are in excess supply their price be zero:

$$X_e^\circ \leqq \bar{X}_e^\circ, \quad P_e^\circ(X_e^\circ - \bar{X}_e^\circ) = 0, \quad P_e^\circ \geqq 0. \qquad [7\text{--}25]$$

As we have seen in our discussion of the nature of the rate of return on capital goods and its relation to the perpetuities we have used in our analysis, it follows that the equilibrium rate of return on capital goods is

$$i_k^\circ = \frac{1}{P_e^\circ}, \qquad [7\text{--}26]$$

for competition in the bond market will bid up the price of bonds to the point where the perpetual stream of net revenue yielded by them is capitalized at the rate i_k°. This latter is, then, the marginal rate of return on any capital good. We have indicated in our treatment of the consumer's desire to save that in our model these bonds will be redeemed in equivalent values of capital goods at the end of the week. Therefore, to the consumer capital goods are homogeneous units of perpetual income in the general equilibrium.

Once more, however, as in the case of the capital goods markets, we finish the analysis unsatisfied with this treatment. It is difficult to treat seriously the case where $P_e^\circ = 0$ (the rate of return on capital goods is infinite), and it is equally difficult to deal with securities independently of the demand for money assets, because the two are perfect substitutes in the model. The *partial* approach, therefore, to the determination of P_e°, neglects relationships so vital to the operation of the securities markets that it is seriously deficient. Indeed, in order to use System [I–3] we had to assume that the equilibrium rate of return on capital goods was no less than the interest rate, which we had no right to do. Therefore, only when we treat the whole economy as a unit, in Chapter 8, can we hope to obtain a satisfactory—if still simple— picture of this crucial price determination.

THE SHORT-TERM PROMISSORY NOTE MARKET

The market on which consumers lend their desired quantities of money balances and firms and consumers borrow their required cash service needs for the week can be handled straightforwardly. Each consumer has been assumed to have a supply-of-cash-balances function, derived from System

[I-10], and we may sum these over all consumers to get a market supply function of cash balances:

$$\overline{X}_u = \sum_c \overline{X}_{cu}. \tag{7-27}$$

From the entrepreneurial sector we have, for each firm, from System [II-16], a demand for cash balances during the week, and they may be summed over all firms to obtain a market demand function for cash balances:

$$X_u = \sum_v X_{vu}. \tag{7-28}$$

In equilibrium we shall require that demand and supply for cash balances be equated in order to determine the equilibrium rate of interest, r°, which is positive. That is,

$$X_u^\circ = \overline{X}_u^\circ, \qquad r > 0. \tag{7-29}$$

We insist upon the equality of supply and demand for money services and refuse to countenance an excess supply of them with $r^\circ = 0$ because if the price of cash balances fell to zero money assets could not exist. The existence of money depends upon its services earning a positive return—a peculiarity of this particular capital good. In our model, therefore, the use of money implies a positive interest rate.

The same basic difficulty with our present method, which we have encountered in the capital goods and securities markets, recurs in a peculiarly strong manner in the explanation of the equilibration process in the promissory note market. For suppose demand and supply are not equal, and all other prices but the price of money services are at their equilibrium levels. This means that fluctuations in the price of cash balances must occur to increase or decrease the demands for and supplies of promissory notes in the previously described manner. But in our model the demands for and supplies of cash balances are very insensitive to changes in the interest rate. Only if the absolute price levels of goods are free to vary can we expect effective equilibration of the promissory note market to be effected. Indeed, as we shall see, this is the way in which demand and supply equality will be achieved, which implies that demand and supply functions do a great deal of shifting, as opposed to the particular analysis depiction of units travelling up and down the same functions. Consequently we have a market that is peculiarly vulnerable to external impacts and dependent upon their occurrence (*changes* in other prices) for equilibration. These other market happenings cannot be abstracted from in the explanation of this market's operations. For that reason we shall be able to depict its equilibration realistically only when we treat the whole economy and its solutions in Chapter 8.

THE MARKET FOR MONEY AS AN ASSET

It is most important to bring into the analysis, not only for the sake of completeness, but to obtain important insights into the operation of the realistic economy, the market for money—not as a cash balance service but as an asset. In effect what our model allows us to do is to split off the cash-balance demand for money from the demand for it as another form of income-yielding asset. The consumer acquires or buys money as an asset (hoards) by failing to spend all of his income on goods and securities or by selling nonmoney assets for money, and relinquishes or sells holdings of money (dishoards) in this sense by spending in excess of his income and drawing down his stocks of money thereby. Therefore, the consumer's net demand for cash as an asset is equal to the value of his initial capital goods and stock of money, plus income, less the value of his capital goods at the end of the week, his purchase of balances in the week, and his purchases of all goods and services over the week. If the amount of money he holds at the end of the week exceeds that with which he began the week, he has enjoyed a net increase in his investment in money. If his money stock has diminished, his investment has decreased. And if his money stocks are equal to those with which he began, his investment in money has remained constant.

The market for money, therefore, considered as an asset, is a peculiar one, because it is scattered over all other markets. That is, money forms the second good in every market, and therefore the agglomeration of all of these *other sides* into one abstract market is necessary to grasp the concept of the market for money as an asset.

Note that in this market demand must equal supply as an equilibrium condition. That is to say, at the equilibrium *price* of money, every individual must be desirous of holding exactly the stock of it which he is in fact holding. Because the supply of money has been fixed at $Q_U = \sum_c Q_{cU}$, the *price* of money (not of money services) proper must be at that level which induces this willingness to hold the stock existing. Now, inasmuch as we have fixed the price of money at unity—the price of a dollar is defined as one dollar—how can there be a price of money that can change as required to equilibrate the money asset market? Of course, the answer is that all other prices must adjust to the disequilibrium of the money market. When the demand for money as an asset exceeds the fixed quantity available, its price must rise, and it becomes more valuable by all other prices falling, including the price of securities. Similarly, a rise in the price of all other goods occurs when the demand for money as an asset falls short of its supply, for then the holders of money go into all other markets to buy goods and securities with it, bidding up prices.

Further, the desire to hold money as an asset must be peculiarly sensitive to the price of its service—r—relative to the rate of return on bonds, i_k, for money and bonds are perfect substitutes in our models. In more realistic models, where we allow uncertainty of the future movements of prices and interest rates to intrude, the distinctive liquidity features of money destroy this perfect substitutability between securities and money, but nonetheless a high degree of substitutability persists. When the short-term interest rate, r, is higher than i_k, the long-term rate of return, consumers will desire to shift out of bonds and physical assets in our model and into money, and when the rate of return on bonds is higher than the interest rate, the reverse movement will be expected. In models with uncertainty, when the rate of return on bonds is expected to rise in the future, units will wish to hold their wealth in money form to take advantage of the expected future fall in P_e, especially because they may lend their cash by buying short-term assets to earn something in the meantime at little capital loss.

Obviously, then, we cannot treat absolute prices as fixed in a partial analysis, and we should be forced in our current analysis to assume rather that all other goods' *relative* prices were set at their equilibrium levels and that absolute prices were free to vary in order to equate the demand for and supply of money as an asset. If we do this, however, and assume that all prices rise and fall in rigid lock step, we *dichotomize* the model into real and monetary sectors, which denies the important fact that money assets are substitutes for real assets and current consumption and that the realistic equilibration process is importantly related to the relative prices of money and such assets, as well as their paper surrogates. Therefore, we cannot truly treat the equation of the supply and demand for money as an asset outside of the model that allows all markets to be in disequilibrium simultaneously and to achieve equilibrium by simultaneous variation of relative as well as absolute prices.

We may use the opportunity to point out a simplification that was frequently used in economic models but that is not present in our models. This is the adoption of what has come to be called *Say's Law*, and has undergone severe criticism for the same type of dichotomization it implies as that which we have referred to in the previous paragraph. By this assumption of behavior, it is explicitly imposed upon the behavior of consumers (in our model) that they do not attempt to change their stocks of money asset holdings. That is, it is arbitrarily imposed that they are in stock equilibrium *re* their money asset holdings at all times: they seek neither to increase nor decrease their investment in cash. The student may sense the difficulties this will imply for the model, for if the consumer is *always* satisfied with his holdings of money as an asset, then the price of money, the interest rate, and the rate of return on capital goods must have no interest to him in their relation to his money assets. Another implication is that money is prevented from becoming an asset or security in the realistic sense, constantly under scrutiny by the investor as an alternative to other security purchases, and providing peculiar advantages of its own in a world of uncertainty. In our model, it will in fact prove true that consumers as a whole must choose to accumulate no increase in their holdings of money assets by the end of the market day, but this result must be brought about by changes in the price of money and most especially the price of bonds and promissory notes. It is, therefore, not a trivial result obtained by assuming that consumers' desires to hold money assets never change, but rather an equilibrium result of the operation of the whole system.

The Factor Service Markets

As we have done in the case of products, let us choose a typical factor service, z_i, and analyze the relevant operational aspects of its market. After we have dealt with this generalized factor service, we may treat some of the special properties of labor, land, and capital more specifically. We continue our assumption that all prices but that under immediate analysis are fixed at their equilibrium levels, and treat the adjustment of the given market in this context.

THE GENERAL FACTOR SERVICE MARKET

From System [I–9] we have derived a supply curve for the consumer's offer of each factor service at his disposal:

$$\bar{X}_{cz_i} = S_{cz_i}(P_{z_i}; \mathbf{P}^{z_i}, \mathbf{Q}_c, K_{cu}, \boldsymbol{\alpha}_c, \boldsymbol{\pi}_v) = Q_{cz_i} - X_{cz_i}. \qquad [7\text{–}30]$$

To obtain the market supply function for the factor service we may sum these supply curves over all consumers:

$$X_{z_i} = \sum_c X_{cz_i} = S_{z_i}(P_{z_i}; \mathbf{P}^{z_i}, \mathbf{Q}, \mathbf{K}_{cu}, \boldsymbol{\alpha}, \boldsymbol{\pi}_v). \qquad [7\text{–}31]$$

As we developed in our analysis of the consumer's decisionmaking, our model implies that if z_i has an alternative consumer use, the individual's offer will reflect the marginal rate of substitution between the factor service and other consumer goods. The market supply function will net out any *purchases* of the factor service which the consumer may be led to effect by virtue of his preferences.

Thus, the derivation of the market supply function for a factor service is rather straightforward in our model. Let us turn, therefore, to the derivation of the market demand function, or the entrepreneurial demand for the service. From System [II–15] we have derived the demand curve for the firm for such primary inputs, and we may write in the specifics of the present analysis,

$$X_{vz_i} = D_{vz_i}(P_{z_i}; \mathbf{P}^{z_i}, K_{vu}). \qquad [7\text{--}32]$$

To obtain deeper insights into the derivation of this function, in the same fashion as we did for the consumer, let us return to the interrelationships that underlie it. We are most interested, in these respects, in [*F*–3–2], which states that in equilibrium the slope of the expenditure line must be no less than the slope of the equilibrium isoquant; in [*F*–3–3] and [*F*–5–4], which state the requirements for maximum-profit output; and in [*F*–5–2], which states the requirement that if the inequality holds in [*F*–3–2] only the minimum amount of the input be taken. The good used as a measuring rod in these comparisons may be any input taken in nonminimal amounts in the equilibrium, and we shall continue to assume that z_1 is such a factor service.

We know that the slope of the isoquant at the critical point is the amount by which factor service z_i must be increased if factor service z_1 is reduced by a small unit amount, in order to keep output at a constant level. That is, if we take the firm's production function for the given good, say Y_j, and allow X_{vz_i} and X_{vz_1} to vary by small amounts in the neighborhood of the equilibrium, we should have output vary as

$$d\overline{X}_{vJ} = T_{J/z_i} \, dX_{vz_i} + T_{J/z_1} \, dX_{vz_1}. \qquad [7\text{--}33]$$

The T_{J/z_i} are the slopes of the production function or the marginal productivities of the two factor services in terms of product Y_J at the initial equilibrium level of output. They indicate the increase in output that results when the respective input service is varied slightly, all other inputs held constant. Let us write, mnemonically, for [7–33],

$$d\overline{X}_{vJ} = MP_{J/z_i} \, dX_{vz_i} + MP_{J/z_1} \, dX_{vz_1}. \qquad [7\text{--}34]$$

But we constrain total output to remain constant if we move along the critical isoquant (or any other isoquant), so that if we impose this, and rearrange the terms of [7–34] we obtain

$$\frac{dX_{vz_i}}{dX_{vz_1}} = -\frac{MP_{J/z_1}}{MP_{J/z_i}}. \qquad [7\text{--}35]$$

Now, the left-hand side of the equation is the slope of the isoquant at the point from which we began, and in our case it is the initial equilibrium of profit maximization for the firm. We may see, then, that the slope of the isoquant is the negative of the ratio of the marginal products of the inputs, a result completely parallel to those achieved in consumer theory.

By applying straightforwardly the same analysis as that for the budget line of the consumer, we may also show that the slope of the expenditure line is the negative of the ratio of prices of the two inputs:

$$E^{\circ}_{z_i/z_1} = -\frac{P_{z_1}}{P_{z_i}}. \qquad [7\text{–}36]$$

Therefore, the equilibrium interrelationship of [F–3–2] may be rewritten as follows:

$$S^{\circ}_{z_i/z_1} \lesseqgtr E^{\circ}_{z_i/z_1},$$

$$-\frac{MP^{\circ}_{J/z_1}}{MP^{\circ}_{J/z_i}} \lesseqgtr -\frac{P_{z_1}}{P_{z_i}},$$

$$\frac{P_{z_i}}{MP^{\circ}_{J/z_i}} \gtreqless \frac{P_{z_1}}{MP^{\circ}_{J/z_1}}. \qquad [7\text{–}37]$$

The magnitude on the right of the last expression in [7–37] is formed by quantities associated with the good which serves as measuring rod. We have assumed that the quantities taken of this good will be nonminimal, and therefore that this magnitude will reflect interior values.

But what is this magnitude on the right-hand side of the relationship? It will be the equilibrium marginal cost of producing Y_j by varying, at the equilibrium point, the absorption of input z_1 only, for the ratio depicts the dollar expenditure per unit of marginal output of the factor service. Therefore, what [F–3] imposes on the system is that as a necessary condition of profit maximization the marginal cost to the firm of using any input contained in the relevant input set must be equal to or greater than the marginal cost of doing so with the measuring-rod input. And, of course, [F–5] states that the inequality can rule only if no more than the minimal quantity of the input is used in production.

That is to say, at the profit-maximizing equilibrium, all inputs that are used in greater than minimal quantities are, in dollar amounts, perfect substitutes for one another at the margin, and, we could show, combinations of them would also be perfect substitutes. The firm is indifferent, for very small changes in output, to obtaining them by small changes in this group of inputs or combinations of them. We may symbolize this common marginal cost at the equilibrium point by λ°, so that [7–37] can be written as follows to eliminate the explicit presence of the measuring-rod good:

$$\frac{P_{z_i}}{MP^{\circ}_{J/z_i}} \geq \lambda^{\circ}. \qquad [7\text{–}38]$$

For a given level of output, therefore, the firm, in order to maximize profits will purchase all inputs down to the point where their marginal costs of production for the product are equal to a common value, or else will purchase only the minimal quantities of them necessary for production.

But now let us turn to the case of profit maximization under freedom to vary the level of output. We have seen that in nonrivalrous competition the production of positive amounts of output under the regime of [F–3], [F–4], and [F–5] implied the equilibrium necessary conditions that marginal revenue of output be equated to the marginal cost under suitable conditions on the slopes of the marginal revenue and cost functions. Let us write the equality condition as

$$MR_J^\circ = \lambda^\circ. \qquad [7\text{–}39]$$

Roughly speaking, this is the condition for choosing the profit-maximizing output, whereas [7–38] is the condition for assuring that this output is produced as cheaply as possible. Let us combine both of these conditions into one by eliminating λ° from the conditions of [7–38] and [7–39]:

$$\frac{P_{z_i}}{MP_{J/z_i}^\circ} \geqq MR_J^\circ, \qquad [7\text{–}40]$$

which we shall write

$$P_{z_i} \geqq MR_J^\circ \cdot MP_{J/z_i}^\circ = MRP_{J/z_i}^\circ, \qquad [7\text{–}41]$$

where MRP_{J/z_i}° denotes the *marginal revenue product* of z_i in the production of Y_j. The marginal physical product of z_i times the rate at which net revenue increases per unit of product at the margin of the equilibrium output under consideration yields the increase in net revenue ascribable to the use of the added quantity of z_i. To maximize profits the firm is then charged to find that level of output and to produce in that way such that if each input is varied slightly, either (1) its marginal revenue product will be less than its price, in which case the firm must be taking only the minimal amount of it necessary for production, or (2) its marginal revenue product will be equal to its price, in which case the firm may be taking more than the minimal amount. For the second case, which is the one that interests us most, the condition merely states that to maximize profits it is necessary to hire inputs down to the point where what they contribute to revenue just equals what they impose in the way of costs.

But this relationship will define the demand curve for factor services for the firm, as it is written in [7–32], for it tells us that at any given price of the factor service, with all other prices fixed (in our case at general equilibrium levels), the firm will buy that quantity of the input which is minimal or which equates its marginal revenue product to its price. We have drawn such a function in Figure 7–9.

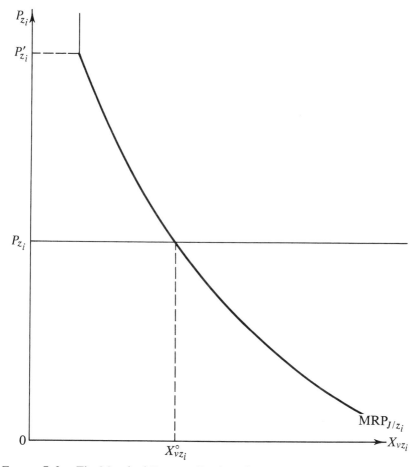

FIGURE 7-9. The Marginal Revenue Product Curve and the Demand for Labor.

The demand curve for the factor service is drawn as negatively sloped in function of its own price, as we have discussed in our displacement analysis of Chapter 5. In pure competition, the marginal revenue of increased outputs will be constant, so that no pressure downward on marginal revenue product will be exerted on this score; however, it will be recalled that the strictly concave production function implies that the marginal product of factor services and groups of inputs falls at least in the neighborhood of equilibrium. With falling sales curves, firms will experience declining marginal revenue with increased output, and the fall in marginal product will be compounded by a fall in the net revenue for which the product can be sold, so that both forces will result in a negative slope for the demand curve for such inputs in the own-price direction. This does not hold, of course, for those segments of the curve where price does not fall low enough to induce a greater-than-minimum purchase of the factor service at a constant output level, and we have drawn in such a segment of the curve in Figure 7–9 from P'_{z_i} upwards.

With this development of the nature of the firm's input demands, we may move forward to obtaining the market demand curve merely by summing the demands for each input over all firms using it:

$$X_{z_i} = \sum_v X_{vz_i} = D_{z_i}(P_{z_i}; \mathbf{P}^{z_i}, \mathbf{K}_{vu}).$$ [7–42]

We may put this market demand curve into juxtaposition with the market supply function obtained in [7–31], and impose the equilibrium condition that supply be no smaller than demand, with the inequality implying that the factor service is a free good:

$$X^{\circ}_{z_i} \leqq \bar{X}^{\circ}_{z_i}, \quad P^{\circ}_{z_i}(X^{\circ}_{z_i} - \bar{X}^{\circ}_{z_i}) = 0, \quad P_{z_i} \geqq 0.$$ [7–43]

Of course, a stability analysis of the equilibrium may be developed as we have done for the illustrative product market, and the same conditions derived for stability.

SPECIAL CHARACTERISTICS OF THE FACTOR SERVICE MARKETS

Although it is a satisfactory and indeed desirable approach to highlight the symmetry of treatment of demands, supplies, and equilibrium conditions relevant to all inputs, certain realistic characteristics of the several primary inputs should be taken into specific account. We shall, therefore, treat in brief fashion some of the salient special qualities of labor, capital, and land. However, these special treatments will be seen to be modifications of the general theory we have presented above; the student should not lose sight of the great advantage that is obtained from the use of such profit-maximization reasoning in unifying the whole field of factor demand. Previous theories developed in economics failed to attain this integration, and its attainment by marginal reasoning springing from maximization outlooks is a great advantage.

The Labor Market. One feature of capitalism that has distinguished it from previous types of economic organization is the existence of a market on which free labor is sold by its possessors in the same way that any other commodity or input is sold. It is a fair judgment, we believe, to say that Western societies have never been quite willing to allow labor to be treated in a perfectly symmetrical manner with other products or factor services. They have, by cultural restrictions of one form or another or by active intervention, imposed certain constraints on the operation of the market that are quite significant in altering the functioning from the presentation given in the generalized analysis. First, of course, although it is possible to sell the flow of factor services from labor, it is impossible to sell the factor itself: Western societies prohibit the institution of slavery or even too one-sided or long-term a labor contract.

Less fundamentally, but more importantly, modern free market economies have allowed or actively fostered the formation of labor unions, whose purpose it is to gain monopoly control over the supply of particular forms of labor and thus affect its price in the interests of their memberships. It is not our purpose, in a book on economic theory, to study in detail the multitude of considerations that led to this encouragement or noninterference. Effectively, however, to the extent the labor union is successful in organizing its membership into disciplined and reasonably comprehensive totals, the effect is to overthrow the market supply function of the type we developed in [7–31] for a monopolistic supply curve of the type we discussed in Chapter 5 for firms with downward-sloping demand curves.

The union might, for example, on the basis of study of the market supply curve of its membership, decide upon a fixed supply of labor (restricted union membership) for which it would aim to obtain employment, and then bargain with firms or the industry to get the highest price it could obtain for that level of employment. Its supply curve for our week, then, would be represented as a vertical line such as $S_o S_o'$ depicted on Figure 7–10. On the other hand, the union might equally simply decide on a given wage rate, $P_{z_1}^o$, as desirable from its point of view, and set it, to allow the industry to take as much labor as it will at that wage, so that the supply curve is the horizontal line through that price. In actual practice, as in the case of monopoly over the supply of a product, the union tends to set a price policy by bargaining over contract stipulations with employers whose primary bearing is upon the price (including all sorts of fringe benefits in addition to money wages) at which an indefinitely large supply of labor service is potentially available.

However, these supply curves are determined in a fashion analogous to rivalrous competition in product markets, in the sense that bargaining is involved in face-to-face confrontations. The outcome of such a process is as indeterminate in general as it was for rivalrous situations on the same side of the market. Many variables, therefore, will enter into the determination of whether an output or a price policy will be decided upon by the union, and the specific level at which the supply curve is set. Such factors include the relative bargaining abilities of the union and its industry or company antagonists, the relative staying power of these parties, the firmness of the union's leadership position in the eyes of the rank and file, the prosperity of the industry relative to others of a roughly comparable character, and any

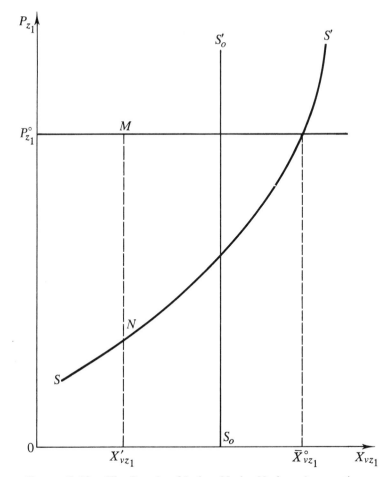

FIGURE 7–10. The Supply of Labor Under Various Assumptions.

number of other variables. Thus, we can say very little beyond the game-theoretic analysis of Chapter 6 without going into specialized and detailed studies.

Monopsony. This is a convenient point to relax our assumption that all buyers in all markets in our economy have no power over price. In the purchase of inputs, particularly, many large firms may have an ability to affect price through the size of their purchases, and if this potential is possessed, the rational profit-maximizing firm must take it into account in its decision-making. In the case of a local labor market, it may very well prove true that a single firm is such a large factor in the purchasing of labor that increases in the firm's demand for labor raise the price of labor to it. This is the analogue on the selling side of a market of finding that increases in the output of the good result in a lowering of the price of the product in order to sell it, and therefore, that profit-maximization considerations must recognize the phenomenon of declining marginal revenue.

One prerequisite for the existence of monopsony power over the price of an input is that the supply curve of the input to the firm in question be rising. Obviously, if the input can be supplied in indefinite amounts at a fixed cost, no matter how large the buyer's demand is, its price will not be bid up by his action. Suppose the input in question is labor: why should the natural supply of labor be rising as we have drawn *SS'* in Figure 7–10?

The answer to this question involves a very important concept in economic reasoning: the concept of *opportunity cost*. We may define this to be the true cost to a particular unit of factor service of serving a particular use during a particular period of time. It is defined to be the value of the opportunity of highest importance that had to be forgone because the resource unit was used in the particular employment defined above. What, for example, is the true cost to the firm in Chapter 5 of using oven capacity or delivery capacity for the week in question? We would define it to be the value of the highest paid alternative use to which these resources might have been put during the week, and by the assumptions of that analysis these alternative uses were nonexistent. Therefore, in terms of its decisionmaking, the firm should value each of these resources at its opportunity cost of zero for the week's operations. It is true that the imputation procedure will put shadow prices upon the inputs that may be nonzero, but these are relevant only for the choice of activity mixes and the maximizing of surpluses. The true cost to the firm of such capacities is zero for the short period because their mobility is zero.

The opportunity cost of an input will vary both with the individual unit of input and with the perspective of the decisionmaker who is contemplating its usage. To illustrate this latter concept, let us consider what the opportunity cost of using a unit of labor this week is to the economy as a whole. In order to answer this question we must ask what the alternatives are for the laborer to working in the economy during the week. Assuming that he has the option of working 40 hours a week in the national economy or not working at all, the laborer has no alternative to working in the economy. Therefore, from the social point of view, the opportunity cost of any worker is zero for the short run, because he has no mobility in the sense of alternative employments.

But now let us ask what the opportunity costs of the same laborer are to the *industry* in which he is employed. Presumably, in the very short run of the week, the laborer may have no alternative to working in the industry named, and therefore his opportunity cost to the industry may well be zero also. But some laborers even in this short a run, and many laborers for periods of a month or so, will have sufficient occupational mobility to leave the industry for another. Therefore, for any given laborer, the opportunity cost of using the labor in the given industry will be the highest alternative wage he can get if he leaves this industry, and it will be positive if such alternatives exist.

What of the alternative opportunities available to the worker from the viewpoint of the firm? That is, what is the opportunity cost of the laborer from its vantage? The laborer can, presumably, even in the short run, leave the firm for another in the same industry. Therefore, to the firm even in the short run the opportunity cost of the laborer will be positive. Thus the same laborer may have a zero opportunity cost to society, a positive opportunity cost to the industry, and a different positive opportunity cost to the firm. The crucial point in determining these opportunity costs is the mobility which the laborer has, and this depends on the number of alternatives that exist outside the set of activities within the orbit of the decisionmaker in question, and upon the time given the laborer to make such moves. Both considerations are contained in the concept of mobility.

Consider now the special characteristics of the unit of factor whose service is in question: in our case, but not of necessity, the laborer. His opportunity cost to the industry or firm (or to the society if his skills are such as to offer opportunities to him abroad) is determined by his versatility and skill in pursuits other than the one currently followed in his present employment. For example, if a tool-and-die maker were employed in the automotive industry, even in the short run he would be able to leave the industry and take the same skills to the electrical machinery industry. Therefore, the opportunity cost to the automotive industry would be what he could earn in the latter industry. Or suppose that a watchmaker were also an automobile salesman: then the opportunity cost of the laborer to the watchmaking industry would be the salary he could earn (plus psychic satisfactions or dissatisfactions of moving, selling cars, and so forth) in the automotive sales line. Or, lastly, assume that a manager of a shoe store was provably more efficient than other such managers in the industry. What is the opportunity cost of the manager to the firm that is currently employing him? It will be the salary he is able to earn from managing other shoe stores.

The opportunity cost to any particular user of the individual, therefore, depends on the special capabilities of the individual, and once more these aspects bear upon the important question of mobility. The greater this mobility, the greater will the individual's opportunity cost be.

Now, consider the natural supply curve of labor *SS'* as drawn in Figure 7-10. The curve tells us that as we add workers to the firm's employ, the *average cost* to the firm of labor rises because the marginal laborer's cost to the firm rises and takes all previous labor's cost along with his. That is, at $X_{vz_1}^{\circ}$ on the figure the cost of employing the first laborer outside the margin currently existing would be slightly above the current wage. Why? Because the marginal laborer's opportunity cost is higher than the wage currently being paid. He may be a worker currently working at another trade in another industry, whose present wage is at a slightly higher value than the going wage in the present industry. To coax him to the firm's employ, again, would require this slightly higher-than-present wage in the firm.

Surpluses to Factors. Note on Figure 7–10 and from the burden of our reasoning concerning the operation of a factor service market, that only the marginal unit of factor service is paid its opportunity cost. All intramarginal units receive more than what would be necessary to induce them to work in the firm (or industry or economy). Thus on the figure, the $\bar{X}_{vz_1}^{\circ}$-th laborer receives only what it is just necessary to pay him to induce him to stay, but all other workers receive the same wage as the marginal worker (we assume that all workers are equally efficient in the firm's employment). Thus, worker $\bar{X}_{vz_1}'$ has an opportunity cost of $N\bar{X}_{vz_1}'$—determined by the wage rate that would make him the marginal worker—yet he receives $P_{z_1}^{\circ}$ as a wage, as though he were marginal at the equilibrium.

Why does the firm (or industry or economy) pay units of factors more than the factor service's opportunity costs to induce them to work in its employ? Let us term the amount a worker gets in excess of his opportunity costs—for worker $\bar{X}_{vz_1}'$, the amount MN—his *surplus*, and we may extend the concept to the amount any factor service gets above its opportunity cost in its current employment. We may immediately see that to the extent factors do not possess mobility among employments most units of factor services in the market society will receive such surpluses. Is this not a wasteful procedure on the part of those who employ them?

The answer is, of course, that the unit in question pays the surpluses only because it has to. In the market in which the factor service is sold, the competition among employers of the services will bid the price of every unit of factor service of equal efficiency in the employment where its use is desired to the amount paid the marginal unit of factor. If any member of the intramarginal units were subtracted from the group of factor services producing, output will in fact decline by the output of the marginal unit, so that the employer will be acting rationally in treating each unit of factor service as marginal in this important sense. Therefore, if it should attempt to lower the return to some unit of factor service whose opportunity cost were less than other units, other firms would immediately bid for the services of the freed factor service until its price were once again on a par with the true marginal unit.

Thus, if the supply curve to the firm (or industry or economy) is rising, as is SS' for the case of Figure 7–10, surpluses will be paid to most of the factors. If the manager of the shoe store is paid $15,000 a year by the shoe store industry, even though his next best employment would yield him only $10,000 a year, the shoe retailing industry pays him a surplus of $5,000 by virtue of the competition among shoe stores for his differential efficiency in this employment. Notice that if the manager is to be assigned to his most valuable employment it is necessary that his salary be set by the market at his net contribution in his highest paid occupation, because only then has the market mechanism assigned him to his best employment and prevented him from being assigned to a less desirable position where his economic significance to society would be less.

If the firm were a single buyer in the market for this factor service (let us continue to assume for simplicity that it is labor, although once more our analysis is quite general) and if it were able to determine each unit's opportunity cost, it could pay every factor unit just this amount, they would continue to work in the firm, and the employer would add the value of rents to his returns from production. Ordinarily, however, this *perfect discrimination* among units is not possible, even to the firm that is a sole buyer of labor in an isolated labor market that has no labor union organization. However, in this situation—called *monopsony* to denote a situation in which a single buyer exists in the market—the firm's profit-maximization reasoning must take into account the upward-sloping nature of the labor supply curve to it.

That is to say, the firm must realize that as it increases its purchase of labor, the cost of the marginal unit rises, and, if all labor receives what the marginal unit receives, the cost of the average unit rises as well. Therefore, if an added unit of labor bids up the wage from $2 per hour to $2.20 per hour, it is not only the marginal laborer who receives the extra 20¢, but the entire previous labor force. The marginal factor service cost, therefore, is not $2.20, but this plus the charge of 20¢ times this labor force. Note the similarity of such reasoning with the firm's problems on the selling side of the product market when its sales curve is negatively sloped.

This leads us to alter our reasoning about the firm's maximum-profit purchases of factor services to a slight degree, fully comparable to the alteration of equating marginal cost to marginal revenue rather than price on the optimum output decision. On Figure 7–11 we have drawn the *marginal factor service cost* curve, which is marginal to the total factor service cost, obtained by multiplying each quantity of the factor service by the amount that would be necessary to induce its employment. Then, the firm will replace P_{z_1} in [7–41] by the marginal cost of employing the factor. That is, the firm will either equate the marginal revenue product of the factor service with its

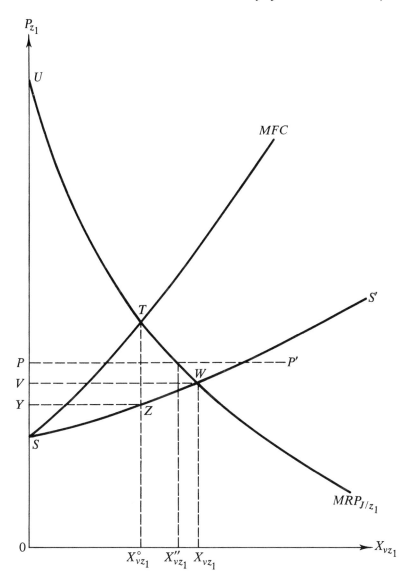

FIGURE 7–11. The Monopsonistic Market.

marginal factor service cost (if the factor service is taken in nonminimal amounts) or make sure that at the minimal quantity this cost lies above the marginal revenue product.

Note at the intersection of the marginal revenue product and marginal factor service cost curves the marginal revenue product of the factor service is more than its wage. We shall see that this implies that the monopsonist is purchasing less labor or other factor service than would be ideal from the viewpoint of society. However, at the moment we can see that the contribution of labor to revenue after paying its wages rises from the triangular area *UVW* in Figure 7–11—which is what it would be if the monopsonist ignored his impact upon wages in the market—to the area *UYZT*, which is what the contribution to net revenue is when he does take this into account.

We have here the possibility of a definition of *factor exploitation*. If the marginal factor does not receive its marginal revenue product which it would be guaranteed by a purely competitive factor service market, we might term it exploitation. Because if all factor units are equally efficient, each is the marginal unit, we might extend this to declare that all units of the factor service in question are exploited; yet this is somewhat clouded by the fact that the purely competitive market yields them surpluses, and the monopsony solution merely reduces the size of these surpluses to those units that continue to work. Perhaps it would be best to limit our concept of exploitation of the stock of factors to the less dramatic comment that such use of monopsony power limits the ability of some units of the factor to work in their best employment, and leads them to find employment in other industries in which their net earnings are less than they would be in the monopsonized industry.

Lastly, in our treatment of the monopsonized labor market, note that this type of situation affords the labor union the rather enviable opportunity both to raise wages and to increase the number of laborers employed. This can be done, for example, if the labor union can set the supply curve *PP'* on Figure 7–11 at a price above the monopsony price of labor, and thus make the supply curve to the firm a horizontal line that eliminates the possibility of monopsonistic departures of wage rate and marginal revenue product. The firm will then find it to its advantage to hire X''_{vz_1} of labor, the quantity at which wage rate and marginal revenue product are equal. This eliminates the exploitation of the marginal worker, but note that because the level of employment is not in general that which the purely competitive labor market would set, the stock of labor is still somewhat hurt insofar as unemployed labor in the industry must now seek jobs outside of it and not receive the rates that most of them would obtain were they able to work in this industry. Nevertheless, the relative results of unionization in such circumstances may well explain the success unions have had in industries that are isolated from other labor markets and in which monopsony was a good approximation to reality. Coal mining, for example, might well serve to illustrate the point.

THE CAPITAL GOOD SERVICE MARKET. The markets for the services of capital goods proper in our analysis are fully coordinate with the market for labor services. Let us now recognize realistically that although this assumption has allowed us and will continue to allow us a desirable simplicity in the analysis of the problems of capital goods, and has permitted us to achieve a long-run mobility in these services during our week, it is not the manner in which firms purchase such services. In the real world, firms purchase capital goods outright, add them to firm-held assets, and harvest annual flows of services from them, expending annual maintenance charges on the factors and accumulating over their lifetimes from the proceeds of use a sufficient amount of funds to replace them when they wear out. Let us step out of our formal model for a brief time to discuss the implications of this realistic procedure.

The Investment Decision. The fact that the firm cannot in general purchase the annual flows of services from the market means that the firm must decide to buy a package of such services over some number of future years—in the form of a capital good—or do without the services. Suppose, for example, that the firm, if it were to purchase a certain capital good, would receive a flow of services each week for three weeks, after which the machine would possess only a scrap value. The profit-maximizing firm, therefore, must decide whether or not to purchase the capital good on the basis of the expected net returns over the lifetime of the good.

How, then, should it proceed? Suppose on the market day of Week 1 the firm may contract to purchase capital good Z_i at a price of $1,000. Suppose the firm expects, after paying all maintenance and other charges (except depreciation), to receive a net stream of earnings of $500 in Week 2, $300 in Week 3, and $250 in Week 4, this latter expected return including the expected scrap value of the capital good when it is disposed of at that time. The following stream of net earnings over the good's lifetime is then expected by the firm:

$$R_{Z_i} = \$500 + \$300 + \$250. \tag{7-44}$$

Inasmuch as this stream of receipts adds up to more than the cost of the capital good, should the firm not make the purchase to obtain a net return of $50? For will it not then be able to repay the loan from whose proceeds it purchased the capital good and pocket a $50 surplus as net return, or else repurchase the machine in Week 5 and benefit again?

The decision process, of course, is not so simple, because the firm, in order to purchase the capital good, must sell bonds on the security market or borrow from its own accumulated funds (which we will allow it to hold for this analysis), on which, week by week, it pays a rate of return, i_k. Let us assume that the firm expects this rate of return to be the same for Weeks 2 through 4. What this rate of return implies to the firm is that a current dollar in Week 1 is not comparable with a dollar in the future. Let us term the price of a dollar in Week 1, $P_{\$,1}$, and set it equal to 1. What, then, is the price or value of a dollar in Week 2? If a dollar may be lent for a week at the rate of i_k, then the value of a dollar obtained in Week 2 in terms of today's dollar is that amount of today's dollars which will grow to equal one dollar in Week 2 at the rate of return i_k:

$$P_{\$,2} = \frac{1}{(1 + i_k)}. \tag{7-45}$$

Similarly, the price of a dollar in today's values that is receivable in Week 3 will be that quantity of today's money which will cumulate to $1 at the end of two weeks:

$$P_{\$,3} = \frac{1}{(1 + i_k)^2}, \tag{7-46}$$

and so forth.

This is an interesting aspect of the market mechanism. The existence of a positive net rate of return on capital goods—whose existence we have not yet explained and will do in Chapter 8—puts a price on the movement through time, much as transport rates arise on the movement through space. In the same sense that a carload of wheat in Chicago must have its value discounted by the costs of moving it to New York in order to calculate its true value at that destination, so the hypothetical movement of a dollar receivable in Week 3 to Week 1 must be discounted by the rate of return to gauge the value of it at the latter desired destination. It is therefore necessary to calculate flows of dollars through time at their true prices, not their nominal dollar prices.

Let us recalculate the stream of anticipated earnings at these true prices, so that [7-44] becomes:

$$R^*_{Z_i} = 500(P_{\$,2}) + 300(P_{\$,3}) + 250(P_{\$,4}). \tag{7-47}$$

Suppose $i_k = .05$. Then we should have

$$R^*_{Z_i} = 500(.952) + 300(.909) + 250(.866)$$

$$= 965.20. \tag{7-48}$$

Thus, under these conditions, the true value in current dollars of the stream of earnings is $965.20. On the other hand, inasmuch as the capital good must be purchased with $1,000 of today's dollars, this cost figure, $C^* = \$1,000$, needs no discounting because it is already in current dollars. It is now possible, therefore, to compare expected revenue flows and expected costs rationally, because they are both on current dollar bases. The opportunity to purchase this machine should be valued at about $965, the costs of doing so at $1,000, so that the firm should not make the expenditure because it would reduce the profitability of the firm over time. Time, therefore, to the firm, is a factor service that must be paid for, and when its cost is introduced into the analysis this opportunity, which appeared to be a profitable one, is seen to be disadvantageous.

One complication which our alteration of outlook introduces into the firm's decisionmaking, therefore, is that it immediately forces the firm to form expectations about time periods other than the current week. Our model up to this point has taken great pains to assure that the firm did not have to look beyond the end of the current week as a time horizon. When we introduce the expectations of the future into the analysis, the student can sense that we introduce a host of complications into the firm's decisionmaking: the problem of how it forms expectations of proceeds in the future, the problems of risk and uncertainty along with the desirability of speculating, hedging, and insuring, and the problems of phasing the production process through time in the sense of arranging the optimal time pattern of using inputs to produce outputs over the length of life of the capital good.

Still another complication which this outlook introduces—although it is less serious in its implications—is the fact of *lumpiness* of the bunch of services: either the firm buys the whole package over time or none at all. For the firm, therefore, marginal productivity analysis must give way to net product analysis of the type we have just illustrated. Consequently, the demand curve of the firm for all capital goods in dollar value will be derived as a function of the ruling rate of return on capital goods in the securities market, and will tend to take the form of a step function. We have illustrated this in Figure 7–12, where i_k is found on the price-axis and where the value of investments is found on the quantity-axis. As we move from high to low interest rates, at crucial points one investment or another becomes profitable and is added to the already profitable investments in lumps. This we may substitute as the supply of securities curve for the firm in this modified model where the firm is recognized as buying and holding capital goods, in lieu of the consumer who owns them only indirectly because of his ownership of the firms themselves. For [7–23], therefore, we may write alternatively,

$$\bar{X}_{ve} = S_{ve}(P_e; \mathbf{P}^e, K_{vu}). \qquad [7\text{--}23']$$

If we aggregate these firms' demands for investment funds over all firms, because the jumps occur at different points and are relatively small in terms of total demand, the *market demand curve* for investment goods may be drawn more smoothly, and is depicted as

$$\bar{X}_e = \sum_v \bar{X}_{ve} = S_e(P_e; \mathbf{P}^e, \mathbf{K}_{vu}). \qquad [7\text{--}24']$$

This curve we may substitute into our analysis of the long-term bond market in order to get i_k°, the equilibrium rate of return, and thereby P_e°.

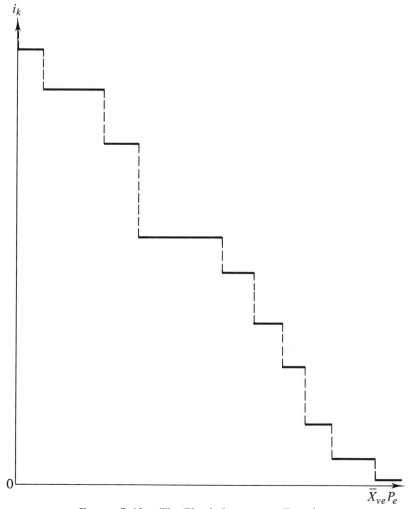

FIGURE 7–12. The Firm's Investment Function.

From this analysis, also, we may derive now a demand curve for each type of capital good as a function of its price, all other prices including that of the price of securities being held constant at general equilibrium levels. That is,

$$X_{vZ_i} = D_{vZ_i}(P_{Z_i}; \mathbf{P}^{Z_i}, K_{vu}), \qquad [7\text{–}49]$$

which, of course, we obtain for each firm and each capital good by allowing the price of the capital good to change. Then, the market demand curve for each type of purchasable capital good is

$$X_{Z_i} = \sum_v X_{vZ_i} = D_{Z_i}(P_{Z_i}; \mathbf{P}^{Z_i}, \mathbf{K}_{vu}). \qquad [7\text{–}50]$$

Using the market supply curve derived from the analysis of capital goods production, when the firm's supply function is

$$\overline{X}_{vZ_i} = S_{vZ_i}(P_{Z_i}; \mathbf{P}^{Z_i}, K_{vu}), \qquad [7\text{--}51]$$

we get

$$\overline{X}_{Z_i} = \sum_v \overline{X}_{vZ_i} = S_{Z_i}(P_{Z_i}; \mathbf{P}^{Z_i}, \mathbf{K}_{vu}), \qquad [7\text{--}52]$$

and we may derive the equilibrium price of each capital good by the conditions that it be nonnegative, that supply equal demand for it, or that supply must exceed demand and the price be zero:

$$X_{Z_i}^{\circ} \leqq \overline{X}_{Z_i}^{\circ}, \quad (X_{Z_i}^{\circ} - \overline{X}_{Z_i}^{\circ})P_{Z_i}^{\circ} = 0, \quad P_{Z_i} \geqq 0. \qquad [7\text{--}53]$$

The alterations we have made in the model now allow specific demand curves for capital goods to be drawn on the basis of profit-maximization reasoning, a task that was not possible when the demand for capital goods was considered to be a generalized demand for future income to be earned by consumers. But, of course, these demands taken jointly must interact with the savings decisions of consumers, and the prices arrived at must satisfy certain generalized price relationships to be discussed in the next chapter.

Note that this analysis, therefore, does away with the active determination of factor service prices, P_{z_i}, where these services are the creation of producible capital goods Z_i. If we adopt this approach we eliminate one market for each z_i, which corresponds to the producible Z_i. Further, our securities E purchased by consumers must now be considered permanent parts of their asset holdings and the rate of return i_k on them generates income instead of the lease of the capital goods which they purchased in the earlier model.

Having analysed this change, we shall revert to the earlier model, but will discuss what implications the present alterations possess for it in Chapter 8.

THE LAND MARKET.   Lastly, the markets for agricultural and urban land, as well as for land that contains natural resources of one type or another, can be subsumed for the best part under the treatment of capital goods with a strong element of the opportunity cost analysis of this chapter. That is, any plot of land will have a potential contribution to make to every type of use to which it might be put, depending upon its location, natural resource content, agricultural fertility, size, and so forth. This can be obtained by forming expectations of the streams of such net products over time for any given level of the rate of return on capital goods. Competition among users should bid up the price of the land such that it receives at least its opportunity cost and perhaps some surplus, so that the sum of the two payments will approach closely to the net contribution of the land in its highest employment.

Land, however, is one form of capital good whose services are sold on a market, because it is essentially nonproducible, so that the P_{z_i} for such services are actively determined as the price of saleable primary inputs. Because the source of such services may also be sold—unlike labor, for example—the price of the land and the price of its service must meet certain constraints to be discussed in the economy-wide consideration of Chapter 8.

The firm, in bidding for these weekly services, must ordinarily sign a lease that commits it to purchase them for rather long periods. Because, presumably, the payment of *rent* each period in the future will be derived and paid from the revenue of that period—there is no need, as in the case of the capital good, to make one lump sum payment for the services in their embodied stock form—the firm is led to subtract weekly rents from weekly expected net products, to capitalize these net receipts, and sum them. For any given rate of return on capital goods and any given P_{z_i}, the firm will then be led to lease the land if the current value of its services is positive. By varying the price of these services, therefore, we may derive the same type of

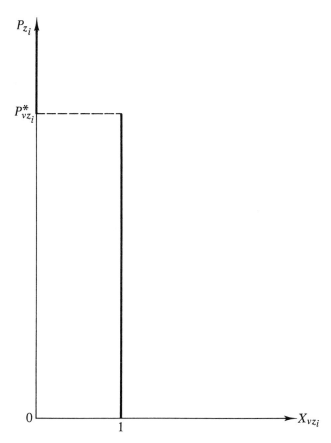

FIGURE 7–13. The Firm's Demand for Land Services.

demand curve for each piece of land in the economy as we have derived for capital goods, except that it will reflect the demand for capital good services. However, it will indicate that the desire to purchase is positive when P_{z_i} is below the critical level where the net value to the firm becomes zero, at which point the curve shows a zero demand for the good. We have illustrated this in Figure 7–13. Let X_{vz_i} be defined as follows: it equals 1 when P_{z_i} is less than or equal to the critical price where the value of the service to the firm becomes zero, and 0 after this level is reached. Let $P^*_{vz_i}$ be this critical threshold. Then, formally,

$$X_{vz_i} = \begin{cases} 1, & \text{if } P_{z_i} \leq P^*_{vz_i} \\ 0, & \text{if } P_{z_i} > P^*_{vz_i} \end{cases}, \qquad [7\text{–}54]$$

which lies behind

$$X_{vz_i} = D_{vz_i}(P_{z_i}; \mathbf{P}^{z_i}, K_{vu}), \qquad [7\text{–}55]$$

the firm's demand for the land service in the market for it.

Then, the equilibrium price for the services of the piece of land will be the maximum of the $P^*_{vz_i}$, or

$$P^{\circ}_{z_i} = \max_{v} (P^*_{vz_i}) \qquad [7\text{–}56]$$

where land is taken to be all capital goods that are saleable and nonreproducible.

Conclusion

With this set of considerations of the specialized characteristics of various factor services and factors, we conclude our statement of the conditions for equilibrium in each market when all other prices are fixed at general equilibrium values. Such analyses of the operations of free markets are the third type of our submodels, forming with the models of consumer behavior and entrepreneurial choice the components of the complete model it is now our intention to build. The pieces of the jigsaw puzzle are now existent, and the next task is to fit them together into the most ambitious anatomical chart of the economy. Note at this point once more that it was all but impossible to use this third submodel to determine the prices of money services, of money as an asset, and of capital goods when they are viewed as being held by consumers.

Selected Readings

1. P. L. BERNSTEIN, "Profit Theory—Where Do We Go From Here?," *Quarterly Journal of Economics*, LXVII (1953), pp. 407–422. An approach to a

spectrum of profit theories dependent upon what group receives profits, and a denial that a single theory can be developed.

2. GORDON F. BLOOM and HERBERT R. NORTHRUP, *Economics of Labor Relations* (Homewood, Ill.: Irwin, Fifth Edition, 1965), Ch. 9, 10, 11. A compact presentation of demand and supply problems peculiar to labor.

3. DONALD DEWEY, *Modern Capital Theory* (New York: Columbia University Press, 1965), Ch. 2, 3, 4, 5. A modern summary of several strands of capital theory.

4. WILLIAM FELLNER, *Probability and Profit* (Homewood, Ill.: Irwin, 1965), Ch. 1. An introductory discussion of the modern Bayesian approach to decision-making and profits in conditions when subjective probabilities must be employed.

, 5. JOAN ROBINSON, *Economics of Imperfect Competition* (London: Macmillan, 1933), Ch. 8. A classic generalization of the concept of rent to that of surpluses to all factor services.

6. J. FRED WESTON, "A Generalized Uncertainty Theory of Profit," *American Economic Review*, XL (1950), pp. 40–60. A development of the uncertainty theory of profits.

7. DEAN A. WORCESTER, "A Reconsideration of the Theory of Rent," *American Economic Review*, XXXVI (1946), pp. 258–277. An excellent summary of classical and modern theories.

PART III

The Complete Model

CHAPTER 8

The Complete Market Mechanism

IT IS TIME now to abandon our parochial view of the attainment of equilibrium which proved so useful in Chapter 7. We must cope with a reality that allows all markets to vary and to be out of equilibrium simultaneously, to affect prices and be affected by the price occurrences in every other market. We must now fit each market into its position among other markets, and seek to develop a physiology for the whole system of economic decisionmaking. By the end of Monday, our market day, there will emerge a price and amount exchanged in every market, which at once equilibrates that market and is consistent with equilibrium ruling in every other market. That is to say, the final result of the activities of actors in the markets is a full or *general* equilibrium of markets and individuals.

This involves another step up in the ambition of the models we seek to build. We have already moved from a construction of submodels for the firm and consumer in which all prices were given among the data to market models in which one price was removed from the data set and determined as a variable. Our next step, therefore, and our final one, is to remove *all* prices simultaneously from the data set, and determine them all simultaneously as variables.

When we do this we are able to grasp the set of markets as in fact a decision-making mechanism of vast complexity whose effectiveness will be judged in this chapter wholly by its ability to arrive at a nonnegative set of prices and quantities exchanged. For the first time we may see in its entirety the problem of a society as it concerns economic variables: how to coordinate and integrate the vast array of individual plans, hopes, and actions with relevance to that economic sphere into one consistent social plan, and to do so in a reasonably efficient manner with results in which all members of the society will at least acquiesce.

317

Let us hark back briefly to the discussion of Chapter 1 that set the problem in the broadest context for the analysis of the book. There we indicated that we were depicting the operation of this decisionmaking system as mechanism rather than organism. That is to say, even if the entity that generates these economic solutions through use of the free market has aspects that are organic in nature—follows internal laws of development, or is capable of autonomous structural adaptation to external stimuli—we shall ignore them as occurring only in the long run rather than in our short-run or medium-run periods. Therefore, our complete market economy consists of component parts called *markets* discussed in the last chapter, and our practical task in stepping up the ambition of the analysis in order to build the complete model is to integrate them into a self-sustaining whole.

We shall be interested in both the *anatomical* and the *physiological* aspects of the market mechanism, as discussed in Chapter 1. However, the complexity of the model to be built is such that we shall do very little in a formal way to discuss the latter. Let the reader recall the like analyses of the preceding chapter, where we discussed the anatomy of the market taken by itself— briefly described by the condition that when the market is in equilibrium the supply of the good or service be no less than the amount demanded. We shall, in the new model, generalize and extend these conditions for all markets simultaneously, as well as add new conditions that must characterize the mechanism's state if it is to be completely at rest. The reader will recall, however, that we briefly presented for one of the product markets a represent- ation of the dynamics of operation for that single market. To extend this analysis to all markets—to attempt to depict formally for specified manners of market price reaction to excess demand in all markets the approach or nonapproach of the many-dimensioned price and amount exchanged solution to a resting place—would require a complex and lengthy excursion into highly mathematical areas. We shall, therefore, limit such examinations to a description in words of the functioning of the mechanism when it has not reached its general equilibrium resting point.

And, finally, we shall limit ourselves in another direction that is familiar from our handling of the previous simpler models. Once we have the statement of the conditions that provide the solution to the market mechanism's equilibrium position, the reader may expect that we will seek further informa- tion about the physiology of the mechanism by shocking it with displace- ments of the data and studying the reaction of the equilibrium points to them. We must, alas, be disappointing on this score as well, for the model we shall build in this chapter will be quite large in terms of the elements in its variable set and the number of conditions that must be stated to determine their values. Even if we make the usual assumption that we have or can obtain an interior solution for the model, the task of seeking sufficient information about the slopes to be able to evaluate the movements of the variables is simply too complex in general.

The Set of Postulates and Data of the Complete Model

We shall retain the following elements in the postulate sets of the consumer and firm submodels, combining them when convenient in order to present the complete model more succinctly.

POSTULATE 1. For every Consumer c, $c = 1, \ldots, s$, there exists a preference function that is unique up to a monotone transformation, smooth, continuous, globally strictly quasi-concave, and strictly rising as any good or groups of goods is increased in quantity consumed, other goods remaining fixed in quantity. Each consumer's preferences are independent of the goods consumed by all other consumers. The domain of this function is the exhaustive set of all goods and services baskets with nonnegative components that it is possible for the consumer to obtain.

POSTULATE 2. The consumer will seek that basket $\mathbf{X}_c^\circ$ which yields the highest preference value for his preference function, subject to (1) the restriction that he choose within his attainable set, defined as that subset of baskets whose total cost does not exceed the value of his assets plus income on these assets for the week, and (2) that setting of his demand for cash balances determined by Postulate 3.

POSTULATE 3. The consumer's demand for cash balances, X_{cu}, will be determined by applying a given constant $K_{cu} \geqq 0$ to the value of his expenditures in the consumer goods proper and promissory note markets.

POSTULATE 4. It is assumed that each consumer enters the week with a vector $\mathbf{Q}_c = [Q_{cZ_i}, Q_{cU}]$ and ends the week with a vector $\mathbf{Q}_c^* = [Q_{cZ_i}^*, Q_{cU}^*]$, the differences in the elements of which reflect changes in the holdings of the various types of assets. Also, we may derive the values $Q_{ce}P_e = \sum_i Q_{cZ_i}P_{Z_i}$ and $Q_{ce}^*P_e = \sum_i Q_{cZ_i}^*P_{Z_i}$. Further, the consumer is entitled to a given proportion α_{cv}, of Firm v's profits, which is contained in the vector $\boldsymbol{\alpha}_c$.

POSTULATE 5. The consumer decides upon a basket that contains nonnegative quantities $\mathbf{X}_c^\circ = [X_{cj}^\circ, X_{cz_i}^\circ, X_{cu}, Q_{ce}^*, Q_{cU}^*]$.

POSTULATE 6. For every Firm v, $v = 1, \ldots, o$, there exists for each good Y_j, $j = 1, \ldots, n$, which are used both as consumer and producer intermediate goods, and for each capital good capable of production, Z_i, $i = 1, \ldots, m$, a production function. It is smooth, continuous, and globally strictly concave over a subset of input mixes M^*, which contains nonnegative values of a subset of inputs Y_j and z_i. The exact nature of M^* is defined more fully in Producer Postulates 4 and 5, in Chapter 3.

POSTULATE 7. Each firm can produce any good, but must choose only one good, because its production completely absorbs the stock of entrepreneurial energy. It chooses this good by producing that which yields the highest profits for the week analyzed. All economies or diseconomies external to the firm and internal to the industry are negligible.

POSTULATE 8. The firm's output, $\bar{X}_{vJ}^{\circ}$ or $\bar{X}_{vZ_i}^{\circ}$, and the firm's input mix, $\mathbf{X}_v^{\circ} = [X_{vj}^{\circ}, X_{vz_i}^{\circ}, X_{vu}^{\circ}]$, are chosen from the nonnegative orthant of input-output space.

POSTULATE 9. The firm's demand for cash balances, X_{vu}, will be determined by applying a given constant $K_{vu} \geqq 0$ to the value of its expenditures on inputs.

POSTULATE 10. The environment of the model is that described in detail in Chapters 2 and 3. This includes the assumption that all markets are purely competitive, so that all firms are in nonrivalrous competition with horizontal sales curves.

We assert the following definition, from which it is possible to obtain certain conditions to be imposed on the model:

DEFINITION 1. A *general equilibrium* of the economy, and a solution to the complete model, is defined to exist if and only if the following conditions are met:

1. given $\mathbf{Q}_c$ and $\mathbf{P}^{\circ}$, the equilibrium price vector, the basket $\mathbf{X}_c^{\circ} \geqq 0$ yields the maximum attainable preference value for every Consumer c;

2. the profit π_v° is nonnegative and the maximum possible profit attainable by every Firm v, given $\mathbf{P}^{\circ}$;

3. excess demand in the cash balance and money asset markets must be zero, in every other market must be nonpositive, and where nonzero, price in that market must be zero;

4. the net rate of return on all assets must be equal; and

5. $\mathbf{P}^{\circ}$ as a vector of equilibrium prices must be nonnegative.

This definition of equilibrium is merely a specification that the anatomical chart of the full economy depict a state of rest. It is, then, the catalog of conditions for a steady state in the economy. Every consumer and firm is maximizing the satisfactions and profits respectively attained by the unit in the circumstances it faces, while in every market every seller is capable of finding at least as many buyers as he wishes for non-free goods, and every buyer can obtain at least as much of the product as he wants. Where more than enough product is forthcoming or more than a sufficient quantity of resource services is provided, the good or service must be considered a free good with a zero price. Because capital goods and money assets are held by consumers as merely homogeneous means of earning future income, consumers have no preferences among them. Therefore, after taking into account the possibly different lengths of life of such assets, the net returns they yield as providers of services must be the same if we are in a steady state, for if they are not, those which earned more net would be sought after and their prices would rise. Lastly, all prices in the solution must be positive or zero, because negative prices make no sense in the conditions of the model. We have already constrained the amounts demanded and supplied to be nonnegative in the postulates.

Interestingly, we may use this definition of a steady state to depict the market process on Monday as an n-person, noncooperative, nonzero-sum game. Let us imagine the consumers of the economy as s players in the game, whose strategies consist of selecting baskets of goods and services; the firms as o players whose strategies consist of selecting levels of output and input mixes; and 1 fictitious *market participant* whose strategy set consists of specifying nonnegative price vectors, **P**. The payoff to the consumer players consists of subjective satisfaction, the payoffs to firm players are profits, and the payoff to the market participant we shall take to be the sum of the value of the excess demands (except that for money as an asset). That is, the market participant multiplies the excess demand in every market by the price in every market, and the total of such products is his payoff.

Now, the market participant plays a strategy (that is, selects a nonnegative price vector, **P**). Consumers, accepting this strategy, select a basket of goods and services within their attainable sets that maximizes their satisfaction. Firms, accepting the price strategy of the market participant, select strategies and thereby determine the profit-maximizing outputs and input mixes. These consumer and firm demands and supplies result in a pattern of excess demands, **E**, or demand minus supply in each market, and the payoff to the market participant from his price strategy is now determined by getting the value of excess demand (except for money assets, which is the negative of the market participant's payoff) in each market and summing. The latter, believing with Cournot-like myopia that **E** is not affected by his stategy, lowers nonzero prices of goods with $E < 0$ and raises prices of goods with $E > 0$, since this lowers the negative contribution of the former and raises the positive contribution of the latter. Then, he makes such adjustments by playing a new strategy **P** to which all the other players respond with new strategies, and this continuing game goes on until, if ever, an equilibrium point is found. From our discussion of game theory in Chapter 6, it will be recalled that an equilibrium set of strategies in n-person game theory is one in which, for every player in the game, given the strategies all other players have selected, he can find no better strategy. It can be proved that for suitable restrictions on the strategy sets of the three participants (and what these imply as restrictions on the interrelationships among the data and variables of our model) at least one such equilibrium point will exist. Thus, in addition to being able to interpret the market mechanism's operation as an *n*-person game and deriving insights into its physiology from such an analogy, we are allowed to prove the existence of a general equilibrium point in the system by following game-theoretic techniques.

More importantly, for the purposes of this book, this view of the market mechanism's state of rest makes clearer the concept of equilibrium: *it is a state in which each player in the game is doing the best that he can do given that all other players in the game are doing what they are doing.* It is in this sense that each player has no desire to upset the status quo: either because he cannot have any impact upon other players' choices of strategies, or, if he can, he cannot induce other players to choose strategies that would benefit himself. Therefore, he is content to play the strategy he does and thereby maintain the status quo.

The Set of Interrelationships of the Complete Model

We must now state the set of interrelationships that we shall employ to obtain a solution meeting the conditions for the definition of equilibrium or a general state of economic rest. For the firm and the consumer we shall take the *solutions* of our submodels to be the *interrelationships* among data and variables for our grand model, but it will be understood by the student that the underlying interrelations of those submodels lie in the background and are available in case we want to manipulate the model, or, more realistically, portions of it.

THE CONSUMER SECTOR

We rewrite the supply and demand functions of System [I] for every consumer in the economy:

1. $X_{cj} = D_{cj}(\mathbf{P}, \mathbf{Q}_c, K_{cu}, \alpha_c, \pi_v),$ $j = 1, \ldots, n,$ $c = 1, \ldots, s$
2. $X_{cz_i} = D_{cz_i}(\mathbf{P}, \mathbf{Q}_c, K_{cu}, \alpha_c, \pi_v),$ $i = 1, \ldots, m$
3. $X_{ce} = D_{ce}(\mathbf{P}, \mathbf{Q}_c, K_{cu}, \alpha_c, \pi_v) - Q_{ce} = Q_{ce}^* - Q_{ce}$

4. $X_{cu} = \dfrac{K_{cu} \sum_j X_{cj} P_j}{1 - K_{cu} r}$

5. $X_{cU} = W_c + Y_c - \sum_j X_{cj}P_j - \sum_i X_{cz_i}P_{z_i} - X_{cu}r - Q^*_{ce}P_e - Q_{cU}$

6. $W_c = Q_{ce}P_e + Q_{cU}$

7. $Q_{ce} = \dfrac{\sum_i Q_{cz_i}P_{z_i}}{P_e}$

8. $Y_c = \sum_i Q_{cz_i}P_{z_i} + Q_{cU}r + \sum_v \alpha_{cv}\pi_v$

9. $\bar{X}_{cz_i} = Q_{cz_i} - X_{cz_i}$

10. $\bar{X}_{cu} = Q_{cU} - X_{cu}$ [I]

Let us review these quickly for the purpose of refreshing the student's memory. Relations 1 state the demand functions for consumer goods proper, and relations 2 the consumer's demand for factor services to consume. Relation 4 depicts the consumer's demand for cash balances to hold during the week. Relations 9 and 10 determine his supply of such factor services and cash balances to the markets of the economy. Relations 3 and 5 yield the consumer's changes in assets during the week, the last of which is stated as a residual after all other expenditures are accounted for, taking into explicit account the consumer's income and wealth. Relations 6 and 8 define wealth and income, and, lastly, relation 7 defines the bond-equivalent of the consumer's initial holdings of capital goods.

THE ENTREPRENEURIAL SECTOR

Next, we may simply rewrite the relations of System [II] for every Firm v in the economy:

1. $X_{vj/J} = D_{vj/J}(\mathbf{P}, K_{vu}),\qquad j = 1, \ldots, n, J = 1, \ldots, n, v = 1, \ldots, o$

2. $X_{vz_i/J} = D_{vz_i/J}(\mathbf{P}, K_{vu}),\quad i = 1, \ldots, m, J = 1, \ldots, n$

3. $X_{vj/Z_i} = D_{vj/Z_i}(\mathbf{P}, K_{vu}),\quad j = 1, \ldots, n, i = 1, \ldots, m$

4. $X_{vz_i/Z_i} = D_{vz_i/Z_i}(\mathbf{P}, K_{vu}), i = 1, \ldots, m, i = 1, \ldots, m$

5. $\bar{X}_{vJ} = S_{vJ}(\mathbf{P}, K_{vu}), J = 1, \ldots, n$

6. $\bar{X}_{vz_i} = S_{vz_i}(\mathbf{P}, K_{vu}), i = 1, \ldots, m$

7. $X_{vu/J} = \dfrac{K_{vu}(\sum_j X_{vj/J}P_j + \sum_i X_{vz_i/J}P_{z_i})}{1 - K_{vu}r}$

8. $X_{vu/Z_i} = \dfrac{K_{vu}(\sum_j X_{vj/Z_i}P_j + \sum_i X_{vz_i/Z_i}P_{z_i})}{1 - K_{vu}r}$

9. $C_{vj} = \sum_j X_{vj/J}P_j + \sum_i X_{vz_i/J}P_{z_i} + X_{vu/J}r$

10. $C_{vz_i} = \sum_j X_{vj/Z_i}P_j + \sum_i X_{vz_i/Z_I}P_{z_i} + X_{vu/Z_i}r$

11. $\pi_{v/J} = \bar{X}_{vJ}P_J - C_{vJ}$

12. $\pi_{v/Z_i} = \bar{X}_{vz_i}P_{z_i} - C_{vz_i}$

13. $\pi^\circ_{v/k} = \max_{i,j}(\pi_{v/J}, \pi_{v/Z_i})$

14. $X^\circ_{vj} = X_{vj/k}$

15. $X_{vz_i}^{\circ} = X_{vz_i/k}$

16. $X_{vu}^{\circ} = X_{vu/k}$

17. $\bar{X}_{vk}^{\circ} = \bar{X}_{vk}$

18. $\bar{X}_{vJ \neq k}^{\circ} = \bar{X}_{vZ_i \neq k}^{\circ} = 0.$ [II]

Let us again refresh the student's memory. Relations 1, 2, and 7 define the demand by the firm for inputs should it produce any given Y_j, and relations 3, 4, and 8 define such demands should it choose to produce any given Z_i. Relations 5 and 6 depict its desire to supply such goods under any given **P** and K_{vu}. Relations 9, 10, 11, and 12 define the firm's costs and profits in the production of all of its potential outputs, and relation 13 defines its highest profit from the production of any good this week. This last relation implies the *actual* demands for inputs indexed by relations 14, 15, and 16, as well as actual outputs as indicated by relations 17 and 18.

THE AGGREGATE CONSUMER SECTOR

We may now sum over the individual relations of System [I] for all consumers, where such relations are of use to the complete model, in order to get aggregate consumer functions:

1. $X_j' = \sum_c X_{cj} = D_j^c(\mathbf{P}, \mathbf{Q}, \mathbf{K}_{cu}, \boldsymbol{\alpha}, \boldsymbol{\pi}_v)$

2. $\bar{X}_{z_i} = \sum_c \bar{X}_{cz_i} = \sum_c Q_{cz_i} - D_{z_i}(\mathbf{P}, \mathbf{Q}, \mathbf{K}_{cu}, \boldsymbol{\alpha}, \boldsymbol{\pi}_v) = S_{z_i}(\mathbf{P}, \mathbf{Q}, \mathbf{K}_{cu}, \boldsymbol{\alpha}, \boldsymbol{\pi}_v)$

3. $X_e = \sum_c X_{ce}$

4. $\bar{X}_u = \sum_c \bar{X}_{cu}$

5. $X_U = \sum_c X_{cU}.$ [III]

These relations, as mere summations of the consumers' relations of System [I], need no further comment, and the reader is referred to our discussion of the individual relations in Chapter 7 if he wishes to refresh his memory of their deeper implications.

THE AGGREGATE ENTREPRENEURIAL SECTOR

In similar fashion we may aggregate over firms in the economy to get relevant functions for the whole of the entrepreneurial sector. Note that we need not take into account industry levels of production in our statement of the firm's functions insofar as we now are allowing all prices to vary and these economies and diseconomies of the industry's operations will be reflected in the varying prices which all firms face. Therefore, we may aggregate as follows:

1. $X_j'' = \sum_v X_{vj} = D_j^v(\mathbf{P}, \mathbf{K}_{vu})$

2. $X_{z_i} = \sum_v X_{vz_i} = D_{z_i}(\mathbf{P}, \mathbf{K}_{vu})$

3. $X_u = \sum_v X_{vu}.$ [IV]

We have aggregated only the input demands for all firms. We have seen from Chapter 7 that under the assumptions of pure competition for the long run the firm's supply curve is never effective except where it intersects the minimum point of the firm's long-run average total cost curve. Even though we are dealing only with the *week*, and therefore with a short-run period in terms of time duration, the characteristics of a long-run equilibrium will mark the solution of the model. This is true because each firm buys all factor services from the market each week rather than owning fixed quantities of some of them, and the competition for such factor services will assure that all differential advantages of factor services will be reflected in their prices by the end of Monday. Therefore, we will expect that every firm that produces will, during the current week, operate at the minimum point of its U-shaped average cost curve. Consequently, the industry's supply curve will be a horizontal line at the level of these costs, and will not follow the sum of these individual firm supply curves, if no economies or diseconomies occur, or will possess rising or falling portions if they do. Therefore, we shall cope with these problems when we discuss industry and aggregate supplies and demands for markets. This is the explanation for not aggregating firms' supply curves, however. The remaining functions of System [II] are not needed for our purposes and therefore have not been aggregated.

THE MARKET DEMAND FUNCTIONS

We have already defined most of the demand functions for goods and services in Systems [III] and [IV], with an exception: we must simply add together consumer and entrepreneurial demand for consumer-intermediate goods to get total demand.

$$X_j = X_j' + X_j'' = D_j(\mathbf{P}, \mathbf{Q}, \mathbf{K}_{cu}, \alpha, \pi_v, \mathbf{K}_{vu}) \qquad [V]$$

This yields the market demand function for the goods Y_j. Let us review the definition of the demand functions in all other markets in the economy:

1. Factor Service Market: defined in System [II–15] and [IV–2].
2. Money Service Market: defined in System [II–16] and [IV–3].
3. Bond Market: defined in System [III–3].
4. Money Asset Market: defined in System [III–5].

We have not yet defined the demand functions for the capital good markets, and indeed will not do so explicitly, but rather will set explicit restrictions upon the values of amounts demanded that must eventuate. Note, however, that if we had wished to keep the alteration of environment which we made in Chapter 7 so that firms were viewed as purchasing and owning specific forms of capital goods, these demand functions would be forthcoming from such equations as [7–47] and [7–48].

THE MARKET SUPPLY FUNCTIONS

Once more, as in the case of market demands, most of our markets already have had their market supply functions defined. This is not yet true of the market for paper assets, however, and to this task we must turn.

Money in our economy is a paper asset fixed in quantity for the week. Therefore, the market supply of it each week must be the total amount of it existing, and the market supply function must be a vertical line through this existing quantity:

$$1. \quad \bar{X}_U = \Sigma_c \, Q_{cU}. \qquad \qquad \text{[VI]}$$

The supply of bonds this week springs from the value of the capital goods which suppliers of them are desirous of producing; by virtue of our construction of the aggregate consumer demand for bonds, in System [III–3], the issuance of bonds by consumers who want to spend from their stock of assets is netted out of the aggregate demand for bonds. The market demand, therefore, is a demand net of any negative demand by some consumers, and if the market demand is positive it can be met only by the production of capital goods.

Suppose $X_e < 0$ at some **P**. This would mean that consumers as a group were attempting to sell some or all of their existing capital equipment in order to obtain money assets or to consume in excess of their aggregate incomes. The price P_e must therefore fall towards zero, and as it falls i_k rises in an attempt to induce consumers to find future income more attractive and present income less attractive, or money assets less attractive relative to holding capital goods as assets. Of course, this must have reactions on r and the *price* of money (the absolute price level), as well as on the value of factor services and factors themselves. Should these physiological reactions throughout the economy fail to prevent the demand for bonds from being negative even when $P_e = 0$, the economy is confronted with a difficult situation to define. The rate of return on factors, i_k, is infinite, so with finite prices for their *services*, such capital goods and land will have zero value. Therefore, those consumers who happen to hold title to them will be forced to hold capital goods whose future services are valueless; none of these capital goods will be produced, because the demand for bonds is negative.

Suppose, now, that $X_e = 0$, at $P_e > 0$. Then consumers as a group are saving nothing, if we recall the assumption that all capital goods have an infinite life so that no depreciation expenditures are required week after week to repair the capital stock. At the ruling **P**, therefore, some consumers will be selling bonds and thereby offering existing capital goods and others will be buying bonds and taking delivery of existing capital goods at the end of the week, but no new capital goods will be produced. The demand function for bonds will intersect the supply function for bonds at a value P_e on the P_e-axis. If some consumers are buying bonds and others selling them, then these consumers are not in stock equilibrium. If $X_e = 0$ and *all* consumers are content to hold their assets, that is, $X_{ce} = 0$ for all c, then all consumers are in stock equilibrium. In either case we may interpret the *economy* as being in stock equilibrium, or in the classic *stationary state* in which no net saving is being done and no net investment is eventuating.

Lastly, if $X_e > 0$, new capital goods must be produced, the economy is growing in its capital goods dimension, and when this condition occurs in the market the supply of bonds may be positive. We write, therefore, as a supply function for bonds:

$$2. \quad \bar{X}_e P_e = \sum_i \bar{X}_{z_i} P_{z_i}. \qquad \text{[VI]}$$

Next, consider the case of consumer-intermediate goods, Y_j, for which we have refrained from defining a market supply function by adding firms' supply functions. From our analysis of Chapter 7 we know that at the equilibrium point the market supply function will be a horizontal line at the equilibrium price. Effectively, therefore, each industry is led, in a non-purposive, decentralized manner, to form a price policy, just as a firm with a sloping demand function might be. As in that case, we need not inquire what the function depicting the desire to supply would be under all possible conditions of sale curves, in terms of their shapes and positions. We need merely define their desires in terms of the sales curve as it exists this week. So in the case of our model: given the statement of a price vector **P**, a given set of firm supply curves will be defined, entry or exit will occur into industries in order to equalize profits and make proper adjustments in factor prices until all firms actually producing are producing at the same minimum costs for the same product. We shall consider only these latter points and define the industry's market supply curve in the peculiar-appearing form

$$3. \quad \pi_v^\circ = 0. \qquad \text{[VI]}$$

That is, in the equilibrium, profits for all active firms must be zero. Therefore, in the production of all goods, equilibrium price must equal equilibrium average costs, which the reader will recall is the industry supply curve under these conditions, as given in [7–6] in the last chapter.

With these exceptions, the market supply functions are given in previous systems:

1. Factor Service Markets: defined in System [III–2].
2. Money Service Market: defined in System [III–4].

3. Capital Goods Markets: defined in System [VI–3] implicitly.
4. Money Asset Market: defined in System [VI–1].

INDIVIDUAL MARKET EQUILIBRIUM

In the complete model each market must be in equilibrium taken individually when the equilibrium price set is ruling. Therefore, we impose the conditions that excess demand in each market must be nonnegative, and if positive, price must equal zero:

$$
\begin{aligned}
&1. \quad X_j^{\circ} - X_j^{\circ} \leqq 0 \\
&2. \quad P_j^{\circ}(X_j^{\circ} - X_j^{\circ}) = 0 \\
&3. \quad X_{z_i}^{\circ} - \bar{X}_{z_i}^{\circ} \leqq 0 \\
&4. \quad P_{z_i}^{\circ}(X_{z_i}^{\circ} - \bar{X}_{z_i}^{\circ}) = 0 \\
&5. \quad X_{Z_i}^{\circ} - \bar{X}_{Z_i}^{\circ} \leqq 0 \\
&6. \quad P_{Z_i}(X_{Z_i}^{\circ} - \bar{X}_{Z_i}^{\circ}) = 0 \\
&7. \quad X_u^{\circ} - \bar{X}_u^{\circ} = 0, r > 0 \\
&8. \quad X_U^{\circ} - \bar{X}_U^{\circ} = 0 \\
&9. \quad X_e^{\circ} - \bar{X}_e^{\circ} \leqq 0 \\
&10. \quad P_e^{\circ}(X_e^{\circ} - \bar{X}_e^{\circ}) = 0. \qquad\qquad [VII]
\end{aligned}
$$

Note that we cannot allow the price of money services to equal zero, for if this were to happen the only basis for the existence of money—to facilitate transactions—would disappear, and transactions would either be conducted by barter using some real good as a unit of account, or transacted by use of credit instruments that would be cleared at the end of the market day. Therefore, if the value of money services is constrained always to be positive, the value of the instrument rendering them costlessly must also be positive at a defined positive rate of return, and this preserves our ability to use money as *numéraire*. Finally, note that condition [VI–2] requires that if $P_e = 0$ the supply of capital goods be zero unless one or more are free goods.

INTERMARKET EQUILIBRIUM

Finally, there are certain conditions that must hold *between* pairs of markets in order that no *player* in the *market game* will have an incentive to change his strategy. First, under our simplifying assumption that all capital goods are permanent in nature and never wear out, the gross return on a unit of capital good asset, P_{z_i}, is also a net return. Because consumers purchase capital goods only indirectly as a result of their purchase of securities, and because consumers are interested in them only because of their ability to provide net returns in the future, we have defined as one of the conditions of equilibrium that the net *rate* of return on capital goods be equal for all of them. We have seen in Chapter 2 that the price of securities, P_e, is actually, in equilibrium, the reciprocal of the equilibrium net rate of return on securities, i_k, so we may write:

$$1. \quad P_e^\circ = \frac{1}{i_k^\circ}.$$

[VIII]

Therefore, because equal values of capital goods must yield equal earnings in the future, we require that the rate of return on each capital good in equilibrium should earn this rate of return:

$$2. \quad i_k^\circ P_{z_i}^\circ = P_{z_i}^\circ.$$

[VIII]

Note, too, that at a positive i_k° (and we shall bound i_k° away from zero in the next condition) if the price of a capital good is zero its service must also be a free good.

But we have a second type of security in our economy: the promissory note, or, more directly, the securities created in the lending and borrowing of cash balances. We may term the net rate of return on money the *interest rate*, r, and it will be by definition the price of money service over the price of money ($\equiv 1$).

We are now able to cast light upon the role of money in the economy as a store of value. We have emphasized that money is a type of security or asset, which can be purchased by those who desire to save, because such assets yield flows of saleable resources (can be lent at short term). Therefore, in equilibrium we should suspect that the net rate of return on capital goods and the net rate of return on money should be equalized by competition:

$$3. \quad r^\circ = i_k^\circ.$$

[VIII]

In the real world, where uncertainty rules about price and interest rate movements, money as a security possesses the quality of absolute liquidity, or the ability to be turned into itself at no loss in value. This additional feature would dictate that the equality of [VIII–3] not hold, but that the advantage of money as an asset be reflected in a lower return (short-term assets revealing lower interest rates than long-term in general). Nonetheless, in our idealized model of the market mechanism, these advantages do not exist.

Note that we can tolerate no zero rate of return on money, so that in equilibrium it must be positive. Therefore, what this last equilibrium equality requires is that in our economy the rate of return on securities at the end of the weekly market day be positive. Indeed, we receive the interesting insight that in an economy that has paper money, the interest rate can never decline to zero, for if it did the use of money would cease. For suppose that $r^\circ = 0$: in an economy such as ours no one would desire to hold money as an asset because its price would be infinite, and inasmuch as its only function in such an economy is to be a means of transaction, money would pass out of existence.

With one last system we have finished the construction of the complete model:

$$4. \quad \mathbf{P} \geqq 0. \qquad\qquad\qquad [VIII]$$

Note that we will have met the conditions set up in our definition of equilibrium: every consumer will be maximizing the value of his preference function subject to his wealth-income constraint; every firm will be maximizing its profit at zero levels; excess demands in every market but those for money services and money assets will be nonpositive, and in these latter two markets will be zero; the net rate of return on all assets will be equal at some positive level; and all prices will be nonnegative.

One last finessing touch may be brought into the picture at this time to point up the nature of a multimarket system. We may eliminate one of the equilibrium conditions of System [VII–7] or [VII–8] as redundant, on the basis that if all markets but one are in equilibrium, the remaining one must be by the nature of markets. That is, if either supply equals demand for all but one good, or supply exceeds demand for some that are free goods, the demand and supply of the remaining good must be equal or its price must be zero. It is simplest to develop this outlook for money as an asset; it is the opposite side of every other market in the economy. If every one of these markets is in equilibrium, it follows that the supply of and demand for money in those markets is in equilibrium. Put in another way, if any market has an excess of demand over supply or supply over demand at any price, that excess is reflected directly in an excess supply or demand for money in that market. Therefore, if all other goods are in equilibrium in this sense, so that if demand does not equal supply for any good its price is zero and does not involve any expenditure, then if all goods are in equilibrium excess demand for money assets must be zero. All individuals in the economy must also be content with their holdings of money assets. Therefore, to impose such a condition explicitly is to repeat a condition contained implicitly, and we may remove the former.

The Set of Variables of the Complete Model

Using rather deep theorems of mathematics, and constraining the data and the postulates in rather severe and perhaps unrealistic ways, we can prove that such a model as the one just presented does in fact always yield at least one equilibrium point of the type described in our definition. Indeed, this is done by showing that the market game played by the three types of participant has an equilibrium mixed strategy set. Assuming these restrictions hold, therefore, our simple model of reality will yield equilibrium values for the following variables:

THE CONSUMER SECTOR

1. $X_{cj}, j = 1, \ldots, n$. Consumer c's demand for consumer goods.
2. Q^*_{ce}. The terminal holdings of capital goods by the consumer in equivalent units of bonds.
3. Q^*_{cU}. The terminal holdings of money assets by Consumer c.
4. X_{ce}. The change in holdings of capital goods by Consumer c in equivalent units of bonds.
5. X_{cU}. The change in holdings of money assets by Consumer c.
6. $\bar{X}_{cz_i}, i = 1, \ldots, m$. Consumer c's supply of factor services.
7. $\bar{X}_{cu}$. Consumer c's supply of cash balances.
8. W_c. Consumer c's wealth.
9. Y_c. Consumer c's income.

THE FIRM SECTOR

1. $X_{vj}, j = 1, \ldots, n$. Firm v's demand for intermediate goods.
2. $X_{vz_i}, i = 1, \ldots, m$. Firm v's demand for factor services.
3. $\bar{X}_{vJ}, J = 1, \ldots, n$. Firm v's supply of consumer-intermediate goods.
4. $\bar{X}_{vZ_i}, i = 1, \ldots, m$. Firm v's supply of capital goods.
5. X_{vu}. Firm v's demand for cash balances.
6. π_v. Firm v's profits.

THE AGGREGATE CONSUMER SECTOR

1. $X'_j, j = 1, \ldots, n$. The aggregate consumer demand for consumer goods.
2. $\bar{X}_{z_i}, i = 1, \ldots, m$. The market supply of factor services.
3. $\bar{X}_u$. The market supply of cash balances.
4. X_e. The market demand for bonds.
5. X_U. The market demand for money as an asset.

THE AGGREGATE ENTREPRENEURIAL SECTOR

1. $X''_j, j = 1, \ldots, n$. The aggregate firm demand for intermediate goods.
2. $X_{z_i}, i = 1, \ldots, m$. The market demand for factor services.
3. X_u. The market demand for cash balances.
4. $\bar{X}_J, J = 1, \ldots, n$. The market supply of consumer-intermediate goods.
5. $\bar{X}_{Z_i}, i = 1, \ldots, m$. The market supply of capital goods.

THE MARKETS

1. $X_j, j = 1, \ldots, n$. The market demand for consumer-intermediate goods.
2. $\overline{X}_U$. The market supply of money as an asset.
3. $\overline{X}_e$. The market supply of bonds.
4. X_{Z_i}. The market demand for capital goods.
5. $P_j, j = 1, \ldots, n$. Money prices of consumer-intermediate goods.
6. $P_{z_i}, i = 1, \ldots, m$. Money prices of factor services.
7. $P_{Z_i}, i = 1, \ldots, m$. Money prices of capital goods.
8. P_e. The money price of bonds.
9. r. The interest rate.
10. i_k. The net rate of return on capital goods.

The model, by assumption, yields the equilibrating values of each of these variables for the end of Monday, the market day.

The relationships of Systems [I]–[VIII] constitute the large-scale *anatomical chart* of the market economy discussed in Chapter 1. It depicts, by virtue of its interrelationships and conditions, the relations that hold among the variables and the state of the components in which values are decided when the mechanism is functioning in a steady state. Its chief virtue is to present the economy as an integrated whole once it has got to the set of values that constitute a solution. It demonstrates that for admittedly unrealistic conditions, but with obvious relevance for realistic processes, the uncoordinated, unplanned market economy, if it can reach it, has a price-quantity solution that can satisfy all participants simultaneously in the game-theoretic interpretation previously given. The proof of the existence of this chart is the culmination of a strain of political economy that may be dated from Adam Smith and earlier, which saw dimly that the egoistically dictated actions of individuals could be harmonized in the game theory sense without conscious coordination.

Further, the fact that this quasi-harmonization can be demonstrated for the pure and idealized environment of pure competition leads us to believe that if we could introduce *all* the relevant detail that leads to the solution in particular oligopoly situations and treat all oligopolies simultaneously the existence of a determinate solution might be proved. This must be merely inspired faith, at the present, and probably will never be proved in sufficiently close approximation to real world conditions. Nonetheless, this insight of the model should not be ignored or dismissed lightly because a rigorous proof is not possible.

But is it possible to gain any insights into the physiology of this complete model, perhaps by shocking its data set? The answer is a flat no: the data shock would ramify through such a very large system that the amount of specific information concerning slopes that we would need is much too large to offer much prospect of fruitful displacement analysis with the whole model. On the other hand, we have demonstrated that if the model is decomposed into its submodel components, such analysis can yield useful insights. Further, current dynamic analysis of such large systems is yielding some useful physiological insights, but their explanation would require a substantial investment in mathematical apparatus.

The Intermarket Determination of Certain Crucial Variables

In Chapter 7 we pointed out the fact that certain variables could not truly be viewed as having their value determined primarily by demand and supply factors within a single market—in the sense of movement up and down given supply and demand functions—by demanders and suppliers. Disequilibrium within the given market set off forces in all other markets such that reactions upon the original market shifted the curves, and these movements dominated the determination of the new equilibrating price for the good in question. We found this to be true of the promissory note market—or the market in which cash balances were lent at the price r—because both demand and supply curves in the market for cash balances were so insensitive to the level of r, being determined by the value of consumption and productive input transactions. And we found that because the money asset market is in fact the obverse of every other market in the economy, changes in demand and supply for other goods and services are immediately implied by changes in supply of and demand for money assets, so that all other markets are intimately involved. Let us now turn to the wider adjustments that must be considered to depict the manner in which the relevant prices and quantities in these two markets were determined in our model.

THE SHORT-TERM PROMISSORY NOTE MARKET

Suppose that at a given interest rate r the demand for and supply of cash balances in the market are equilibrated. Let us now shock the system by assuming that consumers as a group suddenly increase their demand to hold money: that is, that some or all K_{cu} rise by given amounts. This implies, on Figure 8–1, that the market supply of cash balances, as a function of r shifts to the left, so that at the old equilibrating interest rate there exists an excess demand. However, as we have drawn the curves, the interest rate elasticity of both supply and demand curves is very slight, and consequently changes in r would have to be mammoth to reequilibrate the market by themselves.

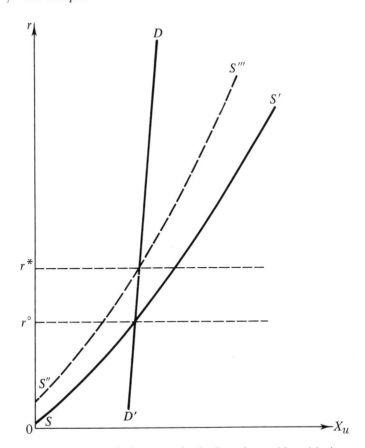

FIGURE 8-1.   A Displacement in the Promissory Note Market.

That is, the price of cash balances would have to rise so high in the absence of other price changes as to wholly disequilibrate the mechanism. Rather, the existing situation sets off impacts upon other markets, which react back upon the promissory note market by shifting the curves to get to an interest rate much closer to the initial one than that which would eventuate if the curves did not shift by virtue of extramarket reactions.

THE NEOCLASSICAL REEQUILIBRATION PROCESS. Let us study one pattern of readjustment that may be presented as an illustration of forces in a self-adjusting mechanism. With the inability to obtain cash balances to cover their purchases, firms reduce their demands for factor service and intermediate inputs, and thereby cut outputs too. But consumers now find themselves with unemployed factor services, and the prices of such services fall, and with them the prices of goods. As goods and factor service prices fall, the demands of consumers and firms for cash balances fall, so the supply curve of Figure 8–1 shifts to the right and the demand curve to the left. In the new equilibrium all factors are fully employed and the prices of inputs are such that firms can finance the full employment output levels at the reduced quantities of cash available to them. Nothing in any real sense has changed: money prices have fallen proportionately to free the cash balances consumers desire to hold, but the price *structure*—or prices relative to some real good rather than money—are the same, and the interest rate and rate of return on capital goods are unchanged from the old equilibrium. With no existent stock of securities to be affected by such changed desires to hold money balances, and with the demand for money balances almost perfectly interest inelastic, the demand for and supply of securities this week will change in inverse proportion to the price level.

The process by which the new price level is achieved operates by virtue of so-called *real-balance* effects, of changes in the value of money on the purchase of promissory notes in our model, and the ramifications on other securities and goods of such interest rate changes. In our economy, however, the demand for and supply of cash balances is not that strategic a factor, even though their price is the interest rate, because increased or decreased cash balances are not obtained by substituting against other goods or services except to the extent of their interest costs. Much more important, however, is the desire to change the holdings of money as an asset, for to do so requires the direct substitution of money for goods and services. We shall, therefore, present the neoclassical adjustment process as it involves changes in money asset holdings, as well as an alternative explanation of that process.

THE MONEY ASSET MARKET

Let us now assume that at a full, general equilibrium near the end of a Monday market day, demand equals supply for money as an asset, so that all consumers are satisfied with their current holdings of money assets. Now, once more, let us disturb the equilibrium by assuming that suddenly consumers generally wish to increase their holdings of wealth in money form, either at the expense of their holdings of assets in other forms or as an addition to their holdings financed by income, or both.

To obtain these increased holdings of money assets—to buy money—consumers must increase their sales of factor services, reduce their purchases of consumer goods, increase their sales of securities or reduce their purchases, or some combination of these actions. This means that demands for goods —consumer goods and capital goods via the bond market—will shift to the left, and supplies of factor services will shift to the right, and both forces will lead initially to a price fall in these markets. Now, let us study, on the one hand, the essentially neoclassical analysis of ensuing events, and, on the other, a Keynesian analysis of developments in markets.

THE NEOCLASSICAL READJUSTMENT PROCESS. When prices fall, the consumer would find that he had more real money assets even at his expanded demands for money, and proceed to reduce them by spending. This induced spending would, let us assume, lead to a shift of prices upward slightly, but in all probability prices would not return to their former level, so unemployment of resources would remain to bid down factor prices. But, once more, with the fall in price, consumers will spend some of their cash balances on goods and securities, as the value of money rises, and thus increase demand for inputs somewhat. Only when all factors have ceased the bidding down of prices because of their full employment will prices stop falling, and this will continue until prices reach a level that is lower by an amount necessary to permit consumers to hold the existing stock of money as the real value they wish to hold. Nothing else need be altered in the economy but the price level, however.

THE KEYNESIAN READJUSTMENT PROCESS. A major challenge to this depiction of the smoothness of the adjustment process in the complete model was thrown down by Lord Keynes in the midst of the great depression of the 1930's, and the analysis was convincing enough to have had great impacts on the outlook on the physiology of the market mechanism and policy recommendations. We may exploit the complete model as we have developed it to compare the Keynesian adjustment mechanism—the Keynesian physiology of the system, so to speak—with that of the neoclassical model we have presented.

We shall begin again with the complete model at a full and general equilibrium for all goods and factor services. Now, once more, let us shock the system by assuming that consumers suddenly increase their desire to buy money assets by decreasing their purchases of consumer goods and capital goods (reducing purchases of new securities) and retaining the cash as money assets. This excess demand for money assets (there being only a fixed quantity of money that can be purchased) is matched in factor service, consumer goods, and capital goods markets by an equal value of excess supply. Keynes was most interested at this point in the occurrences on the labor market, but we may broaden this interest to that of all factor service markets, remembering that by far the most important of these would be the market for labor service.

Inasmuch as excess supplies would exist for factor services, let us suppose that on each of these markets the unemployed factor service owners bid prices down by (say) 5 per cent. Thus, in our analysis, the prices received by all employed factor services fall 5 per cent, and, roughly speaking, initially income falls by 5 per cent. Thus, for approximative purposes, we may assume that excess demand in all factor service and goods markets remains about the same, because all real goods and services prices fall 5 per cent and income falls about 5 per cent. Consequently, as a first approximation, nothing changes in the real sector of the economy.

Therefore, if a boost is to be received in the real good and service markets from this generalized price-cut reaction of individual markets, it must come from the people who hold monetary assets. In Keynes's model, more realistically complete than our own, consumers hold stocks of securities rather than the real capital goods that lie behind them, and so let us from this point on assume that these stocks of securities take the place of our stock of capital goods. We shall assume that P_e, the price of these securities, has also changed in the general 5 per cent price fall. Let us group money assets and security assets together as the *paper sector* of the economy, so that we may refer to these two markets by a short-hand phrase. Then, because nothing real has changed in the *real sector* of the economy by virtue of the fall in prices, if something is to happen to push the real sector toward higher employment, increased demand for factor services and goods must be forthcoming from the paper sector.

But what is true of the paper sector? Assume that the security market remains unaffected for the moment. In the market for money assets we find that the supply of money has effectively increased in quantity by about 5 per cent, because all prices have fallen 5 per cent, so real holdings of money wealth have risen by 5 per cent. Now, if some agency of the government were to reduce the supply of money by 5 per cent, then the excess demand for money would decline by 5 per cent, and all would be as it was before the price cut. Consumers—who were desirous of increasing their holdings of money assets by the disequilibrating amount—would, after the 5 per cent reduction of prices throughout the economy and the 5 per cent reduction in the supply of money, persist in the desire to hold the same real increase in money balances. And, on the bond market, excess demand would remain as it was at the going price of securities.

But, of course, there is no reason for this 5 per cent reduction in money assets to occur. Excess demand for money assets must be increased, therefore, by the 5 per cent price reduction. Consumers, in our model, would feel that they had more money than they wished to hold. Their holdings of the same quantity of money, which was now about 5 per cent more valuable, would lead them to feel wealthier than they were before the fall in prices. The promissory note market would have a plethora of demand and a reduced supply, because the nominal needs for cash balances are less and the availability of money great, and r, the interest rate, would fall, making money assets less attractive.

We have seen that in the neoclassical model there would be three sorts of overflows from the paper sector into the real sector whose individual and combined impact would be to reduce the excess supply of goods and services and aid the economy to reachieve a new full employment equilibrium. First, the *real-balance effect* may lead the consumer to increase the consumption of the factor services that he sells. He may, most importantly, choose to enjoy more leisure, which reduces the excess supply of labor on the market and moves the economy toward equilibrium. We shall not put much emphasis on this effect, because presumably it would not be that important realistically. Second, the consumer may be led to buy more consumer goods, thereby shifting the market demand functions in those markets to the right, raising prices so that the net price fall in those markets is less than the full 5 per cent; because marginal costs have fallen 5 per cent and prices less than 5 per cent, output expands, with a consequent reduction of the excess supplies of factor services. This obviously moves the economy closer to the equilibrium. Lastly, the consumer may make shifts in his wealth holdings in the paper sector. As he seeks to use his excess cash to bid up the price of a dwindling supply of promissory notes, thereby reducing the interest rate, bonds become more attractive investments. If, as in Keynes, securities are inherited from the past, the price of such long-term securities is bid up. This implies that the net rate of return falls to match the fall of the interest rate in the promissory note market. This means more capital goods are produced, more inputs taken from the markets for goods and factor services, and, as in the case of increasing consumption, excess supplies of factor services and goods are reduced.

Therefore, in the neoclassical depiction of the market mechanism's physiology, at the end of the round begun by the price cut, excess supplies in many markets have decreased, and consequently some reemployment of resources has occurred. To the extent unemployment still exists in some factor service markets, prices could be bid down again, with the same result, and the process would then continue until all markets were reequilibrated, including the money asset market at a price of money—a new price level— which is necessitated by the increased desire to hold money as an asset. In essence all prices must fall to the level necessary to free the increased amount of money desired to be held. Even though no new nominal money is added to the economy's stocks, stock equilibrium for every individual in his holding of money is reattained by allowing prices to fall sufficiently to give him the real value of money assets he desires. Also, another equilibrating mechanism is that when consumers seek to acquire more money assets, and find that as they increase the supply of cash balances on the short-term promissory note market, the interest rate on money falls very quickly because of the low elasticity of demand for cash balances with respect to the interest rate, consumers shift into the long-term bond market to take advantage of the higher interest rates, and thus the desire to hold money falls as the desire to buy securities rises. We have seen that this can result in more capital goods being built as the rate of return on capital goods falls, in which case less of the adjustment would have to be made through price reduction and more will be made through a lower interest rate and rate of return on capital goods.

It was Keynes's contention that the market mechanism would not in general show these strong tendencies to reequilibrate itself. Inasmuch as we have traced out the real-balance effects as they would work to reinvigorate factor service and goods markets, if Keynes's model is to deny the reequilibrating effects of price cuts in the factor service markets we must here show how it blocks off these effects.

First, and most simply, as we have done, Keynes deemphasized the possibility that greater real balances would lead to a withdrawal of factor services from the market to any great extent. Second, he also believed that such effects would not have a great impact on the purchase of consumption goods. He felt that most consumption was determined by income, not the consumer's stock of wealth, and therefore the consumer goods markets would not receive a direct injection of increased purchasing power from the money asset sector. Moreover, the reduction in the price of labor would lead to changes in the distribution of income that favored increased savings, he felt. There remains, therefore, the capital goods markets, affected directly by an enhanced desire of buyers to buy capital goods because they were wealthier, and indirectly if the real-balance effect is exhausted in purchasing securities by the fall in the net rate of return and the increase in the amount of capital goods built in response.

The direct impact via the enhanced desire of people to buy more capital goods because they were richer, Keynes discounts: the typical businessman, who makes these decisions, in a period of uncertainty when prices are falling and excess supplies characterize most markets, is not likely to give more hostages to fate by increasing his demands for capital goods.

With these postulates, Keynes therefore splits off the real sector from any impacts of a direct nature from the paper sector. As prices fall there is no directly induced increase of purchasing in factor services, consumer or capital goods. There remains, therefore, only one route left by which the injection of purchasing power into real goods markets can give them a fillip. This consists of the possibility that the real-balance effect will remain wholly in the paper sector and be used to bid up the price of securities. In the Keynesian model the stock of securities is held by consumers in lieu of capital goods, and is fixed more or less for the short period of his analysis. The rate of return on capital goods falls as the price of securities is bid up by the influx of real wealth from the consumers' money assets. Will this not increase the values of capital goods and inspire more to be produced until the capitalized value of the flow of the marginal revenue products in perpetuity at the lower interest rate equals cost, thus reducing excess supply in all markets, and moving the economy back toward full employment equilibrium?

Keynes believed that the elasticity of response of capital goods to interest rate reductions was quite small, particularly in depressed times. Therefore, even if some such response was forthcoming in the capital good markets via the indirect route, quantitatively it would not be great. But more importantly, as prices were bid down further and further in the attempt by the economy to reequilibrate itself, and as prices on securities—both bonds and promissory notes in our model—were bid up higher and higher and before the economy had reestablished zero excess demand in all scarce good markets, r and i_k would reach a floor above zero, below which they could not fall. That is, there exists some minimum interest rate in the economy below which consumers would prefer to hold their wealth in cash, even if (in our model) they could not find borrowers for it on the cash-balance market at remunerative prices. At (say) a two per cent level for the rate of return on securities, the return is so low, and the probability of a rise in interest rates so high (implying a fall in P_e) that consumers would become willing to swallow all of the increasingly valuable money stocks that the continuing fall in prices is yielding them. Therefore, no fall in the rate of return on securities occurs, and this last link to the real sector is broken. If prices went on falling, they would fall toward zero, making money more and more valuable, yet never inducing consumers to purchase more factor services or consumer goods and never inducing higher levels of capital goods output. The economy remains in disequilibrium at less than full employment, and, as a matter of fact, price rigidities in the factor service markets prevent or limit the amount of reduction in prices that occurs.

In the neoclassical and Keynesian physiologies of the complete market mechanism, we have the two poles of adjustment. The first assumes implicitly rather good sensitivity of demand of all types, but more especially of capital goods, to price declines, and rather extensive and prompt real-balance effects as money stocks become more valuable with the rise in the price of money (a fall in the price level). The second assumes that price elasticity is rather ineffective, especially in the capital good sector, and that real-balance effects are totally exhausted in the paper sector. The first model is probably more germane to the longer-run period, when the pace of adjustment is slower, where consumers and firms can change their attitudes and readjust to new wealth levels, and where the perhaps slow working forces of real asset changes can permeate the markets. The second is probably more relevant to the shorter-run period, where the pace of adjustment cannot match the pace of movement in prices, where real-wealth effects do not have time to make themselves felt, and where interest rate changes do not have time to induce changes in investment. The Keynesian dynamic is probably closer to the truth in periods of severe general market disturbances, where the time required and the price flexibility that would have to exist would not be accepted by society or would not exist respectively.

The policy implications that Keynes drew from his analysis are most interesting. First, in periods when the market mechanism was struggling to get out of general disequilibrium, most importantly in factor service markets, the weakness of real asset effects and their ultimate failure to be effective in the goods or securities markets assured that attempts to use monetary means to increase demands in real goods markets were bound to be of only transitory and weak potency. Second, the direct intervention of government in such real sector markets as were appropriate was requisite.

THE CAPITAL GOODS MARKETS

In Chapter 7 we developed an analysis that depicted the investment process in which firms decided upon which explicit capital goods to purchase, so that demand curves for the individual capital goods were derived. With the supply curves already obtained for each of these markets, it was thereby possible to determine the supplies of each, subject to the constraints (1) that each good be produced at the minimum average cost, and (2) that the value of all such goods produced not exceed the amount of new savings generated by the economy. We may then use the rate of return on capital goods implied by P_e° to obtain an imputed set of P_{z_i} for the services rendered by the new goods, because there would be no markets for such services in the economy. Under these conditions, therefore, the imputed prices of the services of the goods would identically reflect a common rate of return on all capital goods.

In our original model, however, markets do exist for the sale of factor services, and as we have seen from Chapter 7, the $P_{z_i}^\circ$ will equal the marginal revenue product of the capital good in each of its actual uses. We do not have, however, at any point in the model, explicit demand curves for capital goods in function of their prices; rather, the conditions that are set by the model define implicitly the quantity of each capital good demanded. Let us demonstrate how.

First, the value of new savings (and we assume that $X_e P_e > 0$) sets a limit to the value of new capital goods that can be produced *in toto*. Therefore, a given maximum total value of new capital goods is available. Second, the prices of the new capital goods in equilibrium, $P_{Z_i}^{\circ}$, must be equal to their equilibrium average cost of production when new amounts of the goods are produced. Third, the ratio $P_{Z_i}^{\circ}/P_{z_i}^{\circ}$ must be equal to the price of a security for all capital goods produced, so that the net rates of return on all capital goods produced this week will be equal. Thus, in our model, a given value of new capital goods is produced at minimum cost and zero profits, and the present marginal revenue productivity of the goods' services in equilibrium is used to structure the new additions to the capital stock. This assumes that all consumers project the current earnings of the capital goods into the indefinite future. Given the price of a stream of dollars received each week in perpetuity, we multiply each dollar of marginal revenue product by this price to get the value through all time of this capital good's service; if the equilibrium cost of the capital good (its minimum average cost of production) is greater than this, the good is not produced; if it is less than this, demand for it is stimulated by consumers who demand to be compensated for their securities in the relevant good, or by speculators who see the possibility of redeeming bonds at a profit, and firms enter into increased production of it. If the capital asset is not producible, as in the case of land, the price of the good will be bid up until this common net rate of return is met, although of course these goods do not enter into net savings.

The Physiology of the Complete Model

We have spent some time in the description of the functioning of the complete model as it involves the equilibration of certain markets that either have an economy-wide impact of more than average significance, so that the markets in which their values are determined are subject to external shocks of great force, or in those cases where, although we had explicit markets in which the goods are traded, we did not define demand functions.

As a last exercise we shall try to depict some of the complete model's functioning and adjustments. We have already excused ourselves from attempting to achieve one type of physiological depiction: the displacement of the model with changes in its data. But let us see if we can treat the whole model as it works to get to its general equilibrium on Monday. We might call this an analysis of the stability of the system, for this process, if successful, is the way in which consumers and firms in all markets in our economy would grope their way to their full and final equilibrium solution at the end of the market day on Monday.

Let us suppose that the process is entered before that final resting place is achieved. There is, at our initial break-in point, some going set of prices **P′**, at which all markets reveal an excess demand of positive, zero, or negative value. On the basis of our stability analysis in Chapter 7 we know that if the excess demand is positive, the physiology of the market in which such a state exists dictates that the price of the product rise. This means that the demand functions in all markets that sell substitutes for this product will shift to the right, increasing excess demands on those markets, while the demand functions for all goods that are complements shift to the left, lowering excess demands. Prices in the markets for substitutes rise, setting off the same types of reactions in markets for their substitutes and complements, and prices in the markets for their complements fall, setting off waves of excess demand and price changes in markets for goods that are substitutes or complements for them. As price rises on the original market, less of the good is desired but more is offered, which shifts the demand functions for all inputs that are used in the production of the product to the right and rises in price may be expected (or falls in price prevented) as a result. Markets for inputs that are complements to these inputs may expect decreases in excess supply and markets for substitutes may expect increases in excess demand. These markets in turn, via price changes so induced, set off waves of reactions upon other markets that spread throughout the entire economy.

It is of course conceivable that these waves of change, starting from P', and giving rise successively to P'', P''', P'''', . . . may *never* get to $P°$ by the end of Monday. In order to do so, it is necessary to prove that sooner or later this sequence of price vectors will get closer and closer to some equilibrium price vector or vectors. For simplified conditions economists can show that the necessary and sufficient conditions for such an approach can be stated, and that the model will ultimately set a course for its equilibrium solution. But these conditions are quite complicated, as is the process of describing the nature of the waves of reaction through the whole system, and we shall limit ourselves to this brief, and impressionistic, nonrigorous, description.

The Work Undone

To finish our presentation of a complete model of the economy, it will be well to indicate to the student what aspects of reality we have not attempted to include in the depiction. We must once more recall the presentation of the aims of modelbuilding made in Chapter 1. At that point we indicated that it could never be the economist's hope to construct a detailed scale model of a whole economy, but rather that by selection, aggregation, deletion of detail, and abstraction, it might be hoped that a working *mock-up* of the economy could be built, which would provide insights into the operation of the real economy. It is that task that we have now completed.

We must stand back to judge not only what we have done, but what we have not done. What are the elements of the real economy that have been eliminated from our complete model, and how might their inclusion affect the anatomy or physiology of that model?

THE EXCLUSION OF PROFITS

Although we have built into our model the potentiality for the earning of profits by the firm in pure competition and for their distribution among the consumers of the economy as additions to their incomes, we have required that in equilibrium all profits be zero. We shall deal wholly with profits earned in pure competition at this point, because we will deal explicitly with the exclusion of monopolistic elements in the next section.

Let us first define the rather ambiguous term *profits*. In economic theory, the everyday notion of profits is not the one that is implied by the use of the term. To the economist, profits are a surplus to the firm, in the sense that the term was defined in Chapter 7 in our discussion of factor service markets. At that point we defined a surplus to any factor as any payment over the opportunity cost of the factor in the specific employment under discussion. Thus, profits in our sense of the word are any payment accruing to the firm that is not required to induce it to produce in the industry in which it is producing. These necessary payments—the firm's opportunity costs—are included in the average cost curve and profits are treated as payments over average costs of production, because the firm need not receive them from the economy in order to induce it to continue producing what it is producing. It should be noted that for short-run analyses, this definition of profits implies that all payments above average variable costs are surpluses, and we shall call all such payments *short-run* profits, reserving the term *profits* for all receipts above *total* costs.

Under conditions of pure competition, profits in this sense would occur only in the short-run period, when all factor services may not be mobile and therefore surpluses that would in the long-run accrue to other factors remain with the firm, and, more importantly, when plant and equipment cannot be built, so that new firms cannot enter the industry to eliminate such surpluses. Our environment, with the ownership of all factor services by consumers and their perfect mobility among all uses, gave us the possibility of depicting the long-run equilibrium during the short period that was so convenient for other purposes. Therefore, we were able to impose the condition—with U-shaped cost curves—that profits be zero in equilibrium, because the firm need not earn negative profits and competition would iron out positive profits.

However, we should have no difficulty in introducing short-run elements into the problem that would yield positive profits to some firms, the proceeds of which would accrue to certain consumers in the specified ways given among our data. These potentialities are built into the present model in that we have provided for the potential earning of profits by the firms; however, to permit nonzero profits in equilibrium is to interfere with the adjustments of most important long-run tendencies in the market economy which we have caught in the model as it now exists. We have every reason to believe that a purely competitive industry whose currently operating firms are earning positive or negative profits in our sense will entice new entrants or lose existing firms with the implication that prices will approach average costs. In our opinion, therefore, building in the potential nonzero nature of *this type* of firm surplus would add little of importance to the model, and definitely mask most important realistic phenomena.

THE EXCLUSION OF MONOPOLISTIC ELEMENTS

It is otherwise, however, with our ignoring of profits whose source is not in the temporary lags in adjustment of entry to a purely competitive industry. Our exclusion of all types of industrial structures in which the firm has some price jurisdiction or output policy latitude, and the elimination of profits that arise from this source of market power, is a most serious simplification of reality. Let us study the nature of this limitation of our model.

In our discussion of the firm submodels we indicated that the case of the large group of firms producing slightly differentiated products was very little different in its long-run equilibrium from that of pure competition. Entry of new firms producing new variations of the same basic bundle of product qualities would effectively tend to eliminate profits that spring from the monopolization of the ability to produce the specific commodity the firm produces. This, then, is a second potential source of profits: the ownership of an institutionally protected right to exclude other firms from the production of a specified product. If other firms, however, receive rights to produce goods very close to that of the given firm, the value of the right may be worthless in the end. We have seen that this is the hallmark of the type of nonrivalrous competition which we have termed *the large-group case* or *monopolistic competition*.

We may best consider this kind of profit as a surplus accruing to a property right: a property right of any type in the last analysis is an ability to exclude others from the enjoyment of some object, and in this case that object is some body of knowledge or the means of using it. We will term it *product-monopoly profits*. Our exclusion of it from the present model in the form of the large-group case does not appear to us to be a serious limitation. In our presentation of the large-group type of nonrivalrous competition we indicated that the occurrence of this market structure was so unusual that we might consider it justly as quite unrealistic. We shall, therefore, not be particularly disturbed by its absence from our model.

Moreover, the case of pure monopoly, in which such product-monopoly profits would be earned, was also presented as quite unusual. That is, in the real economy, product competition is so intense, and institutional protection to product monopoly so incomplete in its policing of variant substitutes, that in medium-run periods we may usually count on some effective competition to the product monopoly to arise. Even if this does not occur, technological advance has been so rapid that the product monopoly may be obsolesced by the development of new products in relatively short periods of time.

However, when we allow such dynamic aspects of the problem as the phasing through time of product innovations into the model, such medium-term monopoly becomes much more important. That is, new products are introduced generally by one or two firms, enjoy a specific institutional protection for some time in their manufacture and sale, and may be viewed as essential monopolies, although in many cases the nearness of other existing products as substitutes may be close enough to make the sales curve of the firm for the new product quite elastic. Thus, if we cut through a growing economy at any week of time for a slice-of-time static analysis, monopoly will be a much more common feature by virtue of product development than would be surmised from a model that accepts the number and kinds of products as among the data set and fixed. However, as the weeks go by and new products are developed and innovated, in part specifically in response to the large profits being earned by product monopolies, each of these monopolies will be doomed to losing its monopoly position.

Monopoly profits, to the extent they spring from proprietary rights arising from technological or product innovation, are viewed by Joseph A. Schumpeter as the dynamic opportunity costs that must be offered to entrepreneurs (or firms) to induce them to take the risks and uncertainties involved in introducing new methods and products. In this view, therefore, they are not true surpluses in a dynamic sense, but the necessary spur to innovation in the economy.

But, despite the loss of realism by our neglect of dynamically transient pure monopoly, there can be no doubt that the greatest and most damaging failure to include monopolistic elements, both in terms of frequency of occurrence and pervasiveness of effect, is the elimination of rivalrous competition from the model. We have spent a great deal of time in Chapter 6 explaining the reasons why this was done, and there is no need to repeat them here. The existence of oligopolistic interdependence means that the existence of a solution may be threatened, for, as an example, if one market in which mutual interdependence of decisionmaking is characteristic is in the throes of a price war, it will be impossible for the entire economy to settle down into an equilibrium until this market is equilibrated. Or, given the existence of an equilibrium defined in some status quo sense other than ours, it may be unstable, so even if it is attained, a displacement from that equilibrium may lead to farther and farther departures. Or, lastly, given its existence, it may prove impossible for the dynamic process ever to get to the equilibrium.

We personally do not find any of these possibilities very likely to happen in an economy whose markets are shot through with oligopoly. The strong desire of most oligopolistic firms for a resting point makes it quite likely that some equilibrium can be attained in an *ex ante* sense, even though it may be difficult to define it before the dynamic groping of the economy is begun. Moreover, the prevalence of price policies on the part of oligopolists, setting a supply curve for the short period that is rigid at a given price, should enhance the stability of the economy, because it removes many degrees of freedom of prices to change. And, lastly, oligopolistic firms will be quite willing and able to change their desires and goals to much greater effect than nonrivalrous competitive firms as the groping of the market mechanism occurs on Monday, so that should the market gallop away from the equilibrium of the previous week, the oligopolists might well compromise their ambitions and permit a more quickly achieved new equilibrium closer to the existing set of market values than a competitive environment could achieve. Thus, it would help to ensure that *some* equilibrium was attainable by the market mechanism.

The exclusion of oligopoly, therefore, is a severe limitation of our model. Prices in many of our markets will be too low, given our assumption of pure competition, and outputs of many products too high, compared with reality. Moreover, when we deal with displacements of our submodels, it will prove impossible to evaluate the effects of data shocks upon such prices and outputs, because to do so implies the knowledge of how the prices were originally set. How important these limitations are in defining the usefulness of our complete model we simply do not know. We shall return to this question, however, in the final section of this chapter.

THE EXCLUSION OF THE FUTURE: RISK, UNCERTAINTY, SPECULATION, EXPECTATIONS, AND INSURANCE

Another most damaging limitation of the complete model is our failure to include in it, in truly effective ways, the problems that spring from the existence of tomorrows and, in most cases, our imperfect knowledge of what the values of crucial variables will be in the future. For example, what the price of a television set will be in Week 2 is extremely valuable information for the consumer, because if it will be lower than it is in the current Week 1 he may well decide to postpone his purchase, and increase his demand for money or securities to store value until that period. Indeed, as we shall see, his choice of money or securities as a storage medium depends upon his expectation of future rates of return. Similarly, the price of labor services in future weeks is crucial in deciding how much of his current income or wealth to spend in Week 1. Consequently, among the data set of the consumer in Week 1 we should include a set of expected prices for every relevant good in every relevant week over some time horizon up to which the consumer can be assumed to plan.

The problems of risk within an uncertain future time horizon will also affect the consumer's decisions. His ultimate death is a certainty, but his *untimely* death is a contingency which he may desire to insure against. That is, risk is defined as a lack of certitude in which the outcomes of each event are unpredictable, but the outcomes of all events will follow a determinate probability distribution. Each person can be viewed as a player in a game with Nature as an opponent, her strategies fully known, and the probability distribution over those strategies (her mixed strategy) known as well. The probability of Consumer c's death in Week 2 may be small, but the results in terms of his family's welfare would be so devastating that he may well decide to hedge against the possibility by purchasing *insurance*. Companies will come into existence to sell this commodity with the basic function of pooling the risks of untimely death, so that every insured person pays the certain loss of his small weekly premium to prevent the highly unlikely loss of a huge sum—if we treat only the case of term insurance as the pure insurance commodity. Similar pooling institutions will arise for protection against acts of God, where their occurrence is capable of being depicted by a stable probability distribution.

More important in terms of the implications for consumer behavior, however, is the pervasiveness of a different type of incertitude about the future. This we may call *uncertainty*, and we may define it to exist when we do not have full information concerning the probabilities of Nature's play over her strategies, including cases in which the pure set of strategies is not completely known. This type of incertitude cannot strictly speaking be insured against, in the absence of stable and predictable occurrences in the large, and gives rise to *speculation* in the broadest sense. The consumer is forced to make guesses about future values, particularly about rates of return and the implied prices of securities. A rise in the interest rate tomorrow will mean a fall in the values of securities held (or, in our economy, real earning assets) and should lead today to an attempt at substitution of money for assets. But this would hold only if the price of money were not related to the rate of return, and could move independently of it. In our economy, however, a rise in rates of return in the future would lead to a fall in the price of money. This means, a rise in the price level would occur, which should send the consumer into purchasing goods. However, in the short run where these adjustments cannot occur so quickly, money is a hedge against expected interest rate rises, and the consumer must take this characteristic of the money asset into account in his decisionmaking.

Money in the environment of uncertainty is that security that is most *liquid*. By holding it—actively, among one's cash stocks or even by lending at extremely short term—one has a security that is immune for some time to interest rate changes. Consequently, if the consumer is desirous of protecting himself against an expected rise in the interest rate in Week 2, he will sell off his securities in Week 1 and hold money as an asset, then purchase securities in Week 2 if his speculation was correct. If he expects a fall in the interest rate in Week 2, the opposite procedure is called for. These most important speculative uses of money are eliminated in our model, with its essential abstraction from the problems of uncertainty and risk, and there can be no doubt that a substantial enrichment would accompany the introduction of the complications that inject the future more realistically into the complete model, even on the minimal basis which the Keynesian physiology incorporates.

Although the incertitude of uncertainty cannot be pooled in a true sense, it is possible that some persons may be able to shift it onto the shoulders of others if these latter are willing. When this is possible, the institution of *hedging* may arise, which merely means that a unit in the market makes himself simultaneously a buyer and a seller, with the purpose of eliminating potential loss or gain from price change. Suppose, for example, that a firm buys inputs in Week 1 to manufacture into product that is sold in Week 3, and suppose also that the prices of input and the product fluctuate together in any given week. Suppose now in Week 1 he makes a contract to deliver the product at the ruling price in Week 3: if the prices of the product and the input fall in Week 3, the firm suffers loss. If the prices of the output and the input rise in Week 3, the firm obtains a windfall profit because it sells the product at a price reflecting higher input prices than those paid in Week 1.

If the firm views itself as more properly a manufacturer than as a speculator, it may wish to escape this gambling and to content itself with its normal profits. If there exists a class of persons in the economy who are willing to do this gambling—or a group of *speculators*—there will come into existence in

Week 1 a *futures* market in the input as well as a *spot* market. In the former market contracts are made at fixed prices to deliver or take delivery of inputs in a future week (say Week 3) at prices fixed today, whereas the latter market is a market in which immediate delivery is effected. Now, if our firm buys spot inputs in Week 1 and sells future inputs for delivery in Week 3 at prices reflecting today's input prices he will protect himself against fluctuations in the price of inputs. In Week 3, if spot prices are above those at which he bought spot in Week 1, he makes a profit on the sale of his product, but, inasmuch as he must buy spot in Week 3 to cover his agreement to deliver input, he loses about the same amount. If spot prices in Week 3 are below those in Week 1, he loses on the product but makes on his contract. In either case windfall profit and loss on inventory wash out, and he is left his manufacturing profit only. This type of institution also our model has abstracted from with its elimination of uncertainty.

A Conclusion

With these recognized omissions from the model, added to its essential simplicity and map-like quality, of what value is it? Would it not be better to remain with the submodels, build another submodel for money and securities, and not attempt to fit them together into a whole? If we remained with decomposable submodels, and did not try an integration, we might also allow for the cases of monopolistic and oligopolistic impediments without the need to eliminate them to permit the larger model's construction.

In our opinion the complete model serves important functions, even though it has severe limitations. We have shown that it cannot be used in any rigorous physiological analysis by virtue of the difficulty of evaluating displacements, but nevertheless it may be used valuably for a nonrigorous analysis to state most important hypotheses about the workings of the complete economy, as the Keynesian revolt demonstrates. It is the only framework within which the realistic operation of certain crucial markets—those involving cash balances, money, and securities—can be treated, because their equilibration is subject to strong impacts from outside their own markets. And the strategic importance of these markets upon the short-run stability of the economy is quite great indeed, not to mention longer-run effects.

It serves also to impress the fact of widespread market interdependence on the student, and to give him the view of the economy as a decisionmaking machine that has a functioning coherence, whose solutions are reflective of a system-wide consistency, and whose logic is that of simultaneous consideration of huge amounts of information that must be rendered into values for variables that still the desire of units to change the status quo. And it serves to give the student a map of the whole economic terrain, within which he can integrate submodels to gain perspective and scale.

Lastly, it allows us to attack in the only proper way a final aspect of the functioning of the economic mechanism that we shall consider: what objectively can be said about the social welfare implications of the solution that we have just arrived at, and how close to reality is it in these senses? What social implications do the prices and quantities that are equilibrium values have? Are they good or the best in some meaningful sense? Can they be bettered? Would a State Planning Board setting out to maximize social welfare in some sense do better than the market mechanism as depicted by our complete model?

These questions can be answered only by a simultaneous consideration of all markets—or at least all real sector markets—and we shall conclude the book with a study of these aspects of the complete model's solution.

Selected Readings

1. E. H. PHELPS BROWN, *The Framework of the Pricing System* (Kans.: Lawrence, 1949). A simplified general equilibrium system using linear homogeneous production functions and a few commodities.

2. ROBERT E. KUENNE, *The Theory of General Economic Equilibrium* (Princeton: Princeton University Press, 1963), pp. 354–361. A more advanced and complete presentation of the difficulties of the Keynesian adjustment process.

3. WILLIAM H. MIERNYK, *The Elements of Input-Output Analysis* (New York: Random House, 1965). A good presentation of the basic tool of a complete system approach to empirical economic analysis.

4. R. A. RADFORD, "The Economic Organization of a P.O.W. Camp," *Economica*, XII (1945), pp. 189–201. A fascinating description of the spontaneous development of a complete market mechanism among inmates of a prisoner of war camp. This reading should not be missed.

5. JOSEPH A. SCHUMPETER, *Capitalism, Socialism, and Democracy* (New York: Harper, Third Edition, 1950), Part II, Ch. VII.

CHAPTER 9

Some Welfare Considerations

FROM THE TIME of Adam Smith, when social thinkers were just beginning to view the market mechanism as a Newtonian apparatus, with immutable laws of operation and a divinely designed harmony reflecting reason, the solution to the complete model that we have presented in Chapter 8 has been asserted to have many extraordinary qualities. Some of them, indeed, we have already commented upon. The fact that it can be shown for suitable restrictions that the model *has* a solution is a formal proof of what devotees of the market saw with eyes of faith: the rather surprising phenomenon that a vast multitude of selfish, uncoordinated decisions in widely separated markets can yield a set of answers to *society's* economic problems that is internally consistent. Active, conscious, and purposive direction by a social agency in the field of the individual's economic goals need not be exerted to assure a coherent solution for them. Under the idealized conditions of pure competition, the state could limit itself to decisionmaking on those economic matters that could not be accommodated by the market mechanism—collective types of goods such as roads, national defense, justice, and so forth—and to policing the power structure of the economy to assure the retention of atomized influence, or to redress the balance of power when it was possessed and exercised against the unavoidably weak.

The grasping of the notion of the market system as a self-contained and viable decisionmaker in the eighteenth century was an intellectual achievement of the first mark in the history of social science. Yet the notion became a basis for the support of *laissez faire* ideology during the nineteenth and twentieth centuries, and the failure to have well-defined anatomical and physiological analyses of the complete model allowed many unfounded or at least objectively unprovable assertions about the desirability of the mechanism to be made. The extents to which these claims rested upon the value judgments of the culture, the disputable ethical assumptions of those who asserted the beliefs, and the perhaps unattainable idealizations of the analysis, were not made clear. As is true of most propositions that enter into or emerge from creeds, they asserted selective articles of faith serving the purpose of persuasion or reinforcement rather than analysis.

We will not assert or defend the position that a normative analysis in the social sciences is free of value judgments—or that it should be. The ultimate goodness of individual liberty rests upon the axiomatic weight the analyst gives the worth of minimizing constraints on the individual's will, and that reflects the ethics of the analyst. Whether or not a consumer should pay marginal cost or average cost when the former is declining turns on the distributional-ethical question of whether the consumer of the good should or should not be forced to cover the full costs of producing the good. Whether or not the market mechanism's income distribution is acceptable to the analyst ultimately rests on whether he accepts the market's dictate that a factor should be rewarded according to the relative scarcity and quantity of the factor services he controls. And, in the broader sense, whether or not the individual accepts the market mechanism as an acceptable social decision-maker hinges to a great degree upon his outlook concerning the relative goodness of strong social bonds versus strong individualistic tendencies in society.

However, in view of the use of the vaguest sketches of the complete model of Chapter 8 to build ideologies supporting or attacking capitalism, it is desirable, now that we have a rigorously defined—if incomplete and deficient—model, to seek some clarification of the issues in such debate. It will be worthwhile to see if we can isolate a body of propositions that are derived from an axiomatic basis concerning ethical value judgments to which a substantial consensus can be obtained in Western society. What can we say about the social welfare aspects of the market economy's solution on such a minimal value base? That is the set of problems we now approach as a last consideration of the market economy.

It has been asserted by various social commentators in the past that the marginal productivity method of income distribution is "natural" and therefore (but beyond that) "just"; that this same method of distributing product among members of the society is "exploitative" and therefore "unjust"; that the market mechanism allocates products among consumers in such a way as to "maximize social welfare"; that the market produces huge amounts of "illth" whose consumption does not maximize social welfare; that the market allocates resources in such a manner as to "maximize social product"; and that the market is wasteful in its allocation of resources and does not produce all that it is capable of producing.

We cannot hope to answer all of these assertions in depth, of course, many of them being defended or attacked on the basis of a subtler or more extensive set of value judgments than it would be proper for us to cope with in this work on economic theory. But the perusal of this list of antagonistic positions will give some motivation to our assertion that it will be worthwhile to attempt a scientific and objective appraisal of such positions through the use of the complete model we have spent so much time in building.

An Introduction to the Criteria of the Market Mechanism

In approaching the substantial task that lies ahead of us in pursuit of even these limited goals, let us pause to probe the nature of the market's decision-making to see if we can pull out of the complex process the criteria of decisionmaking it is following in the ideal nonrivalrous environment we have constructed. That is to say, if we construct a mechanism whose sole function is to make and effect social decisions, and if this mechanism is confronted with a wide array of alternatives, then we must build into the mechanism some choice criteria in order to permit it to function. Society need not do this consciously, of course: it may adopt a given mechanism whose inner logic yields the criteria as deductions rather than purposively introduced principles of operation. Indeed, this is the way we shall derive them.

THE SOVEREIGNTY OF INDIVIDUAL WILL

First, the market asserts the rightness of egoistic individual consumer desires as the ultimate end of economic activity: the economic will of the individuals contained in the set determined to be decisive is and should be the determinant of resource use in the production of capital goods for use in future production and goods for current consumption. The provision by the society for goods that would not be produced under the motivation of individuals' search to effect selfish ends must be provided by extra-market means. Such collective goods are defined as goods whose benefit to the individual cannot be readily isolated from the benefits received by other individuals, and whose costs may be escaped by the individual because if provided by his fellows through the market system it may be impossible to exclude him from their enjoyment. Such associations as charitable organizations and, most importantly, such mechanisms as the various levels of government, must make decisions to produce these goods outside the framework of the market mechanism.

It is one of the gaps in economic theory that we have not yet produced a rigorous model, analogous to our complete market model, to depict the decisionmaking of governments. To date, it has not proved possible to repeat the same group of operations we performed for the market mechanism: to specify a set of postulates and data, most particularly for motivational assumptions with maximization constituents, with which to derive a set of interrelations whose solution will yield the amounts of goods purchased by such state agencies. Inasmuch as we may suppose that the state will effect its decisions by confiscating resources from the domain of the market mechanism and by purchasing goods through it, this complete model of the government economic decision process would be a fourth submodel in our system, coordinate with the consumer and firm submodels. However, the complexity of economic decisionmaking within a political context has proved to be so great to date that it has not yielded to analysis in a determinate model.

Therefore, we must at this point merely emphasize that such collective-good decisionmaking must be done outside the framework of the market mechanism, presumably by motivations that are different from those actuating consumers and firms. There is no provision within the market mechanism for forming and effecting such decisions, as has been realized from the earliest presentations of the mechanism. To the extent a society exists, therefore, and must provide collective goods for its members, the market mechanism can never constitute the entire economic machinery in a nation.

But another implication of this first underlying criterion of the market is that the government ought not to interfere with the proper individualistic decisionmaking of consumers and firms, unless such decisionmaking constricts unacceptably, given the values of the nation's culture, other individuals' welfares. Presumably, only the individual can truly assert his likes and dislikes, and because he has a fundamental right to seek his material welfare within the limits already sketched, he should be permitted to act with no more than these minimal restraints.

The implication of this criterion is, therefore, that the state has no claim as an organic entity in the division of the economic product, except as it provides collective goods for individuals to enjoy collectively. For example, the rate of growth of the economy is highly dependent upon the value of new savings, $X_e P_e$, each week in our complete model. However, this magnitude is governed by the willingness of consumers (and, realistically, of firms acting on consumers' or stockholders' sufferance) to save in the long run. Governmental decisionmakers may form the idea that national purposes will be better served with a higher growth rate, and assure that higher savings are generated by the economy through extra-market means. They might, for example, tax away $1 billion in income that would have been consumed, and offer to lend it to firms at (say) 1 percentage point less than the going market long-term rate of return, i_k°.

Let us assume that this increase of $1 billion in investment is in capital goods of infinite life, as we assumed all investment was in our complete model for simplicity, and that these goods give rise to an infinite-time flow of $40,000,000 per period. Has not the government forced the consumer to be better off despite himself? The logic of the market mechanism answers no: the psychology of the market equates the infinite receipt of (say) $50 per $1,000 invested, if the rate of return is $i_k^\circ = .05$, with the present value of spending $1,000 on consumer goods. Because the return obtained by the government is only $40 per $1,000 invested, the social welfare has been reduced if we equate that wholly, as the market mechanism does, with the desires satisfied by consumers within the confines of individualistic goods.

This criterion of the market mechanism holds true even if it is proved true that consumers tend to underestimate their needs in the future, or in any other way are consistently wrong in the event. The market's concern is for the moods of the moment, the state of current information, and the state of consumer psychology, however formed. The individual taking a low interest currently in the inevitability of his old age or in insuring himself against the contingency of illness, must in the market's view be allowed to effect his current consumption decisions despite any provable irrationality by any set of axioms we wish to adopt.

Perhaps we may best summarize this first inherent criterion of the market mechanism by asserting that *consumer sovereignty* is to be absolute within wide bounds set only to prevent the individual's unacceptable interference with others.

INCOME DETERMINATION BY MARGINAL REVENUE PRODUCTIVITY

A second fundamental criterion with social implications that is used by the market mechanism in its decisionmaking under the ideal conditions we have postulated in our complete model is that resources will be allocated in such wise as to make their marginal revenue products equal in all actual employments. This implies, therefore, that in the equilibrium solution every factor service will earn its marginal revenue product as a return in any actual employment. Every individual in the economy will share its output on the basis of the marginal revenue product of the factor services he owns and the quantity of factors he inherits at the start of the period, plus any profits that might be obtained from firms.

The market is neutral in its decisionmaking concerning the manner in which the individual attains the factor service endowments with which he begins the week. However, in pricing the services of these productive resources by the criterion of marginal revenue product it is asserting the rightness of valuing them according to their scarcity relative to the demand for the products into which they enter and their degree of nonsubstitutability in those employments. That is, the market declares that a year of a physician's labor will be worth $25,000 because relative to the demand for doctors' services the supply of doctors is quite restricted and because in the product made with these services the labor cannot be dispensed with. On the other hand, the market declares that the factory custodian's labor should earn $3,700 per year because the availability of such labor relative to the demand for it is quite great and because much of the task can be performed by machines or other low-skill types of labor.

The market mechanism's sole criterion for the reward to the owner of a factor service for its use in production is that that factor service be scarce in the sense just cited—that is, a requisite in at least one production process and with an excess demand in equilibrium that is zero. It dictates, therefore, that agricultural or site land should receive rents on a marginal product (or its variant, marginal net product) basis, even though the opportunity costs of providing the service may be zero, so that all such payments are a surplus from the view of society. Nor, indeed, are most factors rewarded in general in accordance with social opportunity cost, so that most earn surpluses in the equilibrium brought about by this criterion. Further, it dictates normally that the ownership of producible capital goods—which are merely land and labor in a congealed or storable form whose peculiarity is that they provide a greater leverage over nature than the original factors allow—will also earn net returns over and above the costs of the original factor services contained in them.

It is worth noting in terms of what we have been saying that it is not a sufficient condition for the explanation of the receipt of interest by the people who own the goods (or title to them) that capital goods increase the total productivity of the economy. Factor services tend to be rewarded by the market mechanism on the basis of their *marginal* revenue products, not their *total* or *average* enhancements of productivity measured in some sense. Thus, if the opportunity costs of the means of converting original land and labor into capital goods form were zero, then the marginal capital good in every employment should contribute no more to revenue than its equivalent in direct land and labor, and the marginal revenue productivity of capital—reflecting the marginal revenue contribution of the different form of the original factors—would be zero. In this case, capital goods would be free goods in the same sense as other factors whose services sell for a zero price, and earn a zero net return over the depreciated value of the land and labor yielded up during the week (which depreciation is zero in our model). It is the scarcity of capital goods that prevents their presence to this point—a scarcity that is set by the fact that those who provide the savings with which to construct such goods have not historically been willing to do so to the point that capital goods become free goods in this special sense. It is the enhancement of productivity plus the scarcity of the goods that leads to the payment of a permanent, nondisappearing net return on capital goods equal to its marginal net productivity in a market economy.

Does not this tendency of the market mechanism to reward the factor services z_i according to their marginal revenue productivities provide a "natural" or "physical" basis for defending the income distribution of the market mechanism? Is this not an indication that in some such sense the actual contribution of each factor service to the production of product or revenue is this marginal product? Does it not show that the actual participation of each factor service in the joint production process in some essential sense is reflected in this marginal magnitude? Have we not isolated in this criterion of the market's performance not only *a* method of distributing the product of society but *the* method, any departure from which would disturb not only our ethical but our scientific sense?

Our viewpoint in answering in the negative to such questions as these is the following. In any production process in which two or more inputs cooperate to produce a good or group of goods, the end result is in a philosophic sense an indecomposable one. The complex of inputs has produced the complex of outputs, and any teleologically motivated attempt to determine what part of the result was attributable to what part of the means is a meaningless endeavor. That is to say, it is impossible in general to define a set of operations that would rationally determine what each total amount of input contributed to the total amount of output, assuming that it is impossible to remove one such total input without reducing the product complex to zero or changing it qualitatively.

In general, this is true, but it may be possible to find exceptions where some such total allocation of product or revenue to total inputs may be done in a manner that would satisfy most of our axiomatic requirements for plausibility. For example, suppose that grape juice laid down in storage in Week 1 contains current labor and other factor services worth $2 per gallon, but that in Week 5 the same gallon of liquid sells as wine for $10, with time alone being added during the storage process. In this unusual case where there is a clear-cut temporal sequence of unique factor service additions and the possibility of valuation at each step of the production process, we might say that the grape juice considered as input contributed $2 in revenue and time, considered as a factor service, added a total of $8 to the product. But this is the unusual and rather artificial counterexample of limited applicability, and even it may be challenged on philosophical grounds. If the grape juice were not contributed to the production, the value of the product would decline to 0, not $8, and if the time were not available the product would be grape juice, not wine, and thus it also reveals its indispensability. Moreover, we still face the more characteristic problem of dividing up the value of the grape juice—accepting it for the moment as that dictated by its value contribution of $2—among the typically nonunique factors of production.

In general, therefore, we believe it to be impossible to divide up the total product into identifiable contributions by clusters of inputs. In this train of reasoning, the concept of marginal product is not one of physical ascription of product to increments of factor service. If labor is increased by a small amount, and all other factors are held constant, the increased amounts of product or products or of value cannot be ascribed in some essential way to the increment of labor. Obviously, all factor services were present in the production of the added output, and in their absence the added labor would have produced nothing. It is, therefore, in the deepest sense an artificial or a postulated ascription that on *any* basis divides up the total product among the total factors of production or a marginal product among the factors of production. The ultimate justification for choosing any such postulate, therefore, must be stated in terms of analytical convenience, and, where such methods are applied in social practice, some demonstrated instrumentality in achieving other goals of postulated importance.

In our welfare analysis to follow, we shall show that the marginal productivity convention leads to certain desirable properties of the complete model's solution, at least under the idealized conditions of that model. This convention if adopted by firms permits them to achieve the presumably desirable goal of profit maximization in nonrivalrous environments and cost minimization in rivalrous market structures. On both counts the analytical convenience of the convention is established.

That is to say, if when we increase the availability of one factor, holding all other factors constant, we impute the increase of product and revenue to the factor service whose presence has been increased, or, less rigorously, if we increase the presence of one factor and deduct the expenses of complementary inputs associated with its use from the value of product, and impute the remaining portion of the increased revenue to the relevant factor service, and if this increase in revenue is equated to the marginal factor service cost, profits will be maximized. *Adopting the marginal product ascription fiction, therefore, is a most useful device, but a fiction it is and should not be used as an unquestioned philosophical or ethical basis for the determination of social policy.*

The distribution of income by marginal productivity criteria in the ideal market mechanism implies also that the amount of income received by individuals may not be directly and immediately linked to the ability or capacity of individuals to enjoy it. It is difficult to attempt to define what we mean by this without making certain bold assumptions that violate reality. Let us do so boldly, and then attempt to eliminate them while retaining a somewhat clearer idea of what we desire to convey by this statement than we possessed originally. Suppose, first, that it is possible to measure every consumer's satisfactions unique up to a linear transformation, and second, that it is possible to find an absolute zero and a unit of measurement that are comparable for every individual. That is, assume that we may measure the consumer's utility in a cardinal fashion and that it is possible to make interpersonal comparisons of utility levels. We may, of course, object strenuously to both assumptions on the basis of our patient analysis of Chapter 2, but in the spirit of adopting postulates that are unrealistic and treating their theorems with appropriate distrust for limited ends, we shall do so for our present purposes.

From an adaptation of our consumer submodel for this peculiarly ideal set of preference functions, we can see that maximization of preferences would lead every consumer to so spend his given wherewithal that the marginal dollar would yield equivalent amounts of utility in all directions in which he actually spent. That is, taking into account the fact that the individual will not buy some of all goods and services, the marginal utility of a dollar's worth of goods in those areas where he actually does buy will be equal, and it will be greater than the amount of utility available for a first dollar for those goods which he does not buy in equilibrium. The satisfaction derived from this last dollar we may term *the marginal utility of current expenditure.* Suppose, now, the consumer is in stock equilibrium: then we may term this magnitude *the marginal utility of income,* and we shall deal throughout with this more limited interpretation.

Economists explicitly and policymakers implicitly have frequently assumed under these conditions that in relevant portions of the income domain this marginal utility of income declines as income rises. A given individual receives successively less satisfaction from a dollar of income as income rises. In this sense, during a given time period with a given structure of tastes, a given individual gets less and less satisfaction from increases of income: his marginal utility of income declines. Suppose this is true for all individuals: that at least after some value of income is reached, possibly different for different individuals, the marginal utility of income begins to decline and that the decline is reasonably rapid. Then, by the ability of various individuals to enjoy income at varying levels of intensity, we mean that for different individuals the rates at which they find their satisfactions per additional dollar increasing are different.

Thus, given cardinal measurement, interpersonal utility comparisons, and universally declining marginal utility of income, we may still have individuals who have a greater capability of using income than others. Now, if social welfare is defined simply as the summation of the total utility enjoyed by each consumer over all consumers, and if we assume that no consumer has external effects on any other consumer, to achieve a social welfare maximum we should distribute income to individuals in such a way that the last dollar of income given to each would yield equal satisfactions. In that way we should be unable to take a dollar from one individual and give it to another and allow one to receive more utility than the other loses. When this is done with appropriate second-order conditions, the social utility will be at a maximum.

Two points may be made concerning income distribution under these idealized circumstances. First, it is difficult to see in what way the market mechanism's criteria of income distribution would assure that this maximum social welfare position is reached. There may be some correlation between education, intelligence, and the ownership of scarce resources on the one hand, and the ability to enjoy income on the other, but the correlation may have developed as an effect of the income distribution, not solely as the cause of it. And, no doubt, there are none-too-rare exceptions to the correlation rule.

Second, though the above argument may be used to bolster a more liberal outlook on social welfare, we may also use the analysis to support a more conservative view. The mere fact that the marginal utility of income is a decreasing function of the amount of income received is not an *ipso facto* argument for such egalitarian measures as equal incomes or even income taxes that rise more than proportionately with income. Both propositions follow directly from the possible inequality of individuals in their ability to enjoy incomes from native, inherited causes, as reflected directly not alone in positions of their satisfaction curves as functions of income but also in the differing slopes of the marginal utility functions. The rich man's marginal utility of income may decline so slowly relative to the poor man's that even at extremely high incomes for the rich man a straightforward maximization of total social welfare may require income to be taxed away from the poor man and given to the rich.

The use of progressive taxation and the attempt to redistribute income away from the market's determination to some extent, therefore, implies that policymakers have come to the same results that acceptance of measurable utilities, interpersonal utility comparisons, diminishing marginal utility, and slopes of marginal utility functions that do not differ too radically in the relevant ranges would have led them to. Although in fact all of these assumptions may be incapable of test, and therefore be meaningless in the operational sense, they are useful as a postulational basis to describe the vague and ill-thought-out social philosophy that has underlain economic policy measures in the West for the last 30 or 40 years.

This social basis for policy is an implicit admission of the belief that the social welfare optimum is not brought about by the market mechanism. It provides an empirical support—and we may provide a postulational basis for the actions that describe the implicit beliefs of the policymakers even though they are not scientific propositions—for the assertion that society does not believe the untrammeled market mechanism's use of marginal productivity allocation reasoning results in the optimum distribution of income among its members.

THE ROLE OF PROFITS

A third criterion of the market mechanism in its decisionmaking is that those activities should be engaged in that render the largest surpluses over costs to their undertakers. It asserts, therefore, not only the acceptability of selfish profit-seeking, but the necessity of it to allocate resources properly. We may, indeed, broaden our outlook to all factors instead of confining it to entrepreneurs: we have seen that profits are merely (in the idealized purely competitive market mechanism we have depicted in the complete model) surpluses accruing to the entrepreneur. Profit-seeking by the firm is, therefore, merely one aspect of the market's injunction to every factor to seek out that employment in which its return is largest. Only if this is done is the market mechanism satisfied that all resources are properly allocated.

Surpluses, therefore, including profits, are necessary for a proper allocation of resources. To say this is merely to give further proof to the assertion we have made above that the distribution of income is a matter of no concern to the market mechanism except insofar as it reflects the proper allocation of resources in the sense of profit maximization and insofar as attempts to change it do not interfere with this allocation. As we have seen in Chapter 7, surpluses arise when nonmarginal opportunity costs are smaller than marginal. The important point from the view of the market mechanism is that the factor find that employment in which its value contribution, considered in the fictional marginal way we have discussed above, is highest, whatever surpluses accrue to the factors by virtue of this employment.

In the case of profits, this implies that production should be carried to the point where every input's marginal revenue product is equal to its marginal factor service cost to the firm. This assures a maximum of profit, which is a difference between average revenue minus average cost times output. Once it is assured that the firm is recovering avoidable cost (which may mean minimizing losses) by its operation, the market mechanism becomes interested exclusively in marginal magnitudes. To the extent this implies the earning of surpluses, the market insists that it be done. The important point is that marginal costs be a minimum, given technology, and differences between average magnitudes are of little concern.

The measure of social worthwhileness to the market is implicitly, therefore, money value. A good whose marginal unit is worth more than another is, at the same marginal cost, more worth producing. Profits are used to guide resources to these most valuable opportunities and must be earned if the best allocation of resources from the market's view is to occur. If these market-dictated surpluses, or any others occurring anywhere else, can be taxed or otherwise disposed of in such a way as to have no impact on the distribution of resources among uses, the market's basic secondary interest in income distribution would not be violated. But, of course, any redistribution of income must be expected to change goods demands and factor service supplies, and lead to a new resource allocation in which the pattern of surpluses will be different but equally acceptable to the market.

A CONCLUSION ABOUT THE MARKET MECHANISM'S CRITERIA

Perhaps the one red thread of continuity that runs through all of these criteria of correctness that inhere implicitly in the market's decisionmaking is *individualism*. The rightness of the individual consumer's search for maximum satisfaction of his selfish material desires, given his income; the correctness of his desire to maximize that income by selling his services for the highest prices he can receive for them; the correctness and necessity of searching out highest profit opportunities; the nonimportance of collective, that is, nonindividualistic, goods; and the rightness of the dictation by consumers acting individually of the allocation of resources of the economy, both during a period of time and for the future.

The market must be supplemented, therefore, by other economic decision machinery whenever collective projects are asserted by society to have greater priority than individualistic goals. In no social form of existence can it be accepted as the only economic decisionmaker that should operate.

But given the basic decision by society as to what collective goals should be effected, and therefore what amounts of resources should be taken for collective uses, how good a job in the social sense does the market mechanism do with its decisionmaking in the individual sphere? Given these criteria of decisionmaking at its core, what do they imply in terms of the social acceptability of the solution values of Chapter 7? Let us now attack these problems directly.

The State Planning Authority: An Alternative Mechanism

To answer such questions concerning the social implications of the market mechanism's decisions, we believe the best approach is that of studying an alternative economic decisionmaker in the individualistic goods field, which sets out to accomplish purposively a set of socially desirable goals. Then, when we have seen what conditions must be fulfilled to obtain these ends, we can check these conditions against the conditions attained by the idealized complete model of Chapter 8.

Let us envision a State Planning Authority (or Board—we shall use the terms interchangeably) whose task it is to oversee the economic decision-making of the society. We shall assume that it has already made those decisions concerning the amounts and types of collective goods to be produced this week, and that it has deducted the resources necessary to produce them from the quantities available for individualistic goals. We shall now endow the State Planning Authority with the tasks of allocating resources and distributing goods in such a way that social welfare is maximized. We shall insist that it operate within a democratic society in which the individuals' desires will be given as free a play as possible within the matrix of an economy consciously seeking a welfare optimum subject to certain constraints. We must specify these goals and constraints in full detail now.

THE SOCIAL WELFARE FUNCTION

We shall assume that the State Planning Authority has, for all consumers, the ordinal preference functions of Chapter 2. We shall write them without the investment argument, for all investment decisions will now be effected by the Planning Board:

$$M_c = M_c(\mathbf{X}_{cj}, \mathbf{X}_{cz_i}). \qquad [9\text{--}1]$$

We shall eliminate money from consideration in our planned economy for the simple reason that after all other decisions are made in this economy, the State Planning Authority can distribute sufficient money balances to all consumers and firms costlessly to take care of their transactions needs. Money is one of the means of production whose ownership as well as production will be taken over by the state and its services distributed free to those who want them to the extent needed. We may imagine that at the end of the Monday contracting day, after all decisions for the coming week have been effected, consumers and firms are given cash balances to the extent they desire them, and these same balances are returned to the state at the end of the week. No payment is made for their use.

Our planned economy does not allow consumers to own means of production or titles to them other than labor. Future income, therefore, is a good that does not yield individualistic satisfactions to consumers, and the amount of it the society ends the period with is a decision for the Planning Authority to make.

We shall now hypothesize that the State Planning Authority can define an ordinal social welfare function that contains as arguments the (1) individual preference functions of consumers, and (2) the amounts of net perpetual revenue with which the economy is to end the period. That is, we hypothesize that there exists a function,

$$S = W(M_1(\mathbf{X}_{1j}, \mathbf{X}_{1z_i}), \ldots, M_s(\mathbf{X}_{sj}, \mathbf{X}_{sz_i}), Q_e + X_e), \qquad W' > 0, \quad [9\text{–}2]$$

which constitutes a ranking by the Authority over the rankings by individuals of alternative baskets of goods and the amount of investment or disinvestment effected during the week. We assume not only the existence of the function, but further that it is smooth, continuous, strictly increasing in its goods and investment arguments, and strictly quasi-concave globally.

The specification that the function W rises whenever any of the M_c values rise, all other M_c values and X_e remaining constant, means that the social welfare is increased whenever any individual feels better off, if the stock of perpetual revenue is unchanged and no other individual feels worse off, and when investment rises at no sacrifice to any consumer's satisfactions. This implies that goods satiation in the society cannot occur, and we also assume that if more goods are produced and distributed to any consumer or group of consumers, his or their satisfactions will rise (see Consumer Postulate 3) and consequently social welfare will rise. And, of course, we assume that future income never becomes a worthless good to the society.

If the State Planning Authority distributes goods in such a way that all consumers move along given indifference curves while investment remains constant, then we have isolated a special form of social indifference curve on the function S; other such curves exist as some or all consumers' levels of satisfactions change as investment is altered.

This formulation of the social welfare function implies several noteworthy things about the values of the society that employs it. First, as we have seen, it implies that individuals' preferences *do matter* to the Planning Board. In a situation in which investment is equal to that in an alternative allocation and in which all consumers but one enjoy the same satisfactions, but the latter is better off, the Planning Authority must rank this situation above the alternative. The Authority is also bound to view the marginal rate of substitution between increasing investment at the expense of one or more consumers' consumption as increasing (the indifference curve is convex). Between baskets of consumer goods distributions and investment allocations in which no such clear-cut dominance as those mentioned above exists—some consumers are better off and others are worse off while investment levels vary —the existence of the welfare function implies that the State Planning Authority can make consistent pair-wise orderings on the basis of its own preferences. All of this ground we have covered in the presentation of postulates in Chapter 2.

A second implication is that no externalities exist among consumers' goods allocations. Each consumer consults only his own receipts of goods and services to rank baskets: what his neighbor gets makes no difference to his own satisfactions. These assumptions we have also discussed in our presentation of consumer theory in Chapter 2.

A third implication is that firms' activities of all types do not have any potential for contributing to social welfare, other than in their production of goods for consumers and for investment. Consumers place no value on working for one firm rather than another, and no aspects of firms' operations have any direct welfare impact. For example, the familiar case of a firm pouring out smoke and soot over its neighboring community does not inject these undesirables into the social welfare function as negative elements.

In summary, then, we have assumed that it has proved possible in some unspecified manner for a State Planning Authority to derive a complete weak ordering over all possible allocations of goods and services among consumers and investment from the rankings of all individuals over their own field of choice. This ranking, of course, reflects judgments concerning the relative social values of giving more goods to John Johnson and fewer to James Jones: that is, it implies that the State Planning Authority can make decisions over personal goods distributions. It implies that the society has been able to devise a set of rules for constructing from a set of individual preference rankings and investment levels a *social* ranking that (1) meets criteria of sufficient plausibility to be acquiesced in by the society, and (2) permits a reflexive, transitive, binary relation to exist. Both of these are very strong assumptions.

THE CONSTRAINTS UPON THE STATE PLANNING AUTHORITY

We shall now assume that the society has charged the State Planning Authority with the duty of supervising the allocation of resources and the production and distribution of goods in such a manner as to achieve a maximum social welfare for the week in question. However, the search for such a maximum has to be constrained by various socially or naturally imposed limitations on the society's freedom just as was true in our complete market model. Let us now list these. Note, however, that in the specification of the constraints insofar as they involve investment levels, and, more broadly, in our specification of the ability of the Planning Authority to rank baskets in which investment levels are stated as flows of purchasing power in perpetuity, we are assuming that the Board has some firm idea of the future goods flow to which they give rise. We are, therefore, implicitly abstracting from very violent price changes or technological revolutions over a reasonable distance into the future: indeed, to be rigorous we are in a society whose technology remains about constant.

THE RULING TECHNOLOGY. Self-evidently, we require that all firms remain within the limits of their technology. For convenience, we shall continue to assume that each firm can, potentially, produce any good, but in the event will produce only one. We shall write the technological constraints for all firms as follows, where the symbols have been defined in Chapter 8, and where the numbering of the functions will become clear later:

19. $\quad -\bar{X}_{vJ} + G_{vJ}(\mathbf{X}_{vj/J}, \mathbf{X}_{vz_i/J}) = C_{vJ} \geqq 0$ [9–4]

21. $\quad -\bar{X}_{vZ_i} + G_{vZ_i}(\mathbf{X}_{vj/Z_i}, \mathbf{X}_{vz_i/Z_i}) = C_{vZ_i} \geqq 0.$

These state that all firms in the economy can supply no more of any output than the existing technology permits for a given mix of resources. They may supply less through waste and inefficiency, however.

THE FACTOR SERVICE CONSTRAINTS. The State Planning Authority, like the unaided market mechanism, can use no more factor service inputs this week than what are available:

23. $\quad Q_{Z_i} - \sum_v \sum_J X^\circ_{vz_i/J} - \sum_v \sum_I X^\circ_{vz_i/Z_I} - \sum_c X^\circ_{cz_i} = C_i \geqq 0.$ [9–4]

Note that we shall assume all factor services have some potential consumer usage, although, of course, we are most interested in the alternative consumer usage of labor as leisure.

SUPPLY CONSTRAINTS FOR CONSUMER AND INTERMEDIATE GOODS. The State Planning Authority cannot use goods in equilibrium which it has not produced. Also, it must produce goods to the point where all equilibrium demand can be satisfied:

25. $\quad \sum_v \bar{X}_{vJ} - \sum_v \sum_J X^\circ_{vj/J} - \sum_v \sum_I X^\circ_{vj/Z_I} - \sum_c X^\circ_{cj} = C_j \geqq 0.$ [9–4]

SAVINGS AND INVESTMENT RELATIONS. The State Planning Authority is instructed to price a unit of perpetual earning power and capital goods and to ensure that the value of new capital goods does not fall short of the value of savings. Savings are not to be wasted:

$$27. \quad \sum_v \sum_i \bar{X}_{vZ_i} \pi_i - X_e^\circ = C_e \geqq 0, \qquad [9\text{–}4]$$

where the π_i are values whose significance will become clear soon.

THE MAXIMIZATION PROCEDURE

The State Planning Authority's task is now clear: it is to seek a maximum for the social welfare function of [9–2] subject to the nonnegative constraints C_{vJ}, C_{vZ_j}, C_i, C_j, and C_e. Though we have not performed this constrained maximization process explicitly in previous chapters, we will do so at the present point in order to derive some important characteristics of the economic process. The student with little mathematical background is asked to submit to a few pages of technical matter, after which we will be able to deal with the derived interrelationships.

We may maximize S subject to these constraints by setting up an expression called a Lagrangean form, which consists merely of the function W plus the constraints, each of which is multiplied by a factor whose value will be determined by the analysis. We obtain therefore:

$$L = W(\mathbf{M}_c(\mathbf{X}_{cj}, \mathbf{X}_{cz_i}), (Q_e + X_e)) + \sum_v \sum_J \lambda_{vJ} C_{vJ} + \sum_v \sum_i \lambda_{vZ_i} C_{vZ_i}$$
$$+ \sum_i \pi_i C_i + \sum_j \theta_j C_j + P_e C_e. \qquad [9\text{–}3]$$

The function W is strictly quasi-concave. We shall assume that all production functions are strictly concave over M^* (as we did in Chapter 3), and the remaining constraints being linear in quantities, will be quasi-concave. Under these conditions, and given some further weak restrictions, the following conditions for a social welfare maximum are established[1]:

$$1. \quad \frac{\partial L}{\partial X_{cj}} = \frac{\partial W}{\partial M_c} \frac{\partial M_c}{\partial X_{cj}} - \theta_j \leqq 0 \qquad [sn]$$

$$2. \quad X_{cj}\left(\frac{\partial W}{\partial M_c} \frac{\partial M_c}{\partial X_{cj}} - \theta_j\right) = 0$$

$$3. \quad \frac{\partial L}{\partial X_{cz_i}} = \frac{\partial W}{\partial M_c} \frac{\partial M_c}{\partial X_{cz_i}} - \pi_i \leqq 0 \qquad [sm]$$

$$4. \quad X_{cz_i}\left(\frac{\partial W}{\partial M_c} \frac{\partial M_c}{\partial X_{cz_i}} - \pi_i\right) = 0$$

$$5. \quad \frac{\partial L}{\partial X_e} = \frac{\partial W}{\partial X_e} - P_e \leqq 0 \qquad [1]$$

[1] For a qualification see footnote 1, p. 148.

6. $\quad X_e\left(\dfrac{\partial W}{\partial X_e} - P_e\right) = 0$

7. $\quad \dfrac{\partial L}{\partial \bar{X}_{vJ}} = -\lambda_{vJ} + \theta_J \leqq 0$ $\qquad\qquad$ [on]

8. $\quad \bar{X}_{vJ}(-\lambda_{vJ} + \theta_J) = 0$

9. $\quad \dfrac{\partial L}{\partial \bar{X}_{vZ_i}} = -\lambda_{vZ_i} + P_e\pi_i \leqq 0$ $\qquad\qquad$ [om]

10. $\quad \bar{X}_{vZ_i}(-\lambda_{vZ_i} + P_e\pi_i) \leqq 0$

11. $\quad \dfrac{\partial L}{\partial X_{vj/J}} = \lambda_{vJ}\dfrac{\partial G_{vJ}}{\partial X_{vj/J}} - \theta_j \leqq 0$ $\qquad\qquad$ [on²]

12. $\quad (X_{vj/J} - X_{j/\bar{X}_J})\left(\lambda_{vJ}\dfrac{\partial G_{vJ}}{\partial X_{vj/J}} - \theta_j\right) = 0$

13. $\quad \dfrac{\partial L}{\partial X_{vz_i/J}} = \lambda_{vJ}\dfrac{\partial G_{vJ}}{\partial X_{vz_i/J}} - \pi_i \leqq 0$ $\qquad\qquad$ [omn]

14. $\quad (X_{vz_i/J} - X_{z_i/\bar{X}_J})\left(\lambda_{vJ}\dfrac{\partial G_{vJ}}{\partial X_{vz_i/J}} - \pi_i\right) = 0$

15. $\quad \dfrac{\partial L}{\partial X_{vj/Z_i}} = \lambda_{vZ_i}\dfrac{\partial G_{vZ_i}}{\partial X_{vj/Z_i}} - \theta_j \leqq 0$ $\qquad\qquad$ [omn]

16. $\quad (X_{vj/Z_i} - X_{j/\bar{X}_{Z_i}})\left(\lambda_{vZ_i}\dfrac{\partial G_{vZ_i}}{\partial X_{vj/Z_i}} - \theta_j\right) = 0$

17. $\quad \dfrac{\partial L}{\partial X_{vz_i/Z_i}} = \lambda_{vZ_i}\dfrac{\partial G_{vZ_i}}{\partial X_{vz_i/Z_i}} - \pi_i \leqq 0$ $\qquad\qquad$ [om²]

18. $\quad (X_{vz_i/Z_i} - X_{z_i/\bar{X}_{Z_i}})\left(\lambda_{vZ_i}\dfrac{\partial G_{vZ_i}}{\partial X_{vz_i/Z_i}} - \pi_i\right) = 0$

20. $\quad \lambda_{vJ}C_{vJ} = 0$ $\qquad\qquad\qquad\qquad$ [on]

22. $\quad \lambda_{vZ_i}C_{vZ_i} = 0$ $\qquad\qquad\qquad\qquad$ [om]

24. $\quad \pi_i C_i = 0$ $\qquad\qquad\qquad\qquad\qquad$ [m]

26. $\quad \theta_j C_j = 0$ $\qquad\qquad\qquad\qquad\qquad$ [n]

28. $\quad P_e C_e = 0$ $\qquad\qquad\qquad\qquad\qquad$ [1]

29. $\quad P_e \geqq 0, \quad \theta_j \geqq 0, \quad \pi_i \geqq 0, \quad \lambda_{vZ_i} \geqq 0, \quad \lambda_{vJ} \geqq 0$

30. $\quad d^2L < 0.$ $\qquad\qquad\qquad\qquad\qquad$ [9–4]

The conditions become quite complex but let us attempt to interpret them in terms of economics. The Greek symbols, which are the Lagrangean multipliers, look suspiciously like prices and let us take a leap and interpret them as *shadow prices*. Conditions 1 and 2 then state that maximum social welfare requires that the social welfare derived marginally from the distribution of every consumer good to each consumer be equal to or less than some shadow price, θ_j, and that if the inequality holds the consumer get none of the good, because its first unit could not yield as much marginal social welfare as was lost by taking it away from a consumer for whom the equality held. Conditions 29 require θ_j to be nonnegative, and conditions 25 and 26 require that if excess supply exists in equilibrium, θ_j be zero, so that by interpreting this term as a price we require the good in question to be a free good in this circumstance.

For every factor service that has an alternative consumer use, conditions 3, 4, 29, 23, and 24 may be interpreted in exactly the same manner. Conditions 5, 6, 29, 27, and 28 are similarly interpreted, except that marginal social welfare is expressed directly in terms of the Board's preferences, and this marginal value is multiplied by the specified rate of return ($1/P_e$) to get the weekly social welfare dependent upon the marginal bond. Only if the value of capital goods produced exceeds the value of savings can this marginal social utility of investment income be equal to zero.

Condition 7 states that the magnitude λ_{vJ} in the optimum solution must be no less than the equilibrium value of θ_J, and condition 8 requires that when $\lambda_{vJ} > \theta_J$ the output of Y_J by the firm in question be zero. Now, from condition 19 and condition 30 it may be seen that θ_J plays the role of price, as marginal revenue does in the purely competitive market mechanism: it must be nonnegative, and it must be zero if excess supply characterizes its good in equilibrium. From conditions 11 and 12 we may discern most easily the nature of λ_{vJ}, for we may see with our interpretation of θ_J that it is similar to a marginal cost magnitude. Condition 11 states that the marginal cost of producing Y_J by increasing slightly the use of Y_j only must be no less than this equilibrium marginal cost figure, and the second condition states that when the inequality holds the firm should not use the input in the production of this good.

From conditions 23 and 24 we note that the π_i may well be interpreted as the prices of input services z_i, for exactly the same reasons that we adopted such an interpretation for the θ_j. Then, if we jump to conditions 13 and 14 we note that the marginal cost of producing Y_J by using only additional units of z_i must be no less than this same λ_{vJ} magnitude, and when greater the inputs must not be used by this firm for producing this good. Thus, *if* the firm produces Y_J, and if inputs of Y_j and z_i are used, marginal cost with these inputs must equal the common value λ_{vJ}. Therefore, λ_{vJ} may be used as the economy-wide equilibrium marginal cost of Y_J, and by condition 29 must be nonnegative in equilibrium. Conditions 19 and 20 permit waste of outputs of Y_J only when its marginal cost is zero: that is, from condition 7, when it is a free good.

We may now return to conditions 7 and 8 to have a final explanation. They can now be seen to require that for Firm v, in equilibrium, the marginal cost of producing Y_J be greater than or equal to the price of the good. If the equality rules, the firm may produce positive amounts of the good; if the equality does not rule, the firm cannot produce the good efficiently, and must produce zero amounts of it in equilibrium.

With the exception that capital goods must be priced by the State Planning Authority, we can give the same interpretation to conditions 9, 10, 15, 16, 17, 18, 21, 22, and 29. Lastly, condition 30 expresses the strict quasi-concavity of L.

The similarity between the purposive maximization procedures of state planning and economy-wide decisionmaking and results of the complete market model of Chapter 8 are striking even at this early stage of our analysis. Most surprising, perhaps, is the appearance of quasi-prices in the analysis, so that the planning authority in seeking to obtain the conditions for a maximum social welfare position seems to be getting results that have some resemblance at least to those obtained by the thousands of consumers and firms acting independently and in uncoordinated fashion.

THE SIMPLIFICATION OF THE CONDITIONS FOR A WELFARE MAXIMUM

Let us now simplify the conditions for a welfare maximum by eliminating some of them, in order to get a greater economic insight into their meaning. First, let us find some good, say Y_1, which is taken by every consumer in the equilibrium and which is always produced in that equilibrium (leisure, or working fewer than 24 hours a day, is a good choice). Second, for each consumer let us partition the n consumer goods into two subsets: set A_{cy} (affirmative), which contains all goods for which the equality in condition 1 holds, and N_{cy} (negative), for which the inequality in condition 1 holds. Then we may write for Consumer c,

$$\frac{\partial W}{\partial M_c} = \frac{\theta_j}{\partial M_c/\partial X_{cj}}, \qquad Y_j \in A_{cy}. \qquad [9\text{--}5]$$

And, if we eliminate the welfare term on the left, we may write

$$S_{c/j/1} = \frac{\partial M_c/\partial X_{cj}}{\partial M_c/\partial X_{c1}} = \frac{\theta_j}{\theta_1}, \qquad Y_j \in A_{cy}. \qquad [9\text{--}6]$$

Similarly, from conditions 3, 4, 5, and 6:

$$S_{c/i/1} = \frac{\partial M_c / \partial X_{cz_i}}{\partial M_c / \partial X_{c1}} = \frac{\pi_i}{\theta_1}, \qquad z_i \in A_{ci}. \qquad [9\text{-}7]$$

Because every consumer who consumes a pair of commodity or service units must make his marginal rate of substitution for Y_1, or $S_{c/i/1}$, equal to the same ratio of Lagrangean constants, we may write:

$$S^\circ_{1/j/1} = S^\circ_{2/j/1} = \cdots = S^\circ_{s/j/1}$$
$$S^\circ_{1/i/1} = S^\circ_{2/i/1} = \cdots = S^\circ_{s/i/1}. \qquad [9\text{-}8]$$

We may state this set of derived conditions as Rule 1 for the State Planning Authority to follow in seeking a welfare maximum:

RULE 1.   The marginal rate of substitution for a pair of consumable goods or factor services taken in the equilibrium by a group of consumers must be equal for every such consumer to a common value. Consumers whose equilibrium marginal rate of substitution between any of these items and Y_1 (the always-taken good) is less than the given common value should get none of it. (This common rate of substitution between any two items for all consumers who take some of both will be the ratio of the respective Lagrangean constants.)

From conditions 7 through 18 we can obtain the following summarization of requirements. We divide the set of firms into two subsets, according to whether in the equilibrium a firm does or does not produce a given good Y_J. We denote the subset B_{vJ} as that group of firms which produces Y_J and N_{vJ} as the set of those firms which do not produce the specific Y_J. Then, for firms $v \in B_{vJ}$ the equality will hold in condition 7, and we may substitute to eliminate λ_{vJ} in conditions 11 and 13. Further, let us use the symbol $MP_{j/J}$ to denote the marginal physical product of input Y_j in the production of Y_J and $MP_{z_i/J}$ to denote the marginal physical product of z_i in the production of Y_J. Then, we have from the substitution just mentioned:

1. $MP_{vj/J} \lessgtr \theta_j / \theta_J, \qquad v \in B_{vJ}$
2. $MP_{vz_i/J} \lessgtr \pi_i / \theta_J. \qquad [9\text{-}9]$

Let B_{jJ} be the set of intermediate goods for which the equality holds in [9-9], and let B_{iJ} be the set of factor services for which it holds. Then, from [9-9]

1. $MP_{vj/J} = \theta_j / \theta_J, \qquad v \in B_{vJ}, \quad j \in B_{jJ}$
2. $MP_{vz_i/J} = \pi_i / \theta_J, \qquad v \in B_{vJ}, \quad i \in B_{iJ}. \qquad [9\text{-}10]$

In exactly similar fashion, and using symbols that are readily understood in the above context, we can derive the following conditions for the production of capital goods by firms that do in fact produce them in equilibrium:

$$
\begin{aligned}
&1. \quad MP_{vj/Z_i} = \theta_j/P_e\pi_i, \qquad v \in B_{vZ_i}, \quad j \in B_{jZ_i} \\
&2. \quad MP_{vz_I/Z_I} = \pi_i/P_e\pi_I, \qquad v \in B_{vZ_i}, \quad i \in B_{iZ_i},
\end{aligned}
\qquad [9\text{--}11]
$$

where I has been used as a subscript to denote the specific factor output as opposed to factor service inputs.

We may translate these conditions into the following set of principles for use by the State Planning Authority:

RULE 2. In equilibrium a firm should be allowed to produce a given consumer-intermediate good or capital good only if it can transform every input actually used by the firm in the production of that good into output marginally at the same rate as every other firm producing that good and using that input. The marginal rate of transformation of input into output (we have called it the marginal product of an input in terms of some output) for every firm in the relevant subset and every input actually used in greater than minimal amounts must be equalized for all firms producing the good with discretionary amounts of the input. This condition implicitly provides that the marginal costs of all $v \in B_{vJ}$ or $v \in B_{vZi}$ are equal. Firms with higher marginal costs cannot produce the good, or firms with marginal cost levels equal to the common value for which given inputs yield higher marginal costs use them in minimum amounts. These conditions may be written as follows:

$$
\begin{aligned}
&1. \quad MP^{\circ}_{1/j/J} = MP^{\circ}_{2/j/J} = \cdots = MP^{\circ}_{o/j/J}, \qquad j = 1, \ldots, n, \quad J = 1, \ldots, n \\
&2. \quad MP^{\circ}_{1/i/J} = MP^{\circ}_{2/i/J} = \cdots = MP^{\circ}_{o/i/J}, \qquad i = 1, \ldots, m, \quad J = 1, \ldots, n \\
&3. \quad MP^{\circ}_{1/j/Z_i} = MP^{\circ}_{2/j/Z_i} = \cdots = MP^{\circ}_{o/j/Z_i}, \qquad j = 1, \ldots, n, \quad i = 1, \ldots, m \\
&4. \quad MP^{\circ}_{1/i/Z_i} = MP^{\circ}_{2/i/Z_i} = \cdots = MP^{\circ}_{o/i/Z_i}, \qquad i = 1, \ldots, m, \quad i = 1, \ldots, m,
\end{aligned}
\qquad [9\text{--}12]
$$

where it is to be understood that these equalities hold only for those firms which actually use the given input in the production of positive quantities of the output.

Rule 1 states the necessary condition that for each pair of consumable goods or services, every consumer who actually consumes the pair must have the same rate of psychological transformation as every other such consumer. The motivation of this rule can be illustrated in Figure 9–1. Suppose that the State Planning Authority has a two-consumer economy, and suppose further that it has decided to produce given quantities of consumer goods Y_1 and Y_2 for use by consumers. On Figure 9–1 we have reproduced Consumer 1's indifference map in the usual manner, so that it is oriented to the origin at the lower left-hand corner of the figure. Consumer 2's indifference map, on

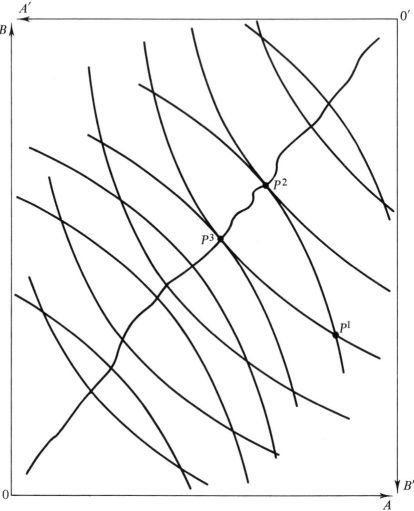

FIGURE 9–1. The Implications of Rule 1.

the other hand, has been revolved 180°, so that its origin is oriented to the upper right-hand corner of the figure. The lengths of the axes OA and $O'A'$ are proportional to the amount of good Y_1 that is available for distribution to the two consumers, and the length of the axes OB and $O'B'$ depict the amount of Y_2 available for the two consumers. It follows, therefore, that any point in the rectangle formed by these four axes depicts a representative distribution of the two goods among the two consumers in such a manner as to exhaust their availabilities. For example, the point P^1 depicts such a distribution of welfare, occurring as it does at the intersection of indifference curves for the two consumers.

We know from the analysis of Chapter 2 that the slope of an indifference curve represents a marginal rate of psychological transformation of two goods into one another for the relevant consumer. The point P^1 therefore depicts a pair of psychological transformation rates for these two goods in the slopes of the respective indifference curves for the two consumers. Because the slopes are not equal at this point, the rates of psychological transformation for these goods are not equal, and so Rule 1 is violated. Suppose we move from P^1 along the same indifference curve for Consumer 2 in such a way as to get to the highest indifference curve for Consumer 1 that it is possible to attain. This will occur at P^2, where Consumer 2's indifference curve is tangent to one of Consumer 1's indifference curves. Note that Consumer 2's satisfaction at P^2 is exactly equal to what it was at P^1, because both baskets lie on the same indifference curve for Consumer 2. However, Consumer 1 has been benefited by the change, because the new basket is on a higher indifference curve on his map. Therefore, merely by redistributing the same quantities of the two goods between the two consumers we have benefited one of them without hurting the other. From our definition of the social welfare function, therefore, we have increased that social magnitude, and at P^2 it is no longer possible to increase Consumer 1's welfare without hurting Consumer 2. Therefore, we have reached some sort of a maximal position, in the sense that given the amount of satisfaction derived by Consumer 2, we have achieved the maximum possible available for Consumer 1. The welfare of the two consumers is now in conflict.

But consider P^3. If we had moved from P^1 by holding Consumer 1 at the level of satisfaction he was enjoying at that distribution and got Consumer 2 to as high a point as was consistent with that constancy, we would have arrived at P^3 as the maximum amount of satisfaction available to Consumer 2 consistent with Consumer 1 remaining on his original indifference locus. Therefore, P^2 and P^3 are symmetrical positions with their only difference being which of the consumers benefits from the redistribution and which remains constant in satisfaction. At both baskets the important characteristic of the solution is the tangency of the indifference curves, which indicates that it is impossible to get higher upon the benefiting consumer's indifference map without reducing the satisfactions of the other. At these points, we know that the psychological rates of transformation of both consumers are equal, because the slopes of the indifference curves are equal, and therefore, that the requirements of Rule 1 and of [9–8] for interior solutions are met.

Let us suppose that we drew in all the indifference curves for both consumers between P^2 and P^3, and that we have drawn the line P^2P^3 through all of their tangencies. We have along this line, then, given the initial distribution P^1, all possible redistributions of the two goods that would benefit at least one of the two consumers and leave the other at least as well off. Any point on the line that is not an end point allows both consumers to benefit from the redistribution, while the end points permit one of the two consumers to gain the whole benefit while the other remains constant in satisfaction.

Rule 1 merely asserts the necessity of distributions of goods among consumers who take both of any pair to lie on the line of tangencies (which we have extended beyond P^2 and P^3 in both directions, because our initial point P^1 was quite arbitrary). This can be seen to be necessary (when the indifference curves yield interior tangencies) because for any point P^1 that is not on the line of tangencies, there must exist at least one point on the line that yields at least as much satisfaction to one consumer and more to another. Therefore, if there is a social welfare maximum, it must occur somewhere over this line of tangencies.

But note that our conditions are not sufficient to tell us yet *where* over the locus of tangencies the highest social welfare is reached. We have no criteria for choosing P^2 over P^3 or vice versa or for choosing any other point on the line because it yields greatest social welfare. To make a determinate choice of a specific point on the line as best would imply our ability to value both of these individuals in terms of their social welfare significance, and that we cannot do. That is, we would require a *specific* social welfare function, rather than the general form we have chosen. Our welfare judgments, then, on the basis of Rule 1 and the general characteristics of the social welfare function W are quite weak; we have not a single *best* distribution of the two goods but a set of points which we know must contain the single best point if it exists. These baskets are marked by the requirement that for all consumers actually taking the pair of goods under consideration, the psychological rates of transformation are equal.

Next, let us motivate Rule 2 with its requirements that the rate of transformation of a given input at the margin into a given output must be the same for all firms producing the given output and using the given input. If, at the Planning Authority's equilibrium, Firm 1 can convert a small amount of labor into wheat at a rate of .25 bushels per hour of labor, then Firm 2, which also uses labor to produce wheat, must also convert labor into wheat at the same rate. If the rates were different it would be possible to transfer labor from the firm with the smaller rate to that which had the larger and get additional product from the same quantity of factors.

On Figure 9–2 we have graphed the product curves for two firms using z_1 to produce Y_j. Firm v's product curves are oriented to the origin O and Firm v''s product curves to the origin O'. The point P^1 depicts the division of a

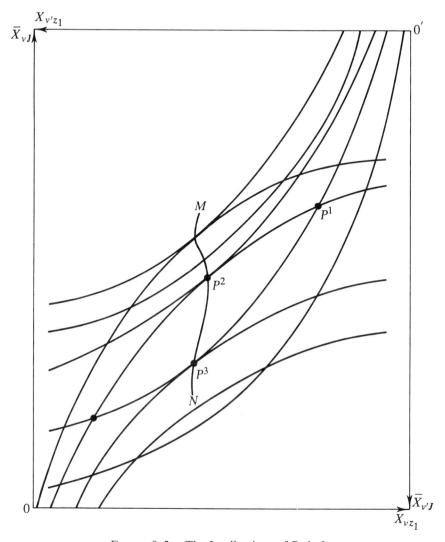

FIGURE 9–2. The Implications of Rule 2.

given amount of z_1 determined by the Board and proportionate to the length of the X_{z_1} axis to the production of Y_J by the two firms (also determined by the Authority and proportionate to the $\overline{X}_J$ axis). By allocating more z_1 to Firm v', however, the Planning Board can reach P^2, where Firm v' is producing on a lower product curve or P^3 where Firm v is on a lower product curve. In either case, the same total product is produced from the same total amount of z_1, but because lower product curves for one or both firms can be attained, other resources are freed to increase the outputs of other goods.

The line of tangencies, of which we have drawn the segment MN, depicts the locus of such *efficient points*. The points of tangency, as we have discussed in Chapter 4, are points where the marginal products of z_1 in each firm are equal in terms of output Y_J.

RULE 3. In equilibrium, the common marginal rate of substitution in Rule 1 must equal the common marginal rate of technological transformation of Rule 2 for all inputs and outputs that have consumer uses. That is, it must be impossible for consumers to transform leisure into bread psychologically at rates different from what all bakers transform labor into bread marginally. If there is a divergence in this marginal equality of transformation rates, social welfare has not yet been maximized.

Rule 3 states that the rate of psychological transformation between any two goods Y_j for all consumers who take them both must be equal to the rate of technological transformation between them by all firms that produce one with the other as input. This same type of equality of transformation rates between consumers and firms must hold for all factor services z_i that have alternative consumer uses. We may state the rule as follows, imposing it for one consumer and one firm, because Rule 1 and Rule 2 will impose it for all relevant decisionmakers if it holds for one pair of such units:

1. $\quad MP^\circ_{1/j/J} = \dfrac{S^\circ_{1/j/1}}{S^\circ_{1/J/1}}, \qquad j = 1, \ldots, n, \quad J = 1, \ldots, n$

2. $\quad MP^\circ_{1/i/J} = \dfrac{S^\circ_{1/i/1}}{S^\circ_{1/J/1}}, \qquad i = 1, \ldots, m, \quad J = 1, \ldots, n$

3. $\quad \dfrac{MP^\circ_{1/j/Z_i}}{MP^\circ_{1/1/Z_i}} = S^\circ_{1/j/1}, \qquad i = 1, \ldots, m, \quad j = 1, \ldots, n$

4. $\quad \dfrac{MP^\circ_{1/i/Z_i}}{MP^\circ_{1/i'/Z_i}} = \dfrac{S^\circ_{1/i/1}}{S^\circ_{i/i'/1}}, \qquad i = 1, \ldots, m, \quad i' = 1, \ldots, m. \quad$ [9–13]

Rule 1 assures that a given number of consumer goods will be distributed optimally when those goods are *already allocated* for consumer use. Rule 2 assures that a given number of factor services and intermediate goods *already allocated* to the production sphere for the manufacture of a given amount of product will be used optimally in the sense of minimizing the amount of other resources used. If either one of these two types of uses were exclusive, so that Y_j were consumed only by consumers and z_i were used only in production, Rules 1 and 2 would be sufficient for allocating these types of goods and services. However, because both Y_j and z_i have alternative uses, we need some rule to allocate them between the two sectors, and Rule 3 accomplishes this. It assures that it is impossible to increase social welfare by taking some amount of input away from the production sector and giving it to the consumption sector or vice versa, for the amount of product thus lost is valued at exactly the same psychological value as the consumption of the inputs thus gained would yield. Similarly, if goods or services were taken away from consumers at the margin and used to produce a small amount of any output, the loss in psychological satisfaction from the sacrifice by consumers of the inputs would only just be made up by the gain from the increased output.

We may motivate this rule by the following analysis. Let us assume that the State Planning Authority must plan for one consumer and one firm, so

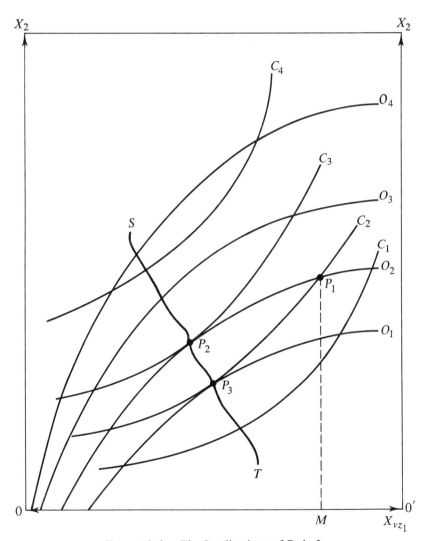

FIGURE 9–3. The Implications of Rule 3.

that we may handle the problem in two dimensions. Let the x-axis be amounts of z_1 used as inputs (measured from the origin O of Figure 9–3) or consumed (measured from O'), the length of the axis representing the amount of z_1 available for allocation to the consumer or the firm.

On the y-axis, measured from either the origin O or O', we denote the amounts of Y_2 produced and consumed by the firm and consumer respectively. The curves $O_1, O_2, O_3, ..$ are the product curves of the firm which we described in Chapter 4. They show the output of Y_2 forthcoming from variable inputs of z_1 when all other inputs are held constant at differing fixed levels, these amounts increasing as we move from O_1 to O_2 and so forth. As we move outward from O, therefore, we consume more and more of the inputs whose amounts are fixed in the definition of the various product curves.

The curves $C_1, C_2, C_3, ...,$ are ordinary indifference curves for the consumer, oriented to O'. Of course, as we move outward from O' the consumer's satisfactions (and therefore social welfare) increases. Let us assume that the Authority must allocate a fixed total amount of z_1 among consumers and firms using it to produce Y_2 for consumption by consumers.

Now, assume that originally we are at the point P^1. This indicates that the Planning Authority has allocated OM of the available z_1 to the firm and MO' to the consumer, in return for an output MP^1 of Y_2, which is given to the consumer. However, at this point the marginal technological rate of transformation of z_1 into Y_2 does not equal the psychological rate of transformation of the consumer. This means that the social welfare can be enhanced. For example, if we slide down the product curve O_2 to P^2, where these rates are equal by virtue of the tangency between O_2 and indifference curve C_3, obviously the redistribution of z_1 from the firm to the consumer with the consequent reduction in Y_2 puts the consumer into a higher indifference curve bracket and yields more social welfare. By staying on O_2, only at P^2 have we reached the highest social welfare.

We might also have moved from P^1 to P^3, which implies that the consumer's satisfaction from the consumption of these two goods is kept constant, but by moving to a lower product curve we have freed fixed resources, which may be used to produce other products and thus enhance social welfare. Which is the better point depends on the whole group of conditions, but we are assured by Rule 3 that a necessary condition for the best point will be that it lie at some such tangency as P^2 or P^3, along the line of tangencies ST.

These conditions for firms and consumers implicitly assert that for the equilibrium production of capital goods the marginal rate at which firms can substitute one input for another in the production of a capital good must equal the common rate of substitution for all consumers taking both goods for consumption. That is, from [9–11] we may eliminate $P_e \pi_i$ to obtain

$$\frac{MP_{v/j/z_i}}{MP_{v/1/z_i}} = \frac{\theta_j}{\theta_1}, \qquad\qquad [9\text{–}14]$$

and so forth, and from [9–8] the equality of marginal rates of substitution follows. Note that because consumers do not consume the goods directly nor have any voice in the quantity produced, this necessary condition merely assures that the capital goods are produced in a manner most conducive to social welfare. These conditions require the tangencies of isoquants and indifference curves, in fashion similar to cost minimization and utility maximization in the complete model of Chapter 8.

By our interpretation of Lagrangean terms as prices it follows that the price of capital goods is $P_e \pi_i$. Be it noted in passing that if π_i is interpreted as the price of the factor good service, and because P_e is the reciprocal of the rate of return over cost set by the Board, this manner of pricing insures that capital goods are valued at the capitalized value of their net earnings. From these conditions we may state Rule 4:

RULE 4. A necessary condition for the social welfare maximum is that the net rate of return on all capital goods be equal.

This may be imposed from [9–4–9] and [9–4–17] for what we will call *own* marginal products; that is, the marginal products of factor services in the production of their own capital good. For Firm 1, which we assume could produce all capital goods economically, a condition would therefore be

$$MP_{1/z_1/z_1} = MP_{1/z_2/z_2} = \cdots = MP_{1/z_m/z_m} \qquad\qquad [9\text{–}15]$$

The Authority must set a price P_e, which is to say that it must declare at the outset the interest rate it would like to have rule in the economy, and its welfare decision will be one relative to this datum. The Authority's decision in this matter will reflect its attitude to growth and the welfare of future generations relative to the present. If it sets a high interest rate, additions to the capital stock will be large, whereas if it sets a low interest rate the amount of savings will be small.

Given that the State Planning Authority has exacted a fixed amount of savings reflecting social welfare at the interest rate it has set, the Authority must now supervise the conversion of these savings into specific capital goods. If it wished for some reason to favor the construction of certain capital goods at the expense of others, it could set high prices upon the favored goods, so that their production would be quite large before marginal costs were equated to the set prices. However, we shall assume that the structuring of the investment of the economy will be undertaken by the state wholly with the object of getting the maximum net perpetual revenue. Consequently, the prices of capital goods should be set by the Planning Board by capitalizing the Lagrangean price of the service of the good by the implied rate of return in P_e. That is, we shall add to the conditions of [9–4] the following definition of capital good prices:

$$31. \quad P_{Z_i} = \pi_i P_e, \qquad\qquad [9\text{--}4]$$

by choice of the Authority.

The next two rules are self-evident in their interpretation:

RULE 5. Input availabilities must not be violated.

If we assume the constraints hold with the equality sign, these conditions are expressed in the m relations of [9–4–23].

RULE 6. Goods can be wasted only if the society is satiated in them.

If we assume satiation does not occur, so that the equalities do in fact hold, these necessary conditions are the *on* relations of [9–4–19], the *om* functions of [9–4–21], the *n* relations of [9–4–25], and the single constraint of [9–4–27].

There remains only one set of transformation rates which we have not dealt with: the rates that dictate the extent to which John Jones's satisfactions can be converted into social welfare compared with the rates of James Brown. All of the conditions which we have derived thus far assume that the equivalent of income distribution in the market's sense is given. That is, all of our conditions can hold at an infinity of points that deal with the distribution of consumption goods and factor services among the consumers of a society. They are *necessary* conditions for the obtaining of a social welfare maximum this week, but they are not yet sufficient in number to yield the *one point* in the space that depicts the distribution of goods and services among consumers over which the social welfare function achieves its highest point. We merely know that that highest point will occur over some one of the many points—each of which meets the conditions we illustrated in Figures 9–1, 9–2, and 9–3—defined by our conditions in Rules 1 through 6.

Before we turn to this most difficult last set of conditions, let us note a few interesting points about Rules 1 through 6 and the necessary conditions for a maximum that they summarize. First, note that we have at no point been forced to define consumers' satisfactions in a cardinal fashion: we have been able to use marginal rates of substitution throughout. Second, note also that it has never proved necessary to make *interpersonal* comparisons of preferences among consumers. We have merely assured ourselves that the marginal rates of substitution between all relevant goods and services for all consumers were equal. From Chapter 2, the student will remember that this implies that the rates at which each consumer substitutes one good for another are the magnitudes equated, and that this is a meaningful procedure.

Third, with the exception of defining a premium on present income over future income we at no point were forced to assume that the State Planning Authority used prices.

This last point is a most important one, and by expanding it we will be able to gain a very fruitful insight into the market mechanism's essential operation. We have used a device that yielded prices in a shadow process, but in the statement of necessary conditions we could have eliminated them all, with the exception of P_e, which was given among the data of the model. That is, the Lagrangean prices are important merely in bringing about certain equalities of rates, and once these equalities are established, could be eliminated as unessential. The important conditions are the equalities or inequalities ruling among the slopes of product curves, indifference curves, and the welfare function, as well as the rates of return on capital goods. The importance of prices is merely to guarantee that all consumers, all firms, and the Planning Board in its investment decisions, are adjusting to the same magnitudes and thereby will end in necessary configurations with respect to crucial *real* rates of transformation.

Let us explore this feature further. In the market economy, we have seen that every market generates a price, whose determination it was one of our prime functions in Chapter 8 and in earlier submodel building to feature. These prices we have already treated as another rate of transformation: rates at which one good or service can be transformed into other goods or services *via exchange*, where that exchange was the principle of organization of the economy. Their function in bringing about a complete model solution has been featured in our discussion, as has their role in transmitting to all independent actors in the market essential information in guiding them toward their own equilibria. In this equilibrating process, indeed, their determination and use were invaluable, and, because we have seen price-like magnitudes determined in the Planning Board's processes, we should expect them to fill the same economical and efficient role in its allocation procedures.

That is, faced with the huge task of allocating variable amounts of resources, including the labor of consumers, among huge numbers of firms potentially capable of producing large numbers of products in varying technological ways, and of performing this allocation in that manner which maximizes social welfare, it would be a foolish Authority indeed that did not recognize the need for an iterative, trial-and-error procedure, and that did not avail itself of the instrumentality of prices. The large electronic computer solves its problems iteratively—not analytically, as, for example, the simultaneous solution of a large number of equations would exemplify—and so does the complete market model of Chapter 8, and no Planning Authority could hope to do otherwise.

We should expect, therefore, the State Planning Board to (1) set the value P_e at its desired level, (2) fix the distribution of purchasing power among consumers in such a way as to approximate the goals discussed in the next section, and (3) make estimates of which prices would lead to the maximization of social welfare subject to the constraints imposed on it. The Board would then establish such prices, and allow consumers and firms to maximize their satisfactions and profits subject to them as well as any income redistribution policies imposed on them by the Authority, which in addition keeps capital goods prices in the desired relation to their service prices. At these initial prices, excess demands would no doubt be nonzero in many markets, and the State Planning Authority would lower those nonzero prices in markets where it was negative. This trial-and-error method of groping for the equilibrium which it was felt yielded the maximum social welfare would continue until the Board was successful in approximating it to some realistic degree, much in the manner of the market game discussed in Chapters 7 and 8.

First, let us assume that the Authority sets P_e, θ_j, π_i, and the implied P_{Z_i}, from which each firm derives its λ_{vJ} and λ_{vZ_i}. Every firm is then instructed to produce any good only if its λ-term equals the relevant θ-term or the implied P_{Z_i}, and to hire inputs down to the point where the relations of [9–10] and [9–11] hold. Consumers are presented with these values and, given the as yet undiscussed purchasing power at their command, make their own decisions about factor service supply under their discretion (labor) and purchases of goods, giving up purchasing power for any of their own leisure they consume.

Second, the Authority aggregates these demands and supplies and compares them by computing excess demands. In the nature of the market participant whom we created in our game-theoretic interpretation of the market's equilibration, the Authority raises the proper Lagrangean term of every market (except for capital goods) in which excess demand exists and lowers it unless it is already zero in markets in which excess supply exists. Firms and consumers once more consult their decisionmaking selves, and choose their strategies, which give rise to another constellation of excess demands, and another change in the Lagrangean terms. If the value of capital goods firms desire to produce exceeds saving, the Planning Board may increase X_e and decrease consumer purchasing power by lowering P_e, which implies raising i_k.

Third, the whole iterative procedure of the two steps just outlined is repeated, until in the end a set of Lagrangean values is found, which reduces all markets to zero or negative excess demands and the goals of the Planning Board in terms of income distribution have been achieved or approximated. At this equilibrium, all consumers are maximizing satisfactions, given their purchasing power, all firms are maximizing their profits, and the Planning

Board is investing at the total level with the structure it believes is best for social welfare.

But once this state has been achieved, the conditions that rule can be stated independently of prices not set in the data. The prices may be precipitated out of the conditions for the social welfare maximum as inessential in the statement of those conditions, once they have brought about the equivalence of the rates of psychological and technological transformation.

Let us, then, eliminate these prices from the solution to the welfare model, and overlook them in the solution to the complete market model given in Chapter 8. If we can arrive at the same conditions in the latter as those that rule in Rules 1 through 6 of this chapter, we will be able to conclude that the *necessary* conditions at least for a social welfare maximum are attained by the idealized complete model of the market economy that we constructed in Chapter 8. Let us proceed to this task with our new insight concerning the unessential nature of prices in the consideration of social welfare.

A Comparison of the Necessary Conditions for a Social Welfare Maximum with the Results of the Complete Model

We shall proceed most smoothly in this attempt to see if we can duplicate the conditions of Rules 1 through 6 in the results of the complete model of Chapter 8 if we take the rules up in order.

Rule 1 requires that for all consumers taking any pair of consumable goods or factor services in equilibrium, the marginal rates of transformation psychologically be equal for each pair. Behind the demand and supply curves of System [I], however, as we have developed them in Chapter 2, we have seen from [C–3] and [C–4] that all consumers adjust their marginal rates of substitution (their psychological rates of transformation) to the *same* price ratios, if we neglect the small cash-balance terms added to prices by the existence of privately owned stocks of money in the market model. It follows, therefore, that the relevant rates of transformation for consumers will correspond to the conditions for Rule 1, and that the important aspect of prices so far as this rule is concerned is that by providing a common exchange rate for all consumers to adjust to the psychological rates of transformation for relevant consumers are equalized.

Rule 2 requires that every firm hire inputs to produce a given good only if the marginal rate of transformation of that input into that output is equal to the same value as that of every other firm producing that output with that input. Behind System [II] of the complete model containing the supply curve of the purely competitive firm's output and the demand curves for its actual inputs lie the conditions [*F*–1] through [*F*–8], which require that if a good is produced every non-minimally-used input must be hired to the point where its marginal value product equals its price. Therefore, because all firms in the complete model face the same product and factor service prices, the conditions of Rule 2 must be met. The inequalities must also rule in the same manner as the inequalities of Rule 2, just as they do for Rule 1, if we neglect the small cost of cash balances as we did for consumers.

Rule 3 requires for all goods and services that have both producer and consumer uses, and for all firms and consumers that use any pair of them, the common factor of proportionality for consumers of Rule 1 and the common factor of proportionality for firms of Rule 2 be equal to each other. But consumers and firms are adjusting to the same prices in the complete model of Chapter 8, and these same prices constitute the same factors of proportionality. Consequently the necessary conditions for a social welfare optimum as defined in Rule 3 will also hold in the purely competitive complete model—again, neglecting cash-balance complications.

Rule 4 requires that all capital goods earn the same net rate of return—a condition specifically met by System [VIII] of the market model.

Rule 5 requires that the economy remain within the limits of its resource contraints, which of course are also enforced on the market model by System [VII].

Further, Rule 6 permits wastage of goods or services if society is satiated in them, and this condition is also imposed on the market model by System [VII].

We arrive at the rather astonishing conclusion that—accepting as given the market mechanism's distribution of income and wealth among producers in the economy and exempting decisions concerning the amount of investment —the purely competitive complete model will meet the six sets of necessary conditions for a social welfare maximum! As in the case of the State Planning Authority, this assumes that neither consumers nor firms have any external impacts upon other firms or consumers when effecting their own decisions.

From our analysis of the economic meaning of the six rules we formulated to this point it will be seen that the necessary conditions for a social welfare optimum are quite weak. At an allocation for which they rule, they merely imply that for the (1) supply of services being provided by each consumer to the economy, (2) the consumption of goods by each consumer from the economy, (3) the kind and amount of each output produced by the firm, and (4) the kind and amount of each input absorbed by the firm, no change in any group of these variables can increase the welfare of all consumers or increase the welfare of some with constant levels for all others.

As we have seen, a very large number of such allocations will meet Rules 1 to 6 if we change allocations of goods or resources. Therefore, this type of social welfare maximization does not yield us a single best position, but a set of them, from which we may choose one by deciding on income distribution criteria. But it is a remarkable result nonetheless, and gives a rigorous definition and proof to what Adam Smith and later economists guessed was true: that selfish, uncoordinated decisions, made in an environment where no decisionmaker has other than negligible economic power, will not only maximize consumers' *own* satisfactions subject to constraints, but for a weak definition of social welfare that takes strong account of consumer welfare, will maximize that *social* welfare in an important sense too.

Indeed, we have shown in our demonstration that the complete model's solution will meet the relevant conditions of Rules 1 through 6: pure competition is a sufficient condition to meet these necessary conditions for a social welfare optimum. In showing that the Planning Authority model meets them by forcing all consumers and firms to adjust to prices as unalterable parameters, which is the essence of pure competition, we have also shown that pure competition is a necessary condition for the meeting of these requirements, when cost conditions are as we have postulated. This point brings us to a final consideration of the implications of Rules 1 through 6 that we wish to consider before we undertake the last analysis of the State Planning Authority's tasks.

The Irrelevance of Profits

A last characteristic of the set of conditions which we have shown rules for both the collectivistic and the purely competitive market model is that none of the rules implies that price must equal *average* cost. We have seen from our analysis of the firm's submodel in Chapter 5 that the conditions of the State Planning Authority require that marginal value product (when the marginal physical product of an input is valued at some Lagrangean factor) of every input be carried to equality with a Lagrangean valuation of the input in actual input uses. These are the conditions for maximum profit, and no other condition requires that this profit be maximized at zero. How can this be? Do we not feel intuitively that social welfare can only be maximized if all goods are produced at the minimum average cost point of the U-shaped cost curve? Granted that profits must be maximized to assure that all resources are going to their best uses, have we not reached a wasteful position if positive profits are being earned?

At this point our analysis of the concept of a surplus payment to a factor in Chapter 7 serves us in good stead. There we interpreted profits in this simple environment as (1) a surplus or rent to superior managerial ability, which therefore is a reward for a more efficient resource, (2) a surplus paid because of insufficient factor service mobilities that prevented an inflow of firms into the given industry, (3) a dynamic frictional return because of the failure of adjustment processes to have time to work themselves out, or (4) a monopoly return, which may be viewed as a return to uncertainty. We may eliminate the latter two types of profits from the collectivist economy, because presumably no institutional protection will be given to new or better technological methods of production.

Because nothing which the State Planning Authority has done to this point is aimed at the elimination of surpluses received from the allocation procedure by other factors of production, it will not come as a surprise to learn that in the allocation procedure the earnings of surpluses by firms is not only permitted but required. The allocation of inputs by the Authority with the purpose of maximizing social welfare is concerned wholly with insuring that every unit of every factor contributes in the fictional sense we discussed earlier at least its imputed worth to the use in which it is committed. Efficiency in the sense of maximizing output and social welfare as defined to this point of our analysis consists wholly of this in the production sector. What the average or total product of any group of factors is, defined in some sense, possesses no interest in terms of this efficiency reasoning, and how this average or total compares with the amount of product paid out to the factors of production also is of no importance. If factor services are allocated on the basis of earning at least some common amount, and no further allocation is made once the factor contributes just that amount, this implies that every factor service is contributing in every actual employment at least as much as it is in every other actual employment *at the only* place where effective action is meaningful: the margin.

If, by following these allocation rules, production conditions are such that the total product would not be exhausted if every factor service were paid the value it earned everywhere else in the economy these rules imply the earning of surpluses in the firm as residuals. *If* a sufficient degree of mobility of resources existed for the period under analysis—for example, if more plant and equipment could be produced for sale in the industry by new firms, or if such plant and equipment could be shifted out of present uses into these uses earning a surplus—they would be eliminated. As we know, surpluses are an indication of imperfect mobility of one type or another, or of differential efficiency of resources. But it is not truly possible to compare the efficiency of allocations in which the number of resources available has changed or the degree of their mobility has changed or the differential efficiency of the factor services has changed. If profits are earned in one optimum allocation and they are not earned in another, we can merely say that the mobility or efficiencies of factors are different in the two situations: the earning of profits in the one does not indicate that it is a less efficient position than the nonexistence of profits in the other. Both cases meet the conditions of Rules 1 through 6, and that is all we can say.

After all, the earning or nonearning of surpluses by specific *individuals* in whatever capacity is a *distributional* problem, and we have in Rules 1 through 6 abstracted from these problems. Consequently, the consideration of the contribution of surpluses (including profits) or their detraction from maximum consumer welfare can only be answered in terms of distributional criteria. This is another indication of the essential neutrality of purely competitive profits in the statement of necessary conditions for a social welfare maximum.

There is another aspect of this question in which the one important role played by average or total revenue and cost in the purely competitive market solution does create a difference in the comparison of the results of the market mechanism and the Planning Authority's allocation. This will not arise in our statement of the models where we have insisted that the equality of marginal costs and prices occur in the portion of the cost curves where marginal costs are rising (that is, in a globally concave portion of the technological function). However, where marginal cost falls through a large segment of the output domain, and where price is equal to marginal costs in that falling segment, the intersection will be below average cost, so that profit will be negative. Therefore, in the purely competitive economy this good would not be produced, because firms must (in the long run) earn at least zero profits in order to produce. However, because, as we have seen, the relation between average and total costs and revenues is nowhere stated in Rules 1 through 6, would this failure to produce not be a violation of the efficient allocation requirements?

The answer is yes, it would be, and this is one of the cases in our complete model in which the purely competitive solution would diverge from the social welfare maximum. Either the good would not be produced, or one or a few firms would come to produce the good and gain monopoly power, thereby restricting its production below the price-equals-marginal cost point and earning a monopoly or oligopoly profit on its production. The criteria of social welfare maximization require that such a good be produced—exactly as in the case of the normal good's marginal cost behavior—and that the quantity reflect the equality of marginal cost and price. Just as the conditions of the rules were neutral to the earning of positive profits, so are they neutral to the earning of negative profits, but the conditions of private enterprise do not permit this symmetry in our purely competitive market model.

In pure competition an argument can be made for having the state undertake the production of such goods, selling them at their marginal cost and taxing to cover the difference between average revenue and cost, or, at least, to subsidize the production of the good by giving firms the difference between average revenue and cost on their outputs. Thus, for example, if the marginal cost of using a privately owned bridge is 5 cents, but the bridge authority must charge 50 cents to make its revenue equal its costs at the volume generated by such a toll, the argument is that the state should subsidize the bridge company, such that perhaps at the new equilibrium, marginal costs would be 3 cents and the average cost at the larger volume 45 cents. Then, the argument runs, the state should force the bridge company to set a toll of 3 cents and pay 42 cents subsidy on every vehicle that goes over the bridge. Now, it must be recognized that the much lower price may generate such a huge amount of new traffic, increasing maintenance and depreciation costs, making necessary new facilities, and increasing both average and marginal costs. All of these effects of the decision must be computed in the calculation of marginal and average costs, of course, and this may in effect eliminate the feasibility of the operation. For example, if the price of 3 cents to cross the bridge, backed up traffic through populous areas, created traffic jams, and generally imposed exorbitant costs on the society, the procedure would, via the sharp rise in marginal costs imputed over the whole economy, eliminate itself.

Even if this were not true, however, an ethical objection can be raised against the procedure. It is useful to consider this argument to impress upon the reader that distributional problems are at their base ethical value judgments. The argument is simply that if the state taxes one group of consumers —under however neutral a program in terms of its impacts on resource allocation—to effect such a subsidy, it is reducing the consumption of some who do not enjoy the subsidized product in order to permit another group to enjoy it. What the implications of Rules 1 through 6 assure us is that because the resource allocation-consumption solution without the good is off the line of tangencies, and because the new position attained with subsidy is on the line of tangencies, that social welfare is enhanced in the sense that the gainers *could* compensate the losers fully for their losses and still be better off. However, the fact of the matter is that Consumer 1 will not have to redistribute his goods to Consumer 2 in the way of compensation, and if this is not done, the tax and subsidy plan may have made Consumer 1 much richer at Consumer 2's expense. The hypothetical recompensation of Consumer 2 may prove that it is potentially a better point, but its potential is never realized.

To accept the subsidy point as better is to judge any point on the line of tangencies as better than any point off the line of tangencies. This is, in fact, what the principle of compensation means: it is always better to move from a point off the line to *any* point on the line.

But to say this is to admit a very strong assumption indeed: that the actual distributive effects of moves from off the line of tangencies to points on it can be ignored on the grounds of ethically neutral potential redistributive surpluses. But is it fair or ethically acceptable for Consumer 1 to be so benefited at Consumer 2's expense? Granted that for purposes of social welfare maxima in some global sense that abstracts from distribution among the individuals of the economy it is required that marginal cost equals price, is there not a basic value judgment in Western society that requires that in most cases where basic life and health are not involved, individuals actually consuming a good pay its full costs? In the case of the purely competitive market economy, this would imply average cost, and might not the distributive considerations of the State Planning Authority also move it to overthrow the nondistributive rules?

It is at this point that we must broach the final set of questions for the State Planning Authority—those dealing with distribution of welfare among all of the consumers of the society. For any society with more than one person in it, we have by virtue of Rules 1 through 6 reached the line of tangencies, but have not designated any single point in it as that which would yield the greatest attainable social welfare. We know, however, that being on the line means that it is impossible to benefit one person in the economy without harming another, and so, if we are to move from one point on the line to another one individual at least must benefit and at least one other must lose. How, then, must the State Planning Authority move in these *s* (the number of consumers in the economy) directions? What rules must it follow to hurt some and benefit others in order to move toward the *maximum maximorum* at which the distribution of goods among consumers as individuals as well as the level of investment—and the allocation of resources that they imply—is the very best attainable?

Obviously, we have reached a most difficult set of decisions—indeed, the set of decisions which economists, by developing only the *necessary* conditions for a social welfare maximum, because such conditions abstract from distributional problems, have been able to evade. The valuation of every individual in such a way as to specify what the worth of his satisfaction is to the society relative to his neighbor's worth is a painful set of decisions indeed. To be forced to form this set of valuations in a personal, explicit, and public way is one of the difficulties which a market mechanism allows a society to avoid. Indeed, it is probably one of the most important advantages which a market mechanism has for achieving harmony in a society; distributional decisions are, for the most part, made by an impersonal mechanism that successfully avoids purposively weighing each person in the social balance, and to a large degree avoids widespread realization of the decision. But how will the State Planning Authority go about doing this task? We shall turn to this problem now.

The Planning Authority's Distributive and Investment Decisions

Let us begin this last task by taking a count of the variables for which the Planning Authority is seeking values to see how many relationships exist in System [9–4] to determine them. Note that an equality of unknowns and equations is neither a necessary nor a sufficient condition for the determinateness of the system, but for systems with simple functions it frequently does permit us to check to see if redundant equations exist or if we have forgotten to provide for the determination of certain variables. Therefore, it is a useful exercise to check the totals, and, if they do not agree, to see if either of these explanations is true.

Now, each condition for the Planning Board's model has been stated in the form of a pair of relations—an inequality-equality pair—such that in the solution at least one equality will rule in each pair. Let us therefore count the

TABLE 9–1: THE UNKNOWNS AND THEIR NUMBER IN THE PLANNING AUTHORITY'S MODEL

UNKNOWNS	NUMBER
1. $\bar{X}_{vJ}$	on
$\bar{X}_{vZ_i}$	om
$X_{vj/J}$	on^2
$X_{vz_i/J}$	omn
X_{vj/Z_i}	omn
X_{vz_i/Z_i}	om^2
2. X_{cj}	sn
X_{cz_i}	sm
X_e	1
3. P_{Z_i}	m
λ_{vJ}	on
λ_{vZ_i}	om
π_i	m
θ_j	n

pairs of such expressions to see how many effective restrictions will rule as a minimum in the equilibrium:

TABLE 9–2: THE NUMBER OF EQUATIONS RULING IN THE SOLUTION TO THE MODEL

RELATIONSHIPS	NUMBER
1. [9–4–1, 2]	sn
2. [9–4–3, 4]	sm
3. [9–4–5, 6]	1
4. [9–4–7, 8]	on
5. [9–4–9, 10]	om
6. [9–4–11, 12]	on^2
7. [9–4–13, 14]	omn
8. [9–4–15, 16]	omn
9. [9–4–17, 18]	om^2
10. [9–4–19, 20]	on
11. [9–4–21, 22]	om
12. [9–4–23, 24]	m
13. [9–4–25, 26]	n
14. [9–4–27, 28]	1
15. [9–4–31]	m

There exists one more equation than unknowns, but we know the nature of the difficulty from our treatment of the complete market model: one of the consumer conditions of [9–4–1] and [9–4–2] may be omitted, because in our closed system if all allocations but that of one good to one consumer have been made, this last follows as a residual. With the elimination of this relationship, the number of relations and unknowns is equal and we will assume (repeat—*assume*) that the form of the relations and the values of the data are such as to yield a solution. These are, then, with the restrictions of [9–4–29] and [9–4–30] necessary conditions for the Planning Board's solution, and sufficient ones as well if our assumption is correct.

But now let us check the unknowns and equations of the *necessary* conditions which we listed in Rules 1 through 6. Because we have eliminated the Lagrangean terms, the set of unknowns is sets 1 and 2 of Table 9–1. The number of equations (and we shall count as if an interior maximum has been achieved) is given in Table 9–3.

A check of these totals will reveal that there are s more unknowns than equations. That is, in general, the statement of the necessary conditions in this form fails to include this number of relationships that may be requisite for a solution to the system. It is interesting to note that this shortfall of equations is equal to the number of consumers in the economy less 1 plus the investment that will be undertaken. Therefore, we may suspect that the necessary conditions in the rules fail to provide for the distribution of goods and services among consumers and for the investment of the economy.

TABLE 9–3: THE EQUATIONS AND THEIR NUMBER IN RULES 1 THROUGH 6

RULE	RELATIONS	NUMBER
1.	[9–8]	$sn + 1 - s - n$
		$sm - m$
2.	[9–12–1]	$on^2 - n^2$
	[9–12–2]	$omn - mn$
	[9–12–3]	$omn - mn$
	[9–12–4]	$om^2 - m^2$
3.	[9–13–1]	n^2
	[9–13–2]	mn
	[9–13–3]	$mn - m$
	[9–13–4]	m^2
4.	[9–15]	$m - 1$
5.	[9–4–23]	m
6.	[9–4–19]	on
	[9–4–21]	om
	[9–4–25]	n
	[9–4–27]	1

We shall find it convenient to return to the equations of [9–8], which state the necessary conditions of Rule 1 as derived from conditions [9–4–1, 2, 3, 4]. These are expressions that require for a maximum to be obtained that the marginal contribution of the individual's satisfaction to social satisfaction or welfare must satisfy a certain condition. The original form of these conditions in [9–4], however, is the following:

$$\frac{\partial W}{\partial M_c} = \frac{\theta_j}{\partial M_c/\partial X_{cj}}, \qquad [9\text{–}16]$$

for all goods Y_j which Consumer c actually takes in the equilibrium. Similar conditions must hold for the consumer's actual purchases of factor services.

In our derivation of the necessary conditions for a social welfare maximum we were able to eliminate $\partial W/\partial M_c$ by forming ratios between such expressions *for the same consumer*. In this way we obtained marginal rates of substitution among goods that are sufficient, as we know, even if derived from ordinal consumer preference functions, to permit us to map the consumer's preferences. Let us go forward with these functions and expressions to see if we can use them to find the consumer transformation rates that we need: those that tell us the rates at which individual consumers' satisfactions are transformed into social welfare.

Suppose we have two consumers, c and c', and that we have the same expression as that of [9–16] for each Y_j for Consumer c'; then, taking these expressions at their face value, we could derive the condition following, by eliminating θ_j:

$$\frac{\partial W}{\partial M_c} \bigg/ \frac{\partial W}{\partial M_{c'}} = \frac{\partial M_{c'}}{\partial X_{c'j}} \bigg/ \frac{\partial M_c}{\partial X_{cj}}. \qquad [9\text{--}17]$$

These conditions say that in equilibrium, the marginal personal satisfactions derived by any pair of consumers from a good they consume must be inversely proportional to their *marginal social contributions* to welfare. The *formal* similarity between these conditions and those we have previously encountered in this book between rates of satisfaction may be exploited in this fashion: consider the social welfare function W, and, holding all other consumers' welfares constant, increase Consumer c's welfare by a small amount. Then a social indifference curve can be obtained by determining the reduction of satisfaction Consumer c' must suffer to keep social welfare constant. Thus the slope of the social indifference curve will depict the inverse ratio of the individuals' marginal satisfactions at this distribution of goods.

In commonsense terms, the condition thus says that social welfare will not be an optimum if Consumer c gets .5 of the satisfaction Consumer c' gets from the last unit of Y_j consumed and Consumer c's marginal contribution to social welfare is 3 times that of Consumer c'. Only by redistributing goods such that (say) Consumer c gets .75 of the satisfaction Consumer c' does from the last unit of Y_j consumed, and the marginal contribution of Consumer c's satisfaction is 1.33 times that of Consumer c' will it be impossible to enhance social welfare by redistribution of Y_j.

The State Planning Authority, therefore, in order to achieve these new conditions, would have to decide upon a specific form of the function W rather than be able to abstract from its specifics, as the conditions that yielded Rules 1 through 6 allowed us to do. This brings out an interesting observation about the nature of the function W to which we have already alluded. We know that the M_c functions that we have placed within it are ordinal functions, representing the rankings of consumers over their fields of choice. Further, W itself is a ranking by the State Planning Authority over all feasible combinations of baskets in the consumers' respective fields of choice. Now, when we hold investment and all other consumers' satisfactions constant, and redistribute goods in such a way as to increase or decrease the satisfaction index of a single consumer, the inclusion of M_c in the social function (and the assumption that $W' > 0$) merely assures that the social welfare function will increase or decrease too. When, however, one individual's satisfactions rise and another's fall, the net impact is yielded by the ordinal function depicting the State Planning Authority's ranking over the set of individuals' rankings. At this stage of our analysis, therefore, we must bring those *social* rankings into explicit play.

The conditions of Rules 1 through 6 have permitted us to define the *generalized locus of tangencies* whose partial projections we have illustrated on Figures 9–1 through 9–3. It contains the sets of baskets distributed to consumers and containing social investment which do not permit improvement in the sense we have explained in our discussion of off-the-line points in those figures. That is, if one or more consumers experience an increase in their satisfactions, at least one other consumer or the social welfare derived from investment must decline, and a rise in the social welfare derived from investment has similar implications for changes in consumers' welfares.

The social welfare function is an ordinal function over the indifference curves of consumers, which in turn are defined on a field of choice. The social welfare function, therefore, is defined on a field of choice which contains one axis for every X_{cj} (that is, *sn* axes), one axis for every X_{cz_i} (or *sm* axes), and an axis for X_e. In that field of choice we may define the generalized locus of tangencies as the following function:

$$H(\mathbf{X}^*_{cj}, \mathbf{X}^*_{cz_i}, X^*_e) = 0, \qquad\qquad [9\text{–}18]$$

by which we imply that when any distribution of goods among consumers plus an amount of investment lies on the generalized locus of tangencies, when put into this function it has a value of zero.

Consider, now, the social welfare function defined on this set of baskets that meet the necessary conditions for a welfare maximum. It will reach a maximum at some point over the set, and it is that maximum we seek, for it will be that distribution of goods and amount of investment which the State Planning Authority believes is optimal. We shall return to [9–3–1] and [9–3–5] to obtain the conditions that will yield the allocation of goods among consumers and to investment which is optimal. From them we obtain,

$$1.\ \ \frac{\partial W}{\partial X_{11}} = \frac{\partial W}{\partial X_{21}} = \cdots = \frac{\partial W}{\partial X_{s1}},$$

$$2.\ \ \frac{\partial W}{\partial X_e} \cdot \frac{1}{P_e} = 1. \qquad\qquad [9\text{-}19]$$

That is, we require that the marginal social welfare of the good that is taken in positive amounts by all consumers should be equal in its marginal employments, which implies that the last unit of it consumed by every individual must yield, in the eyes of the State Planning Authority, equal social welfare. Further, the last unit of perpetual net revenue taken by the Planning Board must yield a weekly flow of social welfare equal to unity. These equations add the s conditions we need to complete those of Rules 1 through 6 and yield the desired point on the generalized line of tangencies. They reflect the Board's interpersonal judgments.

It is necessary to specify the conditions for consumers for only one good that is always taken by every individual because the conditions of Rule 1 will assure that identical marginal social welfare conditions hold for all other goods and services taken by them. Thus, the equivalent of imposing an equality of the "marginal utility of income" in a system in which allocation is accomplished through the use of some such means of generalized purchasing power, is the equation of marginal social welfares for any *one* good taken by all consumers in positive quantities, if marginal rates of substitution are equated for all such goods. We shall return to this interesting observation, with its implications for procedure to attain the goals of the Authority, as soon as we have stated the requirements of [9-19] as a rule.

We may therefore state Rule 7 in this manner:

RULE 7. The contribution to social welfare of the marginal unit of a good or service taken by every consumer must be equal to a common value for every such consumer. Further, when the price of a unit of perpetual net revenue has been set by the State Planning Board at P_e, which by defining a Lagrangean term gives absolute values to the shadow price system, investment must be carried to the point where the marginal social welfare of the weekly flow of value to the society from such resource commitments is unity.

Presumably, the manner in which the State Planning Authority would effect Rule 7, once the definition of W had been made, would be to permit income to be earned from labor, to distribute profits and earnings on the collectively owned resources, and, if necessary, to levy taxes and distribute them among individuals in such a way that the conditions of Rules 1 through 7 would be achieved. To the extent taxation and the distribution of surpluses are required, they must be levied or distributed in such a manner as not to interfere with any of the conditions of these rules. For example, if income taxes are levied in a progressive manner, this implies that the prices of leisure to which consumers are adjusting are different, not to mention the fact that firms are adjusting to a price of labor that is not the same as that to which consumers are adjusting. This is sufficient to guarantee that the economy will be off the line of tangencies. Even if the income tax is proportional, its existence means that consumers are not adjusting to the same prices of labor as firms, and this will accomplish the same derangement.

On the other hand, if excise taxes are levied, there is a direct upsetting of prices in the economy: marginal cost will no longer reflect the true social costs of production in their intersection with the new price, and removal from the line of tangencies will result. The only tax that should not have such effects —that is, which will allow a portion of certain consumers' income to be taken for redistribution to other consumers without any impact on the economy's attainment of the line of tangencies—will be a lump sum tax which cannot be escaped in any manner that permits consumer satisfaction to be sustained.

THE BURDEN OF THE TASK

The awesome burden of defining W for an economy with hundreds of thousands or millions of consumers will be immediately apparent: the word *impossibility* will not seem an exaggeration in this context. Moreover, any society will tend to shy away from such a conscious and purposive sifting of men at the hands of a small number of bureaucrats. These definitions of the worth of men involve nothing less than the explicit judging of the social importance of every consuming unit in the economy, asserting explicitly that John Jones is worthy of 2 or 3 times the enjoyment of Jack Smith and should be allowed to enjoy a larger income. Of course, as we know, the market mechanism *must* perform the same type of distributive decisionmaking, but the mere fact of its impersonality and its private nature is a protection of the individual's privacy and pride.

Added to this, schemes that envisioned a Planning Board were normally inspired by socialist dissatisfaction with the market's decisions, and were therefore basically antagonistic to such judgment processes. Moreover, they were egalitarian in their bias, urging that the inequality of income distribution brought about by the market was inequitable in some ethical sense. Therefore, their advocates frequently asserted explicitly or implicitly the value judgment that every consumer was more or less the same in his capacity to enjoy goods as every other, and therefore, that equality of shares in some sense would more or less bring about the consumer conditions of Rule 7. Indeed, sometimes the assumption was made that W was merely the sum of individual utilities that were measurable unique up to a linear transformation. That is, the assumption was made that individual utility was cardinally measurable and was directly comparable with the utilities so measured for other individuals; further, because all individuals were about equal in satisfactions potential, income equality was the proper rule of the State Planning

Authority to follow. In this way, no embarrassing interpersonal comparisons would be incumbent on the Authority, and the vast impossible task of doing a more precise job of judgment could be avoided.

But individuals do differ in their capacities to enjoy various goods, and, presumably, various levels of income. An egalitarian assumption may be an acceptable ethical judgment that such differences in men should be disregarded in their economic destinies, as such differences are disregarded when all men stand before the law in an ideal legal system. But if this assumption is effected it should be explicitly introduced, not justified on economic grounds, whether as an operational hypothesis that permits decisions to be made which could not be made otherwise, or as an ethical value decision for the society.

A COMPARISON WITH THE MARKET MECHANISM OF REALITY

We have noted already that the market mechanism solves its distributive problem on the basis of property holdings and marginal productivity pricing. We may now make more concrete our assertion that it is difficult to establish that the market mechanism maximizes social welfare in some readily defined sense. What we meant, of course, is that it seems intuitively difficult to see why this basis for the distribution of product should always allows us to attain that point on the line of tangencies which Rule 7 would yield as maximal. Presumably, the market's decision will yield under the ideal conditions we have assumed a point on the line of tangencies but not directly under the maximum point of W. Therefore, we conclude, in the absence of such a well-argued analysis, that the ideal market mechanism may be imagined to maximize product and social welfare only in the sense of Rules 1 through 6, and that, given some acceptably defined W reflecting the society's values and ethical standards, it will not in general meet the conditions of Rule 7. Therefore, in pure abstract theory, this conclusion implies that a society bent on a static welfare maximization would require some interference in the distributive processes of the free market in order to effect lump-sum distributional changes.

This conclusion violates the inner logic of the market mechanism, which we spent some time in developing, and it brings us to a last and more important set of considerations. Up to this point we have been comparing two idealized models: the purely competitive complete market model and the State Planning Authority model for a rather bloodless collectivism. How relevant are our conclusions—and it must be recalled that our analysis of the State Planning Authority's tasks was shaped primarily to understand the welfare implications of the complete model's solutions—to the realistic counterpart of the complete model? As we have seen, the environment in which the complete model functions is most unrealistic in respect to at least two assumptions we have made in its depiction and another that we have thus far projected from the State Planning Authority model. First, the problems of monopoly power must be injected into the model if it is to be realistic, as we have discussed in Chapter 8. Second, the various levels of government, as decisionmakers in the collective submodels whose operation we have largely neglected, must be included in the model when we come to judge the relevance of the welfare conclusions we have just advanced. And, third, the assumption of zero external effects by decisionmakers on other decisionmakers, which we assumed to rule in the State Planning Authority model, must be examined for its implications.

THE PROBLEMS OF MONOPOLY. In the realistic economy, as we know, prices do not tend to equal marginal cost—or at least we should suspect that this is true with a good deal of conviction. Our analysis of Chapters 6 and 8 led to the derivation of this very proposition, and we need not repeat the discussion of those chapters. Further, the presence of market power brings into the model selling costs and product variation, and none of our welfare conclusions assumes an economy in which these elements exist. No propositions have been derived, specifically, about which variations of which products, or which qualities of which products should be produced and which should not. Presumably, consumers in the realistic economy would prefer some product differentiation to none, but we have not obtained any criteria for judgment of the maximal welfare implications of this statement.

The existence of monopoly power, to the extent that it implies the departure of price and marginal cost, means immediately that the conditions of Rules 1 through 6 are violated. The prices to which consumers and buying firms are adjusting their rates of transformation differ from the rates at which factor services are converted into outputs, so that nontangencies occur in these areas. Even, therefore, if all goods prices departed from all marginal costs in the same proportions—so that in this sense all industries enjoyed the same degree of monopoly—the conditions would be violated. Were this true, for example, in [9–13] firms would be adjusting to the same ratios of the Lagrangean multipliers, with some $k\theta_J$ in the denominator, but consumers would be adjusting in their consumption of these goods to a ratio with θ_J. Thus, firms will be producing too little of monopolized products in the general case, and, in the case of a common degree of monopoly will be absorbing too few factor services that have an alternative consumer use.

THE PROBLEMS OF GOVERNMENT INTERFERENCE. We have seen that the normal operations of government require that resources be channeled away from the free market's governance into its own uses, and, moreover, that the chances are quite high that some redistributive functions will also be performed by them. Now, we have noted that there is a method of taxation and subsidization that is capable of effecting these changes without disturbing effects that would take the new equilibrium off the line of tangencies; however, its use requires lump sum taxes, which are determined individual by individual or class by class. But these types of taxes are very seldom practicable in modern economies, and consequently it can be said quite confidently that they will not be used exclusively if at all. Income and excise taxes are relied upon heavily, and they must have nonneutral effects on the allocation of resources; the use of such taxes guarantees that the line of tangencies cannot be attained.

THE PROBLEMS OF EXTERNALITIES. The assumptions that consumers are not affected in their choices by the actions of other consumers and that firms do not affect others' welfares in their operations are also difficult to justify, and do have substantial impacts on the ability of the market mechanism to attain a line-of-tangencies solution. Most particularly, the fact that some firms will, in their operations, inflict costs on other firms or consumers, or, on the contrary, benefit other firms or consumers, means that the marginal social cost of their product will be different from the private marginal cost on the basis of which they act and to which others adjust. Consumers, therefore, even under the assumptions of pure competition, do not adjust to prices that reflect true marginal costs in the social sense, and a departure from the line of tangencies occurs.

It would be necessary, if we were to attempt to remove these sources of interference with the social welfare maximum, to have state determination of these wider cost-and-benefit impacts, and to impose taxes or to subsidize firms in such manner as to have prices accurately reflect true social costs. The number of resources that would have to be involved in governmental mechanisms to gauge these elusive externalities and be lost to the society for other production would probably do much to reduce the net increase in social welfare their discovery brings about. Their existence, however, implies governmental intervention not only in the economic tasks of supervising the collective goods economy, of effecting redistributive decisions, and of policing markets to eliminate monopoly power as well as of modifying the actions of decreasing-marginal cost industries, but also in the additional job of gauging and correcting for the externalities of firms' and consumers' actions.

A FINAL WORD ON THE PROBLEMS

We see from this catalog of three sets of problems that exist in modern economies that there is no hope that the realistic counterpart of the complete model attains (a) a single maximum social welfare point in the sense of meeting the conditions of Rules 1 through 7, or even attains (b) the line of tangencies described by Rules 1 through 6. The existence of monopoly power, the mere operation of governmental economic decisionmaking in practicable manners, and the existence of externalities—taken singly—is a sufficient guarantee of this conclusion. Rates of transformation cannot be assumed to be equal for all relevant decisionmakers in the realistic economy, and certainly no readily perceived reasons exist for believing the income distribution resulting from the hodgepodge of different amounts of monopoly power in free markets, governmental regulation, and governmental redistribution procedures attains a distributional ideal.

But is there not some ability to salvage our results by lowering our hopes and policy measures to operationally available levels, and by compromising with our rather unrealistically global judgments? Can we not, by various social measures, act individually on markets that depart significantly from the purely competitive norm, move the price somehow toward an equality of price and marginal cost, and thereby achieve partial and piecemeal improvements in social welfare? Do not Rules 1 through 6 chart out at least the directions in which the prices of individual markets should be moved to attain the line of necessary conditions depicted for pure competition?

The answer must be that, in general—indeed in all but rare circumstances —such conclusions are unwarranted. Our analysis of the welfare aspects of the complete model is a quite brittle one: it does not yield elastically when the departures we have discussed above are introduced into the complete model as constraints. Rather, the conditions for a welfare maximum must be expected to change in essentially unpredictable directions: that is to say, to continue the metaphor, the conditions that are summarized in Rules 1 through 6 for the purely competitive complete model explode into another and different pattern instead of moving in easily determinable directions when disturbing environmental conditions are introduced.

The problem is simply this. Let us go back to the function L in [9–3], which is the social welfare function to be maximized subject to the conditions we have named. Now, if monopoly rules in some markets, or if income taxes are levied, these imperfections can be entered into the function as new constraints, and to the extent they are numerous and extensive the reader can sense that the derived conditions will change in essentially unpredictable ways. Mathematically, we are saying that if we maximize a function subject to one set of constraints, and obtain one set of conditions for that maximum, then add a whole new set of constraints, in general the *whole set* of conditions will change in directions not readily defined. In other words, such injections of new conditions will not merely move one or a few conditions in rather easily seen ways and leave others alone. The whole set of conditions will change.

The policy implications of this truth are that the piecemeal movement of one market toward a price-equals-marginal-cost-equality cannot a priori in a realistic economy be expected to improve consumer welfare. It may very well be that purely from the view of maximizing social welfare—moving to the equivalent of the line of tangencies we have discussed in previous sections— the divergence of price from marginal cost should be *increased*, not decreased. On wholly abstract grounds for the allocation of resources, it cannot be proved in general that elimination of monopoly from one market, all other environmental conditions remaining the same, will move the economy toward rather than away from the new line of maximum social welfare. These conclusions may be softened for some cases in which a few markets are not purely competitive and the goods involved enter into few uses; but, as our development of the firm's submodel and the reader's knowledge of the all-pervasiveness of governmental operations will suffice to indicate, this cannot be accepted as a realistic depiction of modern market economies.

A Summary and a Conclusion

We have come to the end of a rather long trail—gauging the extent to which we can make objective and rigorous statements about the welfare implications of the market's allocation performance—and must conclude that our ability to do so is most limited. To the demonstrated incapacity which we have displayed must be added the fact that we have discussed only the static performance of the market mechanism's ideal model. We have not included the performance of the market's allocation in the dynamic area: how well it allocates resources for growth, whether its allocations to research and development are sufficient and structured properly, how stable the allocation of resources is over time, whether consumers tend to allocate their income over time in optimal welfare patterns, and so forth. These are needless to say extremely important problems—in the affluent society they may far out-weigh the static aspects of resource allocation—and yet we have neglected them.

To be unable to *prove* a whole case deductively, however, should not be completely discouraging: after all, as we have indicated in Chapter 1, few propositions in the social sciences will be deduced unambiguously, and it is surely unrealistic to hope that we could arrive at global proofs of welfare propositions for an entire economy. Our attempt to do so, however, was valuable, not only in its humbling negative conclusions, but in showing some partial tendencies in which we ground value judgments concerning the market's economic operation. For example, regardless of market structure, every firm in the market mechanism will have a strong interest in profit regimes to act to lower total costs. This is an elementary but surely a most important type of maximization procedure, which tends to ensure not only that the best methods will be used in the static slice of time by the firm, but that the firm will have a strong incentive to develop and/or adopt newer and better modes of production in the dynamic long run. The minimization-of-cost drive, therefore, gives ground for faith that blatant malallocation of resources will be punished, overly wasteful malallocation will be eliminated by bankruptcy, and that economic growth through use of the novel and more efficient will be stimulated. Indeed, it may be much more important in operational senses to pay most attention to the assurance that average costs are minimal and worry less about marginal cost.

That is to say, under a State Planning Authority total costs in firms may not be minimized, by virtue of a failure of sanctions or spurs leading to the adoption of the best technology. Yet, marginal cost based on these inferior methods may be equated to price by planning techniques. The system may well be less efficient—incapable of yielding more of some goods and no less of others—than a market economy with the same resources producing at minimum average costs but without price equality with marginal cost.

Were we writing a book with a broader outlook than that sought by our rigorous analytical methods, the market mechanism could be defended in such terms, with a host of other less rigorous economic norms and, perhaps, more important spiritual and cultural judgments. But these considerations are beyond our present charter, and are left for further work.

Selected Readings

1. KENNETH E. BOULDING, "Welfare Economics," in Bernard F. Haley, editor, *A Survey of Contemporary Economics*, II (Homewood, Ill.: Irwin, 1952), pp. 1–34. An excellent statement of the principles of welfare economics.

2. ABBA P. LERNER, *The Economics of Control* (New York: Macmillan, 1944). A classic nonmathematical—but not a simple—statement of welfare economics.

3. R. LIPSEY and R. K. LANCASTER, "The General Theory of the Second Best," *Review of Economic Studies*, XXIV (1956–57), pp. 11–32. The original presentation of the thesis that welfare economics cannot be a piecemeal analysis.

4. I. M. D. LITTLE, *A Critique of Welfare Economics* (London: Oxford, Second Edition, 1957), Ch. 11. A discussion of average cost versus marginal cost pricing and its welfare implications.

Index